The Neapolitan Recipe Collection

spessa volta cum lo cugliaro. Dapoi frige la
dita carne in bono lardo poi ponela in piatti
coprendola cum questa piperata la quale quanto
he più negra tanto he più bella
Per farla negra piglia una milza di carnero
he pistala cum le predite cose

Brodo consumado

Piglia caponi he starne fasani he
pipioni he columbi salvatici ben nettadi
Et se voy consumare uno capone he far
due menestre di brodo tolle una pila
capace de quattro bucali de aqua he pone dentro
uno capone et gli sia rotta l'ossa cum una
onza di carne salata cum trenta grane di peper
rotto he canella he doi ho tre garofoli et
cinque ho sei fogli di salvia in pezi he una de
lauro he lassa bullire per spatio di sey hore
non ponendoli sale. Item sera meglio ponere
le spetie predite quando sera quasi la mità
parte del brodo consumado etc.

Cuoco Napoletano

The Neapolitan Recipe Collection

(New York, Pierpont Morgan Library, MS Bühler, 19)

A Critical Edition and English Translation

by

Terence Scully

initially with the collaboration of Rudolf Grewe †

Ann Arbor

THE UNIVERSITY OF MICHIGAN PRESS

First paperback edition 2015

Published in the United States of America by
The University of Michigan Press
Manufactured in the United States of America
♾ Printed on acid-free paper

2018 2017 2016 2015 5 4 3 2

A CIP catalog record for this book is available from the British Library.

Library of Congress Cataloging-in-Publication Data

Cuoco napoletano.
The Neapolitan recipe collection: (New York, Pierpont Morgan Library, MS Bühler, 19): a critical edition and English translation / by Terence Scully; initially with the collaboration of Rudolf Grewe.
p. cm.
Includes bibliographical references and index.
ISBN 0-472-10972-3 (cloth : alk. paper)
1. Cookery, Italian—Southern style—Early works to 1800. 2. Cookery—Italy—Naples—Early works to 1800. 3. Cuoco napoletano. I. Scully, Terence, 1935–. II. Pierpont Morgan Library. III. Title.
TX72.2.S65C86 1999
641.59457—dc21 98-51414

ISBN 978-0-472-03636-3 (pbk.: alk. paper)

Contents

I. Introduction

A. The Manuscript: Description

(i) Physical description of the manuscript

The *Checklist of the Bühler Manuscripts* in the Pierpont Morgan Library in New York City offers the following description of MS B19:

> Cuoco napolitano (Neapolitan recipes). Naples, end of the fifteenth century.
>
> Paper, 90 leaves (213 X 145 mm), 1 col., 21 lines (150 X 93 mm).
>
> Script: gothica cursiva. Binding: old cloth over pasteboards.
>
> Provenance: Abbé Celotti; his sale, London, Sotheby's, 14 March 1825, lot 109; Sir Thomas Phillipps (Ms. 921); Katharine Fenwick; Thomas FitzRoy Fenwick; Alan George Fenwick; purchased in September 1953 from William H. Robinson Ltd., London (Cat. 77, no. 921; Cat. 82, no. 514).
>
> Bibliography: Phillipps, 11, no. 921; Faye and Bond, 390; New York, Metropolitan Museum of Art, *The Secular Spirit: Life and Art at the End of the Middle Ages*, New York, 1975, 36, no. 24, fig. on 36.

The manuscript Bühler 19 contains 91 paper folios measuring roughly 14.5 cm by 21 cm. Of these folios, the last belongs to a single folded sheet of newer material, the second half of which is glued onto the end board and is blank. The original manuscript proper ends at f° 90v (the folio that is now numbered 92). The arrangement for the binding of the manuscript is similar at its beginning, where the first folio of a single fold of paper is glued onto the front board. There, however, the second half of the folded sheet has been torn away; only a small tab of this folio remains at the lower edge of the spine.

The foliation throughout is in pencil in a recent hand, and at the extant f° 90 a number has been erased and 92 written in its place, presumably in order to include in the overall count the two folios that preceded this folio but have been cut away. A good centimeter of each of these two folios still remains, but without any writing visible on either of them.

If we ignore the first and last folds of paper, that essentially form part of the book's binding, the folios of the manuscript are arranged in eleven gatherings of varying numbers of folded sheets of paper. These gatherings have been identified alphabetically in the lower margin of their first page by at least three different hands and, in two places, without agreement in the sequence of the gatherings. The first hand is similar to that which is read in the text throughout the manuscript, and is in an ink which is somewhat brownish in color as is now the ink of the main body of the manuscript; the second hand (notably for gatherings from "*b*" to "*f*" inclusive) is a small, fine script in black ink; the third sort of identification is in pencil and is undoubtedly modern.

As the manuscript is now bound and foliated in pencil, the arrangement of folios and gatherings is as follows:

1. A[1]: four folded sheets (that is, eight folios: 1r–8v);
2. *b*[2]: four folded sheets (that is, eight folios: 9r–16v);
3. *c*: four folded sheets (that is, eight folios: 17r–24v);
4. *d*: five folded sheets (that is, ten folios: 25r–34v);
5. *e*: five folded sheets (that is, ten folios: 35r–44v);
6. *f*: four folded sheets (that is, eight folios: 45r–52v);
7. *g*[3]: three folded sheets (that is, six folios: 53r–58v);
8. *k*[4]: four folded sheets (that is, eight folios: 59r–66v);
9. *k*[5]: five folded sheets (that is, ten folios: 67r–76v);
10. *l*[6]: four folded sheets (that is, eight folios: 77r–84v);
11. *m*[7]: four folded sheets (that is, eight folios: 85r–92v).

In the bottom margin of f° 71r a signature, "*k*," is written. This is in the same fine black script that identifies gatherings "*b*" through to "*f*" and "*m*". This folio, 71r, is not at the beginning of a gathering, but is contained within the ninth gathering, itself identified originally with the large brown letter "*k*" that was corrected to "*i*".

A catchword that identifies a following gathering is found at only one place in the manuscript, the foot of f° 24v: *cosa*. At the end of gathering "*b*" in the bottom margin of f° 16v the word *spine* is written in very fine script, but this does not seem to be a catchword to gathering "c".

In all, there exists evidence of a fair amount of uncertainty about the sequence of folios in those gatherings that immediately follow "*f*" — that is, after f° 52v. It is apparent, as well, that one whole gathering ("*h*") is missing, and perhaps one or several double folios elsewhere. Furthermore, a serious problem is posed by the arrangement of the folios in the bound codex that has come down to us. This is most clearly apparent in the gathering that begins at f° 67r and has been identified successively as "*k*", "*i*", and "*i*" again: the contents of the pages in this gathering, and of the pages immediately before and after, suggest that the present book is not as it was originally written and intended to be bound.[8]

---

1 In pencil.

2 Folios "*b*" through "*f*": fine script in black ink.

3 A hand, whose ink is now brownish, resembling that of the manuscript's scribe. The letter G is also pencilled in.

4 A hand, whose ink is now brownish, resembling that of the manuscript's scribe. The letter *H* is also pencilled in.

5 A hand, whose ink is now brownish, resembling that of the manuscript's scribe. This letter *k* has been stroked out diagonally and the letter *i* written beside it, also in an early hand now in brown-colored ink; another letter *i* is pencilled in as well.

6 A hand, whose ink is now brownish, resembling the manuscript's scribe.

7 A hand with the same fine black script as on gatherings "*b*" and following. The folios that, according to the modern foliation, would likely have been numbered 90 and 91 have been cut away.

8 For our conjectures about the shape of the original manuscript, see section C, The Neapolitan Manuscript: Textual Questions, (iii) Composition of this collection.

Pages have been ruled to mark the left and right margins (about 10 cm apart) and for lines of script (about 7 mm apart).

The contents of the manuscript are divided into two major sections. From f° 1r up to f° 76v a series of culinary recipes is copied; the last recipe is unfinished at the end of the gathering in which it began. From that point, f° 77r (the beginning of gathering "l"), up to f° 89r the menus of five rather sumptuous meals or banquets have been transcribed. At the foot of the last page of these menus is written the word *Finis*; the word may apply either to the record of this last menu, whose stages have been carefully rubricated, or to the whole series of banquet menus.

On the *verso* of this f° 89 a hand that is very similar if not identical to the scribe of the whole manuscript has appended another recipe,[9] at the foot of which is again found the word *Finis*. Following the stubs of the two excised folios, on f° 92r a more modern hand has written several very tentative lines in ink:

> *Per fare Quatro taze de . . .* [10]
> *Quando uolenō venire a casa di mg nōlo per uenire poi a touarla a casa sua e il sig*re
> *siofatelle . . . quando Irenege . . .*

Several words here are illegible. As well, there are a couple of doodles, that include a heart with a sword through it! On the *verso* of f° 92 more miscellaneous material has been written and drawn:

> [in black ink] *Sabbe .i. mustekocht*
> [in brown ink] *a far ova fritellada*
> *Recipe*
> *A far ova fritellate*
> *Anj manola*

Then there follows a sketch of a lion rampant, in black ink, and beneath this the notation "Sir T. P / Nidelli Hill / 1921."

On the *recto* of the folded sheet whose second half is glued to the back boards, is drawn the very large figure of a man who is either running or dancing. He seems to be wearing a buttoned frock coat of either the seventeenth or eighteenth century.

Two peculiar anomalies in the principal scribe's habits strike the reader of this manuscript. Firstly, at several places the scribe has added in the bottom margin of a *recto* a catchword found at the top of the *verso* of the same folio.

> f° 43r, *lavala*;
> f° 44r, *queste*;
> f° 52r, *cocere*;
> f° 61r, *piste*.

---

[9] We have assigned to this recipe a number, 220, in the sequence of the recipes of the collection and, despite the very faint ink in several passages, have attempted a transcription and translation of it.

[10] It may be observed that these are the opening words of the recipe for Zabaglone, appended on f° 89v.

The catchwords written in this position seem to serve no purpose — certainly not the conventional one of providing a cue for the binder of a sequence of gatherings. Unless, perhaps, they were intended to remind the scribe just where he was in the text when the ink on the *recto* had dried and he flipped the folio in order to resume copying on the *verso*, their use seems to be inexplicable.

A second peculiar practice of the scribe is occasionally to write a word — again, only on the *recto* of a folio — in the bottom right margin in the same position of the conventional catchword, but this word is an integral part of a text that continues on the next page, and that word is not repeated at the beginning of the next page. Instances of this procedure are found on

f° 23r, *batilo*;
f° 26r, *se veda*;
f° 49r, *miseda*;
f° 59r, *late*.

Watermarks are visible on roughly half of the folded sheets. Without exception these are located in the center of the sheet — that is, now at the fold. However, because of the fold and the manuscript's present binding, it is difficult to identify these watermarks with any assurance as to their precise detail.

The scribe has used paper with one of at least three different watermarks. The most common of these shows a set of scales, with suspended cups, within a circle except for the indicator needle, the central suspender and hook which together project above the circle. This design seems to correspond most closely to one catalogued by Briquet as #2511 (found in Florence in 1494).[11] Briquet calls the type *Balance*. This watermark is found, for instance, on the fold between ff° 25 and 34, 28 and 31, 36 and 43, 37 and 42, 45 and 52, 48 and 49, 59 and 66 and 60 and 65. The second most common watermark is of a sun, with six rays or flames shimmering from it. It bears some resemblance to Briquet, #13924, though apparently without the outline of a human face that shows in this latter; Briquet's design has been found in Zurich in 1461. The sun watermark is found on the fold between ff° 2 and 7, 4 and 5, 10 and 15, 12 and 13, 19 and 22, 53 and 58, 54 and 57. The third type of watermark is rare: it represents a siren holding her split tail with her hands, within a circle. This mark resembles Briquet, #13880, attested in documents from Naples, 1480–97. It appears on the fold between ff° 62 and 63.

We may summarize the manuscript's use of paper thus — at least as far as we have been able to scrutinize the watermarks:

In gathering "A" two of the four sheets have the watermark of the sun;
in gathering "*b*" two of the four sheets have the watermark of the sun;
in gathering "*c*" one of the four sheets has the watermark of the sun;
in gathering "*d*" two of the five sheets have the watermark of the scales;
in gathering "*e*" two of the five sheets have the watermark of the scales;
in gathering "*f*" two of the four sheets have the watermark of the scales;

[11] C. M. Briquet, *Les Filigranes*, ed. J. S. G. Simmons (facsimile of the 1907 edition, with supplementary material), 4 vols. (Amsterdam: Paper Publications Society, 1968).

in gathering "g" two of the three sheets have the watermark of the sun;
in gathering "k"/"H" two of the five sheets have the watermark of the scales and one has the siren.

The regularity with which we find a watermark on roughly half of the sheets of a gathering suggests that the paper was originally twice the size that the codex used, and that each original sheet—at least those with watermarks—was cut in half before being folded, lined and written upon.[12] There is evidence also, in the incomplete state of several marginal sketches, that a certain amount of some margins has been cut away at some time after the manuscript was written, perhaps at a time that the book was bound. The final two gatherings in the manuscript, "l" and "m," use paper that, except for the sheet of ff° 77 and 84, appears to lack a watermark. From this peculiarity we might conjecture that the banquet menus were not part of the original scheme but appended to the recipe collection at some later date, even though the scribal hand responsible for the main parts of the manuscript—recipes, menus and the appended recipe for Zabaglone—appears to be the same.

The watermarks of the paper used in the recipe section of the manuscript seem to indicate that this section was written in the second half of the fifteenth century, and perhaps in the fourth quarter.

(ii) The whimsical character of this compilation

One scribal hand seems to have been responsible for all of the substantial material of this manuscript—that is, for both the recipe and menu sections. Generally speaking the copy is carefully executed and virtually free of errors that might be attributed to this scribe. Where the scribe is aware of having made an error, his usual means of correcting it is to run a stroke through the error and to continue with the correct version. On the whole, though, errors are few and the script is consistently careful and legible.

Abbreviations are few and of only the most common sort: nasals, the *que* of *cinque*, the *er* of *verde*, the *ra* of *sopra*, the *re* of *capreto*, the *ro* of *probatura*, and so forth. Punctuation is rare; primarily, though not always consistently, the scribe depends upon capital letters within the text. A symbol vaguely resembling a script *s* — ʃ — is likely meant to signal a partial stop, a semicolon. With few exceptions this sign is found appended to a word at a break in the sense of a passage. Peculiarly, that word always ends in *-o*. The symbol's use is far from frequent, there being only seventeen clear instances of it in the whole of the manuscript.[13]

---

[12] It is perhaps significant that, for his directions for *Ova cotta in carta papirea* (Recipe 142), our author makes use of *uno mezo foglio de papiro*.

[13] The symbol is seen after words as follows: *carnero*, in Recipe 1; *consumado*, 2, twice; *carnero*, 46; *castrado*, 46; *carnero*, 78; *castrado*, 78, twice; *pistado*, 84; *netado*, 88; *scachero*, 90; *brusculado*, 101; *acarpionado*, 194; *salado*, 199; *carnero*, in Menu [3] at f° 81r; *carnero sano*, after both words, in Menu [4] at f° 84r. In three instances, after the words *scachero* in Recipe 90, *salado*, Recipe 199, and *carnero*, Menu [3], f° 81r, a smaller, more condensed execution of the same symbol looks similar to a modern "roman" letter *s* — ꞩ. After the words *castrado* in Menu [2] at f° 78v and *carnero*, Menu [3], f° 82r, a somewhat different sign is attached; it resembles a carelessly formed 6.

Additions in the side and bottom margins may in the odd instance be corrections to the scribe's copy, but seem for the most part to be supplementary material, whether additional recipes, clarifications or observations.

Several peculiarities mark this compilation of recipes: the marginal notations just mentioned, some modest efforts at decoration, and an occasional personal comment. The notations are generally limited to the lower edge of a page and seem to be additions made, significantly, by the same hand as is responsible for the manuscript as a whole. Some of these notations are further recipes meant to be included along with others of the culinary *genre* then being presented: for instance, the recipe that we have numbered 102, for *Sapore bono,* is inserted at the foot of f° 40v among other sauces — and, in fact, interrupts the text of Recipe 101.[14] Other insertions specify procedures that the text of a particular recipe does not mention or mention clearly: for instance, at the end of Recipe 125 for a *Torta biancha,* we find, "Note that, when it is done, the top of this pie should be sprinkled with an egg yolk beaten with saffron, and then put on plenty of well ground sugar." Other appended material constitutes practical advice of a general nature which the recipe or recipes of that page appears to have elicited: for instance, on f° 72v in the midst of the fish section, the note is added that "Every fish should be boiled slowly." A curious form of this same sort of advice, though not marginal and not directed to the professional cook, is the sort of exhortation that our author extends to his reader, whether this be the cook's employer or the kitchen steward. An instance of such advice is found at the end of Recipe 70: "And note, my lord, that if your cook is not skillful he will never prepare anything good that *is* good, no matter how hard he tries!"

Generally speaking these comments are intended to offer practical counsel to guide the working cook. They represent wisdom or tricks of the trade garnered by one professional in his experience and transmitted to help ensure culinary success in another's kitchen. This advice is, however, generally appended to recipes which the scribe is writing down or copying. We must therefore assume either that the scribe is a professional cook himself (or, expressed another way: that the cook is his own amanuensis in compiling this collection of recipes), or that the scribe is working under the close instruction of a professional cook, inserting these comments exactly where and as directed. They are personal notations. As such, they are found in the same form in no other recipe collection.[15]

The manuscript containing the Neapolitan Collection is by no means an elegant production. The little ornamentation of the text that has been attempted is very much of the homemade, amateurish variety. A few capital letters have invited a modest scribal flourish; large capitals regularly have the enclosed areas in them filled with a wash of what is now a light brown color.

The manuscript further contains several rather incompetent and rudimentary sketches outlined in ink in the bottom margins of certain folios. The open areas of many of these, too, have been

---

[14] We have found the text of this Recipe 102 in no other recipe collection of the time.

[15] See below, however, the observation that a few of these appended notations are incorporated, in modified form, into the texts of the manuscripts of Riva del Garda and Urbinate latino 1203, and of the Vatican and Washington copies of Martino's *Libro de arte coquinaria.*

given a wash, now light brown in color. It is difficult to tell whether these sketches are from the pen of the manuscript's scribe or of some later clerk, copyist or owner imbued with a penchant for doodling. There exist in all some twenty such sketches. A peculiarity of the placement, *recto* and *verso*, of several of these "illuminations" reflects in part the artist's mediocre skill and his artlessness: one sketch is merely an inverted tracing of the other through the paper. The artwork is found as follows:

f° 3r: some sort of doodle or flourish at the end of a faint line separating *de quaresma* from *Bianchomanghiare*
f° 3v: a hand with a finger (or rod) pointing at the word *Nota* in the text; partly cut away in the left margin
f° 4r: a hand with a finger pointing to the beginning of Recipe 8
f° 8r: a snake (?) that terminates in a hand holding a rod pointing at the text *Et simile*
f° 22v: a monkey standing on its tail (?)
f° 23v: a chicken
f° 25r and v: a bird with its wings spread
f° 26 v: a cow
f° 28r and v: a bird, picked out in pointillé on the *recto*
f° 29r: a peacock, in the lower margin but standing on the right edge of the page
f° 29v: a ewe
f° 32: a flower (?)
f° 46r and v: a horse
f° 53r and v: a grotesque of a bird with a human face
f° 58r and v: a snail
f° 73v: a series of four sea creatures: a moray eel, a sturgeon, a turtle and another fish, perhaps a pike.

On f° 66v a small head in profile is attached to the capital *P* of the word *Piglia*. Except for the light colored wash on very large letters that was mentioned before, this is the only instance of an illuminated letter in the manuscript. There are, however, occasional examples of a scribal flourish added to large letters: for instance, on f° 23v, the *I* of *Incipiunt* and the *P* of *Piglia*; on f° 31r, the *F* of *Farcimenti*.

A final sort of peculiarity in this Collection is a tendency, presumably on the part of the compiler, whom we shall with the cataloguer of the Pierpont Morgan Library call the *cuoco napoletano*, to insert facetious remarks about a foodstuff or dish. So at the end of the delicacy described in Recipe 98, our author uses a sardonic tone to address the colleague who is reading him: *Non he cosa per tua boca, coco mio!* Or in Recipe 113, at the conclusion of the directions for making Saracen Sauce, we read, " . . . Make up platesful of this sauce and serve it to Saracens"! Similarly the recurrent reference to "Catharina fasanica" suggests a certain playfulness that breaks from the sober, earnest professionalism that is the Collection's fundamental trait.

(iii) Editorial principles

The editors' handling of the manuscript text tends to be conservative. Emendations are proposed only when errors are patent, and only when such corrections clearly represent what was intended by the scribe or his source. In all cases the actual textual reading is scrupulously noted.

B. Italian Recipe Collections: A Brief Survey

Our current knowledge about cookery and gastronomy in the European Middle Ages is most developed for the fourteenth and fifteenth centuries, and generally concerns the taste and habits of the aristocracy and upper bourgeoisie. These are the classes that could afford to choose the foods and dishes they wished to eat. They are also the classes that could in most cases afford the services of professional cooks. On the payroll of such members of the wealthier classes, along with those professional cooks usually went an extensive corps of kitchen workers, such as roasters, pastry chefs and sauce-makers, specialists whose talents were dedicated to excelling in some particular domain. From the kitchens of the wealthy ultimately came the dishes whose recipes entered into the manuscript compilations which yield the most detailed knowledge that we possess of the specifics of late-medieval cookery.

Recipe collections exist in all of the major European languages of this time. Close to one hundred of these cookery manuscripts, or discrete sections within manuscripts, have been identified. Something of the order of fifty recipe "books" have been studied closely and made available in modern editions. Some collections are larger than others; some are more significant, perhaps because of the variety, richness or uniqueness of their contents; some can be seen as exerting a perceptible influence on practices beyond the sphere in which they were compiled. A few collections reflect a relatively local usage, whereas others are the product of a cosmopolitan cookery embodying customary dishes of more distant regions.

One may simplify by identifying four general streams or traditions of recipe collections of primarily Italian provenance, and to them we may add at least two further, unique compilations of recipes.[16] Hitherto unknown or unrecognized recipe collections seem to be unearthed yearly. Our understanding of the subject is still growing.

To begin with the last. Two substantial collections remain to date apparently unconnected directly with any other known work. There is the untitled, unpublished work copied in the manuscript London, Wellcome Institute for the History of Medicine, MS 211. As Italy entered the sixteenth century its professional cookery incorporated material from a relatively broader range

---

[16] We are aiming to provide only the briefest of outlines here. For more detail on the question, see Claudio Benporat, *Cucina italiana del quattrocento* (Florence: Olschki, 1996), 9–15; Jean-Louis Flandrin and Odile Redon, "Les livres de cuisine italiens des XIVe et XVe siècles," *Archeologia medievale* 8 (1981): 393–408; Bruno Laurioux, "I libri di cucina italiani alla fine del Medioevo: un nuovo bilancio," *Archivio Storico Italiano* 154 (1996): 33–58; and, by the same scholar, "Les livres de cuisine italiens à la fin du XVe et au début du XVIe siècle, expressions d'un syncrétisme culinaire méditerranéen," *La Mediterrània, àrea de convergència de sistemes alimentaris (segles V–XVIII)* (Palma: Institut d'Estudis Balearics, 1996), 73–88.

of sources, in an eclectic and innovative fashion. The *Manoscritto Lucano* is a significant reflection of this later cookery.[17]

Then there are the four manuscript "families" of collections. Related in one way or another with the Latin *Tractatus de modo preparandi et condiendi omnia cibaria* and the *Liber de coquina*[18] are the Italian manuscript "A" edited by Boström;[19] an Italian collection in a Tuscan dialect known as the *Libro della cocina*;[20] an unpublished Latin collection in Châlons-sur-Marne, Bibliothèque municipale, MS 319; an Italian collection in the Biblioteca Universitaria of Bologna;[21] and another unpublished version of this basic material, in the Vatican Library, Palatino latino 1768.

A second tradition is marked by four compilations: the fourteenth-century Venetian *Libro per cuoco*;[22] a work in the Biblioteca Riccardiana of Florence[23] part of the Bolognese manuscript mentioned above;[24] and the rather brief set of recipes copied in the manuscript at Nice, Musée Masséna, Bibliothèque de Cessole, MS 226.[25]

A third tradition is represented by the unpublished manuscript London, British Library, MS Add. 18165, ff° 1r–20r, and by the second manuscript edited by Boström.[26] Yet even here, though many of the dishes in that collection resemble those of our series, the over-all contents of

---

[17] Edited by Michael Süthold, *Manoscritto Lucano. Ein unveröffentlichtes Kochbuch aus Süditalien vom Beginn des 16. Jahrhunderts*, Kölner Romanistische Arbeiten, 70 (Geneva: Droz, 1994).

[18] Both of these fundamental texts were edited by Marianne Mulon, "Deux traités inédits d'art culinaire médiéval," *Bulletin Philologique et Historique (jusqu'à 1610)* (1968, publ. 1971), volume 1: 369–435; the texts proper are found at pages 380–395 and 396–420, respectively. The full title of the second collection is *Liber de coquina ubi diversitates ciborum docentur*.

[19] Ingemar Boström, *Anonimo Meridionale, Due libri di cucina*, Acta Universitatis Stockhommiensis, Romanica Stockholmiensia, 11 (Stockholm: Almqvist & Wiksell, 1985); "Libro A", pp. 5–31.

[20] Edited by Emilio Faccioli in *Arte della cucina*, 2 vols. (Milan: Il Polifilo, 1966), 1:19–57. The work's author is usually known as the Anonimo Toscano.

[21] Published by Francesco Zambrini, *Il Libro della cucina* (Bologna: Gaetano Romagnoli, 1863; repr. Bologna: Commissione per i Testi di Lingua, 1968).

[22] Edited by Emilio Faccioli, *Arte della cucina* 1:61–105. The unknown author of this collection is usually referred to as the Anonimo Venziano.

[23] Published by Domenico and Giacomo Zanichelli and Salomone Morpurgo, *LVII Ricette d'un libro di cucina del buon secolo della lingua* (Bologna: Nicola Zanichelli, 1890).

[24] Edited by Olindo Guerrini, *Frammento di un libro di cucina del secolo XIV edito nel di delle nozze Carducci-Gnaccarini* (Bologna: Nicola Zanichelli, 1887).

[25] Edited by Giovanni Rebora, "La cucina medievale italiana tra oriente ed occidente," *Miscellanea storica ligure* 19 (1987): 1431–1579.

[26] Ingemar Boström, *Anonimo Meridionale, Due libri di cucina*, Acta Universitatis Stockhommiensis, Romanica Stockholmiensia, 11 (Stockholm: Almqvist & Wiksell, 1985); the text of "Libro B" is found at pages 32–48. The Neapolitan Collection seems in particular to bear some relation, whether of provenance or of influence, with this second "anonymous southern" collection of Boström.

the Neapolitan manuscript, and especially the sequence or order of its contents, do not diminish the clear primary links between it and Martino's work.

And, finally, the fourth tradition, to which the material of the Neapolitan manuscript belongs, at least in part. This tradition owes very much to contributions from the master cook Martino (see below), provided Platina's *De honesta voluptate*, printed about 1474, with most of its substance, and was still able to inspire the author of the *Epulario* when this work was printed in 1516. It seems advisable to speak of a Martino tradition because versions of the recipe collection to which the name of Martino have regularly been attached point to a history that has been both durable and almost certainly more complex than has been apparent. For instance, the recently published *Libro de cosina* in a late-fifteenth-century manuscript in the Biblioteca Comunale of Riva del Garda[27] seems to represent a slightly earlier version, and name, of Martino's *Libro de arte coquinaria* as this is read and has until now been known solely in the Washington and Vatican copies; and a manuscript in the Ruskin Gallery in Sheffield, England, R. 3550, has an initial section which is derived from recipes found in Martino.[28] A manuscript held in the Vatican Library[29] presents a close copy of what was eventually to become the *Libro de arte coquinaria*. A further, smaller recipe collection in manuscript, from the sixteenth century but also owing much to some stage of Martino's work, has been called *Modi singulari de cocina*.[30] Of the position of the Neapolitan Collection in the Martino tradition on the one hand and the relationship between the Neapolitan manuscript and Catalan traditions on the other we shall write later.

◈

---

[27] The text of this manuscript has recently received a diplomatic transcription (with some evidence of haste and misreadings, it should be observed) and published by Claudio Benporat in his *Cucina italiana del quattrocento*, Biblioteca dell' "Archivum Romanicum," 272 (Florence: Olschki, 1996), 157–231. One may still usefully have recourse to a facsimile reproduction of the manuscript offered by Aldo Bertoluzza in *Libro di Cucina del maestro Martino de Rossi* (Trento: Edizioni-U.C.T., 1993). Here the photographs of each of the manuscript recipes are accompanied by a very sketchy and occasionally untrustworthy translation into modern Italian.

[28] This Sheffield collection is currently being edited by Gillian Riley.

[29] Rome, Biblioteca Apostolica Vaticana, MS Urbinate latino 1203. The text of the recipes has been transcribed by Claudio Benporat, *Cucina italiana del quattrocento*, 79–155.

[30] London, British Library, Egerton MS 1985. Unedited.

C. The Neapolitan Manuscript: Textual Questions

(i) Date and place of origin of this collection

The script of this codex relates it roughly to the middle or second half of the fifteenth century. The watermarks in its paper likewise point to the second half of this century. Its contents, specifically the nature of the cookery that is found in the recipes between ff° 1 and 76v, belong to this same period and show an affinity with culinary practice in the region of Naples. Finally, the language in which the recipes are written is not incompatible with the dating that is suggested by the other evidence; as do a good number of the recipes themselves, the language also points to an area in Italy that was influenced by Catalan culture: Naples. No extant evidence would seem to invalidate a conjecture that the manuscript Bühler 19 was written during the second half of the fifteenth century in or about the Aragonese court at Naples.

(ii) Language

We can attempt to tabulate the syntactic forms used by the scribe and/or author of the recipes texts in this manuscript.

Definite articles

Singular : *el* (masculine), *lo* (masculine), *la* (feminine); plural: *li* (masculine), *le* (feminine). Other forms, such as *il, i, gli,* do not occur.

Contracted forms

chel (*che* + *el*): 13, 54, 68, 69, 71, 89, 108, 129, 187; *sel* (*se* + *el*): 69, 71.

Personal pronouns, third person: masculine forms

Nominative singular forms

el: 180 (*quando el sera ben cotto*), *passim*; *lui*: 194 (*tute le dolce cose che lui fara*).

Contracted forms

chel (*che* + *el*): 77 (*fa chel non sia tropo salato* [*el pastizo*]), 85, 90, 104; *sel* (*se* + *el*): 1 (*sel te piace* [*el aceto*]), 44, 163, 188; *el* + *e* [verb] contracts in *le*: 115 (*se le tropo forte* [*el aceto e*]), 161 (*se le tempo de carne*), 171 (*quando sera spisso, le cotto* [*el biancho manghiare e*]), 188 (*se le vivo* [*el polpo e*]).

Dative singular forms

gli: 2 (*che gli sia rotta l'ossa* [*capone*]), 67, 69, 70, 71, 132, 148, 167, 219; *li*: 67 (*non li rompere la pelle* [*pizone*]), 182 (*non li lassi spine* [*sturiono*]), 199, 218; *-li*: 5 (*dalli suso doi botti* [*peto*]), and *passim*.

Accusative singular forms

lo: 37, 69 (*quando lo vorai mandare a tavola* [*lo pavone*]), and *passim*; *-lo*: 1 (*pistalo* [*pane*]), and *passim*.

Plural forms

li: 197 (*che non li resti nulla de bruto* [*calamari*]), and *passim*; *-li*: 2 (*non ponendoli sale* [*capone*], and *passim*.

Note the use of *loro* as a nominative: 197 (*che loro siano primo tagliati in pezi* [*calamari*]).

Personal pronouns, third person: feminine forms

Nominative singular form

la: 70 (*como la sera cotta* [*vacina*]); in conjunction with *che*: 10 (*che la sia bene cotta* [*cinna*]), 67, 88; in conjunction with *se*: 52 (*excepto se la fusse vitella* [*carne*]), 57, 68. Note: *ella* does not occur explicitly in the manuscript.

Contracted form

la + *e* [verb] contracts to *le*: 61 (*quando le bene calda* [*la starna e*]), 203 (*se le grossa* [*la orata e*]), 212.

Dative singular forms

gli: 132 (*de sopra gli ponerai* [*tiela*]), 218 (*in bocha gli ponerai una noce moscata* [*lampreda*]); *li*: 15 (*non li mettere piu che doi rossi d'ova* [*farina*]), 218 (*de sopra li ponerai uno poco de sale* [*lampreda*]); *-li*: 1 (*giongendoli specie* [*materia*]), 10, and *passim*.

Accusative singular forms

la: 28 (*alla quaresima la puo fare cum* ... [*cemolella*]), and *passim*; *-la*: *passim*.

Accusative plural forms

le: 50 (*tu le potrai fare dolce* [*cose*]), 55 (*quando le harai cotte* [*galine*]), and *passim*; *-le*: 4 (*falle stare in moglio* [*amandole*]), and *passim*.

Dative plural forms

li: 83 (*che siano bene nete che non li resta niente del grasso* [*budelle*]); 195 (*che non li resta alcuna immonditia* [*testudine*]).

Note the use of *loro* as a genitive: 3 (*piglia lo petto loro* [*galine*]), 112.

Other forms

essi 75, 88; *essa* 214. Note: *ella, ello, esso, lei, ei* do not occur.

alesso, arosto

These words seem to be used as indeclinable, as if they were adverbs with a verb, such as *cotto* or the like, implicitly understood. There is no exception in the manuscript. No form, such as *alessi, arosti* occurs in it. For instance: 10, *cocila alesso*, 45, *polastri alesso*; 37, *conzali como se fa arosto* [*pizoni o polastri*], 52, *qualunche altra carne che meritasse esser posta arosto*.

The infinitive *esser*

Esser is the form used almost throughout the manuscript. There are only three occurrences of *essere*: 104 (note), 125, 199. The final *e* is likewise not written for the infinitive *comer*.

ben and *bene*

The form *ben* is most often used when it precedes the term it qualifies, *bene* when it follows it. For instance: *ben tritto, tritto bene*.

serane

In Recipe 1, the recipe directs that the meat be boiled; then the scribe writes: *Cotta che serane la dita carne, cavala fora.* This sort of postclitic fusion of *ne* (having the sense of "with the salted broth") is unusual on a finite verb that is not imperative.

(iii) Composition of this collection

Whatever the immediate source of the recipes copied in the Neapolitan Collection, a question we shall be examining briefly later, their sequence is the result of some deliberation.[31] A few sectional titles in large lettering announce main divisions or chapters within the body of the work:

> across ff° 23v–24r, *Incipiunt Mirabilia Gule;*[32]
> at f° 31r, *Farcimenti sive Impiture;*
> at f° 40r, *Sapori de Piu Sorte;*
> at f° 43r, *Salsa de Piu Sorte;*
> and at f° 59r, *Menestre de Quadragesima.*

In each case these rubrics certainly apply to the recipes that immediately follow them. They are not, however, entirely satisfactory as divisional markers in the collection as a whole. Most notably, no rubric identifies the *genre* of the initial sixty-five recipes before f° 23v—which are, in fact, quite diverse in nature. And, furthermore, in most of the cases where a rubric is inserted, it is obvious in the series of recipes apparently so designated that there comes a point at which the section title no longer applies. Only between ff° 40r and 42v is it clear that the recipes are homogeneous, that *all* are indeed *Sapori de Piu Sorte.*

There is, moreover, a major problem with the section titles in that the compiler has not been at all consistent in inserting an appropriate rubric to mark what is clearly a significant sequence of a particular type of preparation. At f° 46v, for instance, there begins a series of *torte* and, following them, at f° 53r, a similar series of egg dishes, neither of which series certainly is meant to be covered by the last rubric to precede them (at f° 43r): *Salsa de Piu Sorte.* The inconsistency here is somewhat bothersome. Perhaps the most serious omission of a title occurs at the head of the last section in the work as we have it, the section containing ways to prepare more than thirty fish. However, at the point in the manuscript where we might reasonably have expected some such rubric as *Pesce*, it is apparent that we do not still have the complete manuscript as it must originally have been written. Because of what seems to have been the loss of either one or two double-folios—the folded sheet on which four pages of text were written—the text, and even

31 The order in the arrangement of the recipes can be appreciated in the table of Appendix A (p. 237). The order adopted for the Neapolitan Collection is not that of the Riva del Garda collection nor of the late copies we possess of Martino's *Libro de arte coquinaria* (Vatican and Washington manuscripts), even though Martino's work will eventually incorporate the majority of those recipes.

32 Any of these "marvellous" dishes might serve as a diversionary dish, a *divertimento* or *intermezzo* in the course of a meal.

the contents, of this part of the work are not at all certain (see above: The Manuscript). We may suppose that a rubric for this final section of the collection likely did originally exist here and has been lost along with whatever was on some missing folio or folios.

In gathering "*k*" (reidentified twice subsequently as "*i*"), the text interrupts a series of *torte* with a series of preparations for sea-fish. Contrary to the scribe's practice previous to this point in the manuscript, there is no general rubric announcing this abrupt change in matter. Furthermore, the next gathering, also of a single folded sheet, returns to fried and baked dishes (*fritate* and *tartari*). The gathering that follows, what looks like a full normal gathering and is identified as "*k*", continues with recipes for fish, but the beginning of its first recipe (Recipe 196, for eel) is missing: this beginning of the eel recipe most certainly occupied the *verso* of some previous folio.

We believe that we are right in proposing that ff° 69r–70v, containing recipes for two *Fritate* and two *Tartari*, must originally have been bound to follow f° 66v, after three *torte*. The sequence of dishes (Recipes 182-183-184) over the "join" between f° 66v and f° 69r is exactly that which is copied in the Riva del Garda manuscript at Recipes 170-173-172; in that latter compilation Recipe 171, for *Una bona torta papalle per fare collatione*, is likely a new addition by Martino de Rossi, perhaps at a time when his new duties took him to Rome.

The sections of the book, the culinary genres, as it were, tend to be copied into their own gatherings: the beginning of gathering "*e*" marks a break between *Farcimenti sive impiture* and three extensive recipes for jellies; the section on Eggs opens at the top of f° 53r at the beginning of gathering "*g*"; and Lenten dishes begin at f° 59r at the beginning of gathering "*k*". The single fold of paper now foliated 69r–70v contains, as we have just mentioned, two *Fritate* and two *Tartari*. There is therefore some indication that, for the latter part of the collection at least, some effort was made to assemble the book's material by *genre*, to write this into gatherings, and then to incorporate the various *genres* into the book as a whole.

Despite their rarity and occasional imprecision, the extant divisional rubrics do let us perceive with some clarity what was intended regarding the internal arrangement of the collection as a whole. The most serious exception to this general utility of the rubrics occurs at the beginning of the collection: the long section of 65 recipes with which the book opens has no special rubric itself. This lack may simply indicate that this part of the book contains the wide range of dishes that normally composed a "standard" compilation of recipes in the Italian peninsula during the fourteenth and fifteenth centuries. The book begins with the sort of recipes anyone could find, say, in the *Libro della cucina* or in the *Libro per cuoco*.[33] In this initial section we find a spicy sauce, a broth of fowl, spices and herbs, four versions of a Whitedish, dishes for rice, various forms of pasta, an egg and cheese dish (Recipe 22), vegetable dishes, tripe, a porridge, melons, two sickdishes, pottages, legumes, boiled meats and fowl (from Recipe 43), roast meats and fowl (from Recipe 52). The section ends with three dishes that in a way anticipate the *Mirabilia Gule* that are supposed to constitute the next division of the book. The variety of types of dish found in the first 23 folios of the manuscript is wide, with the consequence that in some places here the compiler has either

---

[33] For these collections, see earlier notes. Both works have been edited by Emilio Faccioli, *Arte della cucina* 1:19 ff. and 61 ff. respectively.

not tried or not been able to sort out his material very categorically: the Catalan *Mirausto*, for instance, a dish in which fowl is half-roast and then half-boiled in a sauce of almond milk, egg yolks and spices, is copied between a recipe for melons and another for stewed herbs.

In short, what we seem to have in the opening section of the collection is a fairly broad, almost miscellaneous selection of what may well have been fairly common recipes. These belong in particular to the categories that we might call graminaceous, farinaceous, stewed fruits and vegetables, and meats. Missing here generally, though by no means entirely, are those types of preparation that will be gathered into their own divisions later: the *intermezzi* or marvellous dishes, preserved meats, serving sauces, cooking sauces, pies, egg dishes, Lenten dishes, and fish. The general organization — such, at least, as it is perceptible — in the initial section of the book is by foodstuff; in what follows in subsequent divisions, again generally (and obviously except for the section of fish recipes), the organization is by dish-type or function. If there is a "category" into which these initial dishes fall, it is perhaps a negative one: whatever does not fit within the clearly cut categories of which the remainder of the collection will be composed.

While the compiler of our collection may not have been entirely successful in arranging all of his material in obvious and exclusive *genres*, he has nevertheless insisted upon a much more rigorous order in the sequence of recipes than is found in such antecedents as, say, the *Libro della cocina* or either of the collections edited by Ingemar Boström.[34]

Certain of the recipes show a mark, always in the right margin opposite the recipe's title or its first lines, that resembles a number "6" and is similar to those numeric 6's that are written in the Menus section of the manuscript. This mark is reproduced as an italic 6 in the catalog of Appendix A (p. 247), and placed beside those recipes that show it in the manuscript. The mark seems to be a private notation of some sort, whether of the compiler, the scribe or some subsequent user of the manuscript. It may indicate a source of the recipe; alternatively and perhaps more convincingly, it may identify recipes chosen (by someone) to be recopied elsewhere. A further guess about the sense of the sign might be that those recipes so marked were seen as lending themselves in some way to a dinner for six persons.

One final observation should be made about the presentation of the assortment of recipes such as we have it, and that is that this copy of the "work" found in the Neapolitan manuscript lacks a general table or index. The absence of such bibliographic material in late-medieval cookbooks is certainly not unusual, but calls for comment. Several explanations are conceivable. The compiler may have assembled these recipes primarily for himself; he was sufficiently familiar with the layout and sequence they occupied in the codex that he needed no reminder of them. Alternatively the generic order of the recipes was more or less recognized within the professional circle around the compiler where this copy was intended for use or was apt to circulate. It is also possible that for the book's contents there was indeed at one time an index that was written onto its last pages, onto those very folios following f° 76v that in all likelihood, unfortunately, originally contained as well the final recipes of the collection.

---

[34] Ingemar Boström, *Anonimo Meridionale*.

Sickdishes

It is surprising that there are relatively few recipes in this collection that are designated as appropriate for the sick or sickly. Only Recipe 32 is explicitly *ad homo infermo*. The recipe that precedes this one in the collection, *Brodo a homo delicato*, was in fact universally considered to belong generically to that category since its ingredients and manner of preparation satisfied the medico-humoral requirements of a dish whose net properties were temperamentally proximate to those of the normal human being. Likewise later, in Recipe 161 for *Limache in tempo grasso*, snails are presented in medical terms as *restaurative et lubriche al corpo*. These three recipes are a very meager representation of a *genre* which is richly developed elsewhere in Italian and French collections of the period.

Cooks employed in large households had inevitably in the normal course of their work to prepare dishes to feed those members of the household or those guests of their master who were either of a sickly disposition, were actually indisposed with some slight distemper, or were convalescent.[35] Late-medieval recipe collections usually reflect this aspect of the cook's professional concern. For instance, the *Libro della cocina* offers recipes for fifteen dishes which are explicitly designated as appropriate for the sick, thirteen of which are grouped in a sequence which we might call a chapter of sickdishes.[36] The first of the anonymous southern Italian collections published by Boström likewise assembles eight sickdishes into a corresponding area of the book.[37] And the Italian collection now in the Library of the Wellcome Institute, and whose manuscript dates from roughly the same period as our own, contains at least seven preparations identified as suitable for the sick.[38]

The paucity of sickdish recipes in the Neapolitan Collection calls for some explanation. Reasonable guesses might include these two: either this selection of recipes originates in circumstances that were too humble for sickdishes to constitute a significant part of the cook's activity; or just the opposite, that this Collection was associated with a court so great that the physicians attached to it had alone the authority to prescribe any and all foods to be prepared for the sickly, sick and convalescent who were members of its household or who frequented it.[39] In any case the seeming unimportance of sickdishes as such remains a remarkable feature of the Neapolitan Collection.

---

[35] An entire chapter of the Latin *Tractatus de modo preparandi et condiendi omnia cibaria* is devoted to twelve "sickdishes" whose preparation is intended for those whose digestive systems were by nature fussy or temporarily out of sorts: *IV. Modo narrandum est de condimentis delicatis dominorum, ad naturam confortandam et appetitum provocandum.* This collection is assumed to have had an Italian origin. Edited by Marianne Mulon in "Deux traités inédits d'art culinaire médiéval," *Bulletin Philologique et Historique (jusqu'à 1610)* (1968; publ. 1971), 2 vols., 1:369–435.

[36] Emilio Faccioli, *Arte della cucina* 1:19–57, Recipes 8, 132, 162, 164–166, 168–176.

[37] Ingemar Boström, *Anonimo Meridionale*, "Libro A," Recipes 84, 85, 88, 89, 91, 94, 95, 96.

[38] Unpublished manuscript: London, Wellcome Institute for the History of Medicine, Library, WMS 211: Recipes 9, 115, 125, 128, 156, 157, 164.

[39] Such physicians would have access to medical treatises in which various regimens included the appropriate foods to prescribe for their patients according to each patient's indisposition.

We may relegate to this footnote a third possible explanation: That any Cook, Kitchen Clerk or Master of the Household who might wish actually to consult this collection of recipes would be medically

(iv) Sources used in its composition

Martino and his legacy

The recipe collection entitled *Libro de arte coquinaria*, the work of Maestro Martino, has generally been recognized as the most significant culinary work of the Italian fifteenth century.[40] The existence of at least four manuscripts of this work testifies to the respect in which it was held, and further suggests the likely influence it exercised on several generations of professional cooks in the latter half of that century. Its authority is recognized in several works that derive from it or incorporate numbers of its recipes more or less textually. Even Bartolomeo Sacchi (*alias* Platina) explicitly acknowledges the enormous debt he owed to Martino when he came to compile his own *De honesta voluptate et valetudine*:

> About the cook.
>
> One should have a trained cook with skill and long experience, patient in his work and wanting especially to be praised for it. He should be lacking in all filth and dirt, and should know properly the force and nature of meats, fish and vegetables so that he may understand what ought to be roasted, boiled, or fried. He should be alert enough to discern by taste what is too salty or too flat. If possible, he should be completely like the man from New Como [*i.e.*, Martino], the prince of cook of our age, from whom I have learned the art of cooking food. . . .[41]

---

competent enough to recognize dishes appropriate for use as sickdishes for specific disorders or ailments, even though they are not so designated in the text of the recipes.

40 The text of the manuscript in the Library of Congress, Washington, has been edited by Emilio Faccioli, *Arte della cucina* 1:117–204. The text in the manuscript of the Biblioteca Apostolica Vaticana, Urbinate latino 1203, differs little from it; it is untitled and unattributed. This text can be seen in Benporat, *Cucina italiana del quattrocento*, 79–155. A third Martino manuscript, which until 1897 belonged to Baron Jérôme Pichon, may presently be in a private collection in Milan; much mystery surrounds its whereabouts. According to a description and a single-page reproduction of this manuscript in *Printed Books, Manuscripts & Autograph Letters* (London: Christie, Manson & Woods, Nov. 13–14, 1974), p. 89, on the occasion of its being auctioned — to a book dealer in Milan — it was an elegantly executed codex of parchment. In it Martino is designated merely as "cook" (without the qualification "formerly" that is found in the Washington manuscript) to the Patriarch of Aquileia (*i.e.*, Ludovico Trevisani, Cardinal of Aquileia, who died in 1465). Bruno Laurioux, "I libri di cucina italiani," 43, speculates that this volume may have been a presentation copy produced by the author for his patron, the Patriarch of Aquileia, in or about 1465. On this copy see also Benporat, *Cucina italiana del quattrocento*, 35.

41 *De coquo. Coquum habeat arte et longa experientia doctum patientem laboris et qui laudari in ea re maxime cupiat. Careat is omni squalore ac spurcitia cognoscat apposite carnium piscium holerum vim atque naturam ut quid assum quid elixum quid frictum fieri debeat deprehendat. Caleat gustu decernere quæ salita nimis et quæ fatua sunt. Novicomensi nostra ætate coquorum principi et a quo obsoniorum conficiendorum rationem accepi, sit omnino, si fieri potest, persimilis. . . .*
Book I, chapter 11. Mary Ella Milham, *Platina. On Right Pleasure and Good Health. A Critical Edition and Translation of De Honesta Voluptate et Valetudine*, Tempe, Arizona (Medieval & Renaissance Tests & Studies), 1998.

If we accept the testimony of both Platina and the Martino manuscript now in the Library of Congress[42], Maestro Martino functioned for a while, previous to 1465, as cook to the Patriarch of Aquileia. The version of his work with the somewhat puffed-up Latin title, *Libro de arte coquinaria*, likely originated in the Papal circles of Rome.

Yet Martino himself seems to have had a professional existence before Rome and further north in Italy. In the Archivio of the Comune di Riva del Garda, an uncatalogued manuscript has been identified by the Civico Museo e Archivio Storico di Riva as "Metodo di cucinar bene: manoscritto; secolo XV." Following six folios of a table that lists the recipes contained in the collection, the *incipit* of the book proper reads:

> *Libro de cosina composto et ordinato per lo egregio homo magistro Martino de Rossi dela Valle de Bregna, mediolanensis diocessis, descenduto dela villa de Turre, nato dela casa de sancto Martino Vidualis, coquo del illustre signore Jo[vanne] Jacobo Trivultio, etc., expertissimo in questa arte et, como legeray, prudentissimo.*

Because of such close textual parallels between certain of the Neapolitan recipes and readings in the Martino works — whether the Riva del Garda's *Libro de cosina* or the *Libro de arte coquinaria* — it is clear that the Neapolitan Collection, though unnamed and unattributed, is an integral part of the Martino tradition. At the same time, when we compare the Neapolitan texts on the one hand and, on the other, those texts expressly attributed to Martino, in the *Libro de cosina* and the *Arte coquinaria*, the nature of the variants indicates that the Neapolitan Collection antedates those Martino texts. We would posit that we have in the Neapolitan Collection a trace of the earliest version of any Martino recipe compilation.[43] This Collection does have material in it whose origin is outside of what will become the Martino canon, particularly recipes drawn more or less directly from Catalan sources; but the recipes that turn up in the *Libro de cosina* or the *Arte coquinaria* are represented in a form that points clearly to an early, proto-text of what will become known as the Martino canon. This proto-text of Italian recipes may have originated under

---

42 Medieval Manuscript 153. The *incipit* of this version reads: *Libro de arte coquinaria composto per lo egregio maestro Martino coquo olim del reverendissimo monsignor Camorlengo et Patriarcha de Aquileia.* We have already pointed out the significance of the *olim* written in this manuscript, the patriarch having died in 1465. For a biography of Martino, see Claudio Benporat, *Cucina italiana del quattrocento*, 17–24; and, in less detail, G. Chiesi, "Martino Rossi: un cuoco bleniese alla corte ducale," in Bertoluzza, *Libro di cucina*, 11–15. See also the study of Maestro Martino and his work in Benporat, 17 ff.

43 Claudio Benporat, *Cucina italiana del quattrocento*, 21, suggests that Martino may have spent some formative part of his professional career exposed to elements of Catalan culinary practice: "Partito dal villaggio di Torre perfeziona il suo magistero in un ambiente legato alla cultura alimentare catalana (Napoli?) con una serie di proposte sconosciute alla passata tradizione italiana che ritroviamo puntualmente in tutte le redazioni del suo ricettario. Passa quindi a Roma al servizio di Lodovico Trevisani e qui ha occasione di incontrare Platina che all'inizio del 1462 ha abbandonato Firenze . . . ." While this view presumes that Martino was enriching his experience in a way that would ultimately determine the nature of the *Libro de arte coquinaria*, it does not consider just as likely an occurrence: during the acquisition of this "Catalan" experience, Martino might well have found and adopted a collection of recipes which he would later modify and endow with his own name.

the pen of Martino himself—or perhaps not—but it was certainly neither the text attributed to Martino de Rossi that we have in the Riva del Garda manuscript nor the one attributed to the Maestro Martino of the *Arte coquinaria*. In Appendix B (p. 245) we present textual arguments for considering that, where the Neapolitan Collection and those collections attributed to Martino contain common material, the first work derives from a version of that material that is older than any extant work attributed to Martino.

The Martino texts of Riva del Garda and the *Arte coquinaria* are, we believe, essentially a literary rewriting, in a humanistic style, of some earlier text. In this process the earlier text was considerably inflated, and not always properly understood. New material was occasionally added during this revision. We can offer a random illustration by examining versions of the recipe for Marzipan Torte. The first version is from the Neapolitan manuscript (Recipe 180, beginning).

> *Torta de Marzapane. Piglia amandole he falle stare a moglio una notte, poi spellale che sian ben bianche, he pistale molto bene, et poi pone equale zucaro he equale amandole; per far questa torta megliore, che sia una libra de una—cio'e, de amandole—he una de zucaro fino ...*

The same part of the same recipe is from the Riva del Garda manuscript (Recipe 163[44]):

> *Per fare torta de marzapane, piglia armandolle ben piste mondate, per che non si passano per la stemegna; et per farli piu bianchi, piu dolzi et piu gustosi, se vogleno tenere a moglio nel'aqua frescha per uno di o una nocte, et se stesso, premendolle, se mondarano; e pistandole, le bagneray con pocho de aqua rossata azio non fazino olio et se volli fare bona la dicta torta, mettigli tanto zucharo quanto armandolle a pexo piu o mancho como ti pyace ...*

And finally, the same passage in the *Arte coquinaria* (Recipe 146)[45]:

> *Marzapane. Monda l'amandole molto bene, et pistale quanto piu sia possibile perche non fanno a passare per la stamegna. Et nota per fare le ditte amandole piu bianche, piu gustose et piu dolci a la bocca, se vogliono tenere a mollo nell'acqua frescha per un di et una nocte o tanto piu, che da se stesse premendole con le ditte se mondino. Et pistandole le bagnerai con un pocha d'acqua rosata, perche non facciano olio. Et se vol fare bona la ditta torta, metteragli a peso equale tanto zuccaro siano quanto amandole—cio e una libra dell'uno et una dell'altro ....*

It is clear that Martino's legacy, even as we are still discovering it, is extensive and complex. It is equally clear that the texts of the *Libro de cosina* and the *Libro de arte coquinaria* are not the first form that most of the recipes in those books had, nor perhaps what Martino first wrote. Both the compilation in the Riva del Garda manuscript and that of the *Arte coquinaria*, whether

---

44 As mentioned before, the text of the Riva del Garda manuscript may be read in Claudio Benporat, *Cucina italiana del quattrocento*, 157–231. In this present study, however, I prefer to use my own transcription. My numbering of the recipes differs from that of Benporat only from Recipe 228 on, where my numbers are greater by one than what is seen in Benporat. The photo-facsimile of this manuscript by Bertoluzza, as noted above, regrettably contains neither recipe numbers nor any indication of folio numbers.

45 With few, insignificant exceptions the texts of the *Libro de arte coquinaria* follow the reading of Faccioli in his *Arte della cucina*. The recipe numbers, lacking in Faccioli's edition, have been assigned serially by myself.

directly from the pen of an older Martino or not, represent a serious revision, an advanced stage in the evolution of his work. It is evident that whatever set of recipes Martino originally found or compiled was far from being set permanently in stone.

One should not too much lament the obscurity that still surrounds this hypothetical "original" form of the work that would be associated with Martino's name. The evolution of any cookbook is an entirely natural phenomenon. Each stage, each version is a discrete product of its times and circumstances. The evolution itself is not at all a case of removing the work further and further from its perfect, original form. Fidelity to a source is not in itself a primary virtue of cookbooks, either today or in the fifteenth century. In many respects each new version of a recipe collection supercedes its source or sources; its very existence declares that its sources are obsolete or foreign, and so no longer valid in different circumstances.

Furthermore, there may be a danger in treating written recipes as just so many texts. Written recipes in the Middle Ages necessarily *follow* practice (whether local or "foreign"), try to keep up with it and, occasionally, to reflect it as contemporaneous activities. Medieval cookery existed quite well *without* texts; professional cooks produced satisfactory meals whether they had written recipes or not.

As we perceive parallels between particular cookery texts we should always consider that, as a genre, the medieval recipe collection is concerned primarily not with instructing a cook but with recording the best sort of practice in a given place at a given time. Recipe collections were of strictly secondary significance to what was actually being done in kitchens across Europe in the late Middle Ages.

Based solely upon textual similarities, the pursuit of a stemma or "family" of recipe manuscripts is an undertaking fraught with risk. We must also take into account a large number of variables having inter alia to do with taste, economics, memory, ambition, openness to novelty, time, accidental influence and talent. It may be useful to abandon the notion of a manuscript "copy" when dealing with early culinary recipes.

The contents of the *Cuoco napoletano* indicate certain connections and influences that are far from fully clear. As the Martino canon evolved, the person responsible for manuscript Bühler 19 benefitted from the professional abilities of an enormous number of cooks, whether directly or indirectly, whether in written, oral or purely practical form — abilities that become embodied in the person named Martino. Similarly our *cuoco napoletano* benefitted from sources that later heirs of Martino's expertise may not have known or cared about. That the person whom we call the *cuoco napoletano* was patently a professional cook leaves room to surmise that he may have been a respected master, contemporary or apprentice of Maestro Martino, a colleague with considerable initiative. Some direct antecedent of his work may have inspired Martino himself; alternatively the Neapolitan cook may have enjoyed access to an early draft of his *compagno*'s masterwork. In any case, the Neapolitan collection sprang from a legacy at some point before this had given rise to either the *Libro de cosina* or the *Libro de arte coquinaria*.

Catalan influence

Both the Neapolitan Collection and the collections attributed to Martino contain a certain number of Catalan recipes, some acknowledged, some not. It is likely that Catalan cuisine became favored in Naples and Rome during the pontificate of Cardinal Alonso de Borja (1378–1458) as Calixtus III (1455–1458). As secretary to Alfonso of Aragon, this Catalan potentate had accompanied his king to Naples. Alonso's nephew, Cardinal Rodrigo de Borja (1431–1503), became Vice-Chancellor of the Church (1456–1492) and ultimately Pope (as Alexander VI, 1492–1503). These famous Borgia prelates were from Játiva, Valencia, a part of the Catalan-Aragonese dominions. It is known that their retinue, including their cooks, remained for the most part Catalan when the family transplanted itself to Naples and Rome. The Catalan dishes recognized in Italy may well have derived directly, perhaps orally, from the Borgia kitchens.

Despite the wide respect enjoyed by Catalan cookery, a surprisingly small number of early Catalan culinary texts subsist in manuscript form. These manuscripts are the following:

BC: Barcelona, Biblioteca de Cataluña, MS 2112. (Probably late-fourteenth or early-fifteenth century.) Contains *De apereylar bé de menyar*, with a large fragment of the *Libre de sent soví* (unedited).

UB: Barcelona, Universidad de Barcelona, MS 68. (Second half of the fifteenth century.) Contains a late, modified and expanded version of the *Libre de sent soví* and the *Libre de totes maneres de confits* (both edited: Grewe, Faraudo[46]).

UV: Valencia, Universidad de Valencia, MS 202. (First half of the fifteenth century.) Contains a smaller fragment of *Libre de sent soví* (edited: Faraudo).

A newly discovered manuscript

A recently discovered manuscript of the Biblioteca de Cataluña[47] has considerably enlarged our knowledge of Catalan medieval culinary practice. This recipe collection was written probably in the late fourteenth or early fifteenth century. It contains some 167 recipes and seemingly draws upon two sources: (i) *De apereylar bé de menyar*, and (ii) a large fragment of the *Libre de sent soví.*

Until now the first work has been known only by name, since an inheritance document of 1428 lists a book with this same title;[48] this designation may well refer to the volume that is now in the Biblioteca de Cataluña.

Guided by the table of recipe titles that appears at the beginning of the *Libre de sent soví* in the MS UV, we suggested in our edition of that work that this was the list of recipes actually constituting the original text. The newly discovered text contains almost all of the recipes in this table and, furthermore, in the order listed in the UV MS. The list contains close to one hundred

---

[46] See the Bibliography (p. 36).

[47] MS 2112. This is in paper, bound in parchment, and is catalogued as from the middle of the fourteenth century. All forty folios are given over to the culinary recipes. See also Cristina Borau, "*D'Aparellar de menjar*: Un altre receptari de cuina medieval en català," *Ir Col.loqui d'Història de l'Alimentació a la Corona d'Aragó Edat Mitjana*, 2 vols. (Lleida: Institut d'Estudis Ilerdencs, 1995), 2:801–12.

[48] " . . . *Altre libre ab cubertes de cuyro blanch, libre appelat* De perellar de menjar." See J. M. Madurell, *Manuscrits en català anteriors a la imprenta (1321–1474)* (Barcelona, 1974), 53, document 58.

items; the new text in the MS BC presents close to eighty. This text probably originated in the first half of the fourteenth century.

Some additional forty recipes, likely of more recent origin, complete the contents of this manuscript.

This manuscript of the Biblioteca de Cataluña seems to have been written down hastily. Some words have been skipped or miscopied; a transcription that is faithful to the intent of the compiler is at times difficult.

Other manuscripts

Before the recent discovery just mentioned, only two culinary manuscripts in Catalan were known to exist: the MS UV, containing a fragment of the *Libre de sent soví*; and the MS UB, which also contains a fragment of this text but with its recipes in a modified order and with a substantial number of additional recipes. These added recipes, it turns out, derive from *De apereylar bé de menyar*.

Two other texts should be mentioned. Firstly, the *Libre de totes maneres de confits*, a book on confections, is included in the MS UB and has been edited by Faraudo;[49] this work is one of the earliest of its kind. Secondly, there exists a booklet on carving. This latter treatise has not survived as an independent work but appears both at the beginning of the *Libre de sent soví* and in the *Libre del coch* of Mestre Robert (or Rupert de Nola). This carving text is likewise one of the earliest of its kind.

We may remark that the total number of known medieval Catalan recipes is not very large, probably below four hundred, if one does not count repetitions and variants. With few exceptions all appear in one or the other of these two books, the *Libre de sent soví* and *De apereylar bé de menyar*. Given the wealth of culinary advice offered in these two collections, one is tempted to wonder if by the middle of the fifteenth century there may not have existed at least another major collection of Catalan recipes.

(v) Catalan recipe manuscripts in Naples

King Alfonso V of Aragon conquered the Kingdom of Naples in 1442. At his death his natural son Ferrante became King of Naples and reigned from 1458 to 1494. Ferrante built a brilliant court there, enlisting the contributions of a great many talented artists and humanists.[50] Lavish banquets were arranged by the court nobility and incorporated such impressive presentations as roasted peacocks displaying their full fan of feathers and blowing fire from their beaks, elaborate

---

49 Lluís Faraudo de Saint-Germain, "Libre de totes maneres de confits. Un tratado manual cuatrocentista de arte de dulcería," *Boletín de la Real Academia de Buenas Letras de Barcelona* 19 (1946): 97–134.

50 On the matter of Neapolitan literature, architecture, sculpture and painting during the latter part of this time, for which Ferrante's son Alfonso, Duke of Calabria, was primarily responsible, see in particular George L. Hersey, *Alfonso II and the Artistic Renewal of Naples 1485–1495*, Yale Publications in the History of Art, 19 (New Haven and London: Yale University Press, 1969).

pasties, dishes with designs in gelatine of different colors, and so forth. Recipes of a few such offerings appear in our manuscript under the rubric of *Mirabilia gule*. Even more complex displays are described in the section of banquet menus appended later in our manuscript. Dining at the Neapolitan court during these decades must have been glorious. It may be assumed that our *cuoco napoletano* was familiar with this noble cookery and with the exuberant style of life that demanded it and sustained it. Likely the person responsible for our collection of recipes held a position in a household of the Neapolitan and Catalan nobility.[51]

During Ferrante's reign over the independent Kingdom of Naples, the intellectual and social exchange remained lively between Naples and the Catalan-speaking areas of the Spanish peninsula, especially Catalonia and Valencia. Many Catalan customs were introduced in Naples; vice versa, through Naples the new trends of the Italian Renaissance arrived back in the Iberian peninsula. As a result of this exchange, the Kingdom of Naples remained in close touch with current practices in Catalan cookery. Some of the culinary preparations that typified this cuisine appear in our manuscript.[52]

Most of the Catalan recipes that have been incorporated into the Neapolitan Collection can be found in both the MSS BC and UB. However, the recipes of MS BC show a text which is closer to the Italian text than that of the recipes of MS UB. For example, the Catalan word *sabrer* (*sebrer, sobrer*) appears in Recipes 110 and 111 of the MS BC, and has been translated into the Italian as *sabrero* (*cf.* Recipes 58 and 113 in our manuscript). The sense of this Catalan word, however, was very likely obscure in the second half of the fifteenth century, and does not appear in the corresponding recipes of the MS UB, where it has been replaced merely by "broth" (*brou*) or "water" (*aygua*).[53] Another example: Recipe 35 of the MS BC requires the use of five almonds,

---

[51] George L. Hersey, *Alfonso II*, 68 and fig. 86, identifies a generously dimensioned kitchen in the grand new villa, Poggioreale, which Alfonso, Duke of Calabria, built just outside the walls of Naples. Hersey (p. 62) also translates a document (from Joampiero Leostello, *Effemeridi delle cose fatte per il duca di Calabria (1484–91)*, in Gaetano Filangieri, *Documenti per la storia, le arti e le industrie delle provincie napoletane*, 5 vols. (Naples, 1883–97), I (1883): 223) which describes the "housewarming" of Poggioreale on June 2, 1489.

> . . . The King arrived at Poggioreale. He rested here for the remainder of the day, amusing himself with instrumental music and singing, and at ten o'clock His Majesty supped with many guests, and in an orderly manner, on infinite varieties of dishes . . . . Having eaten his dinner the King rode out, giving the Duke a chance to eat, for he had not yet done so. Instead he had served the King very circumspectly by taking care of the guests. A little after midnight His Highness [the Duke] sat down at the table, under a great canopy, outdoors in the palace square, with many noblemen, courtiers of the King's who had been invited to the feast . . . .

A cook in a noble Neapolitan household was expected not only to be professionally competent and to work exhausting hours, but to be able to produce "infinite varieties of dishes."

[52] A useful juxtaposition of Italian and Catalan recipe collections can be read in Barbara Santich, "L'Influence italienne sur l'évolution de la cuisine médiévale catalane," *Manger et Boire au Moyen Age*, 2 vols. (Paris: Les Belles Lettres, 1984), 2:131–40.

[53] *Cf.* Recipes 133 and 181 of *Libre de sent soví*.

and so does the Italian translation (*cf.* Recipe 55 in our manuscript), but the corresponding recipe of the MS UB does not specify the precise number.[54]

Such evidence indicates that the older versions of the Catalan texts were the ones that were available in Naples. For this reason, when we suggest Catalan sources for recipes of our manuscript, the recipes of MS BC have always been chosen and reproduced in full, while the corresponding recipes of MS UB, if they exist, are quoted only by title, as in the Grewe edition of the *Libre de sent soví*.[55]

(vi) The Neapolitan manuscript and Mestre Robert

The first printed Catalan cookbook, the *Libre del coch*, was written by Mestre Robert, or Rupert de Nola as his name is spelled in the Castilian translation of this work. The first known Catalan edition of the *Libre del coch* dates from 1520 (Barcelona), and the first Castilian edition is of 1525 (Toledo). This book was a success: there were at least five Catalan editions of it and at least seven Castilian editions during the sixteenth century. It was clearly *the* cookbook of Renaissance Spain.

Some of the recipes presented in the *Libre del coch* derive from older Catalan sources, as has already been pointed out,[56] but there is also a clear Italian influence. This influence is apparent in both the recipes and the language; an instance of the latter may be seen as the Italian word *pignata* ("pot") is occasionally used rather than the Catalan *olla*.

In the first paragraph of the *Libre del coch* it is stated that the author was a cook of King Ferrante of Naples, who reigned from 1458 to 1494. If Nola was his birthplace, he may well have been a Neapolitan since there is a town of this name near Naples. We may conjecture that Mestre Robert (or merely "Nola" as he is often called in the literature) lived in King Ferrante's time, that he worked for him as a cook and that while in his service he assembled a collection of recipes. This compilation was later rewritten, enlarged and expanded in a humanistic style, a style that is very conspicuous in the printed work.

Robert and the author of our manuscript may well have known each other, since they were approximately contemporaries, probably both of them lived in Naples, and clearly had similar professional concerns. However, Nola's book and our manuscript have a few recipes in common — a surprising and important observation for culinary history. We may add that the Italian versions of the handful of recipes common to both collections do not show signs of being translations from the Catalan.

Was Robert's original collection written in Italian or Catalan? Was it written before or after our Neapolitan manuscript was completed? What is the relationship between these two works, Robert's and the Neapolitan Collection? Without a detailed linguistic and culinary analysis of Mestre Robert's *Libre del coch*, which we have not attempted, we believe that it is premature to venture an answer to these questions.

---

54 *Cf.* Recipe 60 of *Libre de sent soví.*

55 Rudolf Grewe, *Libre de sent soví. (Receptari de cuina)* (Barcelona: Barcino, 1979).

56 Grewe, *Libre de sent soví*, 58.

D. The Cookery of the Neapolitan Manuscript

(i) The kitchen and its utensils

The kitchen used by the professional cook in mid- fifteenth-century Italy contained a good variety of pots and pans, cutlery, instruments and furniture of one sort or another, designed and used for specific functions.[57] The most common pot that the writer of this manuscript makes use of is the *pignatta*; he refers to its use forty-two times among these recipes. It was likely a vessel of moderate capacity, a smaller version of which, a *pignatella*, is also called into use on three occasions. Two other pots, a *cazola* and an *olla*, have less frequent use; the second is relatively large, of a size for boiling cuts of meat and fish.

The standard pan, that usually contains hot oil and is used particularly for frying foods, is the *padella* or *patella*. It is in very common use and is specified by our cook on forty-four occasions. It is of iron: Recipe 42 instructs the reader to fry eggs in paper just as if he were using an iron pan. The usual baking dish, probably earthenware and with or without a cover, is the *tegamo*; a larger variety of the same sort of dish is the *tiella*. This latter term derives from the similarity of this dish to a roofing tile.

Mortars of various sizes were in extremely common use in fifteenth-century kitchens. Normally a common mortar was of stone or cast iron; it served to hold and mix ingredients that were to be ground, by means of a pestle of wood or iron. In four instances, however, our Neapolitan cook places the mortar, with its contents, over the fire in order to cook them. We must speculate that the mortar in question here may well have been of brass or bronze.

Among the assortment of knives and strong-tined forks, skewers and spits, skimmers, rasps and strainers that are mentioned among these recipes, a holed spoon is called for in Recipe 26. Filters of cloth are in virtually constant use whenever spices are ground and infused, or almond milk is made. Moist foodstuffs drain on wooden tables; food to be hacked would be placed on a *taglero*, a solid chopping block or board.

(ii) Some culinary techniques

Parboiling, immersion in cold water

Several of the recipes require that meats and vegetables be cooked briefly in water or a meat broth before undergoing the principal cooking procedure, whether this is a frying, a baking or even a further boiling with other ingredients.

The same principle subjecting a foodstuff to a preliminary cooking is seen in recipes that instruct the cook to cook the ingredient only partially, or to withdraw it from the fire before it

[57] See additionally the outline, "The Mediterranean Kitchen," by Barbara Santich in her book *The Original Mediterranean Cuisine* (Totnes, Devon: Prospect Books, 1995), 15–17.

has quite finished cooking. Usually this interruption in the cooking allows the addition of other ingredients to the pot, ingredients such as eggs or spices whose nature would be altered too much by being exposed to a long period of cooking. Pies, likewise, are regularly drawn out of the oven just before their time in order to have flavorants (particularly the volatile rosewater) added through a hole on top.

A counterpart to parboiling is the immersion of a foodstuff in cold water before it is cooked. The procedure is stipulated in Recipe 43 and again in Recipe 52, in this latter case the author providing, in passing, an explanation of this procedure: the meat is boiled and then dipped immediately into cold water—*aquesto se fa cio sia piu bella*—and then finally mounted on a spit for roasting.

Cooking fats

A variety of liquid media are used by the *cuoco napoletano* in which to fry foods. The most common of these is termed simply "oil" and, more often than not, the word is qualified by the adjective "good" or "fino": *bono olio, olio fino* (particularly for the fritters and Recipe 179). Whenever a medium is not specified in the text of a recipe, it is likely safe to assume that what is intended is "oil": in Recipe 33, eggplant is to be boiled, dredged in flour and then fried, following which process the author writes "then drain off most of the oil . . . ." Though never explicitly identified in our collection of recipes, this oil is olive oil. The product was peddled through the streets of most south-European towns and could be purchased in barrels by large households directly from the producers. Because this is a vegetable product, olive oil is an appropriate frying medium for fish on lean days.

Other cooking fats referred to in our collection are animal derivatives. Good *lardo* is mentioned several times (in Recipes 1 and 58, for instance), this being a nonrendered pork fat. *Saimo* or rendered lard (in Recipes 101 and 103, for instance) is also used for finer cooking. Butter is specified or optional in a remarkable twenty-three recipes; some five of these dishes (French toast, for example, in Recipe 91) require a food to be prepared by frying in butter. Generally speaking, the daily products, butter and cheese, play an important role in this Neapolitan cookery.

Thickening procedures

Several methods of thickening a runny liquid mixture are used in these recipes. Bread or toast, whether whole or grated into crumbs, is frequently added to a pot in order to bind liquid ingredients. This is so particularly for sauces (in Recipes 104 and 106, for instance) where the cook does not wish to alter the delicate flavor of the spices that are combined there. A starch, made from wheat flour, likewise functions in the same way (Recipes 169 and 178). Rice flour (as in Recipe 39) similarly will serve as a thickener. In Recipe 72 a mixture of flavorants and eggs is added through the upper crust of a pie after the main contents of the pie have almost finished baking; in all likelihood the eggs are intended, at least in part, to thicken this pie filling. The use of liver (probably chicken liver, where there is no specification) is frequent as a thickener (for example, in Recipes 44 and 58), and often in conjunction with eggs or egg yolks.

One other common procedure is regularly resorted to in order to thicken a liquid or a runny mixture, and that is to reduce it by boiling. In this way must and wine are normally made into syrups, and a simple bouillon (as in Recipes 31 and 163) can yield a base for a relatively thick serving sauce.

Flavoring methods

Several particularities in the taste of the author of this collection may be pointed out. We may observe generally that herbs are not greatly used. The herbs most commonly incorporated into these dishes are, firstly, parsley (in thirty-eight dishes), then marjoram (used on a surprisingly numerous twenty-six occasions) and mint (19); these are followed far behind in importance by sage and fennel. Thyme, basil and chervil appear only once each. Completely absent in this cookery are the herbs coriander, rue, pennyroyal, wild celery, hyssop, bay, orach, cress (either garden cress or water cress), rocket, savory, calamint or dill—herbs that had ensured themselves a valued place in more northly cookery. There is likewise no role for the berries, such as strawberries, mulberries or elderberries. Otherwise, though, the fruits are moderately well represented by apples, quince and cherries, as well as, and extensively so, by the citrus fruits (especially the juice of lemons and oranges) and by pomegranates.

The most commonly used cooking spices in fifteenth-century Europe are all found here. While the peppers had generally lost favor in French kitchens by the end of the fourteenth century, and had been supplanted by the gingery grains of paradise, pepper remains here *the* preferred spice, while grains of paradise appear in only three recipes. Cinnamon, ginger and cloves are used in proportions found elsewhere. Of the spice seeds other than pepper, however, the author makes use of only mustard, cumin, anise and hemp.

The recipes of this collection call for saffron to be included in a mixture on an astounding 78 occasions. In all likelihood saffron was resorted to not for its flavor but for its color: as Recipe 11 for White Ravioli adds at its end, ... *Li poi far ghialdi de zaffrano*: "You can make them yellow with saffron."

In sum, apart from an unusually heavy reliance upon parsley as an herb and pepper as a spice, and an apparent predilection for the golden-russet color of saffron, our anonymous Neapolitan cook presents a set of recipes that make rather temperate use of condiments. In several recipes he even shows himself reluctant to include onions, unless with the master's approval. His own taste appears to have little in it that is exotic or bold, but points rather to a contentment with a repertoire that, for all its openness to "foreign" dishes, remains largely conventional and slightly old-fashioned.

To render dishes sweet (*dolce*), the *Cuoco napoletano* expressly prescribes must syrup (must that has been reduced by boiling: *mosto cotto* and *saba*), honey (*mele*) and sugar (mixed with cinnamon in Recipe 93). For a tart flavor he indicates verjuice or lemon juice.

Garnishes, especially sugar and cinnamon

Of all of the serving garnishes that appear on the dishes prepared by these recipes, by far the most common is a relatively simple mixture of sugar and cinnamon (in Recipes 35 ff., for instance). To these sole ingredients may occasionally be added a dash of rosewater (a distillate of an infusion of rose petals: see, for instance Recipes 39, 53 or 130), but such a modification of the conventional garnish is clearly exceptional. So favored by the cook and his clientele is this particular combination of sugar and cinnamon that the "Good Sauce" of Recipe 102 is nothing more than a mixture of pomegranate juice with sugar and cinnamon, the whole being reduced to a thick syrup by boiling. In Recipe 5, for the Catalan Whitedish, the garnish is merely a sprinkling of sugar; the writer feels that it is advisable to draw attention to this use of sugar alone, unmixed with cinnamon: . . . *cum zucaro di sopra, non ponendoli insieme altra cosa.*

A garnish of sugar-and-rosewater seems to be a distinctive feature of the *tortes.*

Pasta is commonly garnished with a coating of cheese and spices.

(iii) Some new, fashionable preparations

Some of the dishes and foodstuffs presented in the Neapolitan Collection clearly enjoyed the favor of the writer's patrons.

Pasta

The use of dough to make comparatively small, bite-sized morsels of food has a long history in Italian cookery that antedates the mid-fifteenth century, Martino and this present collection. The techniques of making *pasta asciutta,* pasta that is formed, then dried (usually in the sun) for later cooking and use, are described in several recipes here: both macaroni and vermicelli are dealt with, along with the proper ways of serving them.

Lasagne seems to have been a very common dish in the milieu of the Neapolitan Collection, being mentioned in no fewer than nine recipes here. Its preparation is not, however, included among our recipes; we must assume either that lasagne was a staple and, like bread, commercially available, or else that any chef who had advanced professionally in his craft to the point of using this recipe collection would certainly have under him an individual who was entirely competent in the making of such pasta. An interesting use of lasagne is seen in Recipes 128 and 130 where it serves to form the upper "crust" of a torte, and in the Rice Torte of Recipe 181 where it is used for both the lower and upper "crusts." In the Sienese *Tartara* of Recipe 132, lasagne becomes an ingredient within an almond-and-cheese custard.

Ravioli is made here in a variety of sizes and shapes: a walnut provides a model for a veal-and-cheese stuffing in Recipe 10; a finger for a sweet cheese mixture in Recipe 11. The second of these ravioli is made *without* pasta dough, the casing for its contents being provided by flour alone.

Torte

Several of the recipes provide directions for making a *genre* of dish which is named *torta,* either in the titles or the texts. Various indications here and there in these recipes allow us to form a good idea of the nature of this *torta.* A comparison to a modern open-faced sandwich might be useful, although we would have to understand that, in the first place, the "base" upon which the principal ingredients are assembled is frequently a layer of pastry, and, in the second place, that the preparation is baked in a covered dish. Normally this baking takes place on the coals, and sometimes with hot coals over the baking dish as well. Often the recipe for a *torta* will direct that the heat to be applied should be only moderate. In the Neapolitan Collection the main ingredients that are served in the form of a *torta* are varied: various *genres* of custard, pumpkin, rice, and so forth.

It is likely that a *torta* was picked up with the fingers and eaten in much the same way as an open-faced sandwich might be. No directions are copied to the effect that before or after being served on platters the *torte* were to be sliced into smaller segments; individual diners might be expected to slice off what each wanted to pick up.

Though ambiguity may arise because of modern usage of the term, we have kept the English word "torte" in our translation of these texts.

Fritelle

From Recipe 172 a series of no fewer than eight recipes are devoted to presenting varieties of deep-fried fritters. This sort of dish evidently afforded much pleasure at the aristocratic dining tables of the day, in large part because of the rich range of ingredients that could be incorporated into the basic *genre*. Among our *fritelle* we find versions for bitter herbs, elderflowers, rice-and-almond-milk, and stuffed figs. The fritter clearly presented the chef of the time with an opportunity to call his imagination and culinary skills into play; the "empty" fritters of Recipe 179, shaped artistically ad lib. before being fried, provide an instance of the scope of the late-medieval cook's professional initiative.

Sauces for roasts

The cooking and serving sauces outlined in the Neapolitan Collection owe a lot to other collections, particularly to that of Martino, but among these more or less standard preparations our author has interpolated a good variety of other sauces. Some of these are, indeed, derived from Catalan sources, yet the provenance of others is obscure; they may have been the creations of our Neapolitan author himself. Recipes 100 to 124 set out a remarkably broad assortment of sauces. Used either in the cooking of a principal foodstuff or as a serving garnish, or both, these sauce recipes allowed the chef to choose among a good repertoire of seasoning and pungency.

Apparently "new" and "unique" in this collection are the sauces for *Polastri spezati* (Recipe 100: a thick sauce of marjoram, pepper and cinnamon), and for *Pipione spezato he soffrito* (Recipe 103: a sweet, thick, yellow sauce of pepper and cinnamon). A curiously simple combination of pomegranate juice, wine, cinnamon and sugar, hot and reduced to a thick syrup — and then in a delightful understatement called simply a *Sapore bono*—is one of the most appetizing of the lot. Then there are a sauce of marzipan with the sweet-and-sour effect of lemon juice and pomegranate juice; a so-called Lombard Sauce that combined herbs and vinegar; a Papal Sauce, a sweet mixture of carrot (or parsnip) with ginger and cinnamon; a Royal Sauce, a sweet-and-sour blend of ginger and cinnamon; and two garlic sauces (Recipe 119 and 124) that, for the one, imaginatively crush fennel and basil with the garlic, and, for the other, grind walnuts with it. This last sauce is called *Salsa sclavonesco*, suggesting an exotic origin and also underlining the author's attempt to provide tasty and interesting options for his cook and the cook's patrons.

A new foodstuff: eggplant

Recipe 33 is for a dish whose principal ingredient is eggplant (or aubergine): *marignano*. This recipe seems to have no parallel in any other recipe collection of the time, and the eggplant itself seems to be unknown in collections before this time.[58] Appropriately, the author's directions in this recipe are extensive and detailed.

Ostentatious dishes

A section of the collection bears the rubric *Mirabilia gule*. This title applies to the five preparations described in Recipes 66 to 70. Though certainly edible, these "dishes" are intended primarily to amuse the guests at the banquet table, and their host as well, by being other than what they seem at first appearance. For the first the cook will manage to dissolve the bones of a dove without removing them from the carcass; the second makes two doves of one, presenting them as if they were life-like yet still ready-to-eat; the third applies the boat-in-a-bottle puzzle to a chicken; the fourth, a real *tour de force* has life-like (but edible) peacocks breathing fire; and the last stands a large, four-footed, *roasted* animal on its feet but still in its uncooked hide.

The essence of these preparations is that they are, indeed, marvellous. Either the fowl or animals in them will look entirely natural (... *el pavone stara impiede che parira vivo*, reads the direction in Recipe 69), or else the piece will astonish by the amazing technical artifice that it embodies. It is interesting to note in passing that what would be presented as the highlight of our cook's banquet is not gastronomic in nature. Each of these wonderful and amusing preparations is, in fact and literally, a variety of *intermezzo*, an entertainment or diversion that is presented as a sort of delightful change of pace during the meal, inserted as it was *between* the other ordinary servings — the Latin term for these latter being *missa*.[59]

Though these five pieces have been gathered into a section and — exceptionally, in this collection — provided with a rubric, other dishes may well have been considered appropriate for serving as remarkable centerpieces during a grand formal meal. In Recipe 27 the term *imbandisone* is applied to a dish of Garnished Turnips. This designation endows the dish of this recipe with a special status and a special interest; according to the text, this dish will culminate a series in a serving, and possibly in the whole of the meal itself. The difference between this dish of *Rappe armate* and the *Mirabilia gule* seems to be that the *imbandisone* are primarily pleasures for the palate and not just the eye.

---

[58] Claudio Benporat, *Cucina italiana del quattrocento*, 42, note 13, finds that eggplant (written clearly five times *mellegnani* in Recipe 103 of the Riva del Garda manuscript; *melanzane* in modern Italian) becomes known in the Italian peninsula first in the south and there only toward the end of the fifteenth century.

[59] See W. Meyer-Lübke, *Romanisches Etymologisches Wörterbuch* (Heidelberg: Carl Winter, 1911), §5612: *missum*, "Gericht." The French term *entremets* designating this sort of culinary divertissement is relatively common beyond the Alps. While the Italian form *intremesso* does not appear in our Collection, it is written in the Riva del Garda manuscript at Recipe 115: *Per fare uno intremisso chiamato pallotato.*

(iv) Other observations

"Foreign" dishes

An unusual number of dishes copied in this Collection have names that indicate a particular geographic source or nature. For the most part these names — fourteen of them — refer either to Italy (Recipes 8 and 122) or to states in the Italian peninsula: Sicily (15, 28), Rome (16, 23), Florence (47, 50, 134, 155), Bologna (87, 126), Lombardy (115) and Siena (132). To these Italian names might perhaps be added the qualifications Papal (117, 182) and Regal (118), assuming the latter to refer to the state in which the Collection's compiler resided. The other aspect of this use of geographic places in dishnames includes those that refer to nations beyond the Italian peninsula: the Saracen people (113), Slavonia (124), Germany (143), France (62, 116, 121, 185) and, in the Iberian peninsula, Spain (197) and Aragon/Catalonia (5, 30, 37, 61, 92). In all, then, either twenty-seven or thirty dishes here are identified, at least in the names they bear, as having some specific geographic provenance.

What seems apparent in this relatively large number of "foreign" dishes is that the compiler is quite aware of "foreign" tastes and gastronomic customs. It is certainly not likely that he undertook expeditions to foreign parts expressly to garner, for his domestic use or his recipe book, whatever in their national kitchens most appealed to him; all of the "foreign" dishes in his book had undoubtedly become naturalized, in the kingdom of Naples or wherever the compiler was writing, long before he wrote. But the fact that our writer, along with the other food professionals for whom he is writing, are both conscious of what we might call "foreignness" and at the same time willing to keep-by-adoption these other usages shows a significant openness to what other people might consider alien and suspect. There is no evidence of gastronomic xenophobia here, but just the opposite. By being willing to retain in the recipe's title a reference to the foreign origin of the dishes, this Neapolitan Collection acknowledges that the dishes have in a sense been imported, and that perhaps because of this they may even enjoy an increased intrinsic gastronomic interest.

And, finally, if the compiler of the Collection shows a willingness to acknowledge his culinary indebtedness to foreign tastes, then what of his patrons? It would seem likely, as we suggested, that these "foreign" dishes had in fact become naturalized in the local taste of Naples, at least to the extent that the compiler believed that their gastronomic worth had been proven. If so, they reflect on the international spirit of that community. Naples appears to have been home to a community that shared with the author of this Collection an exceptional awareness of other communities and other customs; both are quite willing to adopt and use whatever is worthwhile in other culinary customs.

"Catalan" dishes

In the cookery of the period the qualification of Catalan appears attached to a few dishnames. In our Neapolitan Collection there are four instances of a Catalan origin (or quality) of a dish, in recipes for Whitedish (Recipe 5), gourds (30), *Mirausto* (37) and partridge (61). The qualification does not seem to indicate a particular Catalan way of preparing, of cooking or serving any dish — that is, any dish that might be treated "in the Catalan fashion" — but seems rather to apply to a particular version of each of these dishes. Martino presents all of these Catalan dishes in his collection, and Platina work contains all but the Catalan partridge. The Wellcome manuscript further offers a *Suppa a la Catelanesca*, which consists of a mixture of ground liver, eggs and spices, especially cinnamon, boiled and poured onto bread which has been soaked in fine fat. Again, there seems to be nothing in this recipe to indicate that there was any particular way of cooking that writers in other countries might term "Catalan." And finally, by the sixteenth century the three recipes in the Catalan *Libre del coch* of Mestre Robert (Recipes 141, 142 and 143) that are themselves called "Catalan" have nothing to do with the four dishes so qualified in our collection.

A surprising absence among the recipes in this collection is a version of the persistently popular Parma, or Parmesan, Pie. In the fourteenth and fifteenth centuries no fewer than thirteen recipes can be found for this deep, layered creation.

The cook and his craft

Our anonymous author may be a chief cook or he may be the *maestro della casa* of some important estate, but he shows that he is especially aware of the professional obligations that bear upon him and upon all those companions who are responsible for the food set on the table of their master. In several places the cook is warned in very stern language to be *discreto* as he goes about his exacting labors, and to strive to exert all of the fastidious care that his profession demands. Those professional obligations pertain especially to the relationship between the kitchen and the hall, the cardinal need for the master of the household and the cook to be conscious of the *gusto del patrone*. The professional cook must be devoted wholly to the service of his master; he has one capital rule and that must be always to work to satisfy his master's taste. His profession must exist solely to serve that taste. As our author writes at the end of Recipe 186, *Fa ch'el cocho sia un ghiotto, ma non per se ma per lo suo patrone*: "Let the cook be a gourmand, not for his own sake but for that of his master."

E. The Neapolitan Manuscript: Banquet Menus

The copies of five impressive banquet menus[60] that have been appended to this manuscript likely joined the codex at some date not only after the recipes were copied, but also after the folio or folios disappeared that bore the conclusion of the text of Recipe 219 for *Lampreda grossa*, a text that is broken at the foot of f° 76v. However, the fascicle cue letters of the final gatherings in the manuscript, "*l*" and "*m*," continue the series without a break. The modern foliation of the manuscript likewise continues without a break from f° 76v onto the first page of these menus. This continuity seems to suggest that the pages bearing the menus date from roughly the time that the manuscript was assembled in its present form, rather than from the time that the recipes were copied.

As was mentioned before, the scribal hand that recorded these menus seems to the same as, or certainly very similar to, the one that wrote out the seventy-six folios of recipes.[61]

Of the five menus, there is significant similarity between parts of four of them: the whole menu of First Banquet is closely repeated at the begining of the Fourth Banquet and the whole of the Second Banquet's menu is largely echoed in the Third Banquet, though with different internal subdivisions and numbering.

Two of the menus are "anonymous," unassociated with any particular banquet: the Third Banquet and the Fourth Banquet. In each of these cases they are identified in a remarkably indefinite, even generic, way: *Un'altro convito, Altra rasone de convito*. These are the menus that seem to have a lot in common with the two that precede them in the series. According to the rubric attached to the other three menus, the banquet that each outlines was connected with individuals who are, presumably, historic figures: the *Archiepiscopo de Benevento* (on f° 77r), the *Conte Jeronimo* (on f° 77v), *Monsignore Ascanio* and the *Principe de Capua* (on f° 85r). Presumably also, the banquets outlined here are, or were, historic events — at least those banquets that are associated with proper names.[62] And finally, the banquets are likely to be roughly contemporaneous to the transcripts we have of them here — though not necessarily close in date to the copy of the assortment of recipes with which the manuscript begins.

---

60 We give a popular generic name "banquet" uniformly to all five of the meals described in the menus section of the manuscript, even though in the original the Italian designation varied: *convito* for the first four meals and *pranzo* for the last.

61 A scrolling cruciform symbol which is drawn twice on f° 15v is quite similar to one drawn on f° 84v.

62 For tentative identifications of some of the named personages, see below in our publication of the menus. While attempting to fix the historicity of these personages, though, it is important to bear in mind that they have little significance in indicating the dates either of the particular copy of the recipe collection that precedes the menus or of some "original" compilation of that recipe collection itself.

In every case the servings during the various banquets are in groups of dishes. These groupings are occasionally identified by *genre* with a rubric, though in cases where they are not so identified a comparison with groups of dishes that *are* generically identified reveals certain common elements in the structure of each meal.

The menus vary somewhat in ambition. The First Banquet (*Convito de lo Archiepiscopo de Benevento*) seems a relatively modest affair. With a mere seven courses and seventeen preparations, it is hardly more developed than the formal meal of a wealthy bourgeois. Yet when this and the Fourth Menu are set side by side, it may appear that a little less than a half of the full menu may have been reproduced; Menu [4] may more fully record what was served at this First *Convito*. The Second (*Convito del conte Jeronimo*) lists twenty-three courses — a good proportion of which, it is true, offer the guests a selection between only two prepared dishes. The two "anonymous" menus that follow record a remarkably rich assortment of dishes: the Third Banquet (*Un altro convito*, at f° 80r) offered something in the order of seventy-five preparations, while the menu of the Fourth (*Alra rasone de convito*, at f° 83r) lists perhaps fifty-nine.

While the first four menus are certainly not mean affairs, the final menu, for the Fifth Banquet, is clearly in a class by itself. In terms of the dishes prepared and served, the banquet was perhaps not exceptional, but as a tour de force in the dramatic presentation of these dishes it must have been nothing less than spectacular. It is with such a banquet that the *intermezzo* changed from being an unusual dish served between other dishes to being theatrical divertissement inserted as punctuation within a long, formal event.[63]

An interesting feature in all of these menus is that the writer occasionally mentions quantities. These seem not to be the total that was prepared of any given dish in the kitchen. The number that is attached to a preparation seems rather to indicate the quantity that was dressed out at the serving table and presented, on a platter *per serving*, to the guests at table. In the First Banquet, at the beginning of the seventh serving we find the item, *Dui caponi per piatello cum granate.* In the fifth serving of the Second Banquet, there is *Conigli arosto, tre per piatello*, and in the following serving, *Uno pastello per homo, de medule.* Elsewhere here and in other menus, wherever the meat, such as wild boar, cannot be described in terms of units, the quantities presented in a serving is expressed according to their weight: *Castrado, libre .x.* . Where two figures follow the mention of a dish, these may refer to the charging of platters respectively for the head table and for the other guests: *Caponi, quatro, sei* (Second Banquet, seventh serving).

---

63 On such *intermezzi* and generally on grand banquets at the end of the Middle Ages, see (for the Italian states) Claudio Benporat, *Cucina italiana del quattrocento*, 57–70; and (for France) Agathe Lafortune-Martel, "De l'entremets culinaire aux pièces montées d'un menu de propagande," in *Du manuscrit à la table*, ed. Carole Lambert (Montréal: Presses de l'Université de Montréal and Paris: Champion-Slatkine, 1992), 121–29. For a survey of the menus associated with cookery manuals, see Bruno Laurioux, "Les menus de banquets dans les livres de cuisine de la fin du moyen âge," *La sociabilité à table*, ed. Martin Aurell, Olivier Dumoulin and Françoise Thélamon, Publications de l'Université de Rouen, 178 (Rouen: Université de Rouen, 1993), 273–82.

F. Bibliography

Original Texts

Gathered here is a listing of the most important Italian, Iberian and Latin cookery collections of the Middle Ages.

Iberian

◆ *Libre de sent soví*

Valencia, Biblioteca Universitaria, MS 202, ff° 122r–29v. Beginning of the fifteenth c. Barcelona, Biblioteca Universitaria, MS 68, ff° 185r–258v. Second half, fifteenth c. Original perhaps 1324. 220 recipes.

Grewe, Rudolf, ed. *Libre de sent soví. (Receptari de cuina)*. Barcelona: Barcino, 1979. Also ed. Lluís Faraudo de Saint-Germain. "El *Libre de Sent Soví*. Recetario de cocina catalana medieval." *Boletín de la Real Academia de Buenas Letras de Barcelona* 24 (1951–52): 5–71.

◆ *De apereylar bé de menyar*

Barcelona, Biblioteca de Cataluña, MS 2112, ff° 1–40 (entire). Includes a "primitive" version of the *Libre de sent soví*. End of fourteenth or beginning of fifteenth c. About 167 recipes.

Unpublished.

◆ *Livro de cozinha*

Naples, Biblioteca nacional Vittorio Emanuele III, MS I.E.33. End of fifteenth or beginning of sixteenth c. 67 recipes.

Manuppella, Giacinto and Salvador Dias Arnaut, eds. *O "Livro de cozinha" da Infanta D. Maria de Portugal. Primera edição integra do códice português I.E.33 da Biblioteca Nacional de Nápoles. Prólogo, Notas aos textos, Glossário e Índices de Giacinto Manuppella. Introdução histórica de Salvador Dias Arnaut.* Acta Universitatis Conimbrigensis. [Coimbra]: Por Orden da Universidade, 1967. Diplomatic transcription on left pages; close, regularized translation into modern Portuguese on right. Also ed. Elizabeth Thompson Newman. *A Critical Edition of an Early Portuguese Cookbook.* Ph.D. diss., University of North Carolina at Chapel Hill, 1964.

◆ Mestre Robert, *Libre del coch*

Original likely fifteenth c. Printed in Catalan: Barcelona, 1520; Castillian translation printed 1525. 229 recipes.

Leimgruber, Veronika, ed. *Mestre Robert, Libre del coch.* Biblioteca Torres Amat, 4. Barcelona: Edicions Catalanes, 1982.

◆ *Libre de totes maneres de confits*

Barcelona, Biblioteca Universitaria, MS 68, ff° 172r–184v. Second half fifteenth c.

Faraudo de Saint-Germain, Lluís, ed. "*Libre de totes maneres de confits*. Un tratado manual cuatrocentista de arte de dulceria." *Boletín de la Real Academia de Buenas Letras de Barcelona* 19 (1946): 97–134.

Italian

◆ Anonimo Toscano, *Libro della cocina*

Bologna, Biblioteca universitaria della Università di Bologna, MS 158, ff° 93r–102r. 183 recipes.

Faccioli, Emilio, ed. *Arte della cucina. Libri di ricette, testi sopra lo scalco, il trinciante e i vini, dal xiv al xix secolo.* 2 vols. Milan: Il Polifilo, 1966. The *Libro della cocina* is at 1:19–57.

◆ Anonimo meridionale, "Libro A"

London, Private ownership. 146 recipes.

Boström, Ingemar, ed. *Anonimo Meridionale, Due libri di cucina.* Acta Universitatis Stockhommiensis, Romanica Stockholmiensia, 11. Stockholm: Almqvist & Wiksell, 1985. "Libro A" is at 5–31.

◆ *Buone vivande*

Florence, Biblioteca Riccardiana, MS 1071. 28 loose folios written in the fourteenth c. 57 recipes.

Zanichelli, Domenico and Giacomo, and Salomone Morpurgo. *LVII Ricette d'un libro di cucina del buon secolo della lingua.* Bologna: Nicola Zanichelli, 1890.

◆ *Frammento*

Bologna, Biblioteca dell'Università, MS 158, ff° 86r–91v (5 folios). Part of longer collection which combines several sources. Fourteenth c. 92 recipes.

Guerrini, Olindo, ed. *Frammento di un libro di cucina del secolo XIV edito nel dì delle nozze Carducci-Gnaccarini.* Bologna: Nicola Zanichelli, 1887.

◆ Martino de Rossi, *Libro de cocina*

Riva del Garda, Biblioteca Comunale, Archivio Storico. End of the fifteenth c. 282 recipes.

Diplomatic transcription by Claudio Benporat in *Cucina italiana del quattrocento.* Biblioteca dell' "Archivum Romanicum," 272. Florence: Olschki, 1996, 157–231. Also publ. in facsimile by Aldo Bertoluzza in *Libro di cucina del maestro Martino de Rossi.* De coquina, 3. Trento: Edizioni-U.C.T., 1993.

◆ Maestro Martino, *Libro de arte coquinaria*

Washington, Library of Congress, Medieval MS 153. Written in last decades of fifteenth c. Also Vatican, Urbinate latino, 1203; Milan (private ownership, previously owned by Firmin-Didot). A version of this is in Riva del Garda (see above). 268 recipes.

Faccioli, Emilio, ed. *Arte della cucina.* 1:117–204. The text in the Vatican MS has been transcribed by Claudio Benporat in *Cucina italiana del quattrocento*, 79–155.

◆ Anonimo Veneziano, *Libro per cuoco*

Biblioteca Casanatense, MS 225 (*olim* A.IV.45). End fifteenth c., contents from fourteenth c. 135 recipes.

Frati, Ludovico, ed. *Libro di cucina del secolo XIV*. Livorno, 1899; Bologna: Frati, 1970. Also ed. Emilio Faccioli, *Arte della cucina*, 1:61–105.

◆ Anonimo meridionale, "Libro B"

London, Private ownership. 65 recipes.

Boström, Ingemar, ed. *Anonimo Meridionale, Due libri di cucina*. "Libro B" is at 32–48.

◆ Cuoco napoletano, Neapolitan Recipe Collection

New York, Pierpont Morgan Library, MS Bühler, 19, ff° 1–76v. 219 recipes.

This edition.

◆ Untitled

Wellcome Institute for the History of Medicine, WMS 211. End of the fifteenth or beginning of the sixteenth c. 409 recipes.

Unpublished.

◆ *Dilicate vivande*

London, British Library, MS Add. 18165, ff° 1r–20r. 114 recipes.

Unpublished.

◆ Untitled

Nice, Musée Masséna, Bibliothèque de Cessole, MS 226. 56 recipes.

Rebora, Giovanni, ed. "La cucina medievale italiana tra oriente ed occidente." *Miscellanea storica ligure* 19 (1987): 1431–1579.

◆ Manoscritto Lucano

Naples, Biblioteca Nazionale, XII.E.19, ff° 1–27v. 86 recipes.

Süthold, Michael, ed. *Manoscritto Lucano. Ein unveröffentlichtes Kochbuch aus Süditalien vom Beginn des 16. Jahrhunderts*. Kölner Romanistische Arbeiten, 70. Geneva: Droz, 1994.

Latin

◆ *Tractatus de modo preparandi et condiendi omnia cibaria*

Paris, Bibliothèque Nationale, fonds latin 7131, ff° 94r–96v; also Paris, Bibliothèque Nationale, fonds latin 9328, ff° 129–133v. 82 recipes.

Mulon, Marianne, ed. "Deux traités inédits d'art culinaire médiéval." *Bulletin Philologique et Historique (jusqu'à 1610)* (1968; publ. 1971). 2 vols. 1:369–435. The text of the *Tractatus* is at 380–95.

◆ *Liber de coquina ubi diversitates ciborum docentur*

Paris, Bibliothèque Nationale, fonds latin 7131, ff° 96v–99v; also Paris, Bibliothèque Nationale, fonds latin 9328, ff° 133v–139v; and Halberstadt, MS 97, destroyed during the Second World War. 172 recipes.

Mulon, Marianne, ed. "Deux traités inédits d'art culinaire médiéval." The text of the *Liber de coquina* is at 396–420.

◆ *Doctrine*

Rome, Biblioteca Apostolica Vaticana, Palatino latino 1179, ff° 115v–156v. 55 recipes.

Lambert, Carole, ed. *Trois réceptaires culinaires médiévaux*, Ph.D. diss., Université de Montréal, 1989. Publication pending.

◆ *Modus viaticorum preparandorum et salsarum*

Paris, Bibliothèque Nationale, fonds latin 8435, ff° 24v–28v. Toulouse, Rodez & Montpellier, 1385–90. Latin with provençal features. 51 recipes.

Lambert, Carole, ed. *Trois réceptaires culinaires médiévaux*.

◆ Johannes Herbordi von Bockenheim, *Registrum coquine*. Rome, about 1431–35.

Paris, Bibliothèque nationale, fonds latin 7054, ff° 66r–74v; also London, private collection. 74 recipes.

Laurioux, Bruno, ed. "Le 'Registre de cuisine' de Jean de Bockenheim, cuisinier du pape Martin V." *Mélanges de l'Ecole française de Rome* 100 (1988): 709–60.

◆ Bartolomeo Sacchi, *alias* Platina (1421–81), *De honesta voluptate et valetudine*

Milan, Biblioteca Trivulziana, MS 734 (before 1468), and other later MSS. Roughly 300 culinary recipes.

Milham, Mary Ella, ed. *On Right Pleasure and Good Health.* A Critical Edition and Translation of *De Honesta Voluptate et Valetudine* (Medieval & Renaissance Texts & Studies, 168; Renaissance Society of America, 17). Tempe, Arizona: Medieval & Renaissance Tests & Studies, 1998.

◆ Untitled

Châlons-sur-Marne, Bibliothèque municipale, MS 319. 141 recipes.

Unpublished.

Criticism and History

The following works are some of the more useful resources for understanding the cookery found in the *Cuoco napoletano*.

Benporat, Claudio. *Cucina italiana del quattrocento*. Biblioteca dell' "Archivum Romanicum," 272. Florence: Olschki, 1996.

Benporat, Claudio. "Il ricettario di Martino de Rubeis nel contesto della cucina rinacimentale." *Appunti di gastronomia* 13 (Milan: Condeco, February 1994): 5–14.

Benporat, Claudio. "Maestro Martino e i suoi ricettari." *Appunti di gastronomia* 14 (June 1994): 5–13.

Benporat, Claudio. *Storia della gastronomia italiana*. Milan: Mursia, 1990.

Bertoluzza, Aldo. *Libro di cucina del maestro Martino de Rossi. Cucina tardomedioevale in uso alle corti degli Sforza, dei visconti e nel principato vescovile di Trento*. De coquina, 3. Trento: Edizioni-U.C.T., 1993.

Chiesi, Giuseppe. "Martino Rossi: un cuoco bleniese alla corte ducale." In Bertoluzza, *Libro di cucina*, 11–15.

Laurioux, Bruno. "I libri di cucina italiani alla fine del medioevo: un nuovo bilancio." *Archivio Storico Italiano* 154 (Florence: Olschki, 1996): 33–58.

Milham, Mary Ella. "Platina and Martino's *Libro de arte coquinaria*." *Acta Conventus Neo-Latini (Copenhagen)*, ed. Philip Dust *et al.* Binghamton, N.Y.: MRTS Press, 1994.

Milham, Mary Ella. "Platina and Papal Politics." *Du manuscrit à la table*, ed. Carole Lambert, 81–84. Montréal: Université de Montréal and Paris: Champion-Slatkine, 1992.

Spadaro di Passanitello, Carmelo. "Il codice Bühler 19 della Pierpont Morgan Library di New York." *Appunti di Gastronomia* 9 (1992): 9–14.

Spadaro di Passanitello, Carmelo. "Relazioni tra il *Libro de arte coquinaria* di Maestro Martino e i ricettari italiani rinascimentali." *Appunti di Gastronomia* 14 (June 1994): 119–204.

Vehling, Joseph Dommers. "Marino and Platina Exponents of Renaissance Cookery." *Hotel Bulletin and The Nation's Chefs* (October 1932): 192–95.

Vehling, Joseph Dommers. *Platina and the Rebirth of Man*. Chicago: Walter M. Hill, 1941.

◈

G. Acknowledgments

It was with very great sadness that his many friends and colleagues learned of the passing of Dr. Rudolf Grewe in July of 1994. A gentle scholar of many broad interests, boundless energy and penetrating insights, Rudolf had devoted his intellectual life to the study of Catalan and Italian cookery of the earlier period. At the moment of his death he had five distinct projects at various stages of completion, for one of which he had given himself a good basis of Old Arabic. His research and publications had earned him a world-wide reputation for their solidness; his kind personality had earned him many friends.

This present edition is very largely the result of Rudolf Grewe's scholarly initiative. He proposed the project to the surviving editor and sketched most of its outline. In particular he was interested in the linguistic questions associated with the Neapolitan text and with the historical relationships between Catalonia and Naples. He died in Barcelona while investigating a newly discovered Catalan recipe collection whose significance for the present work and medieval cookery in general he immediately appreciated. In giving form to the work we jointly began, this colleague of his has sorely missed his wisdom and learning.

The remaining editor knows that he speaks also for Rudolf Grewe in thanking the librarians at the Pierpont Morgan Library, without whose assistance the edition would have been impossible. He also thanks Señora Rosa Esteva Grewe and Dr. Barbara Santich for their invaluable help in transmitting Rudolf's last thoughts on our Neapolitan Collection.

◈

II. The Texts

The Neapolitan Recipe Collection

[New York, Pierpont Morgan Library, MS Bühler, 19]

Throughout this transcription of the manuscript, wherever in the various rubrics and titles the scribe has used an initial capital letter, we show a Capital; and wherever the scribe has used a size of script larger, and generally heavier, than that of his normal text, we reproduce the text in a **bold type**. Editorial material is inserted between square brackets: [ ]. The symbols ⌈ and ⌋ are used here to indicate material that the compiler of this manuscript or the scribe himself has inserted or appended as a *quasi* note in the bottom margin of a page.

A. Recipes

[ff° 1r–76v]

[f° 1r] [1.] **Per fare bona Piperata**

Per fare Bona Piperata de capriolo, de lepore, de porcho salvatico ho de altra salvasina, piglia tanta aqua quanto vino rosso he lava la carne dentro di questa aqua he vino, da poi passa questa lavadura per la stamegna; poi coce la dita carne cum questa lavadura, ponendo un pocho di sale; cotta che serane la dita carne, cavala fora. He, volendo fare dui piatti de Piperata, piglia una libra he meza de uva passa he pistala bene, he piglia altro tanto pane tagliato in fetine, brusculado supra la graticula, bagniado bene in bono accito, he pistalo cum la dita uva passa; he, posendo havere de le coradelle de le dite salvasine, serebe optima cosa de pistarle insieme; le quale cose molto bene piste,[1.1] se debano distemprare cum lo brodo de la dita carne cum uno pocho de sabba ho aceto; da poi passa questa materia per la stamegna in una pignata, giongendoli specie d'ogni sorte he pepero assai; poi falla bullire per spacio[1.2] de meza hora lontano dal focho grande — he guardate dal fumo — voltando

⌈Nota che cum la dita carne voria esser, s'el[1.3] te piace, uno bichero de forte aceto he forte zenzaro.[1.4] ⌋

[f° 1v] spessa volta cum lo cughiaro; da poi frige la dita carne in bono lardo, poi ponela in piatti coprindola cum questa Piperata, la quale quanto he piu negra tanto he piu bella.

Per farla negra, piglia una milza di carnero[1.5] he pistala cum le predite cose.

1.1 ms: the beginning of an s (?) before piste.

1.2 The manuscript is partially damaged and illegible here.

1.3 ms., here and elsewhere: *sel*.

1.4 At the bottom right of the page is a signature, in pencil, of the gathering: A.

1.5 ms: *carnero*, with a faint script *s* — ʃ — at the end of the word.

[2.] **Brodo consumado**[2.1]

Piglia caponi ho starne, fasani ho pipioni ho columbi salvatici bene nettadi; et, se vorai consumare uno capone he fare due menestre di brodo, tolle una pila capace, quatro bucali de aqua, he pone dentro uno capone — che gli sia rotta l'ossa — cum una onza di carne salata, cum trenta grane di pipero rotto he canella he .v. ho .vi. garofoli, et cinque ho .vi. fogli di salvia in pezi, he una de lauro; he lassa bulire per spacio de .vii. hore, non ponendoli sale. Item sera meglio ponere le specie predite quando sera quasi la maior parte del brodo consumado.[2.2]

[f° 2r] [3.] **Biancho manghiare** de Galine ho Palumbi

Quando serano ben cotti, piglia lo petto loro he pistalo molto bene; poi piglia riso macinato, he piglia latte de amandole distemperato cum lo brodo de le galine he lo riso a sufficientia; he fa cocere super le braxe; quando sera ben cotto he spisso, piglia zucaro fino he metelo cocendo inseme; he quando sera cotto he spisso como brodeto, cacialo dal focho; he minestra cum de sopra zucaro.

[4.] **.xii. minestre de biancho** Manghiare per Coprire Caponi

Piglia[4.1] due libre de amandole ben biancate he falle stare in moglio uno di in aqua frescha;[4.2] poi piglia uno petto ho piu de capone he pistalo cum le dite amandoli cum una molica di pane biancho bagniato in brodo magro; poi piglia un poco de agresto, meza onza di zenzaro mondato he piu de meza libra de zucaro; et distempera [f° 2v] tute queste cose in brodo magro de capone, he passali per la stamegna in una pignata la quale meterai apresso lo focho, lontano dal fumo, miscolando sempre cum lo cughiaro, et lassa cocere per spacio di meza hora; he quando he cotta, poneli tre onze di aqua rosata; poi fa le menestre, ho vole coprire caponi ho altri volatili che se sia del dito Bianchomanghiare, he manda a tavola; per piu belleza, mette di sopra alcuni grani di melagranata.

[5.] **.xii. menestre** de bianchomanghiare alla Cathalana

Piglia doi buchali de[5.1] latte caprino, he octo onze de farina de riso he ponella a bulire nel dito latte; poi piglia uno petto de capone mezo cotto he disfallo tuto questo peto como fusse in forma de capilli, sotilmente; da poi ponello in uno mortaro he dalli suso doi botti cum lo pistono; poi che hara bulito el latte meza hora, mete [f° 3r] lo dito peto insieme cum una libra de zucaro he lassalo bulire per spacio de quatro hore, misculando·l[5.2] cum lo cughiaro sempre dal principio fina al fine; et per conoscere quando sera cotto, se attacara alo cughiaro; da poi poneli aqua rosa onze .ii. he fa le menestre cum zucaro di sopra, non ponendoli insieme altra cosa.

2.1 ms: *consumado*, with a script *s* — ʃ — at the end of the word.

2.2 ms: *consumado*, with a script *s* — ʃ — at the end of the word.

4.1 The word *piglia* is repeated in the manuscript.

4.2 In the margin: *per che son megliore*.

5.1 In the margin: *alla Cathalana*.

5.2 ms: *misculandol*.

[6.] **Bianchomanghiare**[6.1] per .x. menestre

Piglia una libra he meza de amandole monde, he pistale bene; poi piglia una molica de pane bagnato in brodo de piselli; poi piglia meza libra de polpa de uno bono pesso cotto alesso, he pista cum ogni cosa insieme; he poi piglia onze .viii. de zucaro, he meza onza de zenzaro, he .iii. de aqua rosata, he distempera ogni cosa insieme he passa per la stamegna; he ponerai questa compositione a cocere per uno octavo de hore[6.2] sopra le brase che non pigli fumo.[6.3]

[f° 3v] [7.] **Riso** cum Latte de Amandole

Piglia una libra he meza di amandole per farne dece menestre, he meza libra de riso he lavalo tre volte he fallo ben cocere, he poi fallo bene sugare; he pista le ditte amandole — per fare che non facino olio, pistandole, mettice uno pocho de aqua fresca ho rosata — he passale per la stamegna; he mette a bulire questo latte in una pignata cum meza libra de zucaro fino; et como comenza bullire, meteli dentro del riso, he mette la pignata supra le braxe lontano dal focho, voltando spexe cum lo cughiaro, he fallo bulire per meza hora.

Item: similmente potrai fare cocere dito riso cum latte di capra ho cum altro latte.

Nota: per guardare simile menestre che non pigliano fumo, piglia una peza dopia in tre ho in quatro pige; [f° 4r] ma prima cazarai la minestra fori de la pignata, senza tocar el fondo, he metela in un'altra pignata; poi piglia questa dita peza he bagnila in aqua fresca; da poi preme fora l'aqua he mette la peza cusi dopia supra la pignata he lassa stare per meza hora, ho almancho per uno quarto de hora; poi bagnala un'altra volta[7.1] he rimetela un'altra volta[7.2] sopra la dita pignata, et in questo modo lo fume se caciara fora. Et cusi se fa cum el farro: altro meglior modo non se trova.

[8.] **Riso alla Italiana**

Piglia una pignata he mettice brodo grasso he magro he fa bullire; he poi piglia lo riso bene nettato he piu volte lavato cum aqua tepida, he metello dentro he fa bulire menando [f° 4v] cum lo cughiaro alcuna volta che non se apichi alla pignata; poi, quando serra cotto, piglia ova he caso gratato, sbatuto ogni cosa insieme, cum uno pocho di pipere; poi fa le scutelle.

[9.] **Potagio de farro**

Fa cocere lo farro in una cazola cum brodo grasso he magro; et quando serra bene cotto, mettice uno ho doi rossi de ova cum caso gratato sbattuti he pipero, zaffrano et canella insieme; et quando lo metti ad cocere, mette insieme uno pezo di persuto; he, poi cotto, metti sopra caso, he manda a tavola.

6.1 In the margin: *quaresima.*

6.2 In the margin: *in pila.*

6.3 In the margin: *misculando.*

7.1 ms: *voltra.*

7.2 *voltra,* with *t* crossed out.

[*10.*] **Ravioli**[10.1]

Piglia una libra he[10.2] meza libra de caso veghio he uno pocho de caso fresco grasso he una libra di ventresca ho vero una cinna di vitella he cocila [f° 5r] alesso tanto ch'ela[10.3] sia bene cotta; da poi batella bene; he piglia bone herbe odorifere ben batute, et pipero, garofoli, zenzero he zaffrano, giongendoli lo petto de uno capone ben pisto, et tute queste cose incorpora insieme; da poi falli la pasta sutile et mette questa materia insieme, grossa como una noce, he involtala in la dita pasta; he mete diti ravioli a cocere nel brodo grasso de capone ho[10.4] altra bona carne, he mettelli uno pocho de zaffrano, he lassa bullire per meza hora; poi fa le[10.5] menestre ponendoli de sopra caso gratato misculato cum bone specie.

[*11.*] **Ravioli bianchi**

Piglia de bona probatura fresca he pistala molto bene; poi azonze pistando un pocho de butiro, zenzevero he canella; et per una probatura, azonze tre ghiari [f° 5v] d'ova ben batuta, et del zucaro honestamente; et incorpora tute queste cose insieme; poi fa li ravioli longi he grossi uno dito, poi imbratelli cum bona farina; et nota che questi voleno esser senza pasta; he falli bullire adasio che non[11] se rompano; como hano levato uno buglore, levali fora he meteli in scutelle cum zucaro, canella; he li poi far ghialdi de zaffrano.

[*12.*] **Brodeto biancho**

Piglia amandole he pistale e cum la stamegna passali cum agresto; poi piglia pulastri rostiti; he stempera bene le amandole cum agresto, canella, garofoli, zenzevero; he mete questa compositione sopra diti pullastri, he manda a tavola.

[*13.*] **Brodeto bello**

Per farne .x. menestre, piglia tre rossi d'ova per menestra, he bono agresto, [f° 6r] bono brodo de carne, he uno pocho de zaffrano he specie fine; he miscola ogni cosa inseme he passale per la stamegna, he mittelo in una pignata sopra le braxe, menando continuamente fina tanto ch'el[13] cughiaro se imbrata; he cusi levalo dal focho, continuamente menando per spacio di doi Pater Noster; poi fa le menestre, cum specie dolce de sopra; et fallo dolce ho agro secundo lo gusto del tuo patrone cum agresto ho limoni.

10.1 ms: *Raviolli* repeated in the margin by a later hand.

10.2 ms: *libra he* crossed out (by a different hand?)

10.3 ms: *che la.*

10.4 ms: *ha.*

10.5 ms: *falle.*

11 In the margin: *Et se cum pasta li vorai, falli.*

13 ms., here and elsewhere: *chel.* Written this way, the masculine article may be either *el* or *lo*; a transcription could read either *che·l* or *ch'el. Cf. che la,* rendered as *ch'ela,* in Recipes 10, 67 and 88.

[*14.*] Brodeto de pane he caso he cum ova

Fa bullire mezo uno pane gratato per uno quarto de hora in brodo de carne bona; poi piglia uno pocho de caso gratato he sbatelo inseme cum tre ova; et lassa alquanto refredare el pane, poi mete dentro el dito caso he ova he miscola bene, he falla ghialda de zaffrano; et manda a tavola.

[f° 6v] **[*15.*] Macharoni Ciciliani**

Piglia farina bianchissima he impastala cum uno biancho d'ova he cum aqua rosata et, volendone fare doi piatelli, non li mettere piu che doi ho tre rossi d'ova; he fa questa pasta bene dureta, da poi fane bastonceli longi uno palmo he sutile quanto una pagla; he habi uno filo de ferro longo un palmo, grosso quanto uno spago, he ponelo supra lo dito bastoncello he dalli una volta cum tute due le mane sopra una tavola; da poi cacia fora lo ferro he retira lo macharone bussato in mezo; et quisti machoroni[15] vogliano secare al sole, he se manterano doi ho tre anni; coceli in aqua ho in brodo de bona carne, he meteli caso gratato quando li harai aconci in piatelli cum butiro frescho et specie dolce; et falli bullire per spacio de una hora adasio adasio.

[f° 7r] **[*16.*] Macharoni Romaneschi**

Piglia bella farina he fane pasta uno pocho piu grossa che quella dele Lasagne, et rivoltala in torno ad uno bastone, et taglia la pasta larga uno digito che resta como una stringa; et metteli a cocere in bono brodo ho in altra aqua secondo el tempo; et fa prima bulire l'aqua cum uno pocho de sale avante che li mette dentro li macharoni; et se li cocerai in aqua, mettelli dentro butiro frescho.

[*17.*] Vermicelli

Falli cocere in bono brodo grasso per spacio de una hora, he poi falle menestre he metti de sopra caso permesano gratato cum specie dolce; he primo falle ghialdi cum zaffrano. Et similiter potrai fare de le Lasagne.

[f° 7v] **[*18.*] Lasagne de pelle de Caponi**[18]

Coce le pelle de caponi alesso — ho vero piglia le pelle de caponi cotti alesso — he tagliale in peze he falle cocere in brodo de capone grasso, he falle bullire per spacio de meza hora cum uno poco de zaffrano; da poi fa le menestre, ponendoli sopra caso gratato permesano he specie dolce.

[*19.*] Milli Fanti In menestra

Piglia tre pani he levali la crosta he gratali molto bene he metteli supra una tavola, he metteli atorno una libra he meza de bona farina; he mete cum lo dito pane quatro ho cinque ova he batile bene bene cum lo cultello risguardando sempre lo pane cum la dita farina; he quando te parira che sia minuto como [f° 8r] anesi confetti, pone ogni cosa in uno sedazo he cacia fora la farina; poi falli secare alo sole ho alo focho; et quando li vorai cocere, coceli in brodo de carne, he fallo ghialdo cum zaffrano; he falle bullire adasio per spacio de meza hora; et mette de sopra le menestre caso he specie.

---

[15] *machoroni*: *sic*.

[18] In the margin: *la quale se ghiama Menestra Fasanica.*

[*20.*] **Cardinale In menestra**

Piglia carne magra de vitella cotta allesso, he battila quanto piu minuta potrai; poi falla bullire in brodo grasso, giongendoli una molica de pane gratata he uno poco de pipero e zaffrano, he lassa bulire per uno terzo de hora; dapoi lassa uno poco refredare; poi piglia tre ova sbatuta he caso gratato he petrosillo, maiorana poca he menta, he bene bene sbatute ogni cosa insieme; mette in la pignata menando cum lo cughiaro, azongendo un pochetto de bono agresto.

⌈ Et simile poi fare cum coradelle de capreto ho de altri animali. ⌋

[f° 8v] [*21.*] **Piselli cum carne salada**

Piglia piselli cum la scorza he falli dare uno bullore; he piglia carne salata verzellata he tagliata in fette sotile longe mezo digito, he frigele uno pocho; poi mette li diti piselli a frigere cum la dita carne he meteli uno pocho de agresto, uno poco de sabba he zucaro he canella. Cusi se po fare cum li fasoli.

[*22.*] **Giusello** ho Zanzarelli

Piglia, a volerne fare .x. menestre de dito Giusello, octo ova fresca he meza libra de caso gratato he uno pane gratato, he miscola ogni cosa inseme; poi tolle una pignata cum brodo de carne he metila al foco, he como cominza bullire metti dentro questa compositione he dalli una volta cum lo cughiaro, agiongendili uno pocho de zaffrano; et como vedera che se prenda, levala dal foco he fa menestre cum specie de sopra et miscolate insieme.[22]

[f° 9r] [*23.*] **Caule alla Romanesca**

Piglia caule he rompele cum le mane he metele in aqua quando bulle; et quando serano quasi meze cotte, getta via tuta quella aqua, he habi bono lardo he assai, he sbatillo he mettilo in la pignata cum le caule cusi asutto, voltando bene cum lo cughiaro; poi pigliarai bono brodo grasso he cum quello le metterai al foco a bulire per spacio de due[23] hore—che non he trista menestra quando hai fame.

[*24.*] **Lactucha** che para zucha.[24.1]

Piglia lo pede de la lactucha he fallo cocere in forma de le zuche cum ova[24.2] he cum agresto; ho vero cocelle como la boragine sola cum brodo.

---

[22] ms: *et miscolate insieme* added by a later hand?

[23] ms: *due* changed into *tre*?

[24.1] Although the word *Lactucha* begins a new paragraph and is slightly larger than the usual text and more heavily inked, as if it were a title, there is no additional space as for a new recipe.

[24.2] ms: everything after the word *ova* perhaps added by later hand?

[25.] Trippa

Piglia trippe como vorai he falle ben nettare che non sapiano da Catharina; poi falle cocere cum carne salata, he non li metere sale, acio siano piu bianche. Et quando[25.1] [f° 9v] serano cotte, tagliale in peci picoli he meteli uno pocho de salvia he falli dare un altro bullore, agiongendoli[25.2] sale a bastanza; poi fa le menestre, ponendo di sopra pepe, canella he zaffrano.

[26.] Rappe

Netale bene he tagliale in peci grossi, he coceli assai in bono brodo de carne grassa; da poi passale per la cughiara forata, ho vero pistale, he falle rebullire un pocheto cum uno pocho de carne salata; he farai le menestre ponendo di sopra pepe he zaffrano.

[27.] Rappe Armate

Fa cocere le rape soto la braxa, ho vero falle allessare integre; poi tagliale in fette grosse como la costa d'un cortelo; he haverai caso permesano, ho altro bono caso grasso, tagliato in fette large como [f° 10r] quelle de le rappe, ma piu sutile; he habi zucaro, pipero he specie dolce miscolate insieme; he aconzarai queste fette in una padella da torta per ordine, suso el fondo queste fette de caso, ponendo de sopra bono butiro fresco, he poi le fette de le rappe, he cusi de grado in grado agiongendo sempre per tuto de quelle miscolate specie; he cusi farai cocere in la dita padella cum del butiro assai per spacio de uno quarto de hora ho piu al modo de una torta; et questa imbandisone se da da poi ale altre.

[28.] Cemolella Ciciliana

Falla cocere in brodo grasso, ponendola a pocho a pocho nela pignata, menando continuamente cum lo cughiaro; he falla bullire per spacio de meza hora supra le braxe longe dal focho; poi fa le [f° 10v] menestre he meteli sopra caso he specie. Alla Quaresima la po fare cum latte de amandole he zucaro he aqua rosata.

[29.] Zuche

Mondale molto bene et cocele in brodo grasso; poi che serano cotte, passale per la stamegna ho pistale he rimetele in brodo bono, agiongendoli uno pocho de agresto he zaffrano; poi levale dal focho he lassale refredare; poi piglia rossi d'ova secundo la quantita de le zuche he sbatele cum uno pocho de caso veghio gratato he gettalo dentro in la pignata, voltando sempre cum lo cughiaro; poi fa le menestre, ponendoli supra specie dolce.

25.1 At the bottom right of the page is a signature of the gathering, in fine black script: *b*.

25.2 ms: *agiondoli*.

[30.] Carabace alla Catalana[30]

Piglia le carabace — cioe, zuche — he netale bene bene he metele in una pilla cum carne salata he cum bono lardo batuto, [f° 11r] he mette la dita pila supra le braxe he falla bulire voltando sempre cum lo cughiaro; et volano bulire in questa forma per spacio de .ii. hore; poi habi bono caso, bono brodo grasso he zaffrano he specie dolce he un pocheto de agresto, he mete in la dita pignata — excepto el caso che vole esser ultimo cum l'ova.

[31.] Brodo [de Amandolo][31.1] a homo delicato

Piglia[31.2] pullastri he meteli in una olla netta, he reimpila de aqua acio se possa ben spumare; et quando serra spumata, piglia uno pocho de carne salada he subito copre la olla, he cusi venera lo brodo biancho; et se non venesse biancho, piglia lo capo de uno pullastro he rompilo dentro — cioe, cusi roto, fallo bene bullire; et quando li pullastri serano coti et la [f° 11v] carne salata, fa tanto cocere el brodo che torni in una ho due scudelle.

[32.] Farinata ad homo Infermo

Piglia farina de orzo he latte de amandole he brodo de galine, et in lo latte mittice farina passata per sedazo, he mettila a cocere che cocia assai; poi fa le menestre, et in fine del cocere meteli zucaro fino.

[33.] Marignani

Piglia li marignani he falli bene netare he bene mondare sutilmente; poi pone a focho uno pocho de aqua he falli dare uno bullore; che siano tagliati in quarti he pone in quella aqua uno pocho de sale, he non li lassare bullire piu che doi Pater Noster; poi cavali fora sopra uno tagliero he falli sugare; poi infarinali [f° 12r] he frigeli; et como li harai friti, scola fora quasi tuto lo olio; poi piglia una spica de aglio he pistala bene cum uno quarto de quisti marignani; he poi habi uno poco de rigano de quello se mette sopra le alice, he pistalo cum lo aglio cum uno pocho de pane, pipero, saffrano he sale; poi distempera tute queste cose insieme cum agresto he cum uno pocho de aceto; poi getta ogni cosa insiema in la padella a frigere un pochetto; poi meteli in piatti he manda a tavola cum specie fine.

---

[30] The capital letter here and elsewhere in the transcription of these texts reproduces the scribe's choice of character.

[31.1] ms: Following the word *Brodo* were written the words *de Amandolo*; these last two words were deliberately struck out with several squiggles. A fine line was further drawn between *Brodo* and *de*, and extended to bracket the end of the word *delicato*. The revised or corrected title of this recipe was meant to be read as: *Brodo a homo delicato*.

[31.2] ms: *Piglia* followed by *brodo de*, crossed out.

[34.] Senipa di Canepa

Per farne .xii. menestre, piglia una libra de sementa de dita canipa he netala da saxi molto bene; poi falla bullire tanto che se incomenza ad aprire; poi piglia una libra de amandole ben bianche he pistale [f° 12v] molto bene; poi azonze una molicha de pane he distempera queste cose cum brodo de carne; poi pista la canipa he passala per la stamegna cum brodo bono, he mette questo passato cum lo latte dele amandole he mette a bulire supra le braxe lontano dal fumo, he continuamente volta cum lo cughiaro; dapoi azonze meza libra de bono zucaro he meza onza de zenzaro biancho he uno pocho de zaffrano he aqua rosata; he farai le menestre ponendo de sopra specie dolce.

[35.] Menestra de marzapane

Per fare .x. menestre de marzapane, piglia una libra de marzapane he pistalo bene bene he pone inseme una ala de capone che sia ben pisto quanto si po; poi habi una molicha de pane quanto uno ovo [f° 13r] he bagnalo in brodo magro; poi piglia uno pocho de agresto, uno pocho de aqua rosata, un pocho de brodo de capone, he distempera bene ogni cosa insieme, he fa cocere supra le braxe adasio cum uno pocho de zenzaro, he lassa levare uno bullore ho doi; poi fa le menestre ponendo de sopra zucaro he canella.

[36.] Menestra de meloni

Piglia meloni boni he leva el bono; poi pistali in uno mortaro he falli bullire uno pocho in brodo grasso; dapoi levali un pocho dal focho; et per ogni scutella mette uno ovo batuto insieme cum uno pocho de caso bono he un pocho de agresto, he un pocho de zenzaro o pipero, he zaffrano; he quando farai le menestre, mette de sopra zucaro he canella; he vole esser questa minestra uno pocho spissa.

[f° 13v] [37.] Mirausto alla Catalana

In primo piglia pizoni o polastri ho caponi, conzali como se fa arosto, he poneli a rostire nel spido; he quando son mezi cotti, caveli[37.1] fora he divideli in quarti, he ogni quarto in doi parte, he poneli in una pignata; dapoi piglia amandole he pistale molto bene; poi piglia doi fette di pane brusculato et quatro rossi de ova dura; poi pista ogni cosa cum le amandole, he distempera cum uno pocho de acceto ho de brodo, he passa per la stamegna; da poi lo mette nela dita pignata sopra la carne, giongendoli de bone specie, cioe, canella assai, zucaro asai; poi mette la pignata supra le braxe he falla bullire per meza hora, continuamente menando cum lo cughiaro; et quando sera cotto, manda questo Mirausto a tavola[37.2] in piatelli ho in scutelle, [f° 14r] he fallo como el colore gamellino.

[38.] Herbicine

Piglia maiorana pocha, menta, biete, petrosillo assai, he falli dare uno bullore; poi levale dal focho he spreme l'aqua di fora, poi batele cum uno cortello; he poi mettele in bono brodo grasso cum uno pocho de carne salata.

[37.1] *caveli*: *sic*.

[37.2] ms: *a tavola* preceded by *ust*, stroked out.

[39.] **Genestrata biancha**

Piglia amandole he mondale bene he pistale molto bene, he quando serano piste, passale per la stamegna; poi ponele in una cazola he mitice tanto zucaro che basti; poi fa farina de riso he miscolala cum lo latte de le amandole; poi ponela a cocere, continuamente menando; et quando comenzara farsi dura, tu ci metti datili he pignoli he [f° 14v] he falli cocere; he quando vederai che se afferma, levali dal focho he mettela sopra uno pocho de cenere calda; he poi fa le menestre, ponendoli de sopra zucaro he aqua rosa he canella.

[40.] **Potagio de Fave Fresche**

Piglia fave sive scaffe fresche, he ponele a cocere cum uno par de pizoni, cum uno pocho de carne salata del osso; he pone insieme maiorana, menta he finoghio dolce, pipero, canella he zenzaro—cioe, quando quaxi le fave he pizoni son cotti; he como serano cotte, pone in uno piatello le fave he li pizoni nel mezo cum quelle herbuze de sopra.

[41.] **Fasoli**

Coce li fasoli in aqua pura ho in bono brodo; he quando serano cotti, tole cipolle tagliate suttile he frigele in patella [f° 15r] cum bono olio he mette de sopra queste cipolle fritte cum pipero he canella he zaffrano; poi lassali reposare sopra la cinere calda uno pezo; et poi fa le menestre cum specie bone de sopra.

[42.] **Fave piene**

Mette in moglio le fave, poi fendele[42] in quello loco dove hene quello negro, he cava fora pian piano la fava ch'e dentro, che non se rompi la scorza; da poi piglia amandole bianchate he pistale molto bene cum assai zucaro, et cum questa materia imple le fave—cioe, la scorza—he poi restringe insieme; poi mettele ad scaldare in una pignata ho patella ho altro vaso dove non sia aqua, guardandole che non se abrusano; poi, como sono calde, mette le fave in scutelle cum uno pocho de brodo caldo de carne cum etiam pocho [f° 15v] de petrosillo tagliato minuto cum uno pocho de cipolle fritte in bono grasso cum specie de sopra; et a chi non piace cipolle, non ne mette.

[43.] **Alesso**[43]

Divide la carne in pezi he mettela a moglio in aqua fresca per spacio de meza hora; poi lavala bene cum aqua calda he poi cum aqua fresca, he ponela al focho in uno vaso che non stia stretta, he poneli sale a sufficientia; he sopra tuto se debe bene scumare tanto quando fa spuma; et se lo sale he bruto, lavalo cum aqua calda; se la carne fusse veghia, presertim dura como volatili, cavala spesso da l'aqua bullente he infondela in l'aqua fresca, et sera piu cocibile.

---

[42] ms: *fendole*, with the *o* poorly formed.

[43] The title of this recipe is preceded by a pair of large cruciform designs ( ), one in each side margin. Freely executed, they suggest ornamental scrolls. The marks may signal the beginning of a new section of recipes, those having to do with meats.

[44.] Galine cum carne salata

Piglia una galina he falla cocere [f° 16r] in una pignata, he quando he meza cotta pone insieme specie, zaffrano, rossi d'ova he figatelli, pistata ogni cosa insieme, he fa cocere che sia la dita galina ben cotta; poi pista un pocho de alio s'el piace al patrone, he metelo in la pignata.

[45.] Polastri Alesso cum Agresto[45.1]

Voleno esser cotti alesso cum carne salata; he quando sono mezi cotti, piglia agresto sodo he taglalo per mezo he cazali fora le grane he mettelo a cocere cum li polastri; et quando sono cotti, tolle petrosillo tagliato minuto, he pipero he zaffrano, he mette inseme;[45.2] poi che serano cotti, mandali a tavola cum specie fine de sopra.

[46.] Carne de Capretto ho de Carnero[46.1] cum brodetto

Pilgia carne de capreto ho de [f° 16v] castrado[46.2] he fane peze picole, he metele in una pignata cum carne salata; poi piglia salvia, menta, cepa, he coce ogni cosa insieme; poi piglia de bone specie he zaffrano, he distempera cum del brodo de dita carne, he lassa bulire tute insieme fina tanto che la carne si diffacia; poi leva fora la carne in uno piatello cum lo brodetto.

[47.] Carne de Capreto in Tegamo alla Fiorentina.

Piglia li quarti dreto ho denanze del capreto he fane peze; poi meteli in lo tegamo cum uno pocho de aqua, uno pocho de agresto he grasso del capreto ho de vitella; poi mitte fette de carne salata he del lardo, he manda alo forno; et quando harai[47] rostito da una parte, volta da l'altra; piglia [f° 17r] petrosillo, menta, cipolle, figatelli de pulli, rossi de ova he pane gratusato, he miscola ogni cosa insiema; che ogni cosa sia ben trita; poi quando li prediti pezi de carne serano cotti, levali fore, he remette lo tegamo sopra le braxe cum le preditte cose ad bullire un pocheto he, cusi bullendo, remette dentro la carne; poi leva dal focho facendo scutelle cum lo dito brodo, cum specie de sopra bone.

[48.] Testa de Montone

Piglia una testa de monthone he lavala molto bene; poi falla ben cocere et, posendo levare tuta l'ossa, levale; da poi taglia tuta la carne he sbatila minuta he metela in una pignata; poi, quando sera quasi tuta bene cotta, piglia petrosillo, menta, maiorana he cipolla minuzata, he pone insieme in dita[48.1] [f° 17v] pignata; poi piglia specie, ova he brodo, he pane mogliato in brodo,[48.2] he figato, he pista he miscola queste cose insieme, he pone in la pignata lontano dal focho, he fa bullire che siano bene cotte; poi cava dal focho he fa le menestre cum specie de sopra.

45.1 ms: *cum agresto* written in the margin.

45.2 ms: *in seme*.

46.1 ms: *carnero*, with a script *s* — ς — at the end of the word.

46.2 ms: *castrado*, with a script *s* — ς — at the end of the word.

47 ms: a word, perhaps *cost*, follows *harai* and is crossed out.

48.1 At the bottom right of the page is a signature of the gathering, in fine black script: c.

48.2 ms: *brordo*, second *r* crossed out.

[*49.*] **Testa de Vitello**

Tolle una testa de vitello bene bianchata he netta, poi cocela a alesso; et per suo sapore tolle Agliata.

Se tu la vorai rostire nel forno, impela de aglio, herbuze, lardo, specie, cum lo cirvello cavato he miscolato cum queste cose he zaffrano; poi ligala che non eschi lo pieno, he ponella in uno tegamo cum mezo bucale de aqua; he poi mandala al forno, in fine agiongendoli agresto he bone specie, he voltandola nel tegamo alcuna volta.

[f° 18r] [*50.*] **Carne In tegamo** alla Fiorentina.

Piglia carne de vitella ho de altra carne cum l'ossa, he fanne peci picoli uno pugno, he poneli in lo tegamo cum uno pocho de aqua he uno bichero de vino he uno de bono agresto; et se piacesse al patrone, mette qualche rotelle de cipolla ho, non piacendoli[50] cipolle, mette petrosillo — dico, le radice — he uva passa, prune seche he sale; et fà che questa carne non sia coperta de aqua piu che uno digito de sopra, he mette alo forno; he quando parira meza cotta, azonze garofoli pochi, canella assai, pipero he zaffrano assai, sapi da pipero; he como he mezo cotta, dalli una volta; he poi cazala in uno piatello cum specie de sopra he zucaro; ho vero lassa in tegamo.

[f° 18v] **Similmente** potrai fare de pesso, cioe ciffalo he anguilla tagliata in peci largi quatro dita he ben lavati, poi posti nel tegamo cum uno pocho de olio. Nota che queste cose tu le potrai fare dolce he brusche secundo el gusto del patrone.

[*51.*] **Caponi Inzucarati**[51]

Piglia caponi grassi he grossi he morti de doi di, poi, bene netti, falli alessare che non sian troppo cotti; da poi falli sugare fora de la pignata; poi piglia zucaro fino secondo la quantita de caponi che vorai inzucarare he rompe questo zucaro he fallo squagliare cum aqua rosata he fallo uno pocho bullire; da poi getta lo dito zucaro squagliato sopra de quisti caponi che siano coperti per tuto, cum canella bona; he quasi presto se voleno manducare.

[f° 19r] [*52.*] **Per fare bello Rosto** de caponi, polastri, capreto he de qualunche altra carne.

Primo, se fusse carne grossa, falla dare uno bullore excepto s'ela[52] fusse vitella joveneta. Se fusse capone ho vero qualunche altra carne che meritasse esser posta arosto, fa che sia bene nettata, poi cazala dentro de l'aqua bullente, he subito cava fora he ponela in aqua fresca: aquesto se fa acio sia piu bella; poi lardala cum bono lardo he metela in spito, facendo cocere adasio; he poi, quando he quasi cotta, piglia uno pezo de pane gratato he miscola cum sale he sallalo; he cusi lo haverai cotto bello.

---

50 ms: *piacendoti*; it would seem that the condition expressed by this present participle should represent the negative counterpart of the preceding conditional clause, *se piacesse al patrone*, and read . . . *li* rather than . . . *ti*.

51 ms: *In Zucarati*, written as two words.

52 ms: *se la*.

[53.] **Polastri Arosto**[53.1]

Per fare Polastri arosto,[53.2] coceli cum l'ordine sopra ditto he, quando serano cotti, [f° 19v] piglia sugo de marangoli ho agresto cum aqua rosata, zucaro he canella; he poi mette el polastro in uno piatto he getali de sopra questa miscolanza, poi mandalo a tavola.

[54.] **Capreto In piu modi**

Netalo bene he ponelo arosto, he fa ch'el spito esca dal naso, et guarda non abrusarlo; et falli questo per suo sapore: piglia juivert et pane bruscato infuso in vinagro cum uno spico de aglio he pipero, he pista ogni cosa insieme, he stempera cum agresto ho cum vino cotto, facendolo brusco ho[54] dolce como vorai.

[55.] **Galine ho Caponi In spito cum suo sapore**

Piglia, quando le harai cotte bene arosto, cinque amandole mondate he pistale [f° 20r] bene cum zucaro fino — he non havendo zucaro, pone mel — he stempera cum sugo de limoni che sia un pocho spisso; he ponerai sopra le galine, ho vero fa in scutellino[55] el sapore et le galine in piatelli; he manda caldi a tavola.

[56.] **Limonata a galine ho ha caponi**

Piglia galine ho galina, caponi ho capono ho pullastri, che siano cotti uno pocho in aqua; poi cazali dal aqua he meteli in spito; poi piglia amandole mondate ben piste he stemprale cum lo sabrero de le galine; poi piglia sugo de limoni he miscola cum bone specie, ogni cosa insieme, he mette in una pignatella a cocere uno pochetto; he da poi getta de sopra de questo rosto, he cum pocho de grasso, he caldo caldo manda in tavola.

[f° 20v] [57.] **Pariola Con Galine** ho ha Pollastri ho ha Caponi in Spito.

Piglia pipero he gingibero he zaffrano, he pistali bene; poi piglia li figatelli de ditti animali, he rossi de ova bene cotti, he cum uno pocho de cipolla s'ela[57] ti piace, he pista ogni cosa insieme he distempera cum agresto ho cum altro licore dolce; poi piglia le galine ho caponi ho pullastri, he fane peze he mette in una pignata cum le preditte cose insieme, he fa che stia un pochetto stuffate; poi fa un piatto he manda a tavola cum specie de sopra.

[58.] **Appareghio de Ucelletti**

Perbulle li ucelletti, poi frigeli cum lardo bono; poi piglia figatelli he rossi de ova he pane brusculato infuso in agresto he juivert perbulito, he pista ogni cosa simul, distemperando cum lo sabrero [f° 21r] de diti ucelli; he quando li ucelli sono bene fritti, pone de sopra questo sapore; da poi pone ogni cosa in una pila tanto che ogni cosa sia ben cotta.

53.1 ms: written as two words, the second with a large capital, *a Rosto*.

53.2 ms: *arosto* written as a single word, *sic*.

54 ms: *he*.

55 ms: A vertical stroke partially over the *o* may be an *i* with a long descender, and represent an effort to correct this word to *scutellini*. (See the same sort of correction made in Recipe 70.

57 ms: *se la*.

[59.] Bechafichi

Piglia bechafichi grassi, he nettali molto bene, non caciando l'interiora se non ti piace; poi piglia foglie de vite he involtali dentro cum sale, lardo he finoghio; he cusi[59.1] involupati, poneli sotto la cenere calda per spacio de meza hora. Et hancora li poi rostire ligandoli a quatro a quatro sopra uno spito per la testa he per li piedo;[59.2] ho vero poneli in una canna spacata he ligala da li canti cum filo; et se voleno manducare caldi caldi.

[60.] **Tordi** cum Suo Sapore

Piglia tordi he netali bene [f° 21v] he coceli arosto; et per suo sapore, piglia amandole he falle ben bianche, pistale quanto potrai, he pone simul assai sandalo he distempera cum agresto he cum uno pocho de brodo, agiongendoli zucaro he canella; poi passa ogni cosa per stamegna, poi fa dare uno bullore ad questo sapore; et fatto questo, gettalo de sopra ali tordi. Et se non te piace el dito sapore, piglia, quando serano cotti li tordi, sugo de limoni he de marangoli dolce he forti ho de granate, cum specie dolce; miscola insieme he pone sopra li tordi caldi caldi.

[61.] **Starne Al modo Cathalano**

Piglia la starna he cocela arosto; he quando he cotta, cazala dal spito he sparte le ale dal petto, he pone in quelle fixure questo sapore: piglia sugo de [f° 22r] granate ho agresto, sale he garofoli pisti he specie dolce, he ponelo dentro de le dite fixure quando·l'e[61] bene calda; he nota che la starna non vole esser troppo cotta.

[62.] **Tremolette sopra Starne al modo Franceso**

Piglia meza libra de amandole he falle bene bianche, ho vero bruscale sotto la cenere calda che non se abrusano; poi nettale cum uno canevazo he pistale; he piglia cinquanta nevole fatte cum zucaro he mettele a moglio nel vino rosso, poi ponele a pistare he distemperare cum le amandole, giongendoli canella assai he zucaro sufficienter cum grana paradisi et garofoli, tuti bene pisti, he passa ogni cosa per la stamegna cum uno pocho de agresto; dapoi metterai ogni cosa in una pignatta, voltando spesso, cum uno pocho strutto; he poi pone questa materia sopra la starne cotte arosto, cum de sopra zucaro e canella.

[f° 22v] [63.] **La Sancta Porcheta Arosto[63] reversata**

Piglia una porcheta he spelala che sia bene biancha he bene nettata cum aqua calda; da poi fendela per lo dritto de la scina he cacia fora l'interiora, he lavala bene dentro per ogni lato; he riversala como se fa cum le tenghe; poi, per sua impitura, piglia una spicha de aglio minuzato he lo figato dela porcheta bene sbatuto, he petrosillo, maiorana un quatrino, he pipero uno baiocho, he altre bone specie, he caso gratato he quatro ova he zafrano, prune he uva passa, he miscola

---

[59.1] ms: nasal stroke over the *u*, crossed out.

[59.2] ms: clearly *piedo*, although the *o* is blotted.

[61] ms: *quando le*.

[63] ms: *a Rosto*, in two words.

cum lardo ogni cosa insieme; he mette queste cose in la porcheta, he che pertuto ci ne sia; poi cucella bene cusi reversa, he ponela in spito ben ligata cum bastoni, ho vero mettela sopra una graticula; [f° 23r] he falla ben cocere; he poi, mettendola supra la graticula ho arosto in spito, falli questa salmora: piglia aceto bono, pipero pisto, assai zaffrano he sale, he cum questa bagnaralla cum rosomarino: in questo modo sera bona.

[64.] **Figatelli**

Piglia figato de qualunche animale te pare, he tagliali in pezi grossi una noce, he involtali in bone specie cum sale, he poi ligali in una reticella bene nettata ad un per uno, he poneli in spito; che non sian troppo cotti.

[65.] **Tomaselle**

Piglia figatto[65.1] de porcho ho de vitella he falli cocere alesso ma non tropo, poi gratali; he piglia una libra de panzeta de porcho he falla ben cocere, he poi batila

[f° 23v] **Incipiunt mirabilia gule**[65.2]

molto bene; poi piglia uno pocho de caso veghio he del grasso, he gratalo; he piglia petrosillo, maiorana, he tritale bene, he poi piglia uva passa, ova, zaffrano,[65.3] specie bone, he miscola tute queste cose insieme; poi habi una reticella he involta de questa impitura sive sfarcimento tanto quanto una noce in questa reticella — he non voleno esser piu grosse che una noce; he poi falle cocere in bono lardo adasio adasio in patella sopra la cenere calda.

[66.] **Per Cocere uno pizone et Farlo senza ossa**[66]

Piglia uno pizone he netalo molto bene, poi ponelo a moglio — dico, infondelo — in forte aceto per spacio de .xxv. hore; da poi, lavalo bene he falli uno pieno de caso, ova, [f° 24r] specie, uva passa, he metilo in spito ho arosto; he cusi troverallo senza ossa.

[67.] **Per Fare de Uno Pizone dos**

Pellara uno pizone senza aqua, he guarda non li rompere la pelle, poi cazali fora l'interiora; he reversa la pelle in capo tanto destramente ch'ela[67] resta tuta sana; poi, dove sera rotta, cuzela; he da poi falli una impitura como he dito de sopra, he recuce cum l'aco dove et per dove harai impito, he fallo cocere alesso; l'altro, cioe quello corpo spogliato, metilo arosto ho alesso; se arosto,

---

65.1 The manuscript may read *figatto* or *figatti*.

65.2 This section title stretches in large letters across the top margins of ff° 23v–24r. It would seem to begin to apply at Recipe 66.

65.3 The word is inserted in the margin.

66 Two large ornamental scrolls are drawn in the margin, one beside this title and one beside the text that follows. They may indicate that a new section is beginning and that the rubric written large across the head of ff° 23v–24r, *Incipiunt mirabilia gule*, applies here.

67 ms: *che la*. See the same spelling in Recipe 88.

piglia uno pocho de pane gratusato he sale he, quando sera mezo cotto, getta di sopra questo sale he pane simul; he piglia uno rosso d'ovo he sbatilo bene, he onge lo pipione cum una penna tanto che gli doni colore [f° 24v] et in questo modo parira che non sia scorticato; et cusi parano esser d'uno pizone dos.

[68.] Per Cocere una galina in una Caraffa

Piglia una galina morta alla sera per la matina, poi spelala senza[68.1] aqua calda che non rompi la pelle; he poi levali fora le budella he da quello loco comenza scorticare la pelle reversandola sopra del collo; da poi coce la carne senza la pelle; et quando sera cotta, piglia lo petto he pistalo molto bene cum uno poco de caso he petrosillo, maiorana he altre odorifere herbuce, he ponele insieme cum lo ditto petto de la galina he repista cum uno pocho de garofoli, pipero, canella et zaffrano, et uno pocho de grasso de vitella; he miscola ogni[68.2] [f° 25r] cosa inseme, agiongendoli doi ova; he fa che questa materia sia uno pocho tenera; poi piglia una caraffa capace per tenere una galina ho capone, he fa che la bocha de dita caraffa sia uno pocho larga; poi piglia la pelle de dita galina he impila, he cucela dove l'ai[68.3] scorticata; poi mette li pedi in la caraffa he fa ch'el collo avanzi fora de lo collo de la caraffa, perche avante che metti la dita[68.4] pelle, bisogna che vedi se la caraffa sera capace de tenerla; s'ela[68.5] sera capace, impe la galina per lo collo che havanzara fora del collo de la caraffa, he non la impire troppo; da poi liga el collo he lassalo distendere a sua posta in la caraffa; poi assettala cum uno bastone, che stia bene in dita caraffa; poi impe la caraffa de aqua, cum pocho sale, he fa bulire[68.6] [f° 25v] questa caraffa dentro uno caldaro ho vero apresso al focho adasio; ma pur serra meglio impire uno caldaro de aqua he farla bullire, he poi ho d'avante che bulla metterli dentro la caraffa; et sera cotta in termino de una hora; he mandala a donare, he lassa lo impazo ho pensero del tagliare a loro.

[69.] Pavoni Revestiti che parano vivi. Et per Farli gittare Focho per Bocha

Se debbe primo amazare lo pavone cum una penna, ficandola sopra del capo, ho vero cavarli el sangue sotto la gola como ad uno porcho; ma piu bello he meglio seria cavarli la lingua he da poi fenderlo sotto lo corpo, cioe dal petto fina ala coda, tagliando solamente la pelle, et scorticandolo gentilmente che non guasti la dita pelle;[69.1] [f° 26r] he quando harai scorticato, reversa la pelle fina al capo, poi taglia via el dito capo che resta atacato ala pelle; et similmente fa ale gambe, he cusi de la coda, cazando fora l'ossa de le gambe acio ch'el ferro che fara stare in pede el pavone non si veda; da poi piglia el corpo scorticato he aconzalo bene arosto cum lardo infilzato, ho veramente

---

68.1 The word *senza* is repeated in the ms.

68.2 The catchword *cosa* is written in the bottom margin at the end of this gathering.

68.3 ms: *lai.*

68.4 ms: *dita* followed by *g*, crossed out.

68.5 ms: *se la.*

68.6 At the bottom right of the page is a signature of the gathering, in fine black script: *d.*

69.1 In the bottom margin is a sketch of a peacock.

dalli tanto spesso del grasso che non abrusi, he infilzalo cum garofoli sani, he impello de la impitura de la Porcheta excepto non ci ponere aglio; he fallo cocere adasio adasio ch'el collo non abruxi; he s'el collo havesse tropo foco, coprelo cum una peza bagnata; he quando sera cotto, cavalo fora he revestilo cum la sua pelle, laquale haverai aconzata de dentro cum specie, sale he canella; he da poi che gli haverai posto adoso la dita pelle, poi habi uno inzengno de ferro inghiodato sopra uno grosso taglero, he cazali per li pedi he gambe questo ferro che non se veda; [f° 26v] et cusi el pavone stara impiede che parira vivo.

Et per farlo gittare foco per bocha, piglia uno poco de canfora et uno poco de bambace[69.2] fino in cerco he mete questo bambace cum la camfora nel becho del pavone he bagnalo cum uno pocho de aqua vita, ho vero de bono vino veghio fumoso; et quando lo vorai mandare a tavola, apiza lo focho nel dito bambace, et cusi gittara focho per molto spacio de tempo. Et per piu magnificencia potrai coprire lo dito pavone cotto cum foglie de oro, et poi coprirlo cum la sua pelle.

Et similiter se po fare de fasani, grue, oche et altri ucelli.

[70.] A Fare che una Vacina, una Vitella, uno Cervo Parano Vivi,[70.1] primo amaza la vacina ho vitella como he usanza; da poi comenza infra le[70.2] [f° 27r] unghie a scorticare, ma fa che le unghie restano attacate alla pelle, he le corne; et, scorticata che havarai, fa distendere la ditta pelle; da poi habi cimino, fenoghio, garofoli, pipero et sale bene pisti como polvere, et de questa polvere pulveriza sopra la pelle de dentro; poi taglia via li stinchi da le genoghia in gio; poi cava le trippe fora da lo fiancho; dapoi se vorai mettere a rostire caponi, fasani et altri animali, metteli nel corpo de dita vacha; se la vorai rostire al forno, aconzala sopra una scala.

Se la vorai[70.3] rostire al focho, piglia uno legno — cioe, una stanga como uno spito — he mettela dentro, he inlardala molto bene he falla cocere adasio adasio che non si arda; poi falli fare ferri tanti grandi che la possano sustinere in piede; como la sera cotta, inghioda questo ferro [f° 27v] sopra una tavola grossa he ligala in modo che stia[70.4] in piede; da poi conzali adoso la sua pelle como se fusse viva; se in alcuno loco fusso manchata la carne per cocere, pone a loco de la carne lauro, salvia, rosmarino et mortella; poi retira la pella he cusela in modo che non se veda lo ferro; da poi dalli quella attitudine como fusse viva.

Anchora similmente se po fare cum una cervia ho cum una scroffa et cum una galina; item se po fare cum altri animali como te parira. Nota che aconzare quisti ingegni de animali bisogna che lo coco non sia pazo ne semplice, imo gli bisogna havere grande cirvello.

Et nota, patrone mio, che s'el tuo coco non he discretto, mai aconzara cosa bona, sia bona quanto la vole.

69.2 The first letter of the word is hesitant.

70.1 Apart from the large ornamental capital and little additional interline space, this recipe is not clearly set off from the preceding one. It seems to be considered a sort of variation on Recipe 69.

70.2 In the bottom margin is a faint sketch of an animal.

70.3 ms: *vorari*. The second r has a vertical stroke through it, as if it were a letter *i* with a long descender.

70.4 ms: *stiano*, with *no* crossed out.

[f° 28r] [71.] **Pastizi de Vitella** In tegamo[71.1]

Piglia carne de la cossa de vitella he tritala bene cum uno poco de grasso de vitella he cum uno poco de persuto; he poi, cusi tapolata, mettela in una pignata ho tegamo lontano dal foco, he fa che sia ben spumata; he potrai ponere insieme pizoni, turdi he altri ucelli he pullastri; he quando queste carne serano meze cotte, piglia una cipolletta he tritala bene he uno pocheto de lardo he un pocho de bone specie he uva passa, he pone in pignata[71.2] he lassa uno pocho piu cocere; poi piglia agresto, ova sbatuta he altre bone specie, he mette insieme in lo tegamo he fa fornire de cocere; et gli potrai ponere dentro quatro ho cinque rossi d'ova sani.

Et nota ch'el coco bisogna sia descretto ha ponere le cose predite secondo la quantita de la carne he secondo el gusto del patrone.[71.3]

[f° 28v] [72.] **Pastizi de boni Caponi, Polastri, Pizoni et cum carne de Vitella**

Piglia carne magra de vitello ho de quisti preditti animali, he falla molto bene tritare cum cultello cum uno pocho de grasso de vitella insieme; he quando sera bene pistata[72.1] e tritata—dico, in forma de picoli dadi da jocare—miscola inseme bone specie de ogni sorte; da poi fa la crosta de pasta secondo la uxanza deli pastizi he pone dentro li prediti animali cum la carne, he fa cocere nel forno; he quando parano che sian cotti, piglia ova he sbatte, he agresto he bone specie he brodo grasso he zaffrano, he miscola ogni cosa insieme he mettele in lo dito pastizo per un picolo buso in cima.[72.2]

[f° 29r] [73.] **Pastello de Creste de Galli cum li testiculi**

Piglia le creste he tagliale in tre parte, he li ficatelli in quatro, li coglioni lassali integri; poi piglia uno poco de lardo he taglialo bene minutato, he non lo battere; he piglia tre onze de grasso de vitello he batello bene—he meglio seria la medula de vitella ho de bove; poi piglia .xxx. vissole seche he canella e zenzevero he assai zucaro, he miscola tute queste cose insiema; he fa uno bono pastello he fallo cocere nel forno—he falli la crosta como se usa hali pastelli; ho vero ponello in una patella; et quando sera cotto, piglia uno rosso de ova, agresto he zaffrano, he messeda tute queste cose insiema he ponele in lo pastello, he lassali dare un'altra calda; poi cavalo fora.[73]

[f° 29v] [74.] **Pastello de Capreto**

Piglia carne de capreto he taglala in pezi picoli; poi fa la pasta laborata cum rossi de ova he olio fino; he fa la capsa del pastillo he in questa capsa pone la dita carne del capreto: he fa uno corso de pezi de carne he un altro de specie—cioe, de canella, gingibro, pepe he zaffrano—cum

---

71.1 ms: the words *In tegao* with a nasal on the *o*, inserted above the line.

71.2 ms: *he pone in pignata* inserted in the margin.

71.3 In the bottom margin is a dotted outline of a bird.

72.1 ms: *pistasta*.

72.2 In the bottom margin is a sketch of a bird.

73 In the bottom margin is a sketch of a rooster.

uno pezo de persutto bono; poi lo farai cocere nel forno; et como sera cotto, farai questo suo sapore: piglia rossi de ova batuta, aqua rosata, agresto, zucaro, specie he zaffrano, he stempera insieme, et ponerallo de sopra ad questa compositione tanto destramente che non rompi lo coperto fatto de pasta.

El coco vole esser discreto, dico.[74]

[f° 30r] [75.] **Coppo sive Pastizo de Pipioni**

Piglia li pipioni he taglali in pezi—senza lo corpo ho cum el corpo; he fa la capsa cum ova, zucaro he aqua rosata, he poi mettice dentro li diti pezi: he fa uno corso de li diti pezi he un altro de fette de persuto he uno de bone specie, zucaro he zaffrano; poi fa lo sapore cum ficatelli de galina he de essi pipioni he de la carne sua, he pista molto bene he mittice insieme a pistare maiorana, zucaro he rossi d'ova, agresto per distemperare he aqua rosata; et dalli questo sapore quando ogni cosa sera cotta.

[76.] **Pastello de Pesso**[76]

Piglia lo pesso he fanne peze [f° 30v] grossi, he fa cocere lo pesso cum sale he vino e agrore—he cusi de ogni pesso che vorai mettere en pane, e sarde, alose, varats e spinole he muiols en spito, en gradelle, dare quando sera cotto; poi haverai pebre he zaffrano he vinagro he ceba tagliata menuta he miscolato, he getta de sopra.

Io non intendo questo svozato parlare.

[77.] **Pastizi de Pome Codogne**

Aparaghia la pasta como he dito de li altri pastelli; poi habi pome codogne bene mondate he nette he cacia fora quello duro de mezo, he che lo buso dove haverai cazato fora el duro non passi da banda in banda; et in quello busso ponerai de bona medula de bove cum zucaro he canella assai; et li diti [f° 31r] pomi aconzaralli in li ditti pastizi sopragiongendoli de la ditta medula dentro he de fora; he fa ch'el non sia tropo salato; poi mettili de sopra una pasta, facendolo cocere secondo l'ordine de li altri pastelli.

Farcimenti sive Impiture

[78.] **Pieno Ad una Spalla de Carnero**[78.1]

Piglia una spalla he falla trare uno bullore, poi spacala he cazali l'osso fina al nodo; poi piglia bone specie he carne salata he carne de castrado,[78.2] he tritala, he piglia ova he miscola ogni cosa insieme, he mette in la spalla; he quando sera plena, piglia una fetta de altra carne de castrado[78.3] [f° 31v] et coprine tuta la spalla se ti piace; he poi pone ditta spalla sopra la graticula ho sopra le braxe; et quando sera cotta, da per suo sapore salsa cum juivert.

---

74 In the bottom margin is a sketch of a kid or lamb.

76 The punctuation chosen here is very tentative.

78.1 ms: *carnero*, with a script *s* — ς — at the end of the word.

78.2 ms: *castrado*, with a script *s* — ς — at the end of the word.

78.3 ms: *castrado*, with a script *s* — ς — at the end of the word.

[79.] Sfarcimento a pesso

Piglia zenzevero he zaffrano he fiche he mela monda, he pista tute insieme bene; poi piglia boni pignoli he tritali sotillemente; he poi fende lo pesso per la[79] impe lo pesso per la boca — he fa che primo tu lo netti gentilmente da la boca he getta gio una gotta de olio; poi ponelo sopra la graticula cum rossmarino, he falli salmora cum aceto, specie he zaffrano.

[80.] Sfarcimento a Capreto

Piglia una coradella de capreto [f° 32r] bollita, he tapolala che sia bene trita – he primo ben cotta; poi piglia uva passa, datili, pignoli, persutto, canella, pepe, zinzibero he zucaro, he trita tute queste cose insieme; et poi impe lo capreto, he poi ungelo cum olio fino ho cum bono grasso he aqua he sale, che stia bella la crosta.

[81.] Sfarsimento a Capone

Piglia maiorana, petrosillo he pistali molto bene; poi piglia uno ho doi petti de diti caponi he pistali insieme; he poi piglia uno poco de caso permisano he doi rossi de ova he canella, pepe, zaffrano, zenzaro cum uno poco de lardo ho persuto, he pista ogni cosa insieme, he impe lo capone he ponello alesso ho arosto; he falli la crosta cum rossi d'ova et aqua rosata.

[f° 32v] **[82.] Sfarsimento ad uno budello de vitella**

Piglia uno budello he fallo bene nettare he rascalo — he fa che[82] sia grasso; poi piglia noce monde he meza spica de aglio he uno pocho de caso veghio permisano, specie fine, zaffrano he uva passa cum uno poco de grasso de vitella taglato quanto minuto sia posibile, ma non pisto, he due ova, he miscola questa materia tuta insieme; he impene lo budello che sia un pocho piu che mezo pieno.

Et cum questa materia potrai impire capreti — dico, quarti del capreto alesso — he hancho caponi.

[83.] Cirvelato de Carne de porco ho de vitella

Piglia de la carne de la cossa[83.1] [f° 33r] de quisti animali cum del grasso suo, he tagliala minuta che sia bene batuta cum lo cultello; dapoi piglia bono caso permesano et del caso che sia fresco he grasso, he bone specie, tre ho doi ova fresca secondo la quantita de la carne, he miscola ogni cosa simul cum un poco de zaffrano; poi piglia budelle grosse como la usanza he fa che siano bene nette che non li resta niente del grasso, he impeli de questa materia, he stringela molto bene in le budella he falle longe ho curte como ti piace; et coceli alesso; et in perfectione[83.2] serano per dui giorni.

---

[79] A word or phrase appears to be missing here. Perhaps the scribe's eye skipped ahead to the phrase *per la* that follows the next occurrence of *pesso*: a haplological error? Alternatively, *fende* may have been an erroneous first reading of the word *impe*, whose *i* projects abnormally both high and low.

[82] ms: *che non*, with *non* crossed out.

[83.1] In the bottom margin is a rough sketch of a flower or a patterned design.

[83.2] ms: *imperfectione*. The scribe is almost certainly in error here. The phrase *in perfectione* is so written at this place in the Riva del Garda manuscript and in the *Libro de arte coquinaria*.

[84.] Salsize bone

Piglia carne magra de porcho ho de vitella magra he grassa, he falla battere molto bene; he guarda che non ci sia nervi; et se la carne he .x. libre, [f° 33v] meteli meza libra de sale he onze due de finoghio ben nettado, et due onze de pebro grossamente pistado;[84] he miscola tute queste cose insema he lassa stare per uno di; dapoi tolle budella ben nettata he impele de questa materia, poi pone le salzize a sugare al fumo.

[85.] Persutto bono da servare cotto

Prova lo persuto cazandoli dentro in lo mezo uno cultello; se lo dito cultello sapera[85.1] bono, el persuto sera bono, e cusi e contrario; dapoi piglia tanto vino he altrotanto de aqua ho altrotanto aceto — ma meglio seria senza aqua — he fallo cocere, he non troppo; poi levalo[85.2] he pone inseme salvia, rosmarino in la pilla dove he cotto, he lassalo stare [f° 34r] tanto ch'el sia refredato; he cusi sera bono da conservare .x. giorni.

[86.] Somata

La somata non vole esser tropo grassa, vole esser rossa, et cotta nel predito modo del persutto.

Et similiter po fare cum le lingue salate, ma vogliano esser piu cotte che lo persutto. Ogni salado se debe cocere cusi.

[87.] Per Fare Fare boni Salsizoni Bulignesi

Habi .xxv. libre de carne de porco ho de vitella senza nervi de la cossa, he senza grasso, he falla batere quanto potrai; et in queste [f° 34v] vinticinque libre de carne ponerai quindeci onze de sale he una onza he meza de pipero rotto he sano; poi habi budella grossa, he falle molto bene netare he ben lavare, he impile de questa predita carne tanto strettamente quanto potrai, he falli longi uno palmo alla usanza bulignesa; poi poneli al fumo a sugare.

Ad questo modo li face a fare uno Principe. Vero he che hancho meglio seriano ponerli due onze de sale piu he meza onza de pipero hanco piu. Et fare che saltem de queste .xvii. onze de sale ci ne fusse due onze del bianco sano.

Et ancora ne potrai fare de li grassi pigliando mezo magro he mezo grasso, agiongiendoli finoghio assai, ma questi non sono per conservare.

[f° 35r] [88.] Gelatina de Carne ho de Pesso, et de piu colori

Piglia aceto biancho he altrotanta aqua; poi piglia piedi de castrado he de vitella ben netado[88.1] he sfendoli[88.2] per mezo, gitando via quilli[88.3] fusti longi, he meterali a bulire essi piedi in quella

---

84 ms: *pistado*, with a script *s* — ʃ — at the end of the word.

85.1 *sapera* may also be read as *s'apera*.

85.2 Understand: *dal foco*.

88.1 ms: *netado*, with a script *s* — ʃ — at the end of the word.

88.2 *sfendoli*: clearly *sic*. *Cf. fendole* for *fendele* in 42.

88.3 *quilli*: *sic*. *Cf.* the same pronunciation in Recipes 135, 141, 157 and 217.

miscolanza de aceto et aqua, he fa bullire adasio giongendoli grana paradisi he zenzevero; et quando li pedi paranti cotti, cavalli fora, he fa che lo brodo bulla un altro poco; poi habi quatro bianchi d'ova ben batuta he passa per la stamegna cum lo brodo — ho vero, he meglio sera fare colare per uno panno lino, quanto streto sera piu bella sera, he piu biancha; fa ch'ela[88.4] senta bene de grana paradisi; da poi habi caponi ho altra carne cotta, sola ho cum lo dito brodo, he gettala de sopra la dita decoctione, he ponela in loco fresco.[88.5]

[f° 35v] **Per Farla de Varii colori**: quando la prima, che biancha sera gelata, he posta in piato, cava fora uno quarto de dita gelatina del piatto he fallo squagliare al foco he metteli uno poco de zaffrano, poi cusi ghialdo remittelo quaxi fredo al loco suo; quando questo sera gelato, cavane fora un altro quarto, facendolo rosso cum cornali; in quello modo assetaralo como lo ghialdo; et cusi successive potrai fare di quanti colori tu vorai: per farne un quarto verde, piglia grano quando he in herba he del petrosillo, he pistali he cava fora del sugo he fa como he dito; et per fare de pavonazi, piglia carotte cotte he leva un pezo de la scorza he pista, he fa el simile ut supra et servando tale ordine. Manchando, habi sempre de la gelatina bianca, he reazonze dove mancara; et cusi sera de diversi colori.

[f° 36r] [89.] **Gelatina In uno Canistro**

Habi la decoctione fatta como he dito de sopra; poi habi uno canistro novo he aconzali dentro ho pulli ho altra carne; poi habi un altro vaso capaze per tenere lo dito canestro he getta de sopra questa decoctione, he falla gelare in loco fresco; et quando sera bene gelata, piglia uno cultello scaldato he menalo atorno al canistro che se spichi da quello vaso; poi netalo cum uno panno lo dito canestro tuto atorno; et cusi potrai portare dito canestro dove ti piace. Et el simile potrai fare in una gabia; el simile potrai fare de Quaresima, ponendo el pesso dentro de la gabia integro per bello vedere.

Fa ch'el coco sia discreto he non se dia ad intendere de sapere.

[f° 36v] [90.] **Gelatina a modo de Uno Scachero**[90]

Habi de li pedi assai perche sera piu de maior sustantia, he fa uno brodo biancho cum uno pocho de zenzevero; poi che haverai fatto el brodo, piglia quatro ho cinque ale de capone ho galina, he ponele in lo piatello; poi habi brodo — dico, la decoctione de li diti pedi, colata — he fa ch'el sia alto sopra le ale uno dito; poi como questo brodo sera gelato, piglia uno che se intenda de scachi he fallo tagliare; et quando haverai levato fora uno scaco biancho, pone a loco di quello un altro fato verde, secondo l'ordine del colorire como he dito in la Gelatina de Carne; et de quanti colori la vorai, cusi tu la potrai far fare.

88.4 ms: *che la.*

88.5 At the bottom right of the page is a signature of the gathering, in fine black script: *e*.

90 ms: *scachero*, with a symbol resembling an *s* — ꞩ — at the end of the word.

[f° 37r] [91.] **Zupa D'oro**

Piglia fette de pane biancho he mondale he bruscale; poi habi ova fresca sbatuta cum uno poco de aqua rosata, he pone a mogliare queste fette de pane in quella miscolanza de ova he de aqua rosata; da poi cavale fora he falle frigere cum bono butiro, voltandole molte volte; poi che serano cotte — che presto se coceno — cavale fora de la padella he pone de sopra zucaro, aqua rosata cum zaffrano.

[92.] **Suppa de Ragonisi**[92.1]

Piglia ficatelli de galina he falli cocere in aqua, he poi che serano cotti pistali cum una fetta de pane che sia bagnatta in brodo magro, he passa per la stamegna; he quando serano passati, pone insieme pipero, zaffrano, [f° 37v] zinzivero, he poi pone a cocere questa miscolanza in una pignatella lontano dal foco; he quando sera cotta, leva dal foco;[92.2] poi habi fette de pane he bruscula[92.3] le dite fette de pane al fogo he, quando serano brusculate, getali sopra quella compositione calda he manda a tavola.

[93.] **Sofritto de Carne de Pulastri ho de Pipioni**

Primo piglia le dite carne le quale te piaceno, he netale bene, he poi taglia in quarti he falli frigere in bono lardo; he quando pare che la dita carne sia bene fritta, leva fora de la padella la maior parte del grasso; dapoi piglia agresto, doi rossi de ova, specie fine he uno poco de brodo, he miscola tute queste cose inseme cum [f° 38r] uno poco de zaffrano he mette questa miscolanza cum le predite carne a dare uno bullore cum la carne ho pulli ho altro; poi piglia una poco de petrosillo he maiorana, he bate ogni cosa bene he pone in la padella del Suffritto. Se lo vorai questo Suffritto agro ho dolce, piglia ho mosto cotto ho mele ho zucaro he canella.

[94.] **Crostata de Caso, Pane, etc.**

Piglia pane he getta via la crosta, he fa fette sutile he bruscule a lo foco che siano colorite; dapoi inbratale cum butiro fresco, he ponerai de sopra zucaro, canella; et poi habi fette de[94] caso grasso he metelo sopra questo pane cum de sopra ancora zucaro he [f° 38v] he canella; poi mette queste fette in una padella de torta sopra le cinere cum lo coperto de sopra cum braxa; et como lo caso sia squagliato, manda presto a tavola.

[95.] **Pumata**

Piglia amandole he pistale tanto quanto se po, he fane latte; poi piglia dece ho .xii. pome cotte he, como serano cotte, pistale molto bene he passale par[95] la seta he miscola cum lo latte de le amandole he cum uno poco de aqua rosata he zucaro; he fa cocere questo latte cum le pome tanto che ogni cosa sia spissa; poi leva dalo focho he fane menestre.

92.1 ms: *de Ragonisi*, understand *de Aragonisi*.

92.2 ms: *foco* corrected to *fogo*?

92.3 ms: *fruscula*.

94 ms: *pane*, crossed out.

95 *par*: *sic*.

[f° 39r] [96.] **Sfresurato**

Habi una coratella de capreto ben cotta, poi tritala sotilmente cum juivert e maiorana; poi pone tute queste cose in una pignata cum bono brodo grasso cum del pipero, zaffrano, ova batuta cum una fetta de persuto he uno pocheto de aqua rosata he agresto he un pocho de zucaro, he fa ben cocere; he como sera cotto, fa le menestre.

[97.] **Cossa Stillata**

Piglia una pignata grande che sia capace de una cossa, he poi pone la cossa dentro he fa che la cossa sia imbotita de boni garofoli he canella; poi pone in la pignata uno poco de aqua rosata; da poi coprisse la dita pignata cum uno coperto.[97]

[f° 39v] [98.] **Stillato de Cossa ho de Galina in Caraffa**

Piglia una galina he falla in pezi sutilissimi, he ponela in una caraffa cum un poco de aqua rosata he uno poco[98.1] de canella sana; poi pone questa caraffa in uno caldaro pieno de aqua he fa bullire — he guarda che quando lo caldare bulle che la caraffa stia bene attacata he ben coperta; he pone sopra la dita caraffa qualche cosa che la preme a star ferma in l'aqua; he per sapere ch'e [cotta] quella carne ch'e[98.2] in la caraffa, pone un pede de dita galina a cocere nel caldaro: quando quello sera cotto, cusi sera el resto; dapoi cava la caraffa he cava fora quello suco he bevelo, ho vero manghialo cum la carne cotta insieme, cum de sopra zucaro. Non he cosa per tua boca, coco mio!

[f° 40r] [99.] **Matta Fame**

Piglia carne salata, petrosillo, maiorana, cipolle minuzate; he, quando la carne salata,[99] cavala fora, he sbatte cum lo resto qualche ova he specie he zaffrano; poi cotta, manda a tavola.

Sapori de Piu Sorte

[100.] **Sapore a polastri** spezati[100]

Piglia maiorana he ficatelli de diti polastri he rossi de ova, pebro he canella, he pista ogni cosa insieme he passale per la stamegna cum agresto cum uno poco de aqua rosata; he quando sera passato tanta roba che basti per quanti scutellini ne vorai, mette de sopra zucaro quanto basti; [f° 40v] ho vero pone questo sapore sopra de li polastri che primo haverai spezati he fritti in bono strutto; et quando haveralli fritti, cava fora quello saimo he pone lo dito sapore a dare uno bullore cum li pezi del pullastro; he manda a tavola in piatelli.

---

97 The word *coperto* is written to the right in the bottom margin.

98.1 ms: *pcoco*.

98.2 ms: *che quella carne che*. The first *che* could perhaps be understood as *como è*, without the necessity of trying to restore some missing word.

99 A verb seems to be missing: *sera cotta*? Or the phrase should perhaps have read: *quando la carn' e salata*, or *quando la carne e cotta*.

100 The last word extends into the margin and may have been added.

[*101.*] **Sapore a Lepore**

Piglia la lepore he fane peze he falla perbulire; poi falla frigere in bono saimo cum una cipolla trita; et per suo sapore, piglia lo figatto del lepore he arustilo he pistalo; poi piglia una fetta de pane brusculado[101.1] he passa ogni cosa per la stamegna cum mosto cotto; he quando haverai passado, pone simul pebro, canella, zenzevero, garofali he zaffrano, he falla agra cum agresto he dolce cum sabba; he pone questo sapore sopra la dita lepore;[101.2]

⌈[*102.*] Sapore bono[102]

Piglia granate dolce he forte he cava uno bucale de vino, poi fallo bulire cum meza libra de zucaro he meza onza de canella; nota che vole bulire assai he adasio.⌋

[f° 41r] he manda calda a tavola.

[*103.*] **Sapore a Pipione Spezato he soffrito**

Piglia uno pipione he spezalo he fallo frigere cum saimo; poi falli per suo sapore: piglia ova sbatuta he canella, pepe, zaffrano he zucaro, he miscola ogni cosa insiema cum agresto, he ponerai sopra el fritto; he manda a tavola in piatti ho in scutelle.

[*104.*] **Sapore biancho**

Piglia amandole secondo la quantita che vorai fare, he falle ben bianche he pistale quanto tu poi; he habi una molica de pane biancho posta a moglio in agresto he pista cum zucaro he zenzaro biancho; poi distempra queste cose cum agresto ho cum suco de limoni ho de marangoli; he fa ch'el sia ben biancho.

⌈Nota che ogni sapore vole essere uno pocho spisso.⌋

[f° 41v] [*105.*] **Sapore Gamelino**

Piglia uva passa[105] he pistala quanto se po; poi piglia tre ho quatro onze de amandole he pista cum la uva passa, he due ho tre fette de pane brusculado posto a moglio in vino rosso, he pista insieme; poi piglarai uno poco de bono vino rosso, sabba he agresto, facendolo dolce ho brusco como te pare; et passarai tute queste cose per la stamegna, giongendoli poi canella assai he garofoli he noce moscate.

[*106.*] **Sapore dito Fiore de Persico**

Habi amandole mondate bene he pistale molto bene cum una bianca molica de pane he uno poco de zenzaro he canella, he distempera cum agresto, cum suco de pome granate he sandali,[106]

101.1 ms: *brusculado,* with a script *s* — ʃ — at the end of the word.

101.2 The text is continued at the top of the following folio. See after Recipe 102.

102 This entire recipe is added in small script in the bottom margin. Only the initial letter of the dish's name is written somewhat larger than the rest of the name.

105 ms: *uvapassa.*

106 The text is continued at the top of the following folio.

⌈Nota che, quando tu piste amandole, mette inseme un gozolo de aqua fresca ho rosata azo non faciano olio.⌋

[f° 42r] he passa per la stamegna, et sera bono.

[*107.*] Sapore ditto Fiore de genestra

Piglia amandole, zaffrano, rossi de ova, et pista ogni cosa insieme he distempera passandole per la stamigna, giongendoli zenzaro pisto he agresto.

[*108.*] Sapore de Uva negra

Piglia uva negra bona he rompila bene in uno vaso cum una molica de pane, he poneli un poco de agresto acio che l'uva non sia tanto dolce; et queste cose farai bullire—ma primo passa per la stamegna; he bullito che havera, agiongeli canella, zenzaro et altra sorte de specie.

Nota ch'el dito suco passato vole bullire per meza hora tanto che sia un poco spisso.

[f° 42v] **[*109.*] Sapore de Visole ho de cerase**

Sequitarai l'ordine del sapore de uva negra, ma per esser le visole brusce, azonze zucaro he canella assai como vora el patrone.

[*110.*] Limonata

Piglia amandole he falle bianche he pistale bene, poi fane latte; poi fallo bullire cum canella, zenzaro he zaffrano; lo latte—dico, le amandole—passale per la stamegna cum suco de limoni ho granate he un pocoto de agresto he brodo magro; he se la vorai assai forte, mette piu limoni ho altro agrume.

[*111.*] Sapore de marzapane

Piglia quatro dita de marzapane he pistalo cum uno poco de zenzaro bono, [f° 43r] poi distempara cum suco de limoni he de granate dolce he forte; he sera bono sapore.

Salsa de piu Sorte

[*112.*] **Salsa** ad ogni bestia salvatica, ho de cervo ho urso ho capriolo ho de altra carne

Netta bene le carne he ponele arosto ho alesso; poi fa questa salsa: piglia una molica de pane brusculato cum uno pugno de carne loro he cum pebro, gingibero he zaffrano, he pista bene inseme; poi distempera cum brodo magro he agresto he cum mele, he falla bullire tanto che sia ben spessa; he pone in scutelle.

[*113.*] Salsa Sarazinesca

Quando cocinerai alla sarazinesca, fa pezi de la carne he[113.1] [f° 43v] lavala bene cum aqua calda; poi metila in una olla senza sabrero, he metice lardo del grasso, he del vino agro he cipolla tagliata sutile he juivert he salvia he maiorana, he suffrige queste cose cum la dita carne; et quando haverai soffritto uno bono pezo che sia cotto, fa piatelli pieni de dita salsa, et manda[113.2] tavola de Sarazini.

113.1 The catchword *lavala* is written in the bottom margin of this folio.

113.2 Understand: *manda a*.

[*114.*] Salsa Cotidiana

Piglia una onza he meza de zenzevero he onza una de pebro he otto tornesi de zaffrano, he fa bullire cum aceto ho vino agro tanto che queste specierie integre habiano perso el suo odore in lo vino agro.

[*115.*] Salsa Lombarda

Piglia juivert, menta, salvia, alio, [f° 44r] pepe, serpillo, una foglia de biete, pane brusculado infuso in aceto, he pista ogni cosa insieme he distempera cum aceto; he s'el'e[115] tropo forte, mite inseme saba ho uno poco de brodo.

[*116.*] Salsa Ala Franzesa a Pernice, a Galine o Altri

Piglia pignoli e amandole, he pista bene ogni cosa insieme cum bona canella, pipero, garofoli, zenzaro he zaffrano; poi distempera cum vino agro ho cum aceto ho de granate dolce ho brusce; he fa scudelle.

[*117.*] Salsa Papale

Piglia carotte meze cotte sotto le braxe quanto uno dito de quello rosso che pare negro; poi tolle una radice de[117.1] zenzevero rotto he canella assai he zucaro fino, he incorpora tute[117.2] [f° 44v] queste cose insieme he lassa stare una note; da poi fa colare como se cola la gelatina, he fane scudelini.

[*118.*] Salsa Regale

Piglia aceto biancho he forte, poi piglia una radice de gingibero rotto; he, per farne .xii. scudelini, piglia una onza de canella sana bona solamente rotta, he meza libra de zucaro fino, he pone ogni cosa insema in una pignatella netta he lassa bulire sopra le braxe per spacio de una hora pian piano; da poi cola per la stamegna; he farai li scudelini cum zucaro he canella de sopra.

[*119.*] Agresto cum Aglio

Piglia aglio poco, finoghio fresco he basilico, he pista insieme cum pipero poco, [f° 45r] he poi distempera cum bono agresto.

[*120.*] Salsa de Pampani

Piglia pampani de vite, pistali bene cum una foglia de agleto he cum una molica de pane he sale; he queste cose distemperale cum agresto ho aceto, he passale per la stamegna.

[*121.*] Mostarda Franzesa

Solo se distempera cum vino agro ho sabba. Questa he la Mostarda Francesa, senza pede he senza capo.

---

115 ms: *se le*.

117.1 ms: *de p*, with *p* crossed out.

117.2 The catchword *queste* is written in the bottom margin of this folio.

[*122.*] Mostarda ytaliana

Piglia lo seme che se ghiama sinapo he fallo stare a moglio uno ho doi di, mutandoli l'aqua spesso; poi habi amandole biancate he pistale bene,[122.1] [f° 45v] poi metele inseme cum lo dito seme de mostarda pistando ogni cosa insieme; poi piglia bono mosto cotto per farla dolce, he brusca fa cum agresto; he passa ogni cosa per la stamegna he falla spessa.
Pone dele specie se cum specie la vorai.[122.2]

[*123.*] Mostarda Per Portare cavalcando in balotte

Habi de la sementa mostarda he, quando sera stata a moglio uno giorno, pistala molto bene cum[123.1] uno pugno de uva[123.2] passa, garofali, canella, he uno poco de pipero, he cum questa pasta farai balotte picole ho grosse como una noce; poi meteralle a sugare sopra una tavola; et quando serano seche, le potrai portare cavalcando; et per distemperarle, tole agresto ho sabba ho vino ho aceto.

[f° 46r] [*124.*] Salsa O Sapore Sclavonesco, ho Vero Agliata

Piglia noce bone he pistale he, quando serano piste, meteli dentro quella quantita de aglio che tu vorai; da poi piglera una molica de pane bianco he fallo stare a moglio in brodo, he repista, poi distempera cum brodo; he fa scudelini cum de sopra pipero; se la vorai ghialda,[124.1] pone zaffrano; se la vorai pavonaza, pone uva negra o cerase — dico, del suco.

Nota che, pistando noce ho vero amandole, sempre se debe pistando ponere una guta de aqua fresca ho rosata nel mortaro.[124.2]

[f° 46v] [*125.*] A Fare Torta biancha

Piglia ova, .x. ho .xii. ha modo tuo, he batile molto bene; poi piglia una libra he meza de caso fresco taglato minuto, poi bene pistado cum meza libra de zucaro fino he altra meza onza de zenzaro mondato he meza libra de struto ho de butiro he una picola fogleta di latte; he poi miscola lo late, l'ova, lo caso, lo zucaro, lo zenzaro he lo butiro insieme molto bene — nota che voriano essere .xv. bianchi de ova per farla piu bianca; dapoi fa la pasta sotile sotto la padella he meti de sopra questa compositione, he falla cocere adasio cum foco moderato; et falla un poco colorita de sopra cum maior foco quando serra quaxi cotta; et quando parira cotta, levala fora he pone de sopra aqua rosata he zucaro, he manda a tavola.

⌈Nota che de sopra a questa torta quando sera cotta se debbe ungere cum uno rosso d'ovo sbatuto cum zaffrano, he poi mete zucaro assai he ben pisto.[125] ⌋

122.1 At the bottom right of the page is a signature of the gathering, in fine black script: *f*.

122.2 The sentence is inserted in smaller script between this recipe and the following.

123.1 ms: *cun*.

123.2 ms: *aqua* changed to *uua*.

124.1 ms: *ghiada*.

124.2 In the bottom margin is a sketch of a horse.

125 In the bottom margin is a sketch of a horse.

[f° 47r] [*126.*] **Torta Bulignesa**

Piglia una libra de caso fresco he del veghio, he gratalo; poi habi biete, petrosillo, maiorana ben nete, he batile quanto poi cum lo cultello, he poi frigile in bono butiro un pocho; da poi cavale he piglia quatro ova, zaffrano he pepe assai, he strutto ho butiro bono, he miscola ogni cosa insieme; he poi fa una crosta sutile supra el fondo de la padella he poneli dentro questa miscolanza; he de sopra haverai un'altra crosta, ho vero piglia una probatura he fane peze larghe he copre la dita miscolanza in loco de crosta.

Nota che debe sentire bene da bono pebro, he falla cocere adasio; et, quando la crosta de sopra bullira — dico, se levera — alora he cotta.

[f° 47v] [*127.*] **Herbulata de maio**

Piglia una libra de caso bono fresco he grasso he pistalo molto bene; poi habi .xii. ho .xv. ova he una fogleta de latte; poi piglarai assai biete he maiorana poca he menta he assai petrosillo, he poi pista tute queste herbe he cavane el sugo, he questo sugo meterallo cum le predite cose; he metera insieme meza libra de strutto ho butiro he meza onza de zenzaro et otto onze de zucaro, he miscolarai ogni cosa insieme; poi haverai una padella cum una crosta de sotto, he pone dentro questa compositione he falla cocere adasio cum poco foco de sotto he de sopra; et quando sera cotta — dico, presa — pone de sopra [f° 48r] zucaro he aqua rosata.

[*128.*] **Torta de Zuche**

Piglia una bona zuca he rascala he gratala, poi falli dare uno bullore in brodo grasso ho in latte; he piglerai una libra de caso fresco he del veghio, poi piglerai una libra de porco — dico, de ventresca de porco — ho de vitella, he falla bene cocere alesso, poi batila cum uno cultello; et, piacendoti, potrai ponere in loco de la ventresca, bono butiro ho struto cum meza libra de zucaro, zenzaro he canella cum uno bichero de latte et otto ova; et quando haverai fato cocere le zuche in nel brodo, cavale fora he passale per la stamegna; poi fara questa compositione ghialda de zaffrano he poneralla in una padella dandoli [f° 48v] el foco temperato sotto he sopra; et quando te parira meza cotta, pone de sopra lasagne menute; he quando sera bene cotta, pone de sopra zucaro he aqua rosata.

[*129.*] **Torta grassa cum Riso**

Piglia riso he netalo molto bene he fallo cocere in brodo grasso tanto che sia molto ben cotto; poi lo meterai sopra un taglero a refredare; poi habi caso bono fresco he un poco del parmesano he .x. bianchi d'ova he zenzaro e aqua rosata he un mezo bichero de latte — he fa ch'el caso sia ben pistado; poi miscola ogni cosa insieme, servando l'ordine de la Torta Biancha; he cusi manda a tavola. Questa vole poco caso.

[*130.*] **Torta de Farro**

Netalo molto bene he fallo cocere [f° 49r] in brodo grasso, poi fallo sugare; poi piglarai una libra de caso fresco et meza de lo veghio, pistando l'un l'altro ho gratalo; poi haverai una ventresca de vitella ben cotta alesso he quasi diffata, he batila cum lo cultello, he azonze specie fine, zucaro he zaffrano cum .xv. ova he incorpora ogni cosa insieme; he farai sul fondo de la padella una crosta, he de sopra ponerai questa compositione cum butiro a sufficientia; et quando sera meza cotta, meterai lasagne de sopra spesse, poi lassala un poco piu cocere; poi cava fora, he de sopra zucaro he canella et aqua rosata.[130]

[*131.*] Torta Comuna

Habi bono caso he ova he butiro ho altro grasso, zaffrano, pipero, zenzaro, canella, pane gratato, brodo grasso, he miseda[131] [f° 49v] tute queste cose inseme, he biete et maiorana, petrosillo, he falli dare uno bullore; poi cava he sbatile cum lo cultello he pone queste herbe cum le predite cose; poi fa una crosta supra lo fondo de la padella he meteli dentro questa compositione he falla cocere sopra le braxe, he copre la padella che ci sia foco de sotto he de sopra temperato; et como sia cotta qua non ci vole altro de sopra, seno manda a comer.

[*132.*] Una Tartara alla Senese

Piglia vinti amandole he falle ben bianche he pistale quanto se po; da poi habi meza libra de zucaro, .xii. ova he una fogletta di latte [f° 50r] he doi quatrini de canella he sale a sufficientia he mezo quarto de probatura fresca tanto pistata che piu non bisogna pistarla; da poi inbrata una tiela de butiro he poi infarinala, he de sopra gli ponerai la dita compositione; et pone la tiella sive padella lontano dal foco coperta cum foco moderato. Et nota che in la predita compositione ci potrai ponere uno ramaiolo de lasagne cotte in bono brodo; he, como sia cotta, pone de sopra zucaro he aqua rosata.

[*133.*] Tartara Julatica

Piglia una onza de bono caso parmisano he fallo pistare molto bene, che sia ben pisto; da poi piglia vinti ova he sbatile molto bene

⌈Questa he quella megliori de tute le tartare a le calate.⌋

[f° 50v] he mezo bucale de latte he meza onza de zenzaro biancho ben pisto, meza libra de bono butiro he meza libra de zucaro fino, he miscola tute queste cose insieme; he poi habi una padella grande, he sopra lo fondo farai questa crosta: habi pane gratato he primo inbrata la padella de butiro; et se non ti piace metere sopra quello pane atacato al fondo de la padella questa tale compositione, piglia a loco de quello pane[133.1] caso gratato ho farina, he fa che la padella sia bene aconza[133.2] he bagnata de bono butiro; da poi pone dentro questa compositione, he falla cocere adasio; da poi pone de sopra assai zucaro como fusse uno marzapane, et aqua rosata; et falla manducare calda calda a Catharina Fasanicha.[133.3]

---

130 ms: *aqua ro* with a dot after.

131 The word *miseda* is written in bottom margin, right.

133.1 ms: *pane* inserted above the line.

133.2 ms: *aconza*: should perhaps have been written *aconzata*.

133.3 These last three words are written in faint script and appear to have been added, perhaps at the same time as the following marginal notation.

⌈A ire alla Calata mi sera bono; he meglio mi sera de stare cum questa torta sotto L'omo.[133.4]⌋

[f° 51r] [*134.*] **Miliazo Fasanitico** a lo modo Florentino

Per fare bono Miliazo per dece persone, piglia una libra de caso frescissimo he fallo pistare molto bene — tanto, dico, bene che ti para che sia como latte; poi piglia quatro onze de farina finissima he .xii. bianchi de ova he meza libra de fino zucaro, he miscola tute queste cose insieme; et non havendo fiore de farina, piglia una molica de pane gratado in loco de la farina; poi habi una padella senza crosta sopra lo fondo, he meteralli dentro questa materia; ma prima che metti dentro la dita materia, fa uno solo de bono struto alto uno digito in la padella; he ponerai la padella sopra le braxe he, poi che lo butiro ho struto sera [f° 51v] squagliato, pone subito dentro quella compositione dandoli el foco moderato de sotto he de sopra; et quando sera cotta, cavala fora he mette de sopra zucaro he aqua rosata.

[*135.*] **Torta de Fiori de Sambuco**

Habi fiore de sambuco quando sono ben maturi, he scrola che cada tuto el fiore da quilli ramicioli, he questo fiore incorporalo cum la compositione dita de sopra in la Torta Biancha, ma questa compositione de fiore vole esser piu stretta he piu spessa; he falla cocere como he dito de le altre torte non discordanti del zucaro he aqua rosata.

[*136.*] **Torta de Castagne**

[f° 52r] **Piglia castagne** he falle cocere alesso, he poi pistale he passale per la stamegna cum uno poco de latte, azonzendo tute le cose che se contengano in la Torta de Farro.

[*137.*] **Torta de Cerase**

Tolle cesrase rosse ho piu negre che si possa trovare, he poi caverai fora quello suo osso he pista le cerase in uno mortaro; poi piglia rose rosse he batile — dico, solo le foglie — cum uno cultello molto bene tute; poi habi uno poco de caso fresco he veghio cum specie a discretione, he canella he bono zenzaro cum poco pipero he zucaro, he miscolarai tute queste cose insieme, agiongendoli .vi. ova; et farai una crosta de pasta sopra la padella he cum meza libra de butiro, he ponella ha[137.1] [f° 52v] a cocere,[137.2] dandoli el foco temperato; he quando he cotta, pone del zucaro he aqua rosata.

[*138.*] **Torta Verde** se fa como he dito de la Torta Bulignesa, excepto che se cava el sugo da le herbe.

[*139.*] **Torta de Rape** se fa como la Torta Comuna.

133.4 Pehaps to be read *lomo*.

137.1 The catchword *cocere* is written in the bottom margin of this folio.

137.2 ms: *a core*.

[*140.*] **Torta de Codogne** e·l[140] simile.

[*141.*] **Torta de Caule**

Piglia quilli torsi che parano rape he falli cocere in bono brodo grasso; poi che serano ben cotte, cavale[141] [dal] brodo he passa per la stamegna per forza — ho meglio seria pistarle tanto quanto se po; poi habi una libra de bono caso veghio he fresco, he pipero he zaffrano he .viii. ova he butiro assai, he falla cocere como la Torta Bulignesa.

[f° 53r] [*142.*] **Ova Cotta In Carta Papirea**

Piglia una carta — dico, uno mezo foglio de papiro — he aconzalo tondo ho quadrato como una padella che non possa exire olio; poi pone in questa carta olio alto doi dita ho manco; poi pone questa carta supra le braxe lontano tanto che se ascalda, ho vero sopra una candela — cioe, lontano dal foco doi dita, tanto che non brusi la carta; he quando lo olio he caldo, rompe dentro doi ova pian piano he lassa frigere tanto che sera como se fusseno state cotte in padella de ferro; he fa che l'ova sian fresche. De questo ne ha fatto la prova Julino de Sozago, amatore de le gentileze.[142]

[f° 53v] [*143.*] **Ova menata alla Todesca**

Piglia ova he sbatile bene, he azonze un poco de caso; he se sono dece ova, mettice onze .ii. de zucaro he un poco de canella he zenzevero he zaffrano he onza .i. de aqua rosa he uno poco de agresto ho marangoli; poi falle cocere in bono butiro et, quando lo butiro he caldo, mette dentro la padela queste ova, menandole sempre cum lo cughiaro che non siano troppo cotte; poi metele in uno piatello cum zucaro he canella de sopra.

[*144.*] **Fritata de Ova**

Piglia quante ova vorai he batile molto bene he pone insieme uno poco de latte per farla piu morbida; item, mette uno poco de caso gratado cum sale honestamente, he coceralla[144] [f° 54r] cum butiro bono.

[*145.*] **Fritata de Herbe**

Piglia biete, petrosillo, maiorana poca, menta, he fane suco; he poi piglarai caso gratato, canella he zucaro, he distempera insieme ogni cosa; poi habi la padella he falla frigere cum bono butauro;[145] he de sopra pone specie fine.

---

140 ms: *el.*

141 ms: *cavala*, with the last *a* modified.

142 In the bottom margin is a sketch of a bird with a human face. Also at the bottom right of the page is a signature of the gathering, in what may be the same hand as that of the scribe: g. This is accompanied by a pencilled identification: G.

144 In the bottom margin is a sketch of a bird whose head is smudged.

145 Understand: *butiro* ?

[146.] **Ova Fritelata**

Mette uno poco de bono oleo in una padella he fallo caldo; da poi mette dentro l'ova sana—senza gussa, a cio che me intenda; et quando sono prese he fate bianche de sopra, son cotte.

[147.] **Ova Sperduta** in aqua[147]

Fa che l'aqua bulla, he poi rompeli dentro l'ova fresca; he como sono fate [f° 54v] bianche—dico, che te parano bene inbiancate —alora cavale da l'aqua ponendoli de sopra zucaro he aqua rosata he un poco de marangoli he specie dolce cum agresto.

Item, senza altro gli potrai metere solamente caso gratato cum specie.

[148.] **Ova Sperduta In Latte ho in Vino**

Farai similmente como he dito de sopra, excepto non bisogna meterli caso gratado.

[149.] **Ova Piena**

Fa bulire l'ova fresca sane in aqua che siano bene dura; poi le monderai bene he taglarale per mita; he quando serano partite, cava fora lo rosso he non rompere lo bianco; et cum questi rossi ne pistarai una parte cum uno [f° 55r] pocho de[149] uva passa he un pocho de caso veghio he fresco, he cum petrosillo, maiorana he menta taglata bene minuta, giongendoli doi bianchi d'ova cum specie dolce secondo la quantita che vorai fare; et questa tale compositione miscola tuta insieme cum zaffrano he ponela nel loco deli cavati rossi he fa frigere in bono olio pian piano; ma fa che ci sia in lo pieno garofoli, canela assai; he cusi friti, manda a tavola.

[150.] **Ova sopra la graticula**

Bate doi ova fresca, poi fa scaldare[150.1] una padella he getali dentro queste ova lasando[150.2] andare queste ova per la padella como una fritata che sia sutile como una carta; et quando te parira ben cotta, falla in quarti quadrati he quisti quarti [f° 55v] poneralli sopra la graticula rompendo sopra tanta ova quante ne po tenere, che sera a modo de una torta, sopragiongendoli zucaro e canela; he quando te parirano cotte, levale dal foco.

[151.] **Ova In spito**

Scalda molto bene el spito, poi caza l'ova dentro per la ponta ho per traverso, he falle voltare al spito como fusse rosto; et como te parano cotte, levale fora he manda a tavola.

---

[147] ms: *in aqua* extends into the margin and may have been added.

[149] ms: *aqua*, deleted by an underline.

[150.1] ms: *doi*, crossed out.

[150.2] ms: *lansando* with first *n* apparently crossed out.

[152.] Ova In taze

Piglia ova fresca, he poi habi una taza ho scudella he ongela de butiro, he poi rompelli dentro l'ova he poneli de sopra zucaro he [f° 56r] canella he sale, he copre cum un'altra scutella he ponela supra la cenere calda che presto serano cotte; poi ci potrai ponere de sopra suco de marangoli ho agresto.

[153.] Ova In Cenere

Piglia ova fresca he ponella in cenere calda he voltale spesso; poi, quando serano ben bene sudate, son cotte.

[154.] Ova In aqua freda

Pone l'ova in aqua freda he falla trare un bullore; he subito cavale fora che son cotte.

[155.] Ova Fritellate a lo modo fiorentino

Piglia ova fresca he rompella ad uno ad uno in oleo ben caldo [f° 56v] et subito strengele insieme cum la paletta, facendole tonde quanto potrai; he rivoltale spesso, acio siano alquanto colorite he non tropo de dentro dure ne tropo cotto, imo morbide; manghia.

[156.] Ova sopra la brasa

Piglia ova fresca integra he getale sopra la braxa viva, he dalli de sopra de uno bastone che le rompe, he lassale cocere; et quando questa frascaria sera cotta, cava fora he mete de sopra un poco de aceto he petrosillo; he serago[156] buone.

[157.] Ova Fritellate Piene

Aconcerai l'ova afritellate al modo Fiorentino dito de sopra; che non siano tropo cotte; da poi da un lato caverai fora tuto lo rosso ad un per uno; [f° 57r] poi piglia caso veghio gratato, menta, petrosillo, maiorano, uva passa, pipero et quatro de li diti rossi d'ova—he piu secondo la quantita che vorai fare; da poi incorpora ogni cosa insieme he impe le supradita ova per quilli bussi, he faralli un'altra volta frigere tanto che possi presumere che lo pieno sia cotto; da poi caza fora he pone de sopra agresto ho marangoli cum un poco de zenzaro; et fa comer.

[158.] Ova In Forma de Ravioli

Farai una pasta a modo de lasagne, ne tropo grossa ne tropo sutile; da poi, rompeli[158] dentro ova fresca, butando de sopra zucaro he sale; et ad uno ad uno li ligarai—dico, involtarai l'ova—in la dita pasta a modo [f° 57v] che fareste li ravioli, he falli frigere.

---

156 *serago*: *sic*; also written thus in Recipes 196 and 208.

158 ms: *que*, crossed out.

[*159.*] **Offelle**

Piglia bono caso spongoso cum pocho sale he fallo gratare; poi habi ova, uva passa sana, canella, zenzaro he zaffrano, he tute queste cose falle miscolare insieme, he fa che questo dito pieno sia alquanto stretto; poi piglia una pasta sotile como le lassagne he liga la pasta[159.1] in questa pasta como lassagne,[159.2] facendole grande ho picole como a te piace, facendole sopra ghialde; poi falle cocere al forno che non sia tropo caldo; et non volano esser troppo cotte.

[*160.*] **Calisoni boni**

Fa simile pieno como he dito de la Torta[160] de Marzapane scrita [f° 58r] cum li cibi Quadragesimali; poi fa una pasta inpastata cum zucaro he aqua rosata, he distende la dita pasta como se voreste fare ravioli; et cusi involtarai questa compositione in dita pasta, facendoli grandi he picoli como vorai.

[*161.*] **Limache In tempo grasso**

Non piglare lumache se no quelle che trovi sopra lo rosmarino, supra le vite, he sopra lo finochio, he sopra de la vite ho uva, perche queste sono restaurative et lubriche al corpo; per purgarle, piglia semula he mette dentro una pignata de terra le lumache, acio che se purgano; he falle stare uno di he una notte in la dita semula; et quando vorai[161.1] [f° 58v] aconciarle per manghiare, lavale bene che non ci resti quella semula, dapoi farai darli uno bullore et poi getta via quella aqua he relavale molto bene; et piglia tanta aqua quanta vorai che sia per brodo, he falle bullire, he pone insieme rosmarino, pipero, finoghio assai he petrosillo he menta; quando serano ben cotte et s'el e[161.2] tempo de carne, ponelli dentro a bulire uno osso de bono presutto; se non sera tempo de[161.3] carne, poneli dentro olio bono; he poi cazale fora in piatelli cum bone et fine specie dolce; ma nota che voleno sentire assai da pipero, he cavale cum uno spileto. Item, se haverai lumache grosse, falle allessare dentro de uno caldaro, he poi cavale fora he falle molto bene lavare; he poi cava fora la parte denanze he getta via lo budello e·l[161.4] resto farai infarinare et frigere in bono olio.

⌈Nota che cum el gusso tute se coceno, excepto le grosse che se cavano per frigere, pure se coceno primo alesso cum el gusso.[161.5] ⌋

159.1 *la pasta*. The sense here is clearly "the mixture" or "the paste": the word *pasta* is used elsewhere in a similar sense in Recipe 123. The word may also have been in error for *lo pieno*.

159.2 One wonders whether the word *lassagne* should have been *ravioli* as in both Recipes 158 and 160.

160 ms: *torta bianca*, with *bianca* deleted by an underline.

161.1 In the bottom margin is a sketch of a snail.

161.2 ms: *se le*.

161.3 In the margin a double-curved design may refer the reader to the note added below in the bottom margin.

161.4 ms: *el*.

161.5 In the bottom margin beside this *nota* is a sketch of a snail.

[f° 59r] **Menestre**[162.1] de quadragesima

[*162.*] **Amandolata**

Piglia una libra he meza de amandole he falle ben bianche, per farne otto ho .x. menestre, he pistale molto bene, sempre agiongendo un poco de aqua fresca acio non faciano olio; he habi una molica de bono biancho pane infuso in aqua, poi stempera ogni cosa cum aqua fresca he passa per la stamegna he mette in una pila a bulire che sia lontano dal focho, he lassa bulire per meza hora ho vero per uno octavo de hora; he mitte inseme meza libra de fino zucaro; he lassa bullire adasio, che sia uno pocheto liquida he non tropo spessa; in lo pistare he distemperare falla liquida como late,[162.2] [f° 59v] he ponerai insieme uno poco de aqua rosata.

[*163.*] **Brodo de Ciceri**

Per fare otto menestre de brodo de ciceri rossi, piglia una libra de ciceri he lavali cum aqua calda, et ponelli in una pignata dove li vorai cocere sutti; he habi meza onza de bona farina he uno poco de olio he sale he .xx. grani de pipero rotto he un poco de canella pista, he rivolta tute queste cose insieme cum uno cughiaro; da poi mette in la dita pignata tre bucali de aqua—cioe, de quella dove son stati a moglio ala notte; poi falli bullire he, quando son ben consumati, pone insieme rosmarino, salvia he petrosillo cum un'altro poco de bono olio; et s'el te piace, pone insieme uno capo de aglio; he fa le menestre.

[f° 60r] [*164.*] **Menestra de piselli**

Coce li piselli in tempo de Quaresima cum latte de amandole, ho vero como he diti[164] de li ciceri, ma non voleno stare a moglio, ne voleno farina.

[*165.*] **Fava**

Piglia ho acompra la fava menata he ponela in una pignata cum bono olio; poi fa frigere una cipolla he ponela in la dita pignata cum una onza de uva passa; poi fa le menestre cum specie de sopra he zucaro.

[*166.*] **Fava In padella**

Piglia la fava menata he secondo la quantita de la fritata che vorai fare; he poi piglia sarfoglio, salvia poca, he fiche tagliate in pezoli, he pome he menta, petrosillo, he miscola tute queste cose insieme he fa frigere in[166] bono olio; poi cava sopra uno tondo cum specie fine de sopra.

162.1 The script of this word and of the following recipe title is exceptionally large and thick.

162.2 ms: *late* written in the bottom margin. Also at the bottom right of the page is a signature of the gathering, in what may be the same hand as that of the scribe: *k*. Beside this letter is also a pencilled letter *H*. That this first *recto* was an important page in this gathering is evident in the very large, thick lettering at the top of it: the words *Menestre* (*de quadragesima* being added in normal large lettering beneath) and *Amandolata*, as well as the initial letter of *Piglia*, seem formed by a brush rather than a pen. The only letters of comparable size and thickness are found on f° 89v.

164 *diti*: *sic*.

166 ms: between *in* and *bono*, what appears to be the letter *i*.

[f° 60v] [*167.*] **Jonchada de Amandole**

Piglia amandole he falle ben bianche, poi pistale sempre adiongendoli pistando aqua rosata; dapoi habi doi onze de zucaro he doi onze de aqua rosata he una fogleta de brodo de luzo freschissimo, he miscola tute queste cose insieme, he passaralle per la stamegna stretamente, che esca fora tuta la sustancia; dapoi lassa stare questa passada una notte in uno piatello, et a la matina troveralla quagliata como Jonchata de vero latte; poi ponerai sopra lo piatello zucaro he anesi confetti; he falla comer al coco che gli sapera dolce.

[*168.*] **Ricotta Contrafatta**

Piglia una libra de amandole [f° 61r] he falle ben bianche—cioe, falle stare a moglio una note, he cusi serano piu belle pellate—he pistale molto bene; he da poi habi quatro onze de zucaro he onza .i. de aqua rosata he mezo bichero de brodo de pesso—cioe, luzo ho tencha bona; he distempera tute queste cose insieme et le passarai per la stamegna ben stretta; he questa compositione reponeralla in una forma como he quelle che se portano a vendere cridando 'Ricotta! Ricotta!'; he quando haverai posto quella materia dentro, ponella in loco fresco a la sera per la matina; da poi cavala sopra uno tagliero, non discordandote del zucaro he aqua rosata de sopra, he anasi confetti.

[*169.*] **Butiro Contrafato**

Piglia, como he dito de sopra, una libra he meza de amandole biancate he bene[169] [f° 61v] piste; poi piglia mezo bichero de bona aqua rosada he passara le dite amandole per la stamegna—he se non basta quella aqua rosada, pigliane tanto quanta te ne fa bisogno fina tanto che passata sera quella quantita de amandole; he poi, per fare che lo dito latte de amandole se venga bene a stringere, piglia un poco de farina de amido he uno pocho, se te piace, de zaffrano he zucaro fino, he aconza questa materia in una forma como fusse butiro; he cusi sera bon manghiare.

[*170.*] **Pastonache**

Quelle che sono grosse netale molto bene he cazale fore quello steccho che hage in mezo, poi falle allessare; he quando serano cotte, infarinale he falle frigere in bono olio—ma primo falle [f° 62r] ben siccare sopra una tavoleta; he dapoi, per farle megliore, piglia una scutella de fiore de farina he stemprala cum aqua he pone insiema zucaro, canella he zaffrano he aqua rosada he imbrata le pastonache cum questa miscolanza, he ponele nela padella cum l'olio caldo; he poi pone de sopra specie, he manda a tavola cusi honestamente salade.

[*171.*] **Biancho manghiare**

Per fare sei menestre de Biancho Manghiare de Quaresima: una libra de riso—dico, de farina de riso—he uno bucale de latte de capra he quatro onze de zucaro he un poco de zenzaro; he fa bulire, menando continuamente cum lo cughiaro; he dapoi pista una ho due onze de polpa de pesso he due onze de pignoli, he pone insieme a bulire; he quando sera spisso, l'e[171] cotto.

---

169 The catchword *piste* is written in the bottom margin of this folio.

171 ms: *le*.

[f° 62v] [*172.*] **Fritelle amare**

Habi fiore de farina, un pocho de levato, he piglia tre quatrini de herbe amare he cazali fora el sugo — he, non posendo uxire, pone insieme un poco de aqua; poi piglia un quatrino de uva passa he bone specie he zafrano, he falle miscolare tute queste cose inseme alla sera per la matina; he da poi falle frigere cum bono olio.

[*173.*] **Fritelle** de fiore de Sambuco.

Piglia fiore de sambuco; he primo fa pistare una libra de amandole biancate ho pignoli, he passa per la stamegna cum aqua rosata he cum brodo de piselli; poi habi un poco de bona farina tanto che questo late sia liquido [f° 63v] honestamente, he miscola ogni cosa bene insieme cum lo dito fiore — cioe, fa questa compositione a la sera per la matina; he agiongeralli zucaro, he falle cocere in bono olio adasio.

[*174.*] **Fritelle de Riso**

Coce lo riso, poi fallo sugare; he piglia tante amandole monde secondo la quantita che vorai fare, he pistale he passale [per][174] la stamegna cum aqua rosada he brodo del riso, he fa questo latte dele amandole sia spisso; poi piglia fiore de farina he zucaro, he miscola tute queste cose insieme cum tanto riso quanto vorai; he fa le fritelle como te pare longe ho grosse, he falle frigere in bono olio; he quando son cotte, non te discordare de ponere de sopra zucaro, canella; he sbrufalle cum aqua rosada.

[f° 63v] [*175.*] **Fritelle de Fiche Piene**

Piglia amandole he pignoli, he pista molto bene — dico, che ogni cosa sia biancha — he pista insieme due bone fiche he un poco de uva passa; poi taglia un poco de petrosillo ben trito, he habi bone specie he miscola insieme; he se questa materia fusse troppo dura, pone insieme un poco de aqua rosada; poi piglia fiche belle he grosse he falli un buco dove sta el fiore suo he impele de questa materia; poi falle frigere in bono olio, adasio dico.

[*176.*] **Fritelle de Pome**

Monda he neta molto bene le pome he falle allessare ho vero cocere sotto la braxa; he poi cavali via tuto lo bono he pistalo bene, he pone insieme [f° 64r] farina he zucaro, he distempera ho cum aqua rosada ho cum la communa cum bone specie, he frigele in bono olio.

[*177.*] **Fritelle In Forma de ravioli**

Piglia amandole, pignoli neti, noce, uva passa, fiche, latte de bono pesso he li ficatelli, maiorana, menta, petrosillo he bone specie, he pista ogni cosa insieme cum zaffrano; he farai le Fritelle como ha veduto de li Ravioli — cioe, involta questa compositione in una pasta fata cum zucaro he aqua rosada — he falla frigere in bono olio.

---

[174] ms: *passale la.*

[*178.*] Fritelle in Forma de ravioli cum riso

Fa cocere del riso, he pista de le amandole,[178] he primo falle bianche, [f° 64v] he pasale strette — dico, quanto piu spese che potrai — cum aqua rosata, poi fa che incorpori bene lo late de le amandole cum lo riso; poi adiunge zucaro cum un pocho de farina fina de amido; poi fa le fritelle ho in forma de pastelli — cioe, pone questa compositione in una pasta fatta como he quella cassa del pastello picolo, frigendo in bono olio.

[*179.*] Fritelle Piene de vento

Piglia fiore de farina he aqua he sale he zucaro, he distempera questa materia che non resti tropo dura; da poi distende questa pasta cum mane sopra una tavola cum uno pezo de legno tondo, he taglarai la dita pasta tanto grande quanto vorai che sia in forma de fritelle; et [f° 65r] frigeralla cum bono olio. Et cum la dita pasta potrai fare pere, pome, noce he rami de garofoli he de rosmarino he de salvia, reducendo la dita pasta in quello modo che tu vorai, he subito gitandola in bono olio caldo cum pocho cocere. He quando son cotte, falle hanchora ghialde cum zaffrano stemperato cum aqua rosata. Et nota che la dita pasta, volendo tu fare le cose predite — cioe, pere he etc. — fa la pasta larga como una nevola, he dalli una calda in olio; ho vero tinge la padella de olio he gettali dentro quella pasta larga como una nevola, he subito cazala he falla cum le mane in forma de uno pero ho pome ho altro como a te piacera; he da poi fa cocere in olio fino un'altro pochetto queste fritelle fate in forma de pere he pome ho de altra forma.[179]

[f° 65v] [*180.*] Torta de marzapane

Piglia amandole he falle stare a moglio una notte, poi spellale che sian ben bianche, he pistale molto bene, et poi pone equale zucaro he equale amandole; per far questa torta megliore che sia una libra de una — cioe, de amandole — he una de zucaro fino, ho piu ho manco secondo la quantita che vorai fare, he adiungeralli una onza de aqua rosata; dapoi incorpora ogni cosa insieme; poi piglarai bone nevole fate cum zucaro he aqua rosada — he primo bagnate cum aqua rosata — poi distendele sopra el fondo de una tiella he pone de sopra la dita compositione, he spianala [f° 66r] molto bene cum uno cughiaro he fala bassa supragiongendoli zucaro he aqua rosa; poi falla cocere adasio. He cusi te troverai Torta de[180] Marzapane.

[*181.*] Torta de Riso

Piglia una libra de riso he una de amandole monde he piste molto bene, he stemprale cum lo brodo del riso; he poi piglia lo riso he macinalo molto bene quando el sera ben cotto, he incorporalo cum le amandole; he piglia un pocho de ova de luzo, pistale he passale per la stamegna he pone insieme cum una libra de zucaro; he poi habi due onze de pignoli sani he incorpora tute queste

---

178 ms: *amando*, with *le* squeezed in.

179 ms: *fo a*. The abbreviation here for *rm* is found elsewhere in the manuscript with the value of *m*, as in *cu* , *cum*.

180 ms: *he*.

cose insieme; poi habi la padella he falli una crosta [de][181] sotto he de sopra cum lasagne larghe [f° 66v] he sotile; et quando sera fornita de cocere, meterai de sopra zucaro et de l'aqua rosada. Et questa torta non vole esser troppo cotta.

[*182.*] **Torta Papale**

Piglia una libra he meza de sturiono frollo ho de uno bono luzo che sian cotti alleso bene, he guarda non li lassi spine, poi fallo pistare molto bene; he quando he ben pisto, cazalo fora dalo mortaro; poi piglia meza libra de amandole he un pocho de pignoli, he pista insieme; poi pigla meza libra de riso ben cotto in latte de amandole, poi pistalo cum le supradite cose; da poi pone insieme una libra de zucaro he meza onza de zenzaro he un poco de canella he sale he zaffrano he un bichero de ova de luzo, he passa ogni[182] cosa per stamegna, facendo una crosta in la padela como he dito de sopra supraponendoli questa materia.

[f° 69r] [*183.*] **Fritata de Ova de pesso** —dico, de luzo, che son bona.[183.1]

Piglia ova de luzo—cioe, uno bichero—he uno bichero de aqua; poi piglia maiorana, menta he petrosillo batudo minuto minudo, he un poco de pebro he zaffrano,[183.2] he miscola ogni cosa insieme he falla frigere in padella cum bono olio, he rivoltala una volta. He se non haverai herbe, fa cum cipolla cotta primo alesso.

[*184.*] **Fritata de Caviaro**

Pone a moglio in aqua tepida lo dito caviaro per spacio de meza hora, poi geta via l'aqua he pistalo nello mortaro, che sia ben pisto; he se lo dito caviaro he meza libra, pone un bichero de aqua he pebro, zaffrano he quelle cose dite del luzo in quello modo.[184]

[f° 69v] [*185.*] **Tartare Alla Franzesa de Pome**

Fa cocere le pome quale tu vorai ho in aqua ho in mosto cotto, ho in uno tegamo al forno ho sotto le braxe; poi piglia pignoli stati a moglio in aqua una notte, che non siano ranzi, he pistali bene cum le pome; poi piglia assai zucaro he poco de canella, uno poco de zenzaro he un poco de zaffrano, he uno bichero de ova de luzo bene piste he passate per la stamegna, he miscola tute queste cose insieme he passa per la stamegna cum aqua rosada ho altra aqua; poi fa una pasta pigliando zucaro, farina, olio, [f° 70r] aqua he sale, he miscola insieme he fa questa pasta; poi distendela sopra lo fondo de una padella bassa, he poi poneralli dentro questa tale compositione che non sia alta piu de uno digito; poi falla cocere a lo forno ho al foco como he dito de le altre

---

181 ms: *crosta sotto.*

182 From this point the text is written in short lines and slightly smaller script in the bottom margin. This page, f° 66v, is the end of the gathering identified as "*k*".

183.1 These last six words are centered on the page immediately below the recipe's name but in normal sized script. The space that regularly separates name and text is below this phrase.

183.2 ms: *zaffeano.*

184 The words *in quello modo* are to the right in the bottom margin and seem to be added.

torte; poi, quando sera quasi cotta, piglia nevole he spolvarizale de sopra questa Tartara—che siano fate le dite nevole cum bono zucaro; he quando sera cotta, getta de sopra zucaro he aqua rosa.

[*186.*] **Tartari bianchi**

Piglia una panza de uno bono pesso cotto alesso he pistalo bene; poi piglia latte de amandole he ova de luzo he zucaro he zenzaro, [f° 70v] he distempera tute queste cose cum aqua rosada ho cum altra aqua, he passa ogni cosa per la stamegna; da poi falla cocere como le altre torte[186.1] ponendoli hanchora, quando he quasi cotta, de quella polvere de nevole; et quando he tuta ben cotta, poneli dentro pignoli confetti piantati de sopra la dita torta—ma primo bagna la dita torta de sopra cum aqua rosada; da poi caciala fora de la patella, cum de sopra zucaro he poche[186.2] aqua rosata.

Nota che per ogni cosa hai da ponere sale a sufficientia; et se lo cocho non he discreto, sapi che tute le dolce cose che lui fara ho serano tropo salade ho tropo fatue. Fa ch'el cocho sia un ghiotto, ma non per se ma per lo suo patrone.

[f° 67r] [*187.*] **Sardelle**

Al suo naturale he de frigere; he quando sono fritte, ponelli de sopra suco de marangoli he un poco de quello olio fritto he sale; he calde se vogliano comer.

[*188.*] **Polpi**

S'el e[188.1] vivo, batelo molto bene sopra uno saxo cum uno bastone; poi habi uno pocho de aqua calda he fallo ben bianco; dapoi taglalo in buconi longi uno dito, he metteli in una pignata cum uno pocho de olio, de sopra le braxe lontano dal foco; he non metere dentro aqua, se no fallo cusi cocere cum olio pian piano; poi habi un pocho de cipolla fritta he arbuze odorifere cum specie he agresto he un pocheto de aqua; he fa ogni cosa miscolada insieme che bulla uno pocheto; he poi manda a tavola.[188.2]

[f° 67v] [*189.*] **Granci**

Falli cocere in vino he aqua ho senza aqua, he poi sale assai; et per suo sapore, piglia aceto.

[*190.*] **Scinale**

Taglialo per traverso in fette grosse uno dito, he netalo bene he fallo cocere sopra la graticula, he bagna cum aceto, sale he specie he olio miscolado insieme, he volta li diti pezi spesso; he manda a tavola. Item, lo potrai frigere he ponerlo etiam alesso, he farne pezi grossi quanto a te parira. Guarda non sia ranzo.

186.1 ms: *torte* added in the margin.

186.2 *poche*: *sic*.

188.1 ms: *se le*.

188.2 At the bottom right of the page is a signature of the gathering, in what may be the same hand as that of the scribe: *k*. This has been crossed out and replaced with a large *i* or *j*. Beside these is pencilled a letter *i*.

[*191.*] **Raye**

In nullo modo he bono seno alessato, he poi cum una agliata de sopra.

⌈He questo he pasto de Catherina fasaniticha Florentina.⌋

[f° 68r] [*192.*] **Laze**

Cazali fora quella forzina sive budello da la aureghia, he falla arostire sopra la graticula bagnandola cum sale, aceto, pipero he zaffrano he olio; he per suo sapore: marangoli, ho vero piglia un foglio de biete he un pocho de petrosillo, menta he maiorana he pebro, he pista bene insieme cum uno pocho de pane bagnado in aceto, he distempera cum aceto; he questo he per suo sapore. Item, la poi cocere alesso; et per suo sapore: piglia .xv. noghie he pistale cum uno poco de zucaro he bono zenzaro, he distempera cum agresto ho suco de limoni.

[*193.*] **Bessano**

Fallo allessare in vino, aqua he acito; et per suo sapore, vole agliata.

⌈[*194.*] **Fravolino**[194.1]

He bono arosto he alesso et sopra la graticula et acarpionado.[194.2]⌋

[f° 68v] [*195.*] **Testudine**

Piglia le testidine[195] piu grosse, che son miglore, et falle bullire cusi vive in uno caldaro, he lassale tanto bulire finche sian ben cotte; he poi cazale dal gusso he taglia via la testa he la coda he li pedi, he netale bene che non li resti alcuna immonditia, he cava lo fele dal figato; poi piglia lardo he ponelo in una padella; he habi petrosillo, menta he maiorana, meza spica de aglio, he, ogni cosa pistada, stempera cum bone specie he cum agresto, he poi falli dare una fritura insieme cum le testudine; he poi manda a tavola. He fa questa compositione ghialda de zaffrano.

[missing folio(s)]

[f° 71r] [*196.*] [. . .] le peze de dita anguilla serago cotte, poneli de sopra questa salsa; he manda in tavola li pezi de anguilla in piatelli he la salsa in scudellini.

[*197.*] **Salsa Hispana a Calamari**

Piglia li calamari he netali bene che non li resti nulla de bruto; poi piglia le gambe he le teste de ditti calamari he falli perbullire, da poi pistali sive tapolali; he poi piglia noce he pistale cum bone specie he impe li diti calamari de quelle noce, specie, capi he gambe de diti calamari; poi cuceli he mandali al forno in uno tegamo; et quando sono quasi cotti, piglia, per farli un'altra salsa:

194.1 The entire recipe is added in the bottom margin.

194.2 ms: *acuipionado*, with a script *s* — ς — at the end of the word.

195 *testidine*: *sic*, although the title is spelled *Testudine*.

assai pane torrato infuso in vino agro ho in aqua he pistalo cum pignoli he specie assai,[197] [f° 71v] he quando haverai ben pistado, distempera cum aqua; et quando li calamari serano cotti, cazali da la olla o tiella he pone la dita salsa in dita tiella he fa bulire, he poi pone hancho insieme li calamari; et quando haverano bulito un pezo, pone li calamari per piatelli he la salsa per scudelle.

[*198.*] **Calamari**

Quanto sono piu picoli sono megliori per frigere, cum specie he sugo de marangoli de sopra; li grossi se voleno ben netare, he poi impirli con quello pieno de la Tencha Reversa; ho vero, quando son grossi assai, falli cocere in una pilla cum olio, et che loro siano primo tagliati in pezi picoli como fusse trippa; he poneli lontano dal foco, speso voltando; [f° 72r] he quando serano quasi cotti, pone insieme in la pila ogni sorte de specie cum uno poco de zucaro he agresto, he lassa trare un'altro bullore; poi caciali.

[*199.*] **Sturiono cum Sapore**

Amaza lo sturione he fallo stare dui giorni morto per esser piu frolle; poi fallo cocere cum bono vino biancho misculado cum aqua che sia tanto lo vino quanto l'aqua, he del sale a sufficientia; he fallo bulire tanto quanto s'el fusse carne de vitello, he fallo in pezi — ma piu belleza he servarlo integro, perche ogni pesso hene megliore integro che in pezi; quando sera cotto, cavalo he fallo ghialdo cum zaffrano he sugo de aranze se ti piace; el suo sapore vole esser Sapor Biancho, como he dito de sopra, ma cum piu zenzaro.

⌈Nota che ogni pesso vole esser bene salado.[199.1] ⌋

[f° 72v] Et hancho li potrai dare[199.2] Agliata Biancha, ho vero Mostarda.

[*200.*] **Ombrina**

Vole essere aconzata como lo dito Sturione, salvo che debe bulire manco; et per suo sapore, quello medesimo sapore.

[*201.*] **Dentale**

Debbe esser alessato cum aceto perche piu se conserva; he ha migliore gusto che esser cotto cum aqua.

[*202.*] **Corvo grosso**

Vole esser alesso; se serane picolo, volei esser arostito; et per suo sapore, Salsa Verde ho Mostarda.

---

[197] At the bottom right of the page is a signature of a gathering, in fine black script: *k*.

[199.1] ms: *salado*, with a symbol resembling an *s* — ꞩ — at the end of the word.

[199.2] ms: *da*.

[203.] **Orata**

S'el'e[203] grossa, falla alessare; se no, frigere.

⌈Nota che ogni pesso vole bulire adasio.⌋

[f° 73r] [204.] **Rombo**

Fallo alessare, he perche hene tanto frollo, ligalo sopra una graticula de canuze he fallo bulire adasio in uno vaso capace; et per suo sapore, vole de sopra agresto, petrosillo trito, pipero he zaffrano.

[205.] **Triglie**

Se voleno arostire; he per suo sapore: marangoli, specie he sale de sopra.

[206.] **Salpani**

Cavaralli fora le trippe he cocelo arosto; cum marangoli de sopra.

[207.] **Goze**

Sono megliore alesso che arosto.

[208.] **Hoghiali**

Serago meglio fritti che allessati.

[209.] **Sargo**

He bono alesso et arosto.

⌈Nota che ad ogni pesso se vole cavare l'interiora.⌋

[f° 73v] [210.] **Morena**

Scortica la morena, ho vero falla pellare cum aqua calda gittando via la testa he la coda—dico, un pezo—he poi falla frigere; et per suo sapore, dalli Salsa Verde.

[211.] **Zefali ho macarella**

Sono boni friti quando son picoli, et quando son grossi son boni alesso; he quando sono mezo cotti, pone de sopra pipero bono, agresto, petrosillo he butiro ho olio.

[212.] **Passara**

S'el'e[212] grossa, falla alessare; he vole esser aconzata como lo rombo.

---

203 ms: *se le*.

212 ms: *se le*.

[213.] Hostriche

Se coceno sopra la braxa, he quando se apreno son cotte; ancora le poi cavare he falle frigere in olio; et quando son cotte, pone de sopra agresto he specie[213] [f° 74r] forte — he cusi se fa a la Veneciana.

[214.] Lampuge

Vogliano esser fritte; he poi de sopra pone marangoli he pepe.

[215.] Cappe

Habi una padella sutta, et in essa mette le dite cappe al foco; he como se comenzano aprire, son cotte; potrai subito metere insieme agresto, pipero he petrosillo minutato, he darli un'altra calda, he cavarle fora a comere. Item, le potrai cocere supra le braxe. Et per cavarli l'arena, falli stare una note in aqua.

In questo modo son le concule.

[216.] Luzo

Vole esser alessato cum aceto he vino he aqua; et per suo sapore, Mostarda.

⌈Nota che ogni pesso se debbe molto bene nettare da le squame.⌋

[f° 74v] **[217.] Trotte**

Le trotte grosse netale molto bene, poi tagliale in pezi largi una mano; he piglia uno vasso dove le vorai cocere capace de quilli pezi, he poi ponelli dentro li diti pezi per longo — dico, che lo tagliato guarda in su; he cusi sanguinato, metteli de sopra sale assai, he poi pone l'aqua dentro in modo che non lavi gio el sale che li a posto de sopra; he fa che quella aqua avanzi de sopra li diti pezi doi dita he non piu, he fa cocere adasio; he como comenza far spuma, leva de sotto el foco tanto che bulla bene adasio; et quando serano cotti, caciali fora he ponelli a sugare sopra una grande tagliero, cum specie dolce de sopra; et per suo sapore darai Sapor Bianco.

[f° 75r] **[218.] Tencha In Tegamo**

Piglia una tencha bona de tre libre he rascala tanto che se faza biancha, he caciali li denti; da poi piglia dece noce, mezo quatrino de petrosillo he maiorana, he menta pocha, he tanto aglio quanto uno cicero, he assai pipero, he pista ogni cosa insiema cum zaffrano he cum uno poco de olio et uva passa non pistada[218.1] cum lo figato de dita tencha; he quando haverai ben pistado, pone he cacia zo per la gola de la tenca questa compositione; ma primo cacia fora l'interiora de la tencha per la bocha cum qualche rampino che non rompi el fele, ho vero aprila pocho poco apresso al capo, he da li pone la dita impitura; he poi aconzala in uno tegamo capaze de la dita tencha he falla bulire cum mezo bichero de aceto, [f° 75v] mezo bichero de agresto he doi bicheri

---

213 In the bottom margin are sketches of a moray (identified by the word *morena*, of which the last letter is blotched), a pike (or barracuda), a turtle and another fish, perhaps a smaller pike or pickerel.

218.1 ms: *uva passa non pistada* added in margin.

de aqua cum una onza de mosto cotto, ho piu ho mancho secondo lo vorai dolce; he pone insieme uva passa sana he prune he vissole he una cipolla fritta in bono olio; he al fine habi petrosillo trito he menta he maiorana, he pone dentro a dare un bullore; dapoi cava la dita tencha dal tegamo he ponela in uno[218.2] piatello cum bone specie he suco de limoni, he manda in tavola cum ogni cosa che era nel dito tegamo.

Se la tencha he picola, frigela.

Quelle che sono de meza una libra ho de una, fendele per la scina he falle frigere; cum marangoli ho agresto de sopra.

Potrai hanchora far cocere sopra la graticula una tencha grossa, facendoli la impitura de sopra in la Tenca de Tre Libre; [f° 76r] he faralli una salmora de aceto, pipero, sale he zaffrano, facendola cocere adasio he bagnandola spesso cum dita salmora cum uno ramo de rosmarino.

[219.] **Lampreda grossa**

Se vole far morire la lampreda dentro vino amabile; da poi se vole ponere dentro de l'aqua calda per rascare via quella viscosita, ma guarda de non levare ne guastare la pelle; poi caciali la lingua he li denti he vede de cavarli lo budello cum alcuno rampino che non guasti el corpo, perche la lampreda non ha altro de tristo[219.1] seno lo budello; he non lassare perdere el suo sangue perche cum quello se fa lo suo sapore; in bocha gli ponerai una noce moscata, in li busi del collo pone garofoli; et ponerai questa lampreda [f° 76v] in uno tegamo cum .i. onza de olio he agresto he vino bianco bono, et de questo licore farane tanto che venga sopra la lampreda, he poi de sopra li ponerai uno poco de sale; he falla cocere adasio sopra le braxe; et como sia cotta, falli questo sapore: piglia amandole ho noghie he falle bene pistare cum uno poco de uva passa et cum una fetta de pane brusculado, he poi distempera cum agresto ho sabba ho cum altro licore como a te piacera, he passa ogni cosa per stamegna; da poi agionge garofoli, zenzaro e canella, he mandala a tavola.

Aconzale in un'altro modo — cioe, arosto in spido, tenendoli sotto quando tu volti qualche cosa per recoglere lo sangue, el quale he la sua bonta; et con questo potrai fare lo dito suo [sapore.][219.2]

[missing folio(s)]

[220.] **Zabaglone**[220.1]

Per fare quatro taze de Zabaglone, piglia .xii. rossi de ova frasca, tre onze de zucaro he meza onza[220.2] de canella bona he uno bucale de vino bono dolce, he fallo cocere tanto che sia preso

---

218.2 ms: *tegamo*, deleted by an underline.

219.1 ms: *detristo*.

219.2 This manuscript copy of the recipes ends at the foot of f° 76v with the word *suo*.

220.1 This recipe is written on f° 89v, immediately after the banquet menus, and occupies the entire page.

220.2 The word is written *on* with a superscript slur.

como uno brodeto. Et poi levalo fora he ponello in uno grando piatello davante alli Compagnone. Et se vorai, gli potrai ponere uno pezo de butiro fresco.

Finis.

B. Menus

[ff° 77r–92v]

Gathering	Folio	Banquet
l	77r	[1] Convito de lo Archiepiscopo de Benevento
	77v	[2] Convito del conte Jeronimo
	80r	[3] Un'altro convito
	83r	[4] Altra rasone de convito
m	85r	[5] Ordine del pranzo fatto da monsignore Ascanio allo principe de Capua
	89v	220 Zabaglone

The **bold-face** type throughout this transcription of the Menus represents those words that the scribe has written in large, thick script in the manuscript.

[f° 77r]

[1] Convito de lo Archiepiscopo de Benevento[1]

1.[2] Aqua odorifera ale mane

2. Caponi cum zucaro he cinamomo
Interiori cum petrosillo he specie

---

1 In this rubric the word for archbishop (modern Italian *arcivescovo*) is abbreviated as *Arciepo*. Centered on the line immediately following the place-name Benevento, a papal city some 30 miles northeast of Naples, the word *Primo* is written in the same large, bold script. Though this ordinal number would thus seem to qualify the Archbishop, it must rather be a very proclamatory incipit to the first of the "courses" in the menu that follows — and this despite the numeral *1* also written in the margin beside *Aqua odorifera ale mane*.

In his *Cucina italiana del quattrocento*, 39–40, Claudio Benporat tentatively identifies the personage named here with Cardinal Lorenzo Cybo (Lorenzo di Domenico De Mari), a protégé of Pope Innocent VIII and Archbishop of Benevento from 1486 to 1501. See also the same author's *Storia della gastronomia italiana*, Milan (Mursia), 1990, 84, note 18. However, as Bruno Laurioux has pointed out ("Les livres de cuisine italiens à la fin du XVe et au début du XVIe siècle," *La Mediterrània, àrea de convergència de sistemes alimentaris (segles V–XVIII)* (Palma: Institut d'Estudis Baleàrics, 1996), 77, note 32), the papal town and province of Benevento had at least eleven Archbishops during the fifteenth century.

2 These numerals, representing the course number — that is, the sequence in the serving of various groups of dishes in the meal — are sometimes placed in the margin, sometimes in the middle of the page.

3. Pastelli de medule cum polpe de caponi
   Pastalli de caponi de pizoni, uno per pastizo, cum tordi

4. Uno fasano alla cathalana

5. Starne in brodo lardero, una per homo
   Gelanitina[3]

6. Pavoni, uno per piatello, cum cedri
   Vermicelli de capo de latte
   Sapore di pavo
   Fassani vestiti
   Bianchomanghiare[4] [f° 77v]

7. Dui caponi per piatello cum granate
   Sallato[5]
   Sumata, una[6]
   Presutto, uno
   Salsizoni,[7] doi dorati; salvia, rosmarino
   Lengue, due[8]

---

[2] **Convito del conte Jeronimo**[9]

1. Fichi de piu sorte Pera muscatella	in Confetere

---

[3] *Gelanitina: sic.*

[4] At the bottom of the page is a signature of the gathering, in a hand that may be that of the scribe: *l.*

[5] Here and elsewhere this word *Sallato*, salted (spiced) or preserved meats, should likely be read as a rubric for the dishes that immediately follow.

[6] Understand, here and in the next dishes, the number of items *per piatello*, per serving.

[7] *salsizoni*: ms. *salfizoni*

[8] Menu [4], below, reproduces the servings detailed in this Menu [1] up to this point, but then continues with *Rosto minuto, Rosto grosso, torte*, fruit, nuts and "dessert".

[9] In his *Cucina italiana del quattrocento*, 39, Claudio Benporat writes that this *conte Jeronimo sembra identificarsi in Girolamo Riario, nipote prediletto di Sisto IV, intrigante, grossolano, vile e feroce signore di Imola, sposato a Caterina Sforza, figlia illegittima di Galeazzo Maria [Sforza], fratello de quel Pietro Riario "la tavola del quale fu sempre lautissima"* . . . . See also the same author's earlier suggestions (*Storia della gastronomia italiana*, 84, note 18) that this Count Jeronimo may be either the Count of Cariati in Puglia or the nephew of Pope Sixtus V, Felice Peretti (1585–90).

Aqua odorifera[10] ale mane

2. Pignocati cum arme } in confettere
   Pignocati communi

2.[11] Capo de latte in tace
   Pomeranze dolce cum zucaro he aqua rosata in tace [f° 78r]

3. Fasano, uno
   Animelle
   Ficatelli de pulli
   Ficatelli de capreto
   Ova non nate[12]
   Salviata—cio'e, una torta

4. Una pernice
   Uno pavone vestito, cum sapore de pavo

5. Una testa de capreto in scutella
   Conigli arosto, tre per piatello

6. Porchette,[13] due
   Uno pastello per homo, de medule[14]

Alesso

7. Vitella, libre .xl.
   Capreto, uno, doi[15]
   Caponi, quatro, sei [f° 78v]

---

[10] The manuscrit reads *Aqua Arifa*. The scribe may have begun to write *Aqua ale mane odorifera*, as he does later at serving .xiii., and then half-corrected the second word to end in *-rifera*, an *er* abbreviation being understood.

[11] The first occurrence of this "2" (at the first *Pignocati*, above) is written both in the left margin and in the center of the page. This present "2" is written only in the center of the page. When these four dishes are echoed in the following menu ([3], on f° 80r), the first two (the two sorts of *Pignocati*) are grouped with the very first dishes. It is likely that here as well, in this second banquet, the second course should begin with this *Capo de latte*.

[12] *nate*: *sic*. *Cf.* the spelling *nata* on folio 80v.

[13] *Porchette*: *sic*.

[14] That is, one *pastello de medule*.

[15] The double quantities found here and there in this particular menu may refer to the quantities to be served, per platter, to the ordinary guests and to those at the head table, respectively.

Pollastri, .v., .vi.
Pizoni, .4. — menestre[16]
Porcho salvatico, libre .x. — piselli
Castrado,[17] libre .x.
Salado[18] — sapore
Sumata, una — gamelino
Persutto, uno, doi
Salsizoni, tre, quatro
Lengue vestite, tre, quatro
Lengua de bove, una

Rosto minuto[19]

8. Pollastri, 6
Pizoni, 6
Quaglie, 6
Tortare, 6

Cervo[20]
Signale

9. Cirvello vestito [f° 79r]
Crostate

---

[16] A long vertical slur brackets the items between *Pollastri*, at the top of f° 78v, and *Lengua de bove*. To the right of this bracket the word *menestre* presumably complements the numerals, whereas *piselli* and *sapore gamelino* indicate garnishes or side dishes served at the same time as the meats.

[17] A letter or symbol follows the *o* of *Castrado*. Though not shaped similarly, it is reminiscent of the symbol that ends the same word *castrado* in Recipes 46 and 78 of the main body of the manuscript. In Menu [3] below, on f° 81r, the word *carnero*, found at the same place in the meal as this present *castrado*, is likewise followed by the symbol resembling an *s* — ꞩ — that is found after these words (and others) among the recipes.

[18] Properly the previous dish, *Castrado*, concludes the list of dishes that constitute the first part of the course numbered 7 and bearing the rubric *Alesso* in this menu. Here the word *Salado* should be understood as a minor rubric that introduces the five salted meats that follow. The same use of the word is found in each of the other menus, where its spellings are variously *sallato* and *salato*. In Menu [3] the salt-meat course is recognized with its own sequential number (8); in Menu [5] the rubric for the course is quite distinct: *Piatti 7 de salato indorato: per piatto . . . .*

[19] The words identifying the menu for the course of roast fowl, are repeated below in equally large, bold script to the right of the four dishes.

[20] Although there is a break in the text previous to this *Cervo*, the number 9 is written only before *Cirvello vestito*, below. It would seem more reasonable that the beginning of the ninth course, along with a rubric for *Rosto salvatico* (such as is at course 9 in the next menu [3]), should be located here.

10. Caponi, doi, coperti cum zucaro
Pastelli

.xi. Sturione, uno } sapore verdo
Lamprede }

.xii. Torte anglese
Torte alla divisa[21]

.xiii. **Aqua ale mane odorifera**

Zonchata in tace
Cerase in confetere

.xiiii. Zelatina
Una testa de vitella depinta

.xv. Pastelli de caponi he capreti
Fasano vestito, cum l'ova sotto[22] [f° 79v]

.xvi. **Rosto**

Capone coperto de cerase
Starne, 7
Quaglie, 8, in piatelli

.xvii. Papari, 3, arosto, cum sapore bianco he morello
Fasano, uno, vestito, in piede

.xviii. **Rosto grosso**

Vitella, libre trenta, quaranta
Capreto, uno, doi
Caponi, quatro, sei
Pollastri, 7[23]
Pipioni, 8
Anatre, 2

.xviiii. Piperata
Porchette vestite [f° 80r]

---

[21] The name of the dish is written *Torte alladiuisa*. The words are only very slightly separated, *alla diuisa*, when rewritten at the twelfth serving in Menu [3].

[22] At the fifteenth serving in the parallel Menu [3], below, it is more clear that this dish is, like the decorated calf's head previously, a sort of *intermezzo*: *Fasano, uno, vestito in nido cum ova sotto*. The roast and redressed pheasant is sitting on eggs in a nest.

[23] This figure has been changed, perhaps to 4.

.xx. Torte bianche
Torte in herbigli de piselli he scaffe

.xxi. Zonchata, una per homo
Amandole fresche cum zucaro he aqua rosata

.xxii. Artichiochi
Pera muscatella
Finoghio fresco

.xxiii. Marzapani, uno per piatto
Biscotti
Finoghio coperto de zucaro

.xxiiii. Zaldoni de zucaro
Confetti d'ogni sorte

---

[3] **Un'altro convito**[24]

Aqua odorifera ale mane

1.	Fiche de piu sorte Pera muscatella	} in confetere [f° 80v]
	Pignochate cum arme Pignochate commune	} in confetere
2.	Capo de latte in tace Marangoli dolci cum zucaro he aqua rosata	} in tace
3.	Fasano, uno Animelle Ficatelli de pulli he de capreti Ova non nata	
	Salviata, una	
4.	Una starna alla cathalana Uno pavone vestito	} cum sapore de pavo

[24] Three lines below this point, at the foot of this page, f° 80r, this large rubric is echoed, again centered, in a script of identical size and thickness, but now slightly fainter.

5. Una testa de capreto soffrita in scudella
Pullastri, doi, cum sapore verde

6. Bianchomanghiare cum caponi, tre
Pastelli vollatili, sei [f° 81r]
Porchette, due
Uno pastello de medule per homo

7. **Alesso**

Vitella, libre 34[25]
Capreti, .ii.
Caponi, .6.
Polastri, 6
Porco signale, libre .x.
Carnero,[26] libre .xii.

8. Salato
Sumata, .i.
Persuti, .ii.
Salsizoni, 4
Lengue vestite, 4

9. **Rosto minuto**

Pollastri, vi } cum sapore de visole
Pipioni, 4[27] }
Rosto salvaticho[28] [f° 81v]

Rosto salvaticho

9. Caprioli, libre .x.
Signale, libre .xv.
Crostata, una

10. Caponi coperti de zucaro, .ii.
Pastilli de venatione, uno per homo

---

[25] This figure should likely be read as 3, 4, although in the serving of *Rosto grosso* in the previous Menu the scribe has written *Vitella, libre trenta, quaranta.*

[26] A letter or symbol — ꞩ — follows the *o* of *Carnero.*

[27] The figure 4 has a hook on its lower stem.

[28] This *Rosto salvaticho* is the last line on f° 81r. Although written in the same size of script as the other prepared dishes under the large rubric *Rosto minuto*, it is likely that the phrase merely anticipates the large rubric of the next division of servings which begins at the top of the next page.

11. Sturione, uno } cum sapore
Lamprede

12. Torte anglese } cum[29] pome
Torte alla divisa

Item, aqua odorifera ale mane

13. Zuccata[30] in tace
Cerase in confetere

14. Zelatina
Testa di vitella, una per piato [f° 82r]

15. Pastelli de caponi he de capreti
Fasano, uno, vestito in nido cum ova sotto
Rosto de caponi
Caponi, tre, coperti de sapore de cerase, per piato

16. Starne, .ii. } in piatelli
Quaglie, viii.

17. Papari rostiti coperti cum sapore pavonazo
Fasana, una, vestita, in piede

Rosto grosso

18. Vitella, libre .xl.
Capreti, .ii.
Caponi, .vi.
Pipioni, .viii.
Polastri, .viii.
Carnero,[31] libre .x.

Rosto

19. Lengue de vitella, .iii., fresche [f° 82v]
Copiete de vitella, libre .iiii^{or}.
Lombi de vitella, libre .iii.

---

29 After the word *cum*, the word *sapore* has been written and crossed out.

30 In Menu [2], the dish that occupies the corresponding position in the menu is a *Zonchata in tace*. A recipe for the cheese called *Ioncata*—pressed unsalted curds—appears in this manuscript's recipe collection at Recipe 167.

31 A letter or symbol follows the *o*.

Peverata
Porci vesti[32]

Torte bianche
Torte de piselli cum scaffe

Zonchate, una per homo
Amandole fresche cum zucaro he aqua rosa

Ultimo

Aqua odorifera ale mane

Marzapane, uno per piatto
Biscotelli
Finoghio coperto de zucaro
Zaldoni de zucaro, in confetere
Nevole storte, in confetere[33]
Confetti de ogni rasone [f° 83r]

---

[4] **Altra rasone de convito**

Perfumi

Aqua odorifera ale mane

Insalata
Capari[34] cum zucaro e cinamomo
Interiori cum petrosillo he specie

Pastelli
Pastelli de medule cum polpe de caponi
Pastelli de pizoni, uno per pastizo, he tordi, .ii.

Uno fasano alla Catalana
Starne in brodo lardero, una per homo

Gelatina
Pavoni, uno per piato, cum cedri
Vermicelli de capo de latte

Sapore de pavo
Fasani vestiti

Biancho manghiare
Dui caponi per piatto, et uno per homo, cum granate [f° 83v]

---

32 *vesti: sic.*

33 ms: *confetera.*

34 *Capari: sic.* In all likelihood this is in error for *Caponi*, which appears in the dish *Caponi cum zucaro he cinamomo* in the same position at the beginning of the First Banquet.

Salato
Sumata, una
Persutto, uno
Salsizoni, doi, dorati
Salvia, rosmarino[35]
Lengue, due[36]

Rosto minuto

Polastri, para[37] .iiii^{or}.
Starne, para 4
Pizoni, para 4
Tordi, para 4
Ucelletti, para .10.
  Miraustro[38]
Limoncelli

Crostate caponi fredi, doi per piatto
Pavoni vistiti
  Piperata de salvasine pavonaza
  Pastelli sechi volatili
Caponi zucarati, .iii. per piato
Caprioli vistiti [f° 84r]

Rosto grosso

Uno quarto de vitella sano
Uno quarto de carnero[39] sano[40]
Lepore, uno
Conigli, doi
Caponi, 4
Papari, 2
Anatre, 3
Starne he pizoni, para 3
    Sapore de pome granate

---

[35] In the same position in the first banquet these herbs were clearly intended as garnish for the *Salsizoni*.

[36] The record of the Menu for the first banquet, which is an echo of what we have been reading here, ends at this point. The words *Lengue due* seem to have been inserted here, taking up the space allowed above the following rubric.

[37] *para*, that is a "pair," a "brace."

[38] *Miraustro*: *sic*.

[39] A symbol resembling a script *s* — ʃ — follows the *o* of *carnero*.

[40] A symbol resembling a script *s* — ʃ — follows the *o* of *sano*.

Grue vestite

Gialdo manghiare
Anatre, tre per piato, saporite de aglio

Torte bianche ala zanuesa[41]
Pere he pome

Zonchate de late de amandole cum zucaro
Amandole
Ossa de persicho de zucaro fino [f° 84v]

Pera guaste cum zucaro in piatelli
Torte bianche

Castagne
Tartufari

Marzapani

Aqua ale mane[42]

Zaldoni
Ypocras

Confetti d'ogni sorte

Finoghio inzucarato et indorato [f° 85r]

---

[5] Ordine del pranzo fatto da monsignore Ascanio allo principe de Capua[43]

Le tavole aparichiate cum tre tovaglie; et da capo di tavole — cio'e da ogni canto — era uno perfumatore bene ornato.

---

41 *zanuesa*: *sic*; perhaps *zanvesa, zannesa* ?

42 From this point on, in the middle of f° 84v, up to the end of this Menu, each of the items is centered and generously spaced, apparently in order to fill to the foot of the page: *Finoghio inzucarato et indorato* is written over two lines; also centered, a cruciform symbol (-+-), which has been seen drawn twice previously on f° 15v in the recipe section of the manuscript, completes the page. Menu [5] will begin at the top of f° 85r. The same care to mark the break between Menus has not been obvious before: Menu [3] begins three or four lines above the foot of f° 80r.

43 Claudio Benporat, *Cucina italiana del quattrocento*, 39 and 65–68, identifies this *monsignore Ascanio* as Ascanio Sforza. He was the brother of Ludovico il Moro, Duke of Milan and Bari; he was made a cardinal in 1484. Benporat describes this Ascanio as an *amante di banchetti, cacce, lettere d'arte, scrittore di orazioni e versi italiani e latini*. See also Benporat's *Storia della gastronomia italiana*, 66. It should be observed, though, as Bruno Laurioux does ("Les livres de cuisine italiens," 77, note 32), that Ascanio was a relatively common name in the Colonna family.

The Guest of Honor of this banquet, the *principe de Capua*, may possibly be Giovanni Borgia,

Aqua de citrangoli alle mane.
In dare l'aqua, aparebeno[44] certi fochi artificiati apresso alo principe cum sue arme; et in questo era uno aurispice cum uno servo che interpretava lo protento del dito focho.
Poi vene nove confetere alte, piene de pignochati dorati, capo de latte cum zucaro e aqua rosata in tace grande.[45] [f° 85v]

Piatti .7. de figatelli de pulli he de capretti.
Animelle.
Pastizi de medule in piatti cum la pasta fatta de zucaro.

Posti li supraditi piatti in tavola, vene Venere cum Jove he Juno cum fontane, cum uno pavone, doi fasani et due anatre he dece starne per in una fontana, ogni cosa vestita supra la tavola del principe.
Piatti doi: uno pavone, doi fasani, .xi. starne he due anatre per dita tavola.
Piatti cinque per le tavole de li Ambasiatori et Baroni: per piatto uno pavone, dece starne he .ii. anatre; et li pavoni erano tuti vestiti.
Piatti .7.: he per piatto deci caponi, capretti doi, sapori cum granate e zucaro. [f° 86r]
Piatti .7. de salato indorato: et per piatto due somate, doi sopresate he .x. salcizoni bulignesi.
Pastelli .7. de pizoni, quaglie et ucelli.
Piatti .7.: per piatto 4 anatre cum sapore ghialdo de sopra.

Alesso

Piatti .7.: et per piatto libre .xl. de vitella
Capretti, .ii.

---

nephew of Rodrigo Borgia, Pope Alexander VI (1492–1503). Born in 1474, Giovanni was named Papal Nuncio to Naples (1494–96), a Cardinal in 1496, and Administrator (hence perhaps *principe*) of Capua on October 7, 1498. He died in 1500. More convincingly, however, Benporat states (*Cucina italiana del quattrocento*, p. 40) that the titles *duca di Calabria* and *principe di Capua* were bestowed upon the eldest prince of the House of Naples. The former title dated back to 1443; the latter, however, was first borne (according to Benporat, who offers no evidence) in 1494 by Alfonso (November 4, 1448–November 19, 1495), son of Fernando (Ferrante in Italian), an energetic military man also described as despotic, dissolute and avaricious; he succeeded to the throne as Alfonso II on the death of his father on January 25, 1494. Then the title of *principe di Capua* was apparently borne from 1495 by his son, Ferrandino (June 26, 1467–October 7, 1496), who succeeded to the throne as Ferrante II in that very same year when Alfonso II abdicated (January 23, 1495). On his death, childless, the next year (October 7, 1496), Ferrante II was succeeded by his uncle. Consequently, if Benporat's identification (of either Prince Alfonso or Prince Ferrandino) is correct, this banquet would have to have taken place at some date during the period of slightly more than a year previous to January 23, 1495.

The past tense used in this text may be noted: this menu is a record rather than the copy of a prescription.

[44] ms: *aparbeno*.

[45] At the bottom of the page is a signature of the gathering, in fine black script: *m*.

Porcho signale, libre .3º.
Caponi, 12
Pollastri, 10.
Piatti .7. de salato indorato: per piatto
Persutti, .ii.
Lengue, .ii.
Mortadelle, .x.
Manghiare bianchi alla cathalana [f° 86v]
Sapore camellino.

Diana dice certi versi et presenta alla tavola del principe uno cervo, uno capriolo, due lepore, doi conigli in uno boscho revestiti.
Item, uno porco salvaticho, due lepore, dui conigli in uno altro boscho.
Le corne del cervo he de lo capriolo he[46] la lor[47] testa erano dorate. He alora se introduce Diana—cio'e la sua fabula; et sotto el palcho erano due **Ninphe** che cominzarano la fabula de la dita Diana.

Quatro cervali in doi piatti per le tavole de li Ambasatori et Baroni. [f° 87r]
Piati .vii.: uno cervale per piatto, uno porcho, uno lepore e uno coniglo.
Piatelli .vii. de gelatina de caponi, et per la tavola del principe in doi conche de argento.

Teste .7. de vitella in .7. piatti[48] argentate.

Arosto

Piatti .7.: per piatto
uno quarto de Vitella
Capretti, .ii.
Papari, 2 — Salsa regale
Caponi, 10 — marangoli,
Pizoni, 8 — limoni in
Starne, 2 — tace
Fasani, 2

Vitelli .2., integri, dorati, alla tavola del principe [f° 87v]
Torte, .7.
Tartare, .7.

46 ms: *he delo*, with *delo* stroked out.

47 *la lor*: *sic*.

48 ms: *piatti dorate*, with *dorate* deleted by an underline.

Ordine del pasto del pesso

Aqua alle mane di mortella

Marzapane, dece, cum le arme del principe
Pasta regale

Piatti .7. de fritelle de fiore de sambuco
Piatti .7. de lactuca de pasta

Piatti .7. de locuste, raguste
Alefanti et bambari

Scutella[49] per uno cum figati de sturione e de altri pessi, cum zucaro, cinamo he sugo de pome arance.
Comincia la fabula del tagliare [f° 88r]
locuste he altri pessi.

Poi el carro de **Neptune** menato cum deci monstri marini argentati.

La fabula de Neptuno

Piatti .7. de pesso alesso—sturioni et altri pessi grandi—per la tavola del principe
Due sturioni integri

Piatti de salato
Salmoni } indorati
Tarantelli }

Zenestrata per menestra
Sapore biancho

Neptune dice li soi versi

Lamprede cum sapore
Anguille in pastilli, .xii.
Piatti .7. de rombo, lenguatte et altri belli pessi, cum sapori [f° 88v]
Botarge indorate
Pastici asutti de trotte, .xiiii.
Piatti .7. de gelatina de pesso in conche d'argento per la tavola de lo principe.

Tre Serene et Arion cantano versi

Piatti .7. de pesso arosto

---

49 *Scutella*: ms.: *Stutella*.

Mirausto de pome per minestra
Sapore ghialdo
Hostreche
Marangoli
Limoni

Torte verde, .7.
Torte bianche, .7.

Poste le torte in tavola, **Pan** cum una egloga, com zonchate involte in foglie d'oro, recotte in canestro, indorate [f° 89r]

Pomone cum una egloga medesima, cum frutti de diverse sorte
Finoghi verdi
Tartufari

Levata un'altra tovalia

Aqua ale mane moscata
Confettere de diverse sorte, .viii^{c}.[50]
Due confettere per la tavola del principe, .5. per la tavola de li Oratori, .6. per li Baroni
Zaldoni, piatti .7.
Ipocras

Spazare cum[51] scope dorate sotto la tavola.

Fornito el disnare, fureno levati li trespidi et possareno le tavole in terra cum li coperti de veluto.

Finis

[f° 89v]

Zabaglone[52]

Finis

◈

50 *.viii^{c}.*: that is, 800.

51 Several letters have been stroked out following the word *cum*.

52 The *b* was originally written as *z*. Because of its resemblance to other recipes for *Zabaglione* at the time, the text of this appended recipe is reproduced as Recipe 220 in the main section of this edition.

III. Commentary on the Recipes

In the following Commentary, references are to recipe collections and editions as these are listed in the Bibliography toward the end of the Introduction (p. 36).

Texts of relevant recipes from the unpublished Catalan manuscripts may be read in Appendix C (p. 249). For recipe references to Martino's *Arte coquinaria*, see the Table of Recipes in Appendix A (p. 237).

❖ 1. The version of this recipe found in the Riva del Garda manuscript, and in the copies of Martino's *Libro de arte coquinaria* that have survived, is, in many passages, *verbatim* the text read here in the Neapolitan Collection.[1] Where the texts are not identical, the sense is closely parallel. Such lexical variants as the following appear here, and recur commonly throughout the collections: *ponendo* (Neapolitan, Riva) and *agiongendol* (Martino); *cavala, cavila* (Neapolitan, Riva), *cacciala* (Martino); *fetine* (Neapolitan), *fette* (Riva, Martin); *bagniado* (Neapolitan), *mogliato* (Riva, Martino); *voltando* (Neapolitan), *menando* (Riva, Martino); and *ponela* (Neapolitan), *partila, spartila* (Riva, Martino). As is frequently the case in lexical matters in these texts, the Neapolitan author has used one term where Martino prefers a slightly more technically precise or elegant term; the Martino di Rossi who is responsible for the *Libro de cosina* of the Riva del Garda manuscript shows a wording that occasionally remains faithful to the diction and phraseology of the Neapolitan text and occasionally records the modification that will remain in the *Libro de arte coquinaria.*

Five particular variants are a little more significant, though they do not reflect any substantial change in the nature of this Pepper Sauce. Our manuscript directs the cook to take the *coradelle* of the game, whereas the Riva and Martino copies curiously specify *del sangue overo de la coradella.* To correct the humoral temper of these *coradelle*, our manuscript advises an admixture of "wine syrup *or* vinegar," whereas the Riva and Martino versions have modified this to "wine syrup *and* the vinegar in which the bread was soaked."[2] For spices, our manuscript says simply *specie d'ogni sorte he pepero assai*; the extant Riva and Martino versions specify "spices, [that is] pepper [which,

---

[1] For an identification of the recipes in the Riva del Garda manuscript and the *Libro de arte coquinaria* of Martino that are mentioned in this Commentary, please see the Composition of the Neapolitan Recipe Collection in Appendix A (p. 247). Throughout this Commentary, as elsewhere in this edition, the name "Martino" refers generally to the text of the *Libro de arte coquinaria*, as this has been published by Emilio Faccioli in his *Arte della cucina*, 2 volumes (Milano: Il Polifilo, 1966), 1:117–204. For long this edition has been the only readily available version of Martino's work.

[2] There is also evidence of some garbling of the text: *sabba ho aceto* (Neapolitan) becomes *sabba, zoe ben cocto con mosto et cum acceto* (Riva) and *sapa, zio e vino cotto in mosto, et coll aceto* (Martino). Neither the "and/or" variant nor the garbling (often on the part of Riva) is unusual in the transmission of these recipes and shall not normally be referred to in this Commentary.

remarkably, Riva overlooks], cloves and fine or coarse cinnamon [*canella o cinamomo*], according to what you think necessary; and make this Pepper Sauce stong or mild [with vinegar and with spices, writes Martino explicitly] depending on your master's taste and people's preferences." The Neapolitan recipe directs that the sauce should be boiled "away from the hot fire"; the versions in Riva and the *Arte coquinaria* make this "on the hot coals." And finally, the caution that the Cuoco napoletano expresses concerning smoke, takes on two variant forms: in our text, simply "be careful about smoke"; in Riva and Martino, again in a little more explicatory a fashion, " ... on the hot coals so that it not be exposed to any more heat on one side than on the other."

It is seemingly the person responsible for our version who has appended the last sentence about the way to darken this sauce. It is found in neither Riva nor Martino.

This Pepper Sauce for game may be compared with the simpler composition in Recipe 112, which occupies the leading position in the section on *Salse*.

❖ 2. The sense of the word *consumado* is related to the seasoned bouillon having "boiled *away*": the last line of the recipe makes the semantic value of *consumado* clear, whether the word functions as a past participle, adjective or noun.

The *carne salate*, here and in several other recipes of this collection, seems to refer specifically to various cuts of salt pork. In Chapter 21 of Book II of the *Honesta voluptate*, Platina describes the making and use of salt pork: *De succidia*. Toward the end of this section he points out the variety of cuts that can then be had at any time from the salted carcass: ... *Hinc sumes laridum pro tempore, hinc pernam, hinc petasonem, hinc sumen, hinc glandium. Quare non immerito rustici salsuram "succidiam" vocitarunt qui inde succidi ad esum multa possunt* ... : "From it you can take lard at will, ham, shoulder, sowbelly, tenderloin. For this reason farmers not undeservedly call it a 'briny cut' because much can be cut off to eat."**

Several minor variants distinguish the extant versions of this recipe that are found in Riva, Martino and our manuscript. Both Riva and the *Arte coquinaria* allow deermeat among the fowl for which this recipe is suitable; both stipulate that the salt meat be lean. They allow precisely "thirty or forty" ounces (grains in Martino) of pepper; they reduce the allotment of cloves to "three or four," while increasing the laurel to two leaves. To qualify the seven-hour boiling time, the two later texts add, "so that only two servings or less of the broth are left, if you want it to be good."

The practical advice found in the last sentence of our version — which endeavors to retain the potency of the spices by not having their flavor boil away over the seven hours — is unique to our Neapolitan cook.

On the other hand, Riva and Martino (as well as Platina's recipe for *Ius consumptum*, VI,43) conclude by noting that that the broth may be made appropriate for serving to the sick — presumably those suffering from a dry fever — if salted meat is *not* used. Platina states: *Senibus hoc et valetudinariis propinatur*: "This dish is given to the old and infirm."

** Both Platina's Latin text and any English translation of it are throughout those of Mary Ella Milham, *Platina, On Right Pleasure and Good Health*, Tempe Arizona (Medieval & Renaissance Texts & Studies), 1998.

❖ 3. The first of the remarkable series of four varieties of White Dish that we find in the Neapolitan Collection is textually very close to a recipe entitled *Manyar blanch* that is copied in the Catalan *De apereylar be de menyar* (Recipe 40; *cf.* the same recipe in the *Libre de sent soví*, Recipe 49). With only a few changes in wording and a few amplifications on the part of the Catalan author, the two instances of this recipe are clearly related.

The Catalan version sheds some light upon the sense of our own recipe in a couple of places. The Neapolitan phrase, *lo riso a sufficientia*, is rendered *del arros per guise que torn espes*: "enough rice to thicken it." In our text, the pot is set *super le braxe*; the Catalan text has ... *de brases o de carbó per paor de fum*: " ... embers or coals to avoid smoke." The Neapolitan cook has written that the cooked preparation is *spisso como brodeto*: "as thick as a thick broth"; the Catalan cook thickens his White Dish even more, to the point where it is *espes axí com a morterol*: "as thick as a meat paste." The *brodetto* is almost unknown in Iberian cooking, yet it is becoming a standard dish on Italian tables. For instance, when precooking the herb custard for their *Herbolata de maio* (our Recipe 127), the compilers of Riva and the *Libro de arte coquinaria* direct that the cheese-egg-milk-and-herb mixture should thicken until *se comenza a pigliare como uno brodetto*, "it begins to set like a *brodetto*."

On the other hand, the *morterol* of which the *De apereylar be de menyar* speaks — a mixture of ground animal viscera and rice, usually with eggs — is a dish that is common enough in Catalan (and French) cookery but not well enough known in Italian kitchens of the time to serve as a comparison in this recipe. In the present instance the significance of the *morterol* is that, as Grewe wrote in the *Sent soví*, concerning its *Morterol de brou de gualines*: "Ha de tenir una consistència pastosa" (p. 133, n. 2).

❖ 4. The procedure of "blanching" almonds is described in Recipe 168: it amounts to an overnight soaking in water that will dissolve away any discoloring on the outside of the kernel.

As these almonds are ground, Riva and Martino advise in their version of the White Dish that the cook should sprinkle them with a little water so that the grinding produces almond milk rather than oil. Our author (or compiler or scribe) inserts this same advice at the foot of folio 41v, among the recipes for sauces that generally begin with almond milk, as an addendum of universal value. The versions of this recipe are very close, except that both the Riva and Martino versions go on to explain how to make the White Dish in two colors: the second color, yellow, is produced by adding egg yolks and saffron to a portion of the mixture, this (color) being called *fiore di zenestra/ginesta* (misread by Faccioli), or "genista blossom." If two capons are being served, we are told in these two later versions, the white mixture can be poured on one, the yellow on the other.

❖ 5. Several dishes in this collection are qualified as being *a la catalana*:[3] this present variety of

[3] Barbara Santich has suggested that the value of this same qualification in the Catalan *Libre del coch* of Mestre Robert has to do with the garnish accorded dishes that are so qualified. Dishes served with honey and rosewater seem to warrant the qualification. "L'influence italienne sur l'évolution de la cuisine médiévale catalane," *Manger et boire au moyen âge*, 2 volumes (Paris: Belles Lettres, 1984), 1, 138. In the Neapolitan Collection honey is used in none of the so-called Catalan dishes, and only rosewater appears in this recipe, and as an ingredient rather than as a garnish.

White Dish, *Carabace alla catalana* (Recipe 30), *Mirausto alla catalana* (Recipe 37) and the *Starne al modo cathalano* (Recipe 61).[4] It seems likely that, rather than identifying some ingredient or process, the phrase recognizes that certain dishes were thought to be peculiar to Catalonia.

The precise "eight ounces" of rice flour in our manuscript is repeated by the Riva and Martino versions but not echoed by Platina (VI,42) who, though, together with Riva, offers the common counsel about avoiding the possibility that any smoke from the fire contaminate the Catalan White Dish. Later Platina describes the sticky consistency of the preparation as *ut terebinthina, ubi decoctum fuerit* — "like pitch when it is boiled down."

The professional trick for telling when a mixture is cooked (*se attacara alo cughiaro*) is repeated in Recipe 13. Rosewater is added at the very end of the cooking process because its high alcohol content would cause it to evaporate if cooked for any length of time. The same late addition of rosewater is seen in several instances below in the case of covered pies — for example, in Recipe 74.

❖ 6. The marginal notation to the effect that this dish is suitable for Lent is indeed the qualification found in its name in both Riva and the *Libro de arte coquinaria.* In the second of these alone, though, is the recipe placed among several others explicitly intended for use *in Quadragesima.* As a lean dish, it contains no meat but incorporates a paste of fish flesh.

The texts of our recipe and the other versions run parallel, but with several additions and one probable error in the Martino copy. In our copy the bread thickener is prepared with pea broth *brodo de piselli*; in Riva this is written as a fish broth *brodo de pisce* (the last word is repeated twice later as *pesce*). For Martino the alternative is simply *altro brodo.*

The flesh of the *bono pesso* that goes into the thickened almond milk becomes, in Riva, "good sea-fish or fresh-water fish"; in Martino, "good sea-fish or fresh-water pike." Both Riva and Martin add orange juice (or, alternatively, verjuice) to their ingredients. Martino specifies half a *pound* of ginger (*meza libra di zenzevero mondo*) rather than the Neapolitan's half an *onza*![5]

Riva adds a brief final line that this preparation can be served as a dish in itself or as a garnish for fish.

❖ 7. The concern, expressed here and in previous recipes, that ambient smoke might contaminate the delicate taste of a dish is common, and particularly where the delicate taste of a dish is based upon almond milk. The caution is read in both Riva and Martino, whose texts for this recipe are very similar, and also in the recipe for *Aros ab let de amelles* in the *Libre de sent soví* (Recipe 102), a dish quite similar to this one.

❖ 8. It is tempting to "amend" *brodo grasso he magro* to *brodo grasso ho magro*, yet the word "and" is written clearly here, as it is in the same phrase in the following recipe. This must be a fatty, meaty broth. The recipe does not seem to appear in either Riva or Martino.

---

[4] To these expressly "Catalan" dishes we might also add the *Suppa de [A]Ragonisi* (Recipe 92).

[5] This sort of scribal *lapsus* is natural. The person writing the Washington copy of the *Libro de arte coquinaria*, or some earlier scribe, made the same error later on in his copy of the recipe for the *Menestre de seme di canepa* (Recipe 76) where he wrote *meza libra di zuccharo et meza libra oncia di zenzevero* . . . .

❖ 9. In the Riva and Martino versions this dish is called *Faro in brodo di carne aut di capone*; the recipe there is expressly for ten servings. While the dishes produced by the recipes would be similar, the differences in texts and in ingredients (Riva and Martino do not call for cheese or cured ham, for instance) suggest that the dish underwent some slight change.

❖ 10. The preparation known as *ravioli* is quite common in Italian recipe books but otherwise appears in Latin only in the *Liber de coquina* (Recipes II,54, 56 and 60); in English only in the *Forme of Cury* (Recipe 94) and, owing perhaps to a scribal error at some point, *raynollez* in Austin's first cookery book (Recipe 41); and in French in the Savoyard *Du fait de cuisine* (Recipe 56) where *ravioles* are not described but seem to be well enough known to serve as a model in the making of another preparation called *Mortoexes*.[6]

The Riva and Martino manuscripts title this recipe *Ravioli in tempo di carne* and Platina has merely (and strangely undescriptively) *Esicium ex carne* (Recipe VII,50); unlike our version, the others specify that the recipe provides for twelve (Riva) or ten (Martino, Platina) guests. In their conclusion the others also append further possible meats for this recipe: breast of pheasant, partridge or any other fowl.

Textual variants are minor: the later Riva and Martino versions become more specific in directing that the meat be cooked to the point of disintegrating (rather than merely being "well cooked"); the ravioli are to be the size of "not less than a chestnut" and "half a chestnut" (rather than "a walnut"); and they are to be boiled for the length of time of two *Our Fathers* (rather than for "half an hour"; concerning the measurement of time, see the comment to Recipe 13).

❖ 11. *Ravioli bianchi* are named expressly in the Latin collection *Liber de coquina* (Recipe V,6: *Raviolas albos*) and in the Italian collections, *Anonimo Meridionale* "A" (Recipe 1), *Buone vivande* (Recipe 1) and *Dilicate vivande* (Recipes 62 and 64). They bear a certain resemblance with the so-called *Licaproprii* of the *Libro per cuoco* (Recipe 64). They are likely related to the butter-and-cheese ravioli descibed in the Nice Collection (Recipe 46: *Ravioli in Venardie*) and in the *Frammento* (Recipe 64: *Raviuoli in Venerdie*) where they are intended to serve as a meatless dish. In the *Dilicate vivande*, Recipe 64 bears the full title that we read here: *Ravioli bianchi in di che non si mangi charne*. In the sixteenth-century Neapolitan *Manoscritto Lucano* (Recipe 45) the *graffioli* seem remarkably lean, lacking both cheese and butter.

The Neapolitan text is echoed in Riva.

Ravioli made their way to England where a recipe for its preparation appears in the *Forme of Cury* at Recipe 94. The beginning of the Neapolitan's White Ravioli, with its buffalo cheese, may have some remote connection with the English recipe's opening: "Take wete chese & grind hit smal, & medle hit wyt eyren & saffron and a god quantite of buttur . . . ." Both of these versions of the dish are to be coloured yellow, although not according to Riva.

On the cheese that is made from buffalo milk and known (even today) as *probatura*, see the comment to Recipe 132.

---

[6] In his edition of the *Manoscritto Lucano. Ein unveröffentlichtes Kochbuch aus Süditalien vom Beginn des 16. Jahrhundrets* (Geneva: Droz, 1994), 30, note 571, Michael Süthold mentions the presence of *roffioellen* in a Dutch cookbook of the fifteenth century. He refers to F. E. J. M. Baudet, *De Maaltijd en de Keuken in de Middeleeuwen* (Utrecht, 1904), 76.

❖ 12. This recipe is related to the *Broet blanc* that is read in the *De apereylar be de menyar* (Recipe 19). Given that our recipe is classified a *brodeto*, we should likely understand that the meat, in this case roasted pullets, is to be boiled in the spiced almond milk sauce until the liquid is relatively thick. In the *De apereylar be de menyar*, the step is explicitly mentioned: *... puys fes tot bulir ab lart de porch*. A *brodeto* is normally thickened by means of eggs; in the case of this "white" version, though, the cook relies upon the alternative of thick almond milk.

❖ 13. ... *Tanto ch'el cughiaro se imbrata*: in Recipe 5 the author has explained that this is a good indication that the contents of a pot have cooked sufficiently. The person responsible for the text of Riva has obscured the clarity of this advice: ... *longe dal focho menando sempre e como tu vedi chel cugiale se conmenza ad imbratarse non cessando di menare tant che se dicesse duy paternoster* ....

Kitchens in the Middle Ages rarely had accurate time-keeping devices. Dividing a day into twelve units from dawn to dusk made for somewhat longer hours in the summer than in the winter. For a writer of recipes to advise his reader on the length of time that a process should continue, and particularly for any process taking less than a quarter-hour (but see "an eighth of an hour" in Recipes 6 and 162), he usually resorted to referring to more or less universally recognized activities: the time that it takes to walk around a field of such and such a size; the time that it takes to pray the *Miserere* (Psalm 51) or the Lord's Prayer (see also Recipe 33). Such activities fixed a relatively common brief unit of time.

❖ 14. The text of this recipe in the Riva and Martino copies is virtually identical. There the boiling time for the stock is reduced to a fifth of an hour, the number of eggs to be used is not specified, and a brief phrase at the end advises that the preparation is to be "somewhat thick." This consistency would be recognized in the generic dishname *brodeto*; see the comment to Recipe 3.

❖ 15. Because this variety of *pasta asciutta* can be kept, as the recipe indicates, for up to three years, it must have been common to prepare particularly large batches of it at a time. For that reason it is perhaps somewhat surprising that, in specifying quantities here, the author remains faithful to his policy in this regard—and that he follows consistently throughout his work—of setting forth recipes for a relatively small number of diners.

While the name of this dish remains the same in the Riva and Martino versions, Platina curiously calls it simply *Esicium siculum*. All of these later versions are textually very close to what is found in the Neapolitan manuscript, although the other versions parsimoniously reduce the number of egg yolks for two platesful of macaroni to "two" (Riva) and "one or two"; in all other cases the egg yolks become egg *whites*. Riva reduces the cooking time for the macaroni to half an hour, adding the curious explanation, "*per che ogni pasta volle essere ben cocta*." Martino (and Platina with his text) increases that cooking time from one hour to two. In Martino's texts alone is the observation found that dried macaroni is more "durable" when made during the month of August.

As a variety of pasta, macaroni was known beyond Italy even before this time. In the *Forme of Cury* (Recipe 95) it appears under the name of *Makerouns*. Although in the English preparation the noodles are flat rather than tubular, as here, the serving garnish is the same.[7] Several varieties of macaroni seem to have been recognized in mid-fifteenth-century Italy and identified with a region: the present *macharoni ciciliani*, the *macharoni romaneschi* of the next recipe, and a certain *macharoni a la zenovese, o veramente tagliarini* described in the manuscript of Riva del Garda at Recipe 75.[8]

❖ 16. No recipe for the making of lasagne is provided in our collection or in the extant copies of Riva or the *Libro de arte coquinaria* or the *De honesta voluptate*. The size of this variety of pasta seems assumed to be general knowledge; other recipes here (Recipes 17, 18, 158, 179) will refer to lasagne in the same way as here, as if awareness of its size, shape and fabrication were commonplace. The Riva and Martino versions add directions for serving that are similar to what we have just read in the previous recipe: " . . . Put them onto plates with good cheese, butter and mild spices"—to which Platina (Recipe VII,43) adds sugar.

Riva concludes with generalized advice: "*Nota che ogni vivanda di pasta volle essere ben cocta sopra il tutto.*" The sense of the notation will be repeated by Riva two recipes later in its *Macharoni cecilliani* (see our previous Recipe, 15).

Like macaroni, lasagne made its way into several English recipe collections, where its anglicized name may have influenced—and then been confirmed by—a diamond shape to which lasagna seems occasionally to have been cut: in the *Forme of Cury, loseyns* (Recipes 26 and 132) and *losyns* (Recipe 50); in the *Diversa cibaria, losenges* (Recipe 8); in the *Ordinance of Pottage, losynges* (Recipes 30, 133, 159); in the *Noble Boke off Cookry, lossenges* (Recipe 73).[9]

❖ 17. Our author does not describe the actual making of these "little worms," only their final preparation as a dish. Both Riva and Martino (along with Platina) speak of beginng with a dough of flour, as for the Sicilian Macaroni that precedes this recipe in both versions;[10] they direct, again, that the pasta be dried in the sun and state that, dried, it will last two or more years. Both

---

7 For brief sketches of pasta in early Europe, see Charles Perry, "The Oldest Mediterranean Noodle: a Cautionary Tale," in *Petits Propos Culinaires* 9 (1981): 42–45, and "Notes on Persian Pasta," ibid.: 10 (1982), 48–49; and, specifically for Italy, Odile Redon and Bruno Laurioux, "La constitution d'une nouvelle catégorie culinaire? Les pâtes dans les livres de cuisine italiens de la fin du Moyen âge," *Médiévales* 16–17 (1989): 51–60.

8 This same compilation contains a second recipe for *tagliarini*: Recipe 73 begins *Macharoni in alto modo . . .* and ends . . . *et si chiamano tagliarini*.

9 Concerning lasagne, see the study by Charles Perry, "The Oldest Mediterranean Noodle," mentioned before.

10 In Riva the recipe that immediately precedes this one is for *tagliarini* or "Genoese macaroni." This latter sort of pasta is not mentioned in our text nor copied into any other known Martino text. In a similar recipe in the *Vivendier*, called *Vermiseaux de Cecille*, the French author alludes to the name of this pasta when he writes that they are made *ossi petis comme petis vers qui se trouvent es fromaiges*: Recipe 51 in *The Vivendier. A Fifteenth-Century French Cookery Manuscript*, ed. Terence Scully (Blackawton, Totnes: Prospect Books, 1997), 74. The reference to Sicily has already be seen in the Neapolitan Recipe 15, above.

mention a lean-day alternative to cooking vermicelli in fat broth, and that is to use sugared almond milk or, strangely (as a lean-day option), goat's milk. Both echo the Neapolitan direction that the vermicelli should be yellow with saffron, unless the vermicelli are prepared in milk: ... *nisi in lacte decocti fuerint*, as Platina translates (Recipe VII,52). Our version alone specifies that the garnish be grated *Parmesan* cheese; the others say simply "grated cheese."

❖ 18. Both the Riva and Martino versions are very close to the text of this recipe. Again, as in the previous recipe, our text is unique in specifying Parmesan cheese as the garnish. Riva's conclusion contains an unfortunate *lapsus* as well as an interesting comparison: " ... *ponendoli sopra uno pocho de grasso grattato e spezie como faristi le altre lasagne.*"

Concerning the marginal notation opposite this recipe, "which is called *fasanica* dish," see the comment below to Recipe 191.

❖ 19. The name of this recipe is curious. Riva has *Manfrighi sive millifanti in menestre*; Martino shortens this to *Manfrigo in menestre.*[11] For his Latin version of this recipe Platina abandons both of the Italian names, using for the dish a simple generic, *Ius in pane* (VII,58). The Neapolitan name remains alive in modern Neapolitan usage. Quite graphically the name *Milli fanti* incorporates the word *fanti*, "foot soldiers, pages"; it might seem to evoke the image suggested by the German dish called *Armeritlere* or "Poor Knights", but the nature of the two dishes is not at all similar. In the Italian dish the pasta is formed into tiny, grain- shaped *pastine* similar to *ditalini.*

Both the ingredients and quantities of this recipe are the same in all versions. Martino (with Platina) states that these quantities make enough for ten servings. Our version and Riva indicate that the drying of this pasta can be done either in the sun or by the fire. Concerning the size of the pieces into which the meat is to be cut, we may turn to Recipe 50, for an analogous preparation, where the cook is instructed, *fanne peci picoli uno pugno*: fist-size.

❖ 20. In the versions read in Riva and Martino this dish is called simply *Minestra de carne*, "Meat Dish." Its name in the Neapolitan Collection may be a little more descriptive, though perhaps not quite as understandable. A French dish of the time shapes the same thin sheets of veal into birds' wings and calls them "Larks," *Alouyaulx* (see the *Viandier* of Taillevent, Recipe 204, for instance). Our author may well be aiming to reproduce another type of bird here with these *Cardinale.* A final note in the Riva recipe is disappointingly obscure: *Quèsta minestra si chiama carle.* The *r* of the last word is not at all certain, and the letters *le* are superscript, so that a significant part of the word between the first and last syllables remains to be deduced.

The wording of all Italian versions is very close: the other versions increase the cooking time from one-third hour to one-half hour; "three eggs" become just "eggs"; and the others offer advice about consistency: "This preparation should be as thick as a *brodetto.*" What appears to be a marginal addition at the end of the Neapolitan copy is really part of the Martino text and is so written, though abbreviated, by the scribes of Riva and the *Arte coquinaria*: *Et simelle se po fare dele corradelle.*

---

[11] Of this second name Faccioli glosses the first word as "A term perhaps related to *manfregoli* (from *mano*, 'hand' and *fregare*, 'to fry'), a sort of wheaten porridge" (ed. cit., 1, 147, note 2).

❖ 21. The texts of Riva and the *Arte coquinaria* are very close to our text, with, as always, certain slight modifications in terminology. However, the Riva and Martino versions show *sabba o zucharo*, "syrup *or* sugar." At this point Riva draws a generic comparison between the preparation of this dish and *insalata*: *Et se fa al modo de insalata*. Riva further appends an explanation of what is meant by "syrup": *Notta che sabba e mosto bulito*.

❖ 22. The preparation called *giusello* seems to have been known — under some cognate of that name — in Aragon, England, France and Italy. We find recipes for *Jusell* in the Catalan of Mestre Robert's *Libre de coch* (Recipe 97); for *Jusshell* in the English *Forme of Cury* (Recipe 44), and *Iussel* and *Jussal* in the *Diversa Servicia* (Recipe 21) and *Ordinance of Pottage* (Recipe 18), respectively; for *jussel blanc*, where no equivalent Latin name seems to have been available, in the Latin collection *Viaticorum* (Recipe 40); and in Italian collections only in our manuscript.[12]

For this recipe Riva and Martino show only the rubric *Per cocere zanzarelle/zanzarelli* (with a final *e* in Riva), with no mention of the alternate name *Giusello*.[13] The term *giusello* seems to have been a little old-fashioned, giving way perhaps to the more contemporary *zanzarelli*. This latter term may in some way be related to the word *zanzaro*, designating a dissolute young man and qualified by the Accademici della Crusca in their *Vocabolario* as a *vox furbesca*. Barbara Santich points out the similarity between these *zanzarelli* and the dish called *Xinxanella a la veneciana* in Mestre Robert (Recipe 128).[14]

The dish amounts to a thickened bread pudding but, being fundamentally a simple preparation, can avail itself of many slight variations.[15]

The concluding phrase in our recipe, *et miscolate insieme*, apparently appended in the Neapolitan manuscript, does not appear in the other versions.

❖ 23. The recipe is textually close to what is copied in Riva, Martino and Platina with the exception of two passages. Our text directs the cook simply to take the cabbage and *rompele cum le mane*. In Riva we read, *Rompe le caule in torzelle con la mano secondo l'uxanza*; in Martino this passage has become *Rompi li cavoli torzoti con le mani secundo l'usanza*. The phrase *in torzelle* is a detail of technique added to our text. Then, where our manuscript reads "boil for two hours," the Riva and Martino versions shorten this second cooking phase to *per spatio de pocho tempo*; with an explanation, Platina more or less faithfully renders this as *Parum efferveat sines; non enim multum*

---

12 In his *Honesta voluptate* Platina translates Martino's term *brodetto* by the word *iusculum*: so the recipes for *Brodetto, Brodetto biancho* and *Brodetto verde* in Martino (Recipes 44, 45 and 46) become *Iusculum croceum, Iusculum album* and *Iusculum viride* (Recipes VI,44, 45 and 46, respectively. Platina also writes a recipe for Martino's *Verzuso* (Recipe 55) which he calls *Iusculum quod "verzusum" vocant* (Recipe VII,30).

13 The term *giusel* is not completely unknown to Riva, however. Recipe 101 in that collection is for a *Gyusel de caviaro de quaresma*.

14 Barbara Santich, "L'influence italienne sur l'évolution de la cuisine médiévale catalane," *Manger et boire au moyen âge*, 2 volumes (Paris: Belles Lettres, 1984), 1, 138.

15 In Riva there is a series of five variations on the theme, all called *Zanzarelli*: Recipes 47–50 and 118. A corresponding series is copied in the *Arte coquinaria*.

cocturæ requirit: 'Let it boil a little, for it does not require much cooking" (VII,69: *In brassicam romanensem*). Our author has added to his copy the final, personal endorsement of the dish.

Citizens of Rome seem to have had a predilection for cabbage, because a different preparation in the Latin *Liber de coquina* (Recipe I,5) is similarly named *Caulles ad usum Romanorum*.

❖ 24. In the Riva del Garda version of this recipe for lettuce there is some effort made to clarify the meaning of *lo pede* in our text: *piglia quello de sotto piu blanco dela lactuca, zioe lo fustono*—"take the lower, whitest part of the lettuce, that is, the stem." Rather than use the word *fustono*, Martino writes *quello di mezo*: "the whitest part of the lettuce, that is, the middle part." Platina's *Cibarium ex lactuca* suffers from a slight garbling that includes the *zuche* (or *cucurbita*, he adds) among the ingredients of the lettuce dish itself. The alternative procedure that follows the phrase *ho vero* seems to be an addition by our author.

❖ 25. The mysterious phrase that we find toward the beginning of this recipe, *che non sapiano da Catharina*, is not explained in the other versions, which are otherwise fairly close to what we have here. At this point in the recipe, Riva and the *Arte coquinaria* show only that the tripe should be washed perfectly clean, and that "a bone of salted meat" should be added to the pot "to give it a good flavor." Concerning *catharina*, see also the marginal notation to Recipe 191.

Martino adds a little mint to our sage as the tripe finishes cooking. Both Riva and Martino allow cheese as an optional additional serving garnish: in Riva the word here is *formagio*, in Martino *cascio*. The only word for cheese ever used by the Neapolitan author is *caso*.

❖ 26. In the later versions Riva of Martino, because of an omission of several words (*he farai le menestre ponenedo di sopra*), pepper and saffron appear not as garnishes but as ingredients in the cooking pot: " ... then set it to boil in a fat broth with a little salt meat, pepper and saffron."

❖ 27. The term *armate* in this dish's name does not appear to designate any particular garnish or treatment, but rather merely the fact that the turnip is "dressed" in some way.[16] Here the slices of the vegetable are baked in such a way that the spices, cheese and butter will saturate them. A slightly more rudimentary presentation of the same recipe is found already in the *Anonimo Veneziano*, Recipe 65: *Rapa armata*, where the direction "*lassa ... ben confettare insieme*" describes the melding together of the turnip and cheese. The infinitive there describes the making of a confection.

The final clause in our recipe—copied also in Riva and Martino—suggests that the dish (qualified as an *imbandisone* or "banquet dish") must have been considered exceptional in some way, so that it should occupy a conspicuous place in the order of service. In Martino's *Arte coquinaria*, however, this recipe appears well on toward the end of the chapter on the making of pies (*torte*). Though the text there tends to be slightly more wordy than ours, both Riva and

---

[16] See Barbara Santich's comment on Mestre Robert's *Gallina armada* and *Capo armat* in the *Libre del coch* (Recipes 52 and 53, respectively): in these cases *armat* refers to a coating or crust on a roasted fowl (op. cit., 138).

Martino suggest that the first layer of cheese slices functions as a lower crust in what actually amounts to a sort of pie: *... fette di caso a modo che faresti una crosta di sotto.*[17]

The Neapolitan text alone specifies Parmesan or creamy cheese.

❖ 28. With minor variations the text in Riva and Martino is the same as here. In Riva the incipit of this recipe reads *Per fare como se coce la cemolla, la cemolilla se coce ....* In the Washington copy of the *Libro de arte coquinaria* the title of this recipe is missing, but in the Vatican copy the rubric reads, *Per sapere come si quoce la semola.* Nowhere else is there any qualification that this procedure represents Sicilian practice.

At the direction that the cooking gruel is to be placed away from the fire, the other versions provide the standard explanation, "because it readily picks up smoke."

❖ 29. The later texts of this recipe, in Riva and the *Arte coquinaria*, show some amplification, allowing water as an alternative to the initial cooking broth, adding onions to it, and so forth. A further alternative allows the cook to strain the cooked vegetable through a perforated spoon rather than grinding it.

❖ 30. Compare this treatment of squash with the authentic, and somewhat simpler, Catalan treatment found in the *Libre de sent soví*, Recipe 92. The title of the *Carabace alla catalana*—still in Riva's and Martino's *Carabaze ala catalana* and Platina's *Carabazum catellonicum* (Recipe VII,61)—certainly acknowledges the source of the recipe. The way in which the urtext begins—*carabace cioe zuche*—demonstrates clearly the adaptation of Catalan material for an Italian readership for whom the Catalan word has to be glossed with its Italian equivalent. Platina himself begins his version of this recipe by explaining: *cucurbitam, quam "carabazum" Catellonicum vocant.* Elements of both of our recipes for *Zuche* (Recipe 29) and these *Carabace alla catalana* are combined in Platina's single recipe, although there appear to be a number of other modifications as well.

The *Manoscritto Lucano* offers three varieties of *Carabaciata* (at Recipes 7, 8 and 9) in all of which one or two pigeons join the ground squash, salt meat, cheese and spices. In only the second and third versions do eggs appear, and there only the yolks are used. Throughout this early sixteenth-century recipe collection, the Neapolitan Collection's term *zuche* is rendered by *coccoce* (modern Italian *cocuzza*).

The awkward attempt at clarification that is found at the end of our recipe does not occur in either Riva or the *Arte coquinaria* because their texts have not mentioned cheese earlier. Rather, those versions refer back to "the" (Riva) and "the first" (Martino) recipe for plain *Zuche* (presumably our recipe 29), indicating that beaten egg *yolk* and cheese may optionally be added toward the end of the cooking process.

Our text is clearly flawed at this point: the earlier *pila* ("mortar") now becomes *la dita pignata* ("the above-mentioned pot"), and we suddenly find reference to *l'ova* where none has appeared before in this recipe. The close relationship between Recipes 29 and 30 in the urtext is likely longstanding, even though here in the Neapolitan version it is only implicit. Where the Neapolitan

[17] This is the wording in the *Arte coquinaria*. Riva shows *una crostada* and does not have *di sotto*.

Collection has only two closely related recipes for squash (if we exclude the *Torta de zuche* at Recipe 128), Riva has expanded this number to five (Recipes 77–81) and even preceded them with their very own rubric, *Ogni rasone de zuche.* Of these Martino has kept a series of four, copying the fifth by itself among dishes (Recipe 73: *Zucche fritte*).

❖ 31. The scribal hesitation in the title of this recipe, whose ingredients do not include almonds, relates it to the equally mysterious *Brou ab amenles a hom delicat* in the Primitive *Sent soví* (Recipe 205)[18] and the *Con se ffa brou amellat a hom deliquat* in the *Libre de sent soví* (Recipe 187). All three versions of the texts are at least in part very close; none has any almonds in it.

Rather than referring to almonds, however, the original rubric for the protorecipe of what we read here may well have read *Brodo a mallato o a homo delicato.* The words "for a sick person" could at some stage of their transmission be read as *amalado* and so "corrected," with a transposition of the *l* and *d*, into *amadolo* and *amandolo.* If this is so, the original sense of the title and function of the recipe are readily understood. The regimen of those with tender digestive systems (in general principle, those of the aristocracy) was considered in some respects analogous to that of the sick or the convalescent: in the *Tractatus*, for instance, the rubric of Part IV—essentially a series of sickdishes—is *De condimentis delicatis dominorum*, "Dainty Food for Masters."

❖ 32. A barley gruel is a common sickdish in late-medieval recipe collections. Among the more detailed directions for its preparation in the fifteenth century is the recipe for *Orjat* dictated by Chiquart for his *Du fait de cuisine* (Recipe 78). Because barley possesses a humoral temperament that is slightly cool and slightly dry (each in the first degree) it was held to be particularly useful in the treatment of fevers. The Latin version of the *Tacuinum sanitatis* (of the Arab physician Ibn Botlân) that was copied in the Po Valley toward the end of the fourteenth century and is now in the Österreichische Nationalbibliothek of Vienna illustrates *Savich, id est pultes ordei* with the image of a bedridden invalid who is being fed barley broth or porridge by two attendants. The text declares in part that "barley soup, which is very suitable for sick people, should be made with twenty pounds of barley, three pounds of linseed, half a pound of coriander, salt as required, and the whole mixed well before grinding."[19]

The text for *Farinata ad homo inferno* in our collection follows part of Recipe 187 of the Primitive *Sent soví.* The title of that version of the recipe reads *Farine a hom levat de malaltia, e tempre lo ventre*; that text is reproduced in Appendix C (ii) (p. 253). A close copy appearing in the Valencia manuscript of the *Libre de sent soví* can be read at p. 224 of Grewe's edition.

❖ 33. This vegetable seems to be unknown in early European cookery outside of the Italian and Iberian peninsulas. Among Italian recipe collections only ours recognizes it. See a different set of directions for preparing *Albergínies ab let de amelles* in the *Libre de sent soví* (Recipe 149). Concerning the measurement of time here (*piu che doi Pater Noster*), see Recipe 13, above.

---

[18] See the text of this version of the recipe in Appendix C (ii) (p. 253).

[19] See Judith Spencer, *The Four Seasons of the House of Cerruti* (New York: Facts on File, 1983), 53.

❖ 34. The rubric that heads this preparation in the Riva del Garda collection is *Per fare suppa fatta di semitta di canepa*; in the Vatican copy of the *Arte coquinaria*, while in the Washington copy we read *Per fare minestra di seme di canapa*; and in Platina (Recipe VII, 49) the dish is called *Cibarium cannabinum*. The genre to which this preparation is thought by various writers to belong is interesting. Neither Martino nor Platina assign it to any particular category: a *menestra*, a *cibarium*.[20] Riva, however, had identified the dish as a *suppa*, consequently to be served soaking bread or toast. The Neapolitan cook wrote *senipa*. This term, in the form of *sinapidum*, is found in Platina in the sense of a sauce made of mustard seed—that is, our modern "mustard": see the *De honesta voluptate*, Recipes VIII,13–15, 18, 23, etc. When Platina wrote *Sinapidum in frusta* (Recipe VIII,15), this rendered Martino's *Mostarda ... in pezi* (the Neapolitan Collection's *Mostarda ... in balotte*, Recipe 123). Unless our scribe has somehow misunderstood the word *sementa* (which he does later write), what our author intended was a hot, sweet, *mustard-like* sauce made of ground hemp seeds. According to our text, however, it is to be served in twelve bowls as distinct *menestre*—that is, constituting a distinct dish or *minestra* or *cibarium* as Martino and Platina wrote—rather than as a *suppa* or as a sauce that accompanies or dresses some other specific dish.

Elsewhere, in his recipe for *Offa cannabina* (VIII,57), Platina sounds dire warnings about the effects of hemp seed on the stomach. A single German collection contains recipes using hemp seed: *Mittelniederdeutsches Kochbuch*, *Moes van hennepe* (Recipe 52) and *Vlotkese van hennepe* (Recipe 53). A single Latin recipe for hemp seed is copied by the German chef of Pope Martin V, Johannes Bockenheim, in his *Registrum coquine* (c. 1425): *Ministrum de canapo* (Recipe 59). Despite the similarity of this latter name to that of the dish in the Vatican copy of Martino, the recipes are not identical: there is no almond milk in Bockenheim, but roast onion and olive oil appear as ingredients. Furthermore, this dish is expressly approved for the sick: *Erit bonum pro infirmis*.

The plant and its seed seem to have been ignored by French, English and Iberian cooks.

❖ 35. Our author appears to have had some predilection for marzipan. We find it being incorporated here and in a Marzipan Sauce (Recipe 111), as well as in a Marzipan Torte (Recipe 180) and in a dish called *Calisoni* (Recipe 159). Only these latter two preparations are copied in the *Libro de arte coquinaria*. In Riva the present recipe for *Dece menestre de marzapano* as well as the next one, for *Menestra di melloni*, are faithfully reproduced in juxtaposition though both are dropped from Martino.

The preparation of marzipan, whether for eating as such or to be had on hand as an ingredient in some other preparation, must have been such a common kitchen procedure that directions for it were nowhere thought necessary, whether in this collection, in Riva or in the *Arte coquinaria*.[21]

[20] Platina adds at the end of his *Cibarium cannabinum* his belief that the dish resembles the Sienese *Baricocoli*: *Hoc ego baricocolis Senensium persimile puto*.

[21] From the Iberian peninsula of the previous century a remarkable book on "sweetmeats," particularly delicacies and confections, contains directions for the making of *mersepa*: Luis Faraudo de Saint-Germain, "*Libre de totes maneres de confits*. Un tratado manual cuatrocentista de arte de dulcería," *Boletín de la Academia de Buenas Letras de Barcelona* 19 (1946): 97–134; Recipe 28, p. 118.

The beginning of Recipe 180 for a *Torta de marzapane* likely describes the process closely; in the Riva version of the *Torta papale* (our Recipe 182), the writer directs that almonds and pine nuts be ground *como la pasta del marzapane.*

The present recipe is for a chicken preparation of very smooth texture. As with the Marzipan Sauce, it will have a slightly tart (from the verjuice), gingery flavor.

❖ 36. We accept that the word *meloni* designates a fruit similar to the modern melon, although if this is so the dish outlined here is apt to be rather runny, even with the added egg yolk and cheese. Riva copies this text closely.

❖ 37. The name of this typically Catalan dish (which means, quite literally, "half roast") reflects the dual stages of its preparation. The first stage consists of a partial roasting of the meat; its conclusion is marked in our text: " . . . roast [the fowl] on the spit, and when they are *half cooked,* take them down . . . ."[22]

The *Miraustro ala catellana* in Riva, the *Mirrause catalano* in Martino and the *Mirause catellonicum* in Platina (Recipe VI,13) are quite similar in their texts to that of the Neapolitan Collection. The egg yolks of our version are overlooked in Platina. In the *Mig-raust* of the *Libre de sent soví* (Recipe 54) liver rather than egg yolks is used as a thickener.

The *colore gamellino* which is to be the finished hue of this dish is well known throughout the late Middle Ages. Derived from the word "camel," the term describes the camel's rich mid-brown color that in virtually all cases is lent to a sauce, a broth or some other dish by means of a good dose of cinnamon. So closely associated is cinnamon with this color that in some manuscripts the term is actually written *cannellino.*

❖ 38. This is a fairly plain dish of stewed herbs with some meat flavoring. In Riva and Martino a dish called *Menestre de herbette* (Recipes 89 and 80 respectively) involves a similar (though not identical) combination of herbs, beaten and boiled, but is not close enough textually to our recipe to be considered more than a possible variation of it.

❖ 39. Because the *Genestrata* was traditionally named after the brilliant yellow of the flour *ginestra,* "genista" or "broom," the compound name that our compiler places at the head of this recipe, *Genestrata biancha,* seems contradictory. It may, however, indicate merely that what is normally a dish with a distinct yellow hue contains in this version nothing, such as egg yolks or saffron, that would commonly be used to infuse it with that color. The dish has little in common, though, with the well known yellow sauce known as a *Fiore de Genestra*—of which we see a recipe later in this collection (Recipe 107).

Normally the dish called *Genestrata* in Italian bears a slight resemblance to the standard meatless White Dish, but with fruit and nuts and some yellow colourant. In their copies of our Recipe 4 for *Biancho manghiare per coprire caponi,* Riva and Martino append a variation of the dish that adds egg yolks and saffron, *et in questo modo si chiamera fiore di zenestra*; the phrase is faithfully

---

[22] See the extensive review of the *mirastro, miraustro* by Michael Süthold in his edition of the *Manoscritto Lucano,* op. cit., 169–75.

repeated in Platina (VI,41). The *Dilicate vivande* inverts the equivalence, identifying a *Giannetto, il quale alchune gienti chiamono Bramangieri* (Recipe 5).

Our recipe has little relationship with any of the usual White Dishes, however. On the other hand it does have a fairly close similarity with the Catalan *Ginestrada* of the *Sent soví* (Recipe 56) — though there the author directs, naturally, *mit-hi safrá, en guisa que torn a collor de ginestra*; and with two dishes among the Italian recipes in the Wellcome manuscript: Recipe 92 for *Ianetata* (so spelled) and Recipe 375 for *Ienestrata per dodece scodelle*. In that same latter collection, Recipe 398 bears the same name, *Ienestrata*, but there the list of ingredients is so simplified that the dish is really no longer the version of it that we find in the Neapolitan manuscript.

❖ 40. The precise variety of bean represented by the term *scaffe* is uncertain. Claudio Benporat has proposed that at the time of the Neapolitan Collection this was a Roman dialectal term for an ordinary *fava*.[23]

This recipe makes a dish that is somewhat more than a preparation of new beans. The boiled beans, with their condiments, serve to present the fowl, but what should also be noticed is that the beans apparently remain whole: rather exceptionally, there is no mention of pureeing them.

❖ 41. Concerning the *phaseolus*, Platina (Recipe VII,14) points out that "its cold and harmfulness can be reduced to some degree by sprinkling with marjoram, pepper and mustard." All three of these condiments, marjoram, pepper and mustard, are recognized as possessing exceptionally warm, dry humoral qualities, the last two ranging in the highest or "dangerous" degree. The preparation described in the Neapolitan recipe for *Fasioli* may answer the need to warm and dry kidney beans by means of an extended cooking time, and by using spices both in their cooking and as a garnish.

❖ 42. Both the ingredients and the procedures for Stuffed Beans are closely reproduced in Riva and Martino (and thence in Platina). Our version has overlooked the use of rosewater when grinding the almonds for the stuffing of the beans in this dish; it's use — *azo non fazeno olio*, as Riva explains — is commonplace in this operation. The other copies do explicitly mention it.

❖ 43. To begin this new section of meat dishes, the Neapolitan cook copies this preliminary recipe which offers universal advice on the boiling of meats. The text found here is reproduced in Riva with only minor amplifications: an ample-sized cooking pot should be used *azio che sia piu biancha*, "so that the meat is whiter" (later, the *Arte coquinaria* will change this *sia* to *rimanghi*, "remain"); in the case of older, tougher meats, Riva glosses the Neapolitan *volatilli*, "fowl," as *presertim caponi, galline, pollastri*; for the last phrase, *et sera piu cocibile*, Riva substitutes *et cossi sera piu bella et piu ben cocta e presto.* This second change is hardly an improvement; one has the impression of a scribe determined on change for change's sake.

Our text has undergone a little more modification by the time of the *Arte coquinaria*, particularly with regard to the means suggested for dealing with unclean salt: when dissolved in hot water the salt will make a brine from which the dirty, "earthy" part will sink to the bottom of the pot: the pure salt water can then be used.

---

[23] Benporat, *Cucina italiana del quattrocento*, 41, note 9.

❖ 44. This recipe for boiled chicken, along with the following one for cockerels, provide help to prepare some of the most important meats of the day. From this point in the compilation, after the general introduction to "Boiled Meats" copied in Recipe 43, the Catalan influence is strong. The first recipe of the series is similar to what is found in the *De apereylar be de menyar* under the title *Gualines ab carn selade* (Recipe 20: see the text of this in Appendix C). In the *Sent soví*, see also *Con se coen gualines en olla* (Recipe 58).

❖ 45. Stewed verjuice grapes may not have been commonplace to the author of the Neapolitan Collection, to the compilers of the Riva del Garda collection and the *Arte coquinaria*, or to Platina—or at least as common as they were elsewhere in Europe at this time. In each case the writers copy directions for this particular preparation of the grapes. In French cuisine, the equivalent of the *agresto sodo*, "whole verjuice grapes"—written as *agresto in uga* in Riva, *agresto sano* in the *Arte coquinaria* and *grana uvæ sublatis e medio vinaceis* in the *De honesta voluptate* (Recipe VI,16)—which is seeded and boiled with a meat, is the common *grain de verjus* or *verjus en grain*. There is a standard variety of sauce, consisting of slightly mashed and boiled verjuice grapes, that is known in the French cookery of the time as *Rapée*.

What is particularly noteworthy in this recipe is the use of the green herb parsley (to which the Martino version will later add mint as well) and the yellow saffron, a combination that will produce a particularly favored yellow-green ("gaudy-green") hue.

Riva and Martino omit any mention of the spiced serving garnish.

❖ 46. That recipes for goat kid and mutton follow the recipes for boiled poultry again seems to indicate the relative importance of this meat in the local aristocratic diet. See the next two recipes as well. Again, herbs play a significant role in the cooking pot.

It may be noted that the author seems to use the words *carnero* and *castrado* interchangeably in this recipe, as in Recipe 78 and in Menus [2] and [3], below.

Textually this version of the recipe is close to the *Cabrit e moltó ab broet* that is read in the *De apereylar be de menyar* (Recipe 16). At the conclusion of the recipe in this latter collection, however, the cook is advised that "sops are made with the sauce." See also the *Carn ab brou* in the *Libre de sent soví* (Recipe 180).

❖ 47. Four dishes in the Neapolitan Collection are qualified as being "in the Florentine fashion" or "Florentine-style." If the qualification identifies a treatment typical of practice in Florentine kitchens, what it seems to indicate according to this recipe is that the meat is reduced to small chunks which are cooked in a sauce in the oven. This is generally the procedure followed as well in the *Carne in tegamo* of Recipe 50. However, the *Miliazo Fasanitico* described in Recipe 134, though likewise a baked preparation, and the *Ova Fritellate* of Recipe 155 are likely just Florentine dishes rather than Florentine-type dishes.

The present recipe is similar to the *Cabrits en caçola* of the *De apereylar be de menyar* (Recipe 57), and to the *Casola de cabrits ab salsa* in the *Sent soví* (Recipe 136). In neither of those Catalan recipes, though, is any mention made of this dish being "in the Florentine fashion."

❖ 48. Textually, this recipe is close to the *Cabayat* of the *De apereylar be de menyar* (Recipe 85) and the *De aperellar tota cabadura e peus, e con sa deu menyar* in the *Sent soví* (Recipe 182). The Catalan term for an animal's head in a culinary preparation, *cabayat*, has no specific equivalent in the Italian of our compiler.

❖ 49. The "blanching" of the calf's head likely involves an immersion in boiling water. This seems likewise to be the procedure to be followed in preparing the blanched piglet of Recipe 63.

There are two treatments for a calf's head: boiling and baking. For the first, Platina speaks of the Garlic Sauce as a cooking sauce (*fuerit in alliatum mergito*: Recipe VI,30); the Neapolitan Collection, Riva and the *Arte coquinaria* all refer to this *Agliata* as a *sapore*. The second manner of preparation — in which the brains are removed, combined with other ingredients and restuffed into the head, which is then bound and baked — is very much abbreviated in the other versions; in the *Arte coquinaria* there is not even any mention of the calf's brains. In Riva this latter oversight corrected: a final sentence reads, *Et notta che se vole cavare fora lo cervello per fare la impitura*, "Note that the brain should be dug out to make the stuffing."[24]

❖ 50. This *Carne in tegamo alla fiorentina* and the following recipe for *Caponi inzucarati* seem to be *unica* to the Neapolitan Collection. They conclude the series of recipes for boiled meats.

❖ 52. This recipe begins a (brief) series dealing with the preparation of roast meats. As before with boiled meats, the initial recipe in the series consists of practical advice on general procedures. And as with that Recipe 43, the text of these general-purpose directions for the roasting of meats has been slightly amplified in the other collections, of Riva and Martino, that contain it. In particular these other versions include herbs and a number of fruits as possible ingredients with which the roasting meats can be "larded."

❖ 53. As was the case earlier for boiled meats (Recipe 43), the first variety of meat to be dealt with when roasting is poultry, specifically cockerels. Our text refers back to the preceding general advice on roasting meats; however, because Riva and the versions of the *Arte coquinaria* that survive seem to have modified the order of recipes as these were likely originally compiled by Martino de Rossi (or some protocook/author), we can guess that the later authors or scribes suddenly found themselves faced with nonsense at this point (*coceli cum l'ordine sopra ditto, he quando serano cotti,* . . . , "follow the above directions and, when cooked, . . . ") and, remarkably, let themselves reproduce nonsense: *Per fare polastri a rosto, e se vole cocere a rosto, et quando e cocto,* . . . — "To roast a cockerel, it should be roasted and, when it is cooked, ..."

Apart from this revealing blunder, the texts of the Neapolitan Collection, Riva and Martino are close.

---

[24] We may observe, though, that in Riva, the *Arte coquinaria* and the *Honesta voluptate* (Recipe VI,30) this present recipe is followed by another, which is much more detailed, expressly for the preparation and serving of calf's (*del vittello o bove* in Riva) brains.

❖ 54. The *vino cotto* or "wine syrup" that is specified here is a standard ingredient available in large kitchens of the time. Its preparation is described by the *Menagier de Paris*: "Get a tub of the very finest wine that has distilled [*i.e.*, drained gently, perhaps on the first pressing, hence richer] from the grapes before they are pressed, either white or red, put it into an earthenware vessel and boil it very gently over a fire of dry logs with absolutely no smoke; remove the scum with a holed wooden spoon and not an iron one; if the grapes harvested that year are 'green' [*i.e.*, sharp in flavor], let the wine boil down to a third; if the grapes are 'mature' [rich], let it boil down to one quarter; let it cool in a clean wooden tub, then put it into a cask and it will be better after the first year." (§338)

The fourteenth-century Venetian Collection also gives directions for making *vino cocto*, but ensures its fundamental sweetness by reinforcing it with honey: *Toy vino vermeglio el piu fino che tu poy avere e bono miele; mitilo a bolire insieme e alquanto fiore de canella, e bolia tanto ch'el torne el terzo; e per IIII bichier de vino, vole essere uno pien de melle* (Recipe 120). For our author the value of this wine syrup is as a source of a sweet flavor: verjuice will produce a piquant (*brusco*) taste in a preparation, wine syrup a sweet (*dolce*) taste. See also our author's use of must syrup in Recipe 93.

This dish begins another series of five recipes that are related to Catalan sources and have no known immediate connection with any Italian recipe collection (see the corresponding Catalan texts in Appendix C). The text of the present recipe is close to that of the recipe headed *Si vols saber cabrit en totes maneres* found in the *De apereylar be de menyar* (Recipe 58). In that version ground roast filberts (hazelnuts) are included in the sauce, and the cook is instructed that, no matter what liquids are added, this sauce should remain thick.

❖ 55. Given that *galline* (and *caponi* in the rubric) is unlimitedly in the plural, we must wonder whether the quantity of five almonds, so precisely specified by this recipe, is in error. The use of lemon juice relates this dish to the following, and to Catalan cookery in general.

This recipe, too, is found in *De apereylar be de menyar*: *Gualines o capons en ast* (Recipe 35). It is repeated in the *Sent soví* (Recipe 60), where to the same title is added the phrase "without boiling."

❖ 56. See also the cooking sauce known as *Limonata* below, Recipe 110.

A closely related treatment for poultry-in-*Limonata* is described in the *De apereylar be de menyar* under the somewhat misleading rubric *Si vols fer Limonia* (Recipe 31). The Catalan version ends with the notation that for twenty persons the recipe needs four pounds of almonds. There exist as well lean versions of this preparation, a *Limonia de Pescie* in *Anonimo Meridionale* "A" (Recipe 66) and in the Wellcome manuscript (Recipe 391).

❖ 57. The *puriola*, *poriola* or *pariola* seems to be an exclusively Catalan sauce. In known recipe manuscripts this preparation appears in the *De apereylar be de menyar* and the *Sent soví*; in the latter collection, the preparation called *puriola* is mentioned a total of nine times. In the former collection the recipe titled *Puriola a galinas o capons en ast* (Recipe 23) is clearly a close precursor of our Italian one (see Appendix C). Two recipes for the dish are provided in the *Sent soví*, in

Recipes 72 and 87. The latter, entitled *Puriola a gualines ho a capons ho a pols en ast* derives directly from Recipe 23 in the other Catalan collection.

The title as we find it here may be misleading, changing prepositions as it does. The *pariola* is clearly for any of these three varieties of poultry.

The roast poultry that is to be served this way must steep for a short time in the sauce. To designate the manner of this procedure the term *stuffare* is used: the implied vessel, holding meat and sauce and surrounded by a moderate heat, would be either a sort of *bain Marie* (a double-boiler, occasionally of glass) or a covered, earthernware or metal *trapa* with hot coals under and above. The French culinary phrase, *à l'étouffée*, retains this original sense of *stuffare*.

❖ 58. This recipe is very close textually to Recipe 110 in the *De apereylar be de menyar*: *Qui vol apereylar aucels menuts* (see this text in Appendix C), and to Recipe 133 in the *Libre de sent soví* where the rubric is *Con sa deu ffer en alcels menuts alidem*. The mention in this title of the Catalan generic preparation *alidem* is discussed by Grewe in n. 3 to this recipe in his edition.

❖ 59. The *Oxford Companion to Food* has the following entry on the figpecker: "FIGPECKER (or *beccafico*), any of various small birds in the group known as warblers, in the Mediterranean region, especially S Italy and Cyprus. The capture of these tiny songbirds for consumption, entire, as delicacies offends the sensibilities of bird-lovers and efforts are made periodically to end or diminish the practice." Even as far back as the sixth century, Anthimus enumerates garden warblers among good, edible wildfowl.[25]

There are two ways to prepare garden warblers (otherwise known as figpeckers because of their habitual manner of seeking sustenance): under hot coals or on a spit. These are small birds; later Riva, then Martino, qualifies the time allowed for the first cooking method by writing "a half hour or less, because they are quickly cooked under hot coals." Platina explains why in the second procedure these tiny fowl should not be mounted with the spit *through* them: if they were pierced with a spit, he writes, you would have nothing left to eat![26] Our version alone suggests binding the birds inside a split cane, and directs that they should be eaten hot.

❖ 60. A number of significant variants appear in the later versions of this recipe. In Riva and the *Arte coquinaria* (and the *Honesta voluptate*, Recipe VI,29) it is not explicitly clear, as in our version, that the cook is making a *sapore* for these thrush — though they do explain that the use of sandalwood is to give the *sapore* a russet color. This sauce will be a hot Cameline Sauce. It is brownish in color: after sandalwood is mentioned Riva explains *azio chel sapore sia rosso*. It should be bitter-sweetish, but in Martino (and consequently Platina) the word "sugar" seems to have been misread as "ginger."

---

[25] *De ficitulas. Ficitulas et ipsas bonas et apti sunt vel alia genera aucellorum qui albas carnes abent vel alias aves teneras prusumantur*: "Of beccaficoes. Beccaficoes also are good and suitable; so are any other kinds of birds that have white meat; any other young birds may be eaten." Anthimus, *De observatione ciborum*, ed. Shirley Howard Weber (Leiden: E. J. Brill, 1924), 26–7; Recipe 31.

[26] *Assas si voles quaternas simul devincies circa veru capite et pedibus, ne si transfixæ fuerint nil habeas quod comedas. De honesta voluptate*, Recipe VI,32.

The specific use of the juice of *sweet* oranges (*marangoli dolce*), is to be noted, the bitter orange being older and much more common in the fifteenth century. The optional alternative of pomegranate juice mentioned here is not echoed in the other versions which write lemon juice instead. In general the Neapolitan cook tends to make a slightly greater use of pomegranates and their juice than is found in the other versions: in the Glossary (p. 214) see the list of occurrences of *granate, pome granate* and *grani di melagranata.*

❖ 61. As with Recipes 5, 30, 37 and 61, this dish is qualified as being *a la catalana*, "in the Catalan fashion." As was mentioned before, there seems to be no common factor among these dishes that might explain the qualification as having to do with their ingredients or preparation. For the author of the Neapolitan Collection this dish would seem merely to be one that was understood to be common in Catalonia.

As with the recipe for thrush, the Neapolitan author on the one hand and the later Riva, Martino and Platina versions on the other again differ somewhat as to the optional liquids to be used in this mixture for partridge. Our author writes pomegrante juice or verjuice; the others have orange juice, lemon juice or verjuice. Rather awkwardly amplifying the final piece of advice that partridge not be overcooked, the other versions write, " . . . and it should not be overcooked, but raw [*verde*, 'green, underdone'], almost bloody, that is, not greatly cooked, and very hot, and turned [on the spit] quickly and not slowly."

❖ 62. No written source, or close parallel, of this recipe is known.

The *Tremolette* was indeed a French sauce as the title indicates. It appears elsewhere only in French recipe collections: the *Viandier* of Taillevent (Recipe 192), Chiquart's *Du fait de cuisine* (Recipe 12) and the *Recueil de Riom* (Recipe 14). The ingredients in the *Tremolette* seem to have varied a little over time and from place to place: some of the recipes for it include the drippings from the roasting partridge, some chicken or partridge liver, some chopped, fried onions, some bread as a thickener. Our recipe has none of these, but uses instead ground almonds which are nowhere mentioned in the existing French recipes for *Tremolette.*

The presence of grains of paradise in this recipe is interesting. This spice with a gingery taste, which had become so "popular" in fifteenth-century French aristocratic cookery, appears in only two recipes in our collection: in this French sauce and in the *Gelatina* of Recipe 88. In our author's mind the distinctive taste of this particular spice may well have gone some way to justify the qualification he wrote in the title of his dish: *al modo franceso.*

❖ 63. The Neapolitan author's reverence for the "Holy Piglet" does not seem to be shared by either Riva or Martino (or Platina, for that matter), who name this dish merely *Una porchetta* and *In porcello asso* (*De honesta voluptate*, Recipe VI,15). Very generally all versions of the recipe agree, though our recipe is perhaps slightly richer: the others do not include dried fruit (the prunes and raisins) in the stuffing, and quantities are left inexplicit (only "a few eggs" and "ground pepper"). On the other hand the others add a little more flavor to the basting sauce by putting several more herbs (sage and bay leaves) into it along with our author's rosemary.

Contemporary European cookery recognized a standard procedure that could be followed in preparing tench by "reversing" it, that is by folding its outer sides back upon themselves; Riva and

Martino insert an explicatory phrase after the crucial Neapolitan direction, ... *he riversal como se fa cum le tenghe*; they write, ... *zioe, ponendo fora quello ch'e de drento.* The specifics of this procedure are nowhere detailed in the surviving pages of the Neapolitan Collection. Further on in our compilation, however, in Recipe 198, we do find explicitly a reference to the dish which is called *Tencha reversa.* It seems entirely likely that the recipe for this treatment of tench originally appeared among the fish recipes, somewhere on pages that are now missing from our manuscript. The procedure itself was quite straightforward and involved slitting the fish lengthwise, eviscerating it and then folding the two flanks back along its spine. As with the *Sancta porcheta* here, a more or less elaborate stuffing—referred to in Recipe 198 as *lo pieno de la Tencha reversa*—along with a batter coating, could be added before the reversed tench was roasted on a spit or a grill. Explicit directions for the prepation of tench in this way are offered in the *Viandier* (Recipe 104), the *Menagier de Paris* (Recipe 172), the *Buone vivande* (Recipe 45)—and, significantly, in Riva: *Tenche: el secondo modo*[27] (*la potray fare reversa essendo grossa* ... , Recipe 252), Martino: *Tenca reversciata* (Recipe 229), and Platina: [*Tinca*] *Aliter* (Recipe X,43).

❖ 64. The authors, or revisors, of the Riva del Garda collection and the version of the *Arte coquinaria* that we possess have felt it necessary to add a few specifications to what in our manuscript is a relatively simple and generalized recipe. Instead of our rubric we read, "Liver Bits (*Figatelli*) of a calf,[28] cockerels, pig or any other animal." Then for the omentum (whose source is unspecified in our version) the other authors write, " ... bind them in the omentum of a pig or a calf, the best being of a goat kid." These authors further add an herb to the liver's seasoning: fennel.

❖ 65. These *Tomaselle* are generically similar to the preceding *Figatelli* in that they consist of a meat mixture wrapped in small walnut-sized packets in peritoneal membrane (here called the *reticella*) and then slowly deep-fried in lard. The preparation was known back to the time of the Anonimo Toscano (Recipe 141: *Tomacelli ovvero mortadelle*) and the Anonimo Veneziano (Recipe 46: *Mortadelle bone e perfette*). A diminutive, *tomacellum*, of the Latin word for a sausage, *tomaculum* or *tomaclum*, is used in the plural (*tumacella*) as a synonym for *salcicias* in the *Liber de coquina* (Recipe I,12).[29]

As he had previously done in his version of our Recipe 30 (Recipe VII,61), Platina again indicates that his source is using a "popular" dishname: *Tomacella haec vulgus applellat* (Recipe VI,21).[30] His own name for the dish, *Esicium ex iecore*, may be more descriptive but turns its back on a good bit of Italian culinary history.

---

[27] See the text of this part of the recipe in the comment to Recipe 198.

[28] Both the Washington and Vatican copies of the *Libro de arte coquinaria* read *vitello* and not *ucello*.

[29] See a study by Sthold of the word and its use in late-medieval and Renaissance cookery, as well as in more modern dialectal usage: *Monoscritto Lucano*, 193–202.

[30] The concluding sentence of this recipe for *Esicium ex iecore* in the *De honesta voluptate* reads: ... *"Tomacella" haec vulgus appellat quæ fortasse melius "omacula" cum involuta omento fiant dicerentur vel "tomacla"* ... : "The common people call them *tomacella*, which would perhaps be better called *omacula*, since they are wrapped in omentum, or *tomacla* ... ."

There are very few differences between our version and those of Riva and Martino: the former calls for an unspecified number of eggs, the latter two make this two or three eggs, *secondo la quantita*; in our version the inclusion of saffron, noted in the margin, is likely an attempt on the part of our author to improve over his "original." Although Recipe 21 (*Esicium ex iecore*) of Book VI in the *De honesta voluptate* is certainly copied closely from this recipe in the extant version of Martino, Platina's previous recipe (*Esicium ex pulpa*, Recipe VI,20) also offers some similarities to the *Tomaselle*.

❖ 66. With this dish the compiler begins a series of what he terms "Wonders of Gourmandise" or "Gastronomical Marvels." The end of Recipe 65 — for a dish that certainly has nothing marvelous about it — occupies the upper portion of f° 23v. However, because the scribe has felt the need to proclaim the rubric for the dishes that begin with Recipe 66 in letters large enough to cover a two-page spread (ff° 23v–24r), he begins to write *Incipiunt mirabilia gule* in the upper margin even before the end of Recipe 65. The rubric does not actually apply until the midpoint of f° 23v, between Recipes 65 and 66. The placing of this rubric suggests that our scribe was not himself compiling individual recipes into a book but was copying from a recipe collection that he had in front of him.

The interesting feature of the first of the "marvellous" dishes, and clearly the one that qualifies it as an item in this section of recipes, is the way (apparently) that a full day's soaking in highly acidic vinegar will dissolve a bird's bones. For the bird's stuffing, the *Arte coquinaria*, and later the *Honesta voluptate* (at Recipe VI,39), greatly simplify our ingredients list by omitting any mention of cheese, eggs or raisins and by suggesting, the use of what are identified merely as "good things and good spices" (Martino) and "spices and herbs" (Platina)! For the cooking method to which the boneless bird is to be subjected, these other versions also change our "on the spit or roasted" — the latter presumably on the grill — to "boiled or roast, whichever you like."

The collection of recipes compiled in the Riva del Garda manuscript does not contain this "dish." However, we may compare the procedure that is outlined in our recipe with what the *Mittelniederdeutsches Kochbuch* describes in its Recipe 26:

> *Wyltu maken gantze voghele ane knoken, so nym junghe vogele van eyneme jare. Make se reyne. Vorwelle se yn etycke. Nym se dar wedder uth unde nym etick, so du en starker krighen kanst. Legge se darin unde lat se stan eyne nacht. So machst du se seden edder braden.*
>
> If you wish to make whole birds without bones, get young, year-old birds and clean them. Let them come to a boil in vinegar. Remove them and get vinegar that is as strong as you can get, and lay them in it, leaving them there for one night. Then you can boil or roast them.

The potency of medieval vinegar varied, a fact of which professional cooks of the time were well aware. A practical test to determine the strength of any given batch of vinegar is outlined by Aldobrandino of Siena in the thirteenth century: "If you wish to know whether [the vinegar] is good, pour some on the ground and, if it boils and froths, you may be sure that it is good; and if it does not, it is bad."[31] An unspecified condition for the success of this test must clearly be that the "ground" is alkaline.

❖ 67. The second "wonderful dish" in this section relies upon a standard, long-practiced technique of skinning a fowl, complete with its feather, and "redressing" either that fowl's carcass after it has been suitably cooked or the cooked carcass, of a similar size, of another bird altogether. This exercise, or a variant of it, had already entertained a century of banqueters right across Europe. The Neapolitan recipe To Make Two Pigeons Out of One derives directly from this traditional technique.

The versions of the recipe here and in Martino (and Platina) are very similar, although our Neapolitan author insists a little more on the cook's professional responsibility to do a neat job in sewing up the bird's skin. A similar procedure in English can be read in the *Noble Boke of Cookry* at Recipe 20: *To make two capons of one.*

For the ingredients of the stuffing to be put into the bird's skin, where our author can refer back to the detailed list he has set out in the previous recipe, Martino and Platina (Recipe VI,40) are forced to repeat their rather unsatisfactory "fill it with a stuffing made of good things" and *optimo farcimine replebis*.

❖ 68. The recipe for cooking Chicken-in-a-Flask appears in the Riva del Garda compilation in a position whose logic is not at first apparent: it concludes a series of five jellies, whose explicit rubric is *Libro sexto per fare gellatina*, and precedes another of fourteen egg dishes. Nothing similar is copied into the *Libro de arte coquinaria* or into the *De honesta voluptate*. As with the previous dish, this one represents a variant on a long-practiced procedure: fundamentally it is a method of preparing chicken within a sort of double boiler in order to retain and enhance the natural properties and flavor of this preferred meat.

Our author will repeat this general procedure twice more in his collection, in the context of sickdishes where Chicken-in-a-Flask is more traditionally known: Recipes 97 and 98.

❖ 69. This redressed, fire-breathing peacock is a curious hybrid, the redressed fowl that also incorporates the wonder of flames that issue from the mouth of a marvelous beast. The recipe is not copied in Riva but reappears in much the same detail in Martino and Platina (Recipe VI,14). For the stuffing here these other versions cannot write, as our author does, "fill it with the stuffing of the Piglet [the so-called Holy Piglet, Roasted Inside-Out: Recipe 63], but without garlic here"; rather they must content themselves, yet once again, with the unsatisfactorily vague, "fill it with good things with good spices": in these latter two collections the recipe for the Piglet *follows* the redressed, fire-breathing peacock.

Generally our author is slightly more concerned with technical details than the other versions: he directs, for instance, that the peacock's leg-bone must be extracted before the bird is roasted so that the iron bar may later pass through the leg—a detail omitted by the others. These latter do, however, direct the cook to spread out the peacock's tail in order to obtain its full effect.

---

[31] *Le Régime du corps de maître Aldebrandin de Sienne*, ed. Louis Landouzy and Roger Pépin (Paris: Champion, 1911), 120.

Platina abbreviates the text somewhat in detailing the technique for producing the long-lasting flame that is to be exhaled from the bird's beak. The source of the fire was the distilled alcohol known as *aqua ardens* (or, alternatively, an old and "volatile wine"); the other versions do not render the significant word *fumoso* that is copied in our text. A half-century before, in his *Du fait de cuisine* Chiquart described an *entremets* of his invention in which a wild boar, a piglet and a swan are served in towers of a castle and all breathing fire at the same time; the same entremets boasted a roasted goose (non-fire-breathing, this one) redressed into the elegant plumage of a peacock. Normally *aqua vita*, produced by a single distillation of wine, was redistilled repeatedly to refine the alcohol and make an increasingly volatile *aqua ardens*.

The form of the word *inzegno* in the manuscript, along side *ingegni* in the next recipe, illustrates the way in which the letter *z* is occasionally exchanged with the letter *g*. The alteration may result from a dialectal idiosyncracy of the scribe or from what was written in some proto-source in the tradition.

❖ 70. Among the historic banquet menus appended to this manuscript we find (at f° 86v) one during which Diana presents a stag, a deer, two hares, two rabbits and a wild boar, all properly cooked and then redressed, and all standing in lifelike poses at the edge of a forest. The chief cook responsible for this banquet was undoubtedly very familiar with the procedures outlined in this current recipe — and undoubtedly also had the assistance of a good number of underlings. This recipe is the last of the five *Mirabilia gule* of our collection. It has no counterpart in the Riva manuscript, the *Arte coquinaria* or the *Honesta voluptate*.[32]

The care with which the Neapolitan cook describes not only the culinary procedures but also what we might term the mechanical details of this complex procedure reflects his professionalism. The cautionary note addressed to his master, and that he feels impelled to append to this recipe, insists upon any cook's supreme professional qualification: the worthy cook must be *discretto*, "competent." We might even expect some such phrase as *El coco e discretto* to be emblazoned in our cook's heraldic device.

❖ 71. Though no rubric is found at this point in the compilation, we apparently pass from the marvelous, entertaining dishes of the previous section to another sequence of dishes, for *pastizi* and *pastelli*. Seven varieties of these are offered: five for meat and fowl, one for fish and one for fruit.

The term *pastizo* identifies primarily a variety of *olla* or cooking dish. By extension the same term is applied to the sort of pie baked in such a dish. Later, in the title of Recipe 75, an alternative word will be a *coppo*, this being a sort of baking dish or, again by extension, the sort of pie baked in such a dish. The title of Recipe 71 reads *Pastizi de vitella*, yet some corrector, or the scribe himself, perhaps wishing to clarify the meaning of the word *pastizo*, has added *in tegamo* immediately above this name. The dish, then, is a sort of "Veal Pot Pie." We find in the recipe here no mention of dough or pastry or shell, which may or may not be implied. Subsequent dishes for which the term *pastizo* is used (Recipes 72, 75 and 77) do expressly have a pastry crust.

---

[32] Carole Lambert describes a banquet, offered by Cardinal Ceccano to Pope Clement VI in 1343, in which a great stag, although cooked, looked still alive. "La nourriture comme signe de distinction religieuse et sociale de Thomas d'Aquin à Erasme," *Heresis* 26–27 (1996): 111.

The first part of the recipe is clearly concerned with boiling the principal ingredients. Then, toward the middle, with the meat a little better than half-cooked, a marginal addition marks what may be at the root of our problem: *he pone in pignata*. The scribe seems to realize that something has been omitted here. Is it just a matter of directing that these new ingredients be added into *la pignata*? Or are all of the partially cooked foodstuffs to be transferred . . . to another pot? What may have been omitted at some (early?) stage in our text—and, if so, the likely place is here—is a passage in which a pastry crust is laid out in a second heavy pot or baking dish, the *tegamo* that is mentioned a line or two later. It is entirely common for fifteenth-century recipes to add ingredients (such as the verjuice, beaten eggs and additional spices mentioned in the last lines here) into a pie toward the end of its baking; this is, in fact, the procedure prescribed in the next two recipes.

The texts of this recipe that are copied in Riva and the *Arte coquinaria* give no support to any speculation that the foodstuffs may have been transferred from a cooking pot, and the *pastizi* finished in a baking dish: at the crucial place both Riva and the extant Martino versions read, *mettilli . . . cipolla tagliata minuta e fritta con uno pocho de lardo in la pignata*. Platina does not copy this recipe.

❖ 72. There is no question (as perhaps in the preceding recipe) that this *pastizo* is indeed a pie in a shell of pastry dough. What is interesting in the texts of both Riva and the *Arte coquinaria* is a concluding alternative not found in our version of the recipe: "And if you do not know how to make the crusts, cook it in a pan [*nella padella*] as tortes are done." We shall find a series of tortes later (Recipes 125–41). To make them, a layer of fine pastry is laid on the bottom of a baking dish; thick, heavy-duty pastry walls, such as are normal for tall-sided pies, are unnecessary, the dish itself providing the physical support to hold the pie's contents in a relatively thin dough during the baking. The pie is also without a top crust.

In Riva the name of this recipe has changed slightly to become *Pastello di carne de vittello o de capone o de altre qual voglia si sia*; in the *Arte coquinaria*, this is echoed as "Pasty of Veal or Capon or Any Other Meat or of Fowl."[33]

❖ 73. The very specific full name of this recipe, though accurately transcribed in Riva and the *Arte coquinaria*, is strangely changed by Platina to just *In pastillum gallinaceum* (Recipe VI,38). This name would do little to help the cook who might happen to want a quick reminder of the principal ingredients in a dish of cock's combs and testicles. At any rate all the other versions reproduce the Neapolitan text fairly with a few variations: the number of cherries varies between our thirty, thirty to forty in Riva and Martino, and forty in Platina; Riva, Martino and Platina add the sauce to the pasty when it is only half-cooked; Platina increases the single egg yolk of this last mixture to "two beaten egg yolks." Platina explains what is meant by baking in a pan—*in una patella*, rather than the alternative, in the oven—by writing "under a cover on the hearth."

---

[33] The recipe in both the Riva and Martino collections ends with optional alternatives that both amplify on the sense of the title they give it and hark back to the Neapolitan title: *Et nel dicto pastelo si po mettere uno o duy polastri o uno capone o pipioni o qualvoglia altro ucello tagliato o integro.*

This genre of dish, the *pastello*, should not be confused with the sixteenth-century *pastetella* or *pastitella* as this will appear, for instance, in the *Manoscritto Lucano*. The *pastello* is a small pie, baked in an oven; the *pastetella* is a sort of turnover which is deep fried in oil. The latter term is not used by our *cuoco napoletano*.

❖ 74. This *pastello* is a free-standing, double-crusted pie. Its contents are not fluid enough to place an impossible strain upon its unsupported pastry walls—even though recipes at this time often direct that these should be up to an inch thick. The term *capsa* for the pie shell is what English recipes of the time would call a *coffin*. A liquid, seasoning mixture properly called a *sapore* is added, most carefully, under the top crust when the principal ingredients have cooked: this is in effect the serving garnish for the dish. Whenever distilled rosewater, *aqua rosa*, is to go into a pie, it is virtually always added in this way when the pie has finished baking so that its flavor will not wholly evaporate. Occasionally one or several small holes will be made in the upper crust of a pie before it is put into the oven for the purpose of such a final addition of an ingredient or a prepared sauce.

See also the *Pastero de capreto bono* in the *Anonimo Veneziano* (Recipe 52).

❖ 75. As a prepared dish, the genre designated *copo* or *coppo* is a sort of layered pie, baked originally perhaps in the dish from which it borrowed its name. The Accademici della Crusca[34] glossed a *coppo* as a *spezie di vaso, orcio*, to which they added the Latin equivalent, *dolium*; this likely an elongated baking dish, the *tiella* of which our Neapolitan author makes use on several other occasions. The present recipe is the only one in our collection for a dish that is identified generically as a *coppo*. The composition of this particular *pastizo* or *coppo* resembles—at least roughly—that of the previous *pastello*, and a similar sauce is added through a hole in the pastry cover in the same way as before as it finishes baking.

In the version of this dish found in the *Manocritto Lucano* (Recipe 84[35]), called merely a *coppo*, the same layering is specified. It is likewise for pigeons, which are well cooked in a spiced sauce before going into the pie. The sauce itself is then inserted gradually through the upper crust which is to be of a piece, whole (rather than woven, for instance)—*sana, con un pertuso in mezo*: some of the sauce at the beginning of the baking, some when the pie is half done, and the remainder after it is placed on its serving platter.

See also the *Pastero de pipioni* of the *Anonimo Veneziano* (Recipe 50), as well as the *Coppo di polli o d'altri uccelli* of the *Anonimo Toscano* (Recipe 125) and its Latin translation in the *Liber de coquina* (Recipe II,23). In none of these three recipes from the previous century, however, is there any mention of layering the ingredients within the pastry shell.

❖ 76. This recipe is apparently incomplete, or else the copy is faulty: the making and filling of the pastry crust remains only implicit (as in Recipe 71), and in places the sense of the text

---

34 *Vocabolario degli Accademici della Crusca*, (2nd edition, Venice: Iacopo Sarazina, 1623).

35 See also Recipe 50 in this same collection, where the dish in which the *copo* is formed is identified as a *tiella*.

itself is not too clear. The Neapolitan cook himself seems to express his own poor opinion of the recipe — though whether his distaste is aroused by the dish or by the state of the text he is dealing with is difficult to say. The recipe in any recognizable form does not seem to have been picked up by Riva, Martino or Platina.

Our compiler's source for this paragraph is undoubtedly the Primitive *Sent soví*. The text there of *Penades de pex* (Recipe 217) has been translated here more or less word for word — including the various Catalan names of fish.[36] The Catalan text does not continue beyond what we have in the Neapolitan rendition, so that, again, the sense of our compiler's comment remains uncertain.

❖ 77. The precise directions that our author, Riva and the *Arte coquinaria* give for hollowing the center of the quince are not copied by Platina (Recipe VIII,53), who writes merely that the cook should put the filling into cored quinces. Similarly Platina does not mention that marrow should be added to the pie after the quince are set into it.

Earlier in his work Platina comments, interestingly, that as a foodstuff quince are favored particularly in Naples (I,22).

❖ 78. The chapter of ten recipes that begins here and that is headed with the rubric "Stuffings or Fillings" contains an unusual assortment of preparations. We might most easily gloss this rubric with a phrase such as Dishes made with Meat and Fish Pastes. The first five of these seem to have sources other than in the traditional Martino repertoire.

The first of the recipes in this section is for quite a well-known procedure. The compiler seems to have translated a recipe entitled *Spatle farcide* in the *De apereylar be de menyar* (Recipe 88); this Catalan text has been adopted also by the *Sent soví* under the rubric *Com se ffercex espatla de moltó en altra manera* (Recipe 8; see also Recipe 67). In Italian collections something similar can be read in the *Anonimo Toscano* (Recipe 111: *A empiere una spalla*), the *Buone vivande* (Recipe 14: *Spalle di castrone ripiene*), the *Anonimo Veneziano* (Recipe 77: *Spalle de castron implite*), and the Wellcome manuscript (Recipes 189: *Spalla farciata arostita* and 206: *A la spalla de lo castrato*); and in Latin, in the Châlons manuscript (Recipe 62: *De modo preparandi spallam castronis*).

None of these occurrences of the preparation is literally close to our version. The "standard" procedure regularly has ground, seasoned meat wrapped with the shoulder bones in a visceral membrane (caul or omentum: the *rete* or *reticella* already seen above in Recipes 64 and 65), and then roasted on a grill. In our particular copy there is no mention of this *reticella*; what fulfils the function of an envelope is called a *fetta*, a word whose sense elsewhere in our manuscript is simply a "slice." We may speculate that a scribe may not have understood the word *reta* or *retta* in his original, and, having written *fetta* tried to clarify the sense of the passage by adding the words *de altra carne*. In the *De apereylar be de menyar* the direction that we read at this point in the text is *pren hom .i. tela de moltó* . . . , "you get sheep's caul . . . ."

❖ 79. The series of three dishes whose recipes begin here are tantamount to being entertainment pieces such as we saw previously under the rubric *Mirabilia gule*. Being instances of stuffed objects, they all have a close generic relationship with the previous dish of Stuffed Shoulder of Mutton,

[36] See this Catalan text in Appendix C (ii).

but here they present to the diner a complete animal: a fish, a goat kid and a capon. All four of the "stuffed" preparations constitute minor *tours de force* of the professional cook's competence.

The fruit designated here by the name *mela* is uncertain; we have guessed "apple." This is the only occurrence of the word in our collection. Although *grani di melagranata*, "pomegranate seeds," are called for in Recipe 4, the singular *mela* here and its qualification *monda* seem to rule out that interpretation. In other Italian collections *mela cotogna* (quince) and *mela ranze* (orange) are also found. The use of figs in late-medieval European cookery is fairly common, particularly in English and in Mediterranean kitchens, but we do not know of another recipe in which a whole fish is stuffed in this way with spice, figs and (perhaps) apples.

❖ 80. This Stuffed Goat Kid bears some resemblance to the *Cabrit farcit en ast* in the Primitive *Sent soví* (Recipe 189; see this recipe also in the *Sent soví*, Recipe 4, called *Com se ffercex cabrit*). The composition of the stuffing varies significantly, however, there being herbs and onion in the Catalan version but no fruit. An English recipe, called *For to Counterfet a Kidde* in the *Noble Boke of Cookry* (Recipe 29), affords a distant echo of the same sort of procedure: "To counterfet a kidde, take a kid and fley of [off] the skyn and fille it full of swet mete as ye did the capon skyn [*cf.* the next recipe in our collection] and trusse hym on a broche in the maner of a kidde then rost hym and endore hym with yolk of egge and serve it."

At the end of Recipe 82 we find a reference to stuffing boiled, quartered kid.

❖ 81. Among the Wonderful Dishes above, we have already seen a similar stuffing for roast pigeon or dove (Recipe 67, with reference to Recipe 66 for the ingredients). As in Recipe 80 the word *crosta* may refer to a coating or glazing that is to be applied to the stuffed creature before it is roasted.

❖ 82. The concluding advice may refer back to the preceding two recipes, 80 and 81.

❖ 83. With this recipe our cook-compiler begins a series of four recipes that he has incorporated from the collection that, with modifications, will become known as the *Libro de arte coquinaria*. In both Riva and the *Arte coquinaria* (along with Platina's copy of this latter copy, at his Recipe VI,22), the *Cirvelato* remains on the whole textually close to what we read here. Once again our author is alone in specifying Parmesan cheese by name. For Riva and Martino the cheese to be used here is simply *de bon casco vegio*, "some good old cheese." Among all of the Italian recipe collections of the Middle Ages only our collection, Riva, Martino and Platina refer expressly to Parmesan cheese. Other instances here of this particular variety of cheese include Recipes 17, 18, 27, 81, 82, 129 and 133; Riva makes use of Parmesan cheese in only five recipes;[37] and in Martino and Platina we find Parmesan cheese in only one instance.[38]

---

[37] In recipes 87 for *Ravioli gialde*, 105 for *Emelin*, 167 for *Caule* (the Neapolitan Recipe 141), 171 for the *Torta papalle*, and 183 for *Zuppa francese*.

[38] In their Recipes 148 and VIII,50, respectively, for *Ofella*. Curiously, in the Neapolitan Recipe 159 for the same *Offelle* our cook writes only *bono caso spongoso* and does not specify *caso parmesano*.

The phrase *in perfectione* is found in Riva and the *Arte coquinaria* in both its version of the present recipe (Recipe 22 in that latter collection) and later in the recipe on how a sturgeon should not be completely fresh before cooking: *che sia un poco passato, trito o frolo et non frescho se vole che sia bono in perfectione* (Recipe 196).[39] The sense of the phrase has clearly to do with the food being fit to eat, its relative wholesomeness or salubrity. In the Venetian Collection the conclusion of the recipe for *Cervellade bressane* (Recipe 125) reads: *Lassali stare di 2 di saxone*: "Let them hang for two days of maturing (seasoning) [before smoking them]." Riva and the *Arte coquinaria* are uneasy about the value of this two-day period; they add that, *secundo lo tempo e bixogno*, depending on the season and need, and *se serano ben conzi*[40] —provided they are properly prepared—the sausages may, nevertheless, be "good for" fifteen to twenty days or more. Platina's translation is rather remarkably more detailed here than its source: *Bona non nisi biduo durant*: "[They are] not good unless they have hardened for two days .... They can be kept, however, a fortnight or more, if you add more salt and spices or if you dry them in smoke."

The *Cirvelato* sausage is mentioned by name in only Italian and Latin recipes: *Anonimo Veneziano* (Recipe 125), Anonimo "A" (Recipe 1) and "B" (Recipe 52), and the *Liber de coquina* (Recipe 6). In Anonimo "A" and the *Liber de coquina* the sausages are identified as constituting the fifth layer within a Parmesan Pie.

❖ 84. These "Good Sausages" of our collection, Riva and Martino become "Lucanian Preparations" (simply *Lucanicæ*) in Platina (Recipe VI,23). The texts of all four versions are very close. Lucania is a region to the south of Naples. The sausage stuffing is a simple mixture, with quantities of ingredients clearly indicated. The *Anonimo Meridionale* "A" (Recipe 53) contains an interesting lean variety of *Bona Lucanica* that is made of tench. In Chapter 20 of his Book IV Platina explains that a *Patina de linguis aut lucanicis* can also be made of salt tongue.

❖ 85. Ham was preserved and kept in a salted state. When the salt was removed from it, its "shelf life" as an edible meat or ingredient was immediately quite limited. This recipe shows how one may cook such ham but still retain a certain durability for it even in this new state.

Riva, the *Arte coquinaria* and Platina (Recipe VI,36) all reproduce the same method for verifying the freshness of cured ham. The rubric for this recipe that is found in Riva (and the Vatican copy of the *Arte coquinaria*) reflects the relative importance of the first part of the recipe for the later compilers: *Per cognoscere uno presuto se.l e bono o non*: "How to know whether a cooked ham is [still] good." In Riva, bay laurel is added to the herbs sage and rosemary; in neither Martino nor Platina, however, are any of these herbs mentioned, although these warm and dry herbs may have been believed to help preserve the cooked meat by means of an influence analogous to that of salt.

---

[39] The corresponding instruction in the Riva del Garda manuscript has, *Mazello e fallo stare morto per duy di senza cocere che e megliore*—"let it hang, dead, for two days before cooking it, for it is better that way" (Recipe 229).

[40] This is the reading in the Riva del Garda manuscript. The *Libro de arte coquinaria* changes this phrase to *se seranno ben governate*.

❖ 86. *Sommata* is a loin of pork that has been cured by salting.[41] It is a complementary cut to the *persutto* of the previous recipe, and as such the position of the recipe here is entirely reasonable, as are the two addenda concerning salt tongue and any salted meat.

As in the previous recipe, there are in effect two parts to these brief directions: recognizing a good piece of meat, and cooking it. Riva's rubric is as in the Neapolitan manuscript: *Per fare una somata*; as before, though, the rubric written in the *Arte coquinaria* reflects only the first part of the recipe: "How to know when salt loin of pork is good."

❖ 87. This recipe seems to have no counterpart in any known collection of the time.

The second paragraph of the recipe, and particularly the sense of its conclusion, may pose some difficulty. The Latin adverb *saltem*, "at least, at all events, anyhow," indicates that the direction that is to follow is an important variation if one wishes to improve these Bolognese Sausages. The variation bears upon the increased amount of salt and specifies that two of these seventeen ounces of salt should be of the "white" sort. White salt was a universally recognized variety across Europe in the late Middle Ages. The most widely distributed quality of salt was that which was produced on the Adriatic and French Atlantic coasts by the evaporation of seawater, but it tended to be gross in texture and its color was rather dirty from the impurities, animal, vegetable and mineral, in it. Where it was not naturally available for excavation from mineral deposits, a purer, so-called white salt could be produced by a boiling and a second evaporation of the original sea-brine; this "distilling" yielded a product of finer grain, that was more readily soluble when it was used, and whose simple designation, "white," described its distinctive characteristic.[42] Previously, in Recipe 43, our author has already advised the cook against using a coarse, dirty sort of salt: *Se lo sale he bruto, lavalo.*

❖ 88. Our compiler has organized a series of three jellied dishes at this point in his recipe collection. With some apparent enthusiasm for the genre, the Riva compiler amplified this series to six dishes (Recipes 206–11), making up a whole chapter for which he wrote the rubric *Libro sexto per fare gellatina.* Into it he incorporated the Neapolitan recipe for *Una galina in una caraffa* (Recipe 68), which has jelly-like elements. The *Libro de arte coquinaria* retains only three of Riva's recipes for jellied dishes in its shorter series (Recipes 254–56).

Jellied dishes, made from gelatin extracted from animal or fish sources, are gastronomically esteemed compositions in late-medieval cookery. The Riva del Garda manuscript and the *Libro de arte coquinaria* both contain our proceedure for processing animal hooves (alone, despite the rubric, found in all three collections, that refers to fish).[43] While our recipe uses sheep and calf hooves, its counterpart in Riva and Martino uses those of sheep or goat kid.

---

41 It may be noted that the term *sommata* is misread by Faccioli as *sinnata* in his edition of Martino's *Libro de arte coquinaria* (Recipe 37).

42 "Sel blanc, sel noir, l'un éclairait les tables princières, l'autre était destiné au peuple": Jean Claude Hocquet, *Le sel et la fortune de Venise*, 2 volumes (Lille: Université de Lille, 1978); 2, 128–30.

43 The compilers of the Riva collection and the *Libro de arte coquinaria* both write out another variant, longer and slightly more complex, of this animal jelly, at Recipes 206 and 24 respectively. For two servings of it Riva calls for the use four calf hooves and "six or seven" sheep hooves; for the same two

The "woody processes" (*quilli fusti longi*) that are found in the hooves and are to be discarded are perhaps more plainly described in the later versions as *l'osso dele gambe*. The *Arte coquinaria* goes a little further, explaining *l'ossi — cio e, i fusi de le gambe*: "the long leg-bone."

Our cook is conscious of the very unusual flavour that the spice called grains of paradise will give to this dish when he stresses, *fa ch'ela senta bene de grana paradisi*. This direction is not found in either of the other versions. One may well wonder how much influence was exerted on this recipe by French cookery, where grains of paradise enjoyed a much greater vogue by the beginning of the fifteenth century than in Italy.

One of the colorants used to produce a green hue in the jelly is noteworthy. What the Neapolitan author specifies is the first green sprouts or shoots of the wheat plant (*grano*), leaves available in the winter and early spring when, presumably, few other green vegetable colorants could readily be had. The use of the wheat plant for this purpose was relatively common practice: the *Viandier* of Taillevent (Recipe 170) lists *ble vert en yver* among other foodstuffs (parsley, herb bennet, sorrel, vine leaves, vine shoots and currants) that may be relied upon to yield a green colorant. To this *grano* Riva adds another possible source of green — barley sprouts: ... *et per farlo verde, haray della grana o del orzo quando he in herba*;[44] the *Arte coquinaria* further clarifies the word *herba*: *foglia del grano o dell'orzo quando e in herba*.

The production of a lustrous blue-green colorant for the jelly poses a problem. Our text assures us that the ground scrapings (*leva un pezo de la scorza et pista*) from "cooked" carrots will yield the desired peacock blue or violet. On the face of it, this seems doubtful. Even if we were to understand that "cooked" implies roasted (*sotto le braxe*) as the carrots are in Recipe 117, it is still difficult to understand how, combined with such scrapings, the jelly will become any closer to the hue known as *paonazzo*. Two explanations might be suggested. Firstly, that an ingredient with which the carrot might be mixed, has been omitted; again, though, it is difficult to imagine just what this hypothetical ingredient might be. Alternatively we might conjecture that the word *carotte* is a misreading here for some other colorant.[45] For a blue color in a similar multi-colored jelly the *Menagier de Paris* specifies the use of two ounces of *tournesot* — obtainable, the author indicates, from the local spicer — with which the meat or fish jelly is to be boiled (Recipe 252). This colorant,

---

servings the Martino scribes nonchalantly direct the cook to begin with *forty* sheep hooves. Platina's *Gelu — quod vulgo "gelatinam" vocamus* (Recipe VI,24) — translates this recipe in Martino in all details.

44 This same compilation again suggests a use of these sprouts for a green colorant in its version of our Recipe 127 (*Herbollata de mazo*, Recipe 144): *Per farla piu verde, toglieray dela blada quando e alto uno palmo in herba, et pistalla ben insema*: the wheat should have sprouted a palm's width out of the ground.

45 It may be noted that blue was a particularly difficult color for medieval cooks to obtain. One German recipe collection (Hans Wiswe, "Ein mittelniederdeutsches Kochbuch des 15. Jahrhunderts," *Braunschweigisches Jahrbuch* 37 (1956): 19–55; Recipe 93, page 46) directs that unopened columbine blossoms be plucked and ground with honey; the French *Viandier* (Recipe 199) calls for the use of *asur fin*, which is probably the mineral lazurite or lapis lazuli, finely powdered. On lapis lazuli, see the commercial treatise of Francesco Balducci Pegolotti, *La Pratica della Mercatura*, ed. Allen Evans (Cambridge, Mass.: Mediæval Academy of America, 1936), 372.

an orchil lichen now identified as *Gozophora tinctoria*, was much valued in French and English[46] cookery of the time because, like modern litmus, it could be relied upon to produce either a red or a blue color depending upon whether, respectively, it entered an acid or an alkaline mixture.

However, despite our doubts, the version of this recipe copied by the *Riva del Garda* scribe (at Recipe 208) confirms the wording of our text.

> *... Similmente potray fare pavonazo l'altro quarto biancho, havendo delle corate cocte sotto le braxe, et mondate destramente con lo cortello quella parte di sopra che ha collore de pavonaza, et quello metteray nel fondo del sacho in nel quele se colla la decoctione dela gellatina; et tante volte reservando lo metteray sopra quello biancho brodo rischaldato al focho che habia ben preso lo dicto collore ....*

Other than changing Riva's word *corate* to *carote*, the Martino version (at p. 198 in the Faccioli edition) agrees textually with this procedure. It would seem that an upper[47] portion of this root (?) has in itself a *collore de pavonaza* which can be used to color this dish.

❖ 89. The problem for which this recipe suggests an attractive solution is likely originally to have been associated with the presentation of a jellied dish. When the jelly was set, suspending within it, as here, chunks of capon or other meat, was it merely to be dumped out of its container or mold onto a plate and served up unimaginatively as a shapeless, quivering mound? A strikingly charming alternative was to present the jelly in a basket; this option presented a professional challenge to the cook's skill and inventiveness, but also offered a means by which the cook who was truly *discreto* could increase his honor. As the writers of Riva and the *Arte coquinaria* say, concerning the whole fish that will be as if suspended in a wicker cage, it will look alive and be pretty to see: ... *che parira vivo et parira de bello da videre.*

The final admonition to the cook is unique to the Neapolitan manuscript.

❖ 90. The checkerboard pattern is an interesting use of two-colored jelly.

❖ 91. The *Zupa d'Oro* was a relatively international preparation. The modern equivalent would generally be known as "French Toast." The preparation is properly a "sop" only to the extent that the sweet yellow serving sauce covers the toast in the manner of a standard sop. In a late manuscript of the *Viandier* (Recipe 198) a similar recipe is a little less picturesquely called *Tostees dorees*, "Gilded Toast."

This recipe is rather freely reproduced by Riva and Martino (with a lot of sugar added to the egg mixture in which the slices of toast are to be soaked) as *Zuppa indorata* and *Suppa dorata*; Platina does not even bother to include it in his collection. The Wellcome manuscript of Italian recipes contains a *Zuppa de Lauret* (Recipe 155: the name here suggests a scribal error) that resembles this recipe but in which, a little strangely, the eggs are to be boiled first. This preliminary boiling,

---

[46] In the *Forme of Cury* (Recipe 69), for instance, *turnesole* is used to produce the *paonazzo* color — written *pownas* by the English scribe. The term *pavonazo* caused difficulties even for Italian scribes: Recipe 113 in the *Arte coquinaria* for *Mostarda roscia o pavonaza* turns up as *Mostarda rossa padovana* in Recipe 114 of the MS Urbinate latino 1203.

[47] Upper, unless our author's *ut supra* was misunderstood!

which would seem to destroy the function of the eggs, is an integral part of a series of English recipes entitled variously *Soppes dorre* or *Sowpes dorry*, but in which there are no eggs at all, just almond milk and saffron, boiled: *Forme of Cury* (Recipe 84), *Diversa servicia* (Recipe 65), Austin's second manuscript (Recipe 103), *Stere hit well* (Recipe 3) and the *Liber cure cocorum* (in the third course of the menu). The Italian *Manoscritto Lucano* continues to present a *Suppa indorea* (Recipe 24) but which is considerably enriched with ingredients such as ground almonds, liver (as in our next recipe), apples and poultry.

❖ 92. This recipe does not seem to have been copied in the *Arte coquinaria* or the *Honesta voluptate*. These spicy sops of ground spiced chicken liver are understood by our compiler to be typically Aragonese: they turn up later in the *Manoscritto Lucano* (Recipe 25) with the modified name *Suppa a la catelana*.

❖ 93. While the *Soffritto* in Riva and the *Suffritto* in the *Arte coquinaria* conclude by indicating that this dish may be either sweet or tart ("depending on popular taste or your master's taste"), to obtain the relative degree of sweetness or tartness those versions do not reproduce the particular means that the Neapolitan cook suggests: must syrup or honey or sugar. At the beginning of the sixteenth century the *Manoscritto Lucano* affords a separate recipe for each taste, a *Suffritto agro* (Recipe 22) and a *Suffritto dolce* (Recipe 23), each for pigeon; both varieties of the dish contain orange juice (a distinctly bitter element, where the Neapolitan Collection is still using verjuice), but the *dolce* dish contains additionally "a good chunk of sugar."

The "boiled must" syrup that will ensure an optional sweet flavor for this dish is mentioned by the Neapolitan cook in several other recipes; it appears as an ingredient in Recipes 101, 122, 217 and 193 as well as here. Our author uses the term *mosto* only in conjunction with *cotto*; for this syrup he also uses the term *sabba*. Because must is a relatively fresh, unfermented grape juice, the difficulty with keeping it even briefly is that an unwanted fermentation will set in and, eventually, end any particular usefulness of the juice. A way of limiting this sort of spoilage and of extending the life of the juice a little, and at the same time of concentrating its qualities, was to both "pasteurize" and concentrate it by boiling.

The manuscript at Châlons offers the following directions for producing this syrup from the juice of the must grape.

> [Recipe 96; f° 56v] *Modus conservandi mustum coctum pro coquinis et pro mustarda. Recipe mustum novum et tamen coque que remaneat quarta pars, et cave bene a fumo. Et si vis facere* Mustardam, *recipe seminem sinapis mundam et mollificatam in aceto, et maçina bene cum macinis duabus vicibus et cum sale et distempera cum dicto musto cocto; et repone et conservabitur per quatuor menses; et valet pro carnibus porcinis recentibus et salitis et pro aliis carnibus lixatis et assatis et pro piscibus lixis et frictis et aliis; et qui valet dictum mustum coctum pro aliis vivandis et ferculis preparandis acriter et dulciter.*

From this must syrup is made the so-called Italian Mustard of Recipe 122.

❖ 94. This dish is an open-faced, cheese "sandwich" which is baked on the coals in a covered dish. A century after our Collection, according to the Accademici della Crusca, a *crostata* will be defined primarily by its "crusts" without reference to its contents or other ingredients.[48] In two other collections a similar *crostata* is found, the base being either bread or a piece of pastry dough, this latter presumably of much the same size as a slice from a rounded mound of bread. In the *Libro de arte coquinaria* a *Crostata de pippioni o de pollastri, etc.* (Recipe 10) makes up a mixture of partially cooked fowl, fruit, eggs and herbs, and spreads this on the crust; in the Latin collection at Châlons (Recipe 133: *De crostata piscium*) a similar mixture of fish paste similarly covers the crust before being baked in a dish in (and under) the coals. The use of crustless toast in our collection seems a handy shortcut.

❖ 95. In a short sequence here, several recipes, beginning with this *Pumata*, are perhaps indirectly related to counterparts in the Catalan compendium by Mestre Robert, the *Libre del coch*. This dish of applesauce is basically the same as Robert's *De pomada* (Recipe 35), though the latter's mixture is considerably more spicy.[49] By the beginning of the sixteenth century the *Manoscritto Lucano* has a *Pumata bureglia* (Recipe 12) which precooks the apples in honey and then simmers them in a similar spicy broth.

❖ 96. The name of this dish, *Sfresurato*, is influenced by the Catalan word for the Italian *coratella*, "lungs and organs," that we find in the text. In Robert's *Libre del coch* the recipe titled *Frexurat* (Recipe 42) bears some resemblance to ours but makes the pluck undergo a boiling before being cut up and fried, and then boiled again with the sauce. In Robert this cooking sauce has a base of almond milk.

❖ 97. If this recipe appears brief and too simple to be complete, this is because it is, in fact, one of the simplest of recipes. It is also closely related to the following recipe; as there, the important element of the dish lies in the sense of the qualification *stillato*. The word is cognate with the word "distilled": as the leg of meat is cooked in a sealed container, with no other ingredients and very little additional moisture, the liquid that is exuded is held to represent the essence (and in a real sense, the quintessence) of the meat itself. The only foreign substance in the container is rosewater, which is itself a distillate and so considered to contain marvelous properties, particularly for the healing of diseases. In other recipe collections this or the following recipe, or variants of them, are normally included in the chapter devoted to dishes for the sick.

When the distilled potion is served to a sick person, the cooked meat is normally discarded—or at least it does not appear to be used in any further culinary procedure.

❖ 98. This dish, in which the juice of the meat is extracted or "distilled" in a sealed flask which is part of a double-boiler, echoes the *Eaue rose d'un chapon* that is found in the French *Viandier* (Recipe 91) and the *Menagier de Paris* (Recipe 300). In both of these versions the finished preparation is expressly a beverage prepared for the sick. The procedure outlined here is well known in the world of professional cookery in the late Middle Ages, but an interesting and closer use of it is found in

---

[48] *Crostata: Torta, detta così dalle croste di pasta, chela si fanno sopra. Lat. potremmo dire* morettum, *e'l Platina chiamò la torta,* pulmentum.

[49] See the text of Mestre Robert's recipes in Appendix C (iii).

Mestre Robert's *Libre del coch, De estillat* (Recipe 101). Because the juice—whether fortified by rosewater or not—that the chicken yields is produced by a method that bears a certain affinity with the production of liquors by distillation, the chicken water is held to possess properties similar in potency to those of *aqua vitæ*: the flask yielded a virtual quintessence of chicken, and this had virtually miraculous powers as a universal remedy. As Robert adds at the end of his recipe for *Estillat: E sapies que y haura una bona quantitat de brou* [that is, of the "distilled" chicken water]; *e aquest brou e una cosa la mes maravellosa para malalts del mon.*

❖ 99. While apparently a simple preparation and perhaps, if we may judge by its name, a relatively popular one, the recipe here seems to be faulty. There are no explicit directions concerning the preparation of the meat or its cooking. It may be that, as in Recipe 46 for *Carne de capreto ho de carnero*, the salted meat is to be boiled until the point of disintegration; for that dish the text reads, *lassa bulire tute insieme fina tanto che la carne si diffacia.*

Under this name the recipe is not well known. The only other instance of the dish's name, apparently a variant of the dish in both name and ingredients, is found in the *Modus viaticorum preparandorum et salsarum.*[50] If these dishes are the same, our version of the recipe is, if clearer, a little less explicit as far as the procedure to be followed is concerned. According to the *Modus*, the meat is to be formed into moderate-sized balls.

❖ 100. A very rough distinction may be essayed between serving sauces (*sapore*), a series of which begins here, and cooking sauces (*salse*, beginning at Recipe 112). A *sapore* is a garnish with which to eat the preparation; in a sense it is both supplementary and complementary. A *salsa* is integral to the dish; it helps to determine the nature of the final preparation. Earlier, the recipe for a Stuffing for a Shoulder of Ram (Recipe 78) concludes, *et quando* [*la spalla*] *sera cotta, da per suo sapore salsa cum juivert.* The *sapore* is valued for its faculty of imparting flavor to a preparation. Boiled meats are usually cooked *with* a *salsa*; the same "broth" may serve as a *sapore* or "serving sauce" when the cooked dish is presented at the table. Pies have their *sapore* added into them toward the end of their baking (see Recipes 74 and 75). On the other hand roast meats usually have this *sapore* added just before they are served, as is the case for the Roast Kid of Recipe 54. Alternatively, the *sapore* could be brought to the table in bowls for the diner to dip the meats into it.

---

[50] Edited by Carole Lambert, *Trois réceptaires culinaires médiévaux*, Doctoral thesis (Montréal: Université de Montréal, 1989):

> *Matafeam. Ad faciendum matafeam, scinde in partes gallinam. Deinde recipe julvertum et sepe minutatum et sauzenguera cum callinis, cum pinguedine liquefacta, cum modico aque. Deinde recipe unum parum de carne porcii fracta minutatim cum pinguedine mutonis cruda. Postquam recipe gyngibre, granam paradisii, safran et de sale circumposito in carne porci cum speciebus et fac pomellos modicos. Et pone eos bullire cum gallinis. Recipe plus gyngibre, pebre, girofle, croceum, julvertum, mentam, majoranam, mole, distempera cum ovis et conjunge totum in una cassa. Et pone unum parum de caseo fracto in partes et unum parum de brodio carnium et totum hoc conjunge. Et pone super pruynas vivas longe ab igne. Et pone super cassam unam trabam calidam cum pruyna viva. Et custodi ne uratur vel cremetur.* Recipe 18.

The author of the Venetian collection writes of a *civiro over savore* (Recipe 15) as if the term *savore* could be used by itself to designate a variety of broth or stew. The distinction is also recognized in the Anonimo Meridionale "A", although the order there is the reverse: *salse*, from Recipe 37 (and including Garlic Sauce, Must Syrup and Pepper Sauce), and then *sapori*, from Recipe 47, where the preparations include such garnishes as Pepper Sauce and are particularly for roasted meats and fish.

The series from Recipe 100–Recipe 111 in the Neapolitan Collection presents two sorts of recipes: on the one hand, complete dishes that combine a specific foodstuff with an appropriate cooking sauce (properly *salse* which become *sapore*), and on the other a selection of *sapore* in conjunction with which no specific foodstuff is specified. Their particular use would seem to be more general and to depend upon the cook's taste or that of his master. The present recipe for a *Sapore a polastri spezati*, the next one for *Sapore a lepore* and the *Sapore a pipione spezato he soffrito* (Recipe 103) all show the sauce being used after a meat has been cooked by frying. The first sauce is brought into close contact with the meat during a brief boiling; the other *sapore* of this series may be intended to be used in a similar way.

❖ 101. The combination of two ingredients, verjuice and wine syrup, that will explicitly make this dish at the same time both bitter and sweet, is to be noted. The final direction in this recipe is significant: a cooking sauce may simply be discarded, or it may be served to table either *on* the cooked food (as here) or *with* the cooked food, in bowls or dishes alongside the serving platter or trencher on which the food is heaped. In the version of this dish that is found in the *De apereylar be de menyar*, *Cunils ab sosengua* (Recipe 63: see the text in Appendix C), the processes of the preparation are similar but the ingredients are not identical. This Catalan recipe has a counterpart in the *Sent soví* (Recipe 82). On p. 116, n. 1 of his edition of this work, Grewe defines a Catalan *sosengua* or *soengua* as a procedure for preparing meat that consists of three stages: the meat or fish is fried, cut-up parboiled onion is added and the frying continued, and bread (or toast) is soaked in an appropriate liquid, added and the frying completed. Even though the generic classification is missing from the Neapolitan version of this recipe — perhaps because it was untranslatable — this version remains a *sosengua*.

❖ 102. This cooking sauce, for which no appropriate meat is mentioned, has its name to recommend it. Inserted by our scribe as an addition in the lower margin of folio 40v, it seems to be unknown in any other recipe collection.

❖ 103. This recipe is likewise unknown elsewhere in a form close to what is read here.

❖ 104. This White Sauce is basically a variety of ginger sauce, what French recipes of the preceding century generically called a *jance*. Though fairly common elsewhere, in our collection it is called for expressly only in Recipes 199 and 207. The recipe is found in Riva and Martino with the same name and a similar text. The later texts tend by their wordiness to confuse the clear simplicity of our version, though. There the almond mixture is strained with verjuice *or* the fruit juices. Riva and Martino also write that the sauce can be made sweet (with sugar) *and* tart (with verjuice and orange juice) according to taste. A final note in these other collections evinces a slight garbling: originally the note possibly read that White Sauce was suitable anytime for any boiled meat — *ogni carne alesso*; the juxtaposition of *tempo* and *carne* may have suggested the opposition of meat dishes and lean/Lenten dishes. Perhaps as a consequence of this, the notation as written in Riva might befuddle an inattentive reader: *De talle sapore si po fare in tempo di carne alesso et in tempo di quaresma*; in Martino the ambiguity is lessened: *Tal sapore si vol dare con ogni allesso a tempo di carne o di quadragesima.*

In the anonymous Catalan *Libre de sent soví* (Recipe 53) this ginger sauce is called *Gingebrada* and is a cold serving sauce primarily for roast fowl, rabbit and hare.

❖ 105. Two principal varieties of spice sauce were made and eaten everywhere in late-medieval Europe, one made from ginger and one whose basic ingredient was cinnamon. We have just seen the Neapolitan cook's treatment of the ginger sauce, which he knows as White Sauce. The cinnamon sauce follows here; its name, normally *Camellino*, as Riva and the extant Martino compilation later call it, actually derives from the brownish camel-color that the ground cinnamon imparts to it.

This recipe for Cameline Sauce follows the one for White Sauce in the other collections as well. Both of the later works (together with Platina's translation, *Condimentum camellinum*, Recipe VIII,3) entirely omit any mention of almonds, but give a supplementary choice of vinegar rather than verjuice in order to obtain the (really) tart taste that their authors think might hold some interest for their patrons.

❖ 106. Two further sauces that are known known by their color follow here: a peach-blossom sauce and a genista-yellow sauce. The sequence of these sauce recipes in Riva, Martino and Platina (Recipes VIII,7 and 8) remains that of the Neapolitan Collection, but the other collections have enriched their readers' choices in this matter by inserting three additional recipes for sauces not represented in our collection: a so-called Peacock Sauce, a Prune Sauce and a Green Sauce. It is surprising that the Neapolitan cook has not included a recipe for *Salsa verde* in his book: it is certainly one of the most common and simple culinary preparations in Europe at this time.

The name of the *Sapore dito fiore de persico* must derive from its color rather than from an ingredient; the ginger and cinnamon, and particularly the sandalwood, would indeed lend the sauce a "peach-blossom" color.

❖ 107. This sauce is named, as with the previous one, for the resemblance of its hue to that of a flower, in this case genista or broom. Still in the same series of sauces that is followed, with additions, in Riva and the *Arte coquinaria* (and in the *Honesta voluptate*), this quite popular yellow preparation — whose name we saw incorporated into the dish bizarrely called *Genestrata biancha* (Recipe 39) — contains the same ingredients in these other collections. It is basically a cold, yellow, ginger sauce.

❖ 108. To make the *Sapore de uva negra* our author (with those of the Riva manuscript and of the *Arte coquinaria*) writes that the dark grapes should be crushed *in uno vaso*. For some reason Platina was unhappy with this "vessel" because he writes *in mortario* (Recipe VIII,9). As for their Cameline Sauce, Riva, Martino and Platina offer a choice here of using vinegar rather than verjuice, a choice that is not in our manuscript.

❖ 109. This Cherry or Sour Cherry Sauce is the last in the series of *sapore* which are also copied by Riva, Martino and Platina, and copied in the same order. However, between the previous sauce (for *Uva negra*) and this one, the other recipe collections insert a Mulberry Sauce (*Sapore de morroni*) that has no counterpart in the Neapolitan Collection. In setting out the present recipe, Riva and the *Arte coquinaria* are considerably more vague than our text: in our manuscript the recipe that is to serve as model for this Cherry Sauce immediately precedes it and our author can easily refer back to it. In the other collections the Mulberry Sauce recipe now intervenes. Moreover, the compilers of Riva and the *Arte coquinaria* do not seem to understand the nature of the variable between *visole* and *cerase*, and make their title *Cerasse negre o visolli.* Rather than following the optional procedure offered in our collection, those compilers (and Platina, blindly, in Recipe VIII,11) write: " ... but [the cook] can vary the color more or less depending on the ingredients he puts in."

❖ 110. This sauce is not copied in the *Arte coquinaria.* As for Recipe 56, our compiler's source for this recipe may have been the Catalan *De apereylar be de menyar* where the name of the sauce is *Limonia* (Recipe 96). The sauce or broth called *Limonata* does recur in a good number of Catalan, Italian and Latin recipe collections where its name varies from *Limoneha*, *Lamonia* and *Lumonia* to *Limonieyra.* See the *Sent soví* (Recipe 52), *Anonimo Toscano* (Recipe 98), *Anonimo Veneziano* (Recipe 119), *Buone vivande* (1Recipe 3), Wellcome (Recipe 104), *Dilicate* (Recipe 26), *Liber de coquina* (Recipe II,12), *Viaticorum* (Recipe 41). Some of these versions of the sauce, such as in the *Frammento* (Recipe 14, repeated at Recipe 43) have no lemons at all in them; some make use of oranges rather than lemons. The recipes in *Anonimo* "A" (Recipe 127, in Latin) and in Wellcome (Recipe 231) resemble one another, as do those in *Anonimo* "A" (Recipe 18) and in Wellcome (Recipe 192).

❖ 111. This use of marzipan, liquified and seasoned, as a preparatory sauce seems to be unique to the Neapolitan Collection. This sauce will have a tart, gingery taste.

❖ 112. Historically (and etymologically) the *salsa* was originally a means of correcting an inappropriate humoral temperament in a foodstuff. For this reason certain sauces were deemed to be appropriate for certain meats or principal foodstuffs in a dish. While a serving garnish could effect a last-minute modification of the dish's properties, the most efficient means to temper the potentially harmful complexion of a foodstuff was to bring the seasoning into intimate contact with it during the cooking process.

Many of the recipes in the series of cooking sauces (*salse*) that begins here have been derived from outside the Martino tradition. Compare the present recipe with Recipe 1, above, for a Pepper Sauce for game, itself a part of that tradition however faithfully rendered. The Catalan collection *De apereylar be de menyar* has a counterpart for the *Salsa ad ogni bestia salvatica* at Recipe 97, a recipe that is echoed in the *Libre de sent soví* in Recipe 90. This first recipe of the series of *salse* is for a standard variety of thickened, yellowish spice sauce, but with the further unique addition of verjuice and honey. This latter bitter-sweet combination is particularly favored by our cook. Because it is to function as both a cooking sauce and a serving garnish, it is to be presented to the table in bowls and placed beside the platter of meat; the diners will dip their meat into this sauce.

Though far from being unknown in late-medieval European kitchens, honey is not a common ingredient in Italian cookery of this time. As sugar became more available and cheaper, and as European palates formed a taste for sugar, the industry of beekeeping came to depend more upon the demand for wax from the combs than for honey. None of the three occurrences of honey in our collection appears in the *Arte coquinaria*.

❖ 113. The text here is largely identical in wording to the Catalan recipe *Carn a la sarraynesque* in the *De apereylar be de menyar* (Recipe 111) and in the copy made of it and called *Con cuynarets carn a la sarreÿnesca* in the *Libre de sent soví* (Recipe 181). Our version omits instructions that hot water or bouillon be added while the contents of the pot are cooking.

A definition of what it means to "cook in the Saracen fashion" is only implicit here. The phrase describes a process in which a meat, that has been reduced to small pieces and moistened in water, is sauteed in fat and vinegar along with and at the same time as onions and herbs, but with no spices. Unfortunately, this present instance of the qualification "Saracen" in a culinary sense seems to suggest little relationship with what is found elsewhere, where the terms *saracenico* and *sarsoun* qualify dishes in Italian, French and English cookery. In these other broths and sauces (including the French *Sarraginee* of the thirteenth-century *Enseignements* and the popular *Sorengue*), the meat is frequently precooked, various fruits appear, spices are plentiful and the sweetness of sugar often plays against the tartness of vinegar or citrus juices; a thickener, such as liver, rice flour or egg yolks, is often included.

The final instruction, "Serve this up to Saracens!" hints at the author's sense of humor, and perhaps also at his opinion of the gastronomic value of this preparation. The witticism is not found in his Catalan source.

❖ 114. The name of this serving sauce seems to indicate both the breadth of its possible use and it banality. Its name and the beginning of its text are, virtually verbatim, those of the *De apereylar be de menyar* (Recipe 148). Even the quantity of saffron, expressed in terms of its value, remains merely an adaptation: *.viii. diners* becomes our *otto tornesi*.

❖ 115. This Lombard Sauce is a cold green garlic sauce.

❖ 116. It is difficult to say just what is typically French about this sauce. The text here is close to what Mestre Robert wrote in his *Libre del coch* for a *Bona sals francesa* (Recipe 85). As well, Robert directs the cook, "*Assaborir-ho has que sia agra dolç*": the finished sauce should be bitter-sweet.

❖ 117. This recipe for a carrot sauce seems to be unique among all known sauces of the period. We may wonder whether its name reflects a noted gastronomic predilection on the part of a contemporary Pope.

The direction that the carrots be cooked *sotto le braxe* should not evoke an image of carbon-coated vegetables: the author implies the use of a covered baking dish (elsewhere called a *trapa*) of which the concave cover could be filled with live embers or coals. This procedure allowed a foodstuff to be cooked "dry" in only its own moisture, and was an alternative to boiling (see Recipes 176 and 185) or roasting; it did not call for an oven.

❖ 118. Our author continues his reference to what may have been local taste and culinary practice: appropriately, he adds a recipe for a *Salsa regale* following his *Salsa papale*. Both of them seem to be *unica* among the recipes of extant collections. A hot sauce, the "royal" preparation prevents even fine particles of the spices from entering its mixture: the ginger and cinnamon are not ground but merely "broken" so that their flavor infuses, by boiling slowly and at great length, into the vinegar. The combination of strong vinegar and fine, readily dissoluble sugar ensures a bitter-sweet sauce. It is relatively mildly flavored and thin.

❖ 119. This cold sauce is a remarkable and quite unusual compound of ingredients. Riva and the *Arte coquinaria* simplify the mixture considerably by omitting both the basil and the pepper, as little as this latter might have been in the Neapolitan sauce.

❖ 120. The versions of this sauce are identical in our collection and in Riva and Martino. In Riva the name of the preparation is explicitly *Salza deli pampani dele vitte*; curiously this is reduced to merely *Salsa* in the *Arte coquinaria*, although Platina, in turn, is rather more expansive in naming the dish *Moretum pampinaceum quod salsam vocant* in his *Honesta voluptate* (Recipe VIII,21).

The culinary use of the leaves or shoots of fresh garlic, is not common. Riva's Recipe 124 for *Salza verde* (*Arte coquinaria*, Recipe 105) calls for them when only a slight garlic flavor is desired: *. . . e se vole ch'ela* [the Green Sauce] *senta d'aglio, ne potray pistare con le cosse supradicte con qualche fronde de agleto.*

❖ 121. The recipe here is copied from the Primitive *Sent soví*, where Recipe 209 is titled *Mostayla francesa*. Our first sentence alone reproduces the entire Catalan text.

In his second sentence here, in a tone that makes one think of Platina, our Neapolitan author displays a quite exceptional contempt for a particular foreign treatment of a preparation. Apart from the fact that, according to our Neapolitan cook, French Mustard is not based upon must at all (see the following recipe), he avers that it "lacks head and feet"—seemingly because it does not have the smooth, thick texture that almonds lend good Italian-style mustard, and perhaps also because, being made only of a vinegar or wine syrup, it lacks the richer body and bite of must syrup or verjuice.

This recipe does not appear in Riva or the *Arte coquinaria*. Given the poor opinion our Neapolitan author has of French Mustard, that he chose to insert it here at this point in his collection *ahead* of Italian Mustard seems to suggest that his Catalan source or sources regularly enjoyed preference over his Italian ones.

❖ 122. Etymologically, mustard sauce, or simply mustard, is a combination of must and the seed of the plant *Sinapis nigra*, the latter giving the former a "burning" zest. The making of Mustard, with must syrup (see Recipe 93) though without almond paste, is described in the Châlons manuscript.[51]

---

51 *[f° 56v] Modus conservandi mustum coctum pro coquinis et pro mustarda: recipe mustum novum et tamen coque que remaneat quarta pars, et cave bene a fumo. Et si vis facere Mustardam, recipe seminem sinapis mundam et mollificatam in aceto, et macina bene cum macinis duabus vicibus et cum sale et distempera cum dicto musto cocto; et repone et conservabitur per quatuor menses; et valet pro carnibus porcinis recentibus et salitis et pro aliis carnibus lixatis et assatis et pro piscibus lixis et frictis et aliis. Et qui valet dictum mustum coctum pro aliis vivandis et ferculis preparandis acriter et dulciter.* Recipe 96.

According to that source, mustard may appropriately be used on pork and, seemingly, on virtually any other foodstuff.

The Neapolitan recipe for Italian Mustard is picked up in Riva and the *Arte coquinaria*, as well as later in the *Honesta voluptate* (Recipe VIII,13: *Sinapidum*), but without the qualification "Italian." These latter versions allow vinegar as an optional alternative to verjuice but make no mention of the must syrup that we find in the Neapolitan version—as well as in the so-called French Mustard, about which neither Riva nor Martino apparently know.

❖ 123. This recipe for dried balls of enriched mustard allow a glimpse of Italian travelling customs in the mid-fifteenth century. The recipe permits a variety of liquids to be used to moisten the balls when the time comes to eat them, in all likelihood because the traveller is not apt to be able to lay his or her hands on any particular one of them. Both Riva and the *Arte coquinaria* (and the *Honesta voluptate*, Recipe VIII,15) drop pepper from the mustard mixture—pepper seeming to be a spice to which their common source was not overly partial. Rather than specify "walnut-sized" balls, the later collections describe round balls and cubes "of any size you like" into which the mustard paste may be formed.

❖ 124. This Slavonic or (simply) Garlic Sauce may be employed either as a cooking sauce (a *salsa*) or as a serving sauce (a *sapore*). The dual potential of this sauce is not uncommon, but is perhaps appropriate for the final item of the two series of sauces. An interesting walnut-and-garlic mixture, it has a later echo in the Riva del Garda manuscript and in the *Arte coquinaria* where, in the first, almonds are mixed in with the walnuts and, in the second, *noce* are not even mentioned, the preparation having become merely another variety of almond sauce.

Likewise in these other versions a pepper garnish is no longer used,[52] nor is there any interest in coloring the sauce with either saffron, black grapes or cherries. In both of the "Martino" collections this recipe's name has been changed to simply *Agliata biancha*. The sense of the original name, containing the qualification of "Slavonic," as this appears in the Neapolitan Collection, is not obvious. The alternative name the Neapolitan cook provides, ... *ho vero Agliata*, seems to suggest that the qualification hinges merely upon the basis of the composition in garlic. The use of walnuts, the ingredient affected by later reworkings, may also be significant.

❖ 125. With this recipe we pass into a substantial series of recipes for tortes. In Recipe 13 (for a *Crostata de capone, pizoni, pollastri o capreti*), the Riva del Garda manuscript directs that the pan with its small flat patty of dough is to be placed on the fire "as if it were *una torta*." (The same recipe with the same instruction is echoed in the *Libro de arte coquinaria* at Recipe 10.) Similarly in our Recipe 150 an omelet is expressly made to function as a sheet of pastry does in a *torta*.

[52] A subsequent author will develop the final option mentioned by our Neapolitan cook (... *se la vorai pavonaza* ...) and insert it as a new recipe at this point. Recipes 135 in Riva and 118 in the *Arte coquinaria* will represent a distinct variety of sauce, *Agliata pavonaza* or "Violet" Garlic Sauce. Significantly, to it the compiler of the Riva del Garda manuscript appends the following declaration: *Nota che ogni agliato volle havere uno pocho di pipero et fenochio*, "Note that every [sort of] garlic sauce should have a little pepper and fennel."

The White Torte is the first dish in its chapter here as well as in Riva and the *Arte coquinaria* (and the *Honesta voluptate*, Recipe VIII,26). In both compilations the recipe follows a rubric — *Libro quarto per fare ogni rasone di torta* — and begins a sequence of seven pies that more or less faithfully reproduce the same order and texts as are in the Neapolitan manuscript. The *Torta biancha* is essentially a single-crusted cheese custard pie made with fine pastry dough. It is baked in a pan with a lid, the pan being placed into a fire with low heat below and above. The ingredients of the mixture are chosen for their whiteness; only egg *whites* (whose numbers are increased to twelve or fifteen in the later copies, rather than the "ten or twelve" here) are to be used.

A lean counterpart to this dish might be the *Tartari bianchi* of Recipe 186.

❖ 126. Using a little less cheese and fewer eggs than the White Torte, the Bolognese Torte seems to be peculiar in its use of herbs (parsley and marjoram) and chard, and in its green and yellowish-red hue — the saffron yielding the latter color. This "gaudy-green" or *vertgay* coloring was popular in late-medieval cookery; see it used in Recipe 45 as well. Riva, Martino and Platina insist upon a very distinct yellow glazing when they direct that an egg yolk be mixed with saffron. As is usual, none of the later versions directs that the pie "have a good smell of pepper" as we read here; nor do they offer the possible alternative "upper crust" composed of broad slices of *probatura* cheese.[53] All versions refer to the rising of the upper crust as a sign that the pie is done.

❖ 127. This May Herb Dish is, despite its name, still a variety of torte. It bears a certain affinity with the Bolognese Tort that precedes it in the Neapolitan Collection and in the other Italian compilations related to it. The major differences between the two dishes appear to be that this *Herbulata* has many more eggs, more, even, than the *Torta biancha*: this present dish is more like a modern custard pie. As well it has a gingery-herbal flavor and is a bright yellow-green in color. In the version copied in Riva and the *Arte coquinaria*, "a lot" of sage (*salvia asay*) is also added to the greenery, and "fifteen or sixteen" egg whites (alone) leave the final mixture with a predominantly green hue.

❖ 128. Riva, the *Arte coquinaria* and the *Honesta voluptate* (Recipe VIII,29) reproduce all of the fundamental elements of this Squash (or Pumpkin or Gourd) Torte. A torte is normally an open-faced pie; the inventive use of strips of lasagna here in lieu of an upper crust is to be noted.

When the *ventresca de porco* is described as being cooked well enough to be beaten with a knife, it is helpful to read Recipe 130, for *Torta de farro*, where a *ventresca de vitella* is similarly cooked until it is *quasi diffata*, "almost disintegrating."

❖ 129. Before writing out this recipe for a Rich Rice Torte, Riva and the so-called Martino copies (and Platina) insert four other recipes for pies in their collections, including one for a sort of crustless millet pie that appears in our manuscript a little later. Our *Torta grassa cum riso* is renamed slightly in Riva to *Torta grassa in riso*, and to simply a *Torta di riso* and a *Torta ex riso* in the *Arte coquinaria* and the *Honesta voluptate* (Recipe VIII,34). All three of these later works substitute sugar for the ginger we read here, creating a surprisingly bland mixture. Similarly they

---

53 See this cheese also used as an ingredient in Recipes 11 and 132.

allow milk (of unspecified variety) as an alternative to the broth in which the rice is to be cooked. As happens frequently where a Neapolitan recipe is reproduced in Riva and the *Arte coquinaria*, our version is alone in referring explicitly to Parmesan cheese.

❖ 130. The versions of the Spelt Tort found here and in the other collections are the same except that the others limit the amount of saffron to "a little" and leave the cinnamon out of their standard garnish of sugar and rosewater. The sugar-and-rosewater garnish is by itself so regular and ubiquitous for these tortes that it seems almost to be written automatically at the end of most recipes. The other versions make no mention of the unusual upper "crust" that we read about here.

❖ 131. This *Torta comuna* incorporates a spiced herb-egg-and-cheese mixture. It seems to be a variant of several of the previous tortes, in particular of the *Torta bulignesa* (Recipe 126). The *Torta comuna* is not copied in the Riva del Garda manuscript. The versions of it that appear in Martino and Platina are marked by a number of differences: they throw in whole raisins, simplify the spice list and leave out the herbs entirely. The concluding option mentioned obliquely in our recipe is also lost, perhaps having undergone a distortion of some sort, in the *Arte coquinaria* where we read, " . . . And you will have it set out as is said *above* for the White Torte"; or, as Platina puts it, " . . . *Eoque modo coquito quo est tortam albam*" (Recipe VIII,38).

Cooking in a covered baking dish with live embers or coals "above and below" presumably offered an alternative to oven baking, one that afforded a closer control of the heat to which the torte was exposed; the *foco temperato* was important. See the same procedure in Recipe 134 as well.

❖ 132. This and the following recipe seem to have no counterparts in any known recipe collection. The Sienese-Style Torte is a cheese "pie" whose characteristic feature may be that it is crustless: the baking dish is merely coated with butter and flour.

The variety of cheese called *probatura* is still produced in southern Italy—and can still be had in Italian specialty shops around the world.[54] Except for its source in milk of the buffalo cow, it resembles mozzarella in texture and flavor, and is nowdays kept and shipped sealed in its own liquid.[55] We may also add that this recipe itself seems also to be closely related to these south-Italian lands. The cheese, rare in medieval cookery, appears in another unedited work, the *Modi singulari de cocina*, contained in the MS London, BL, Egerton 1985, at f° 22r.

❖ 133. This *unicum* unfortunately presents serious problems in its *genre*, in its name and in its text. The three marginal notations that accompany it[56] suggest that the author, compiler, scribe

---

54 In our own town of 80,000 inhabitants such a shop does a good business in packets of *probatura*.

55 "On trouve encore un fromage du nom de *provatura* dans le sud du Latium et en Campanie; il est à pâte filée comme la mozzarella, mais il n'est pas certain que telle était la *provatura* du XVe siècle. De toute façon, l'usage de ce fromage confirme l'origine méridionale du manuscrit Bühler": Odile Redon, Françoise Sabban and Silvano Serventi, *La Gastronomie au Moyen Age* (Paris: Stock, 1991), 87.

56 One notation (*Questa he quella megliori de tute le tartare a le calate*) is at the bottom of f° 50r; two (*a catharina fasanicha*; *A ire alla calata mi sera bono he meglio mi sera de stare cum questa torta sotto l'omo*) are at the foot of f° 50v.

or an eventual owner felt that this recipe called for some sort of supplementary commentary or clarification; unfortunately, the notations do not help much.

The dish is a sort of torte — that is to say, it is a mixture of cheese, eggs, milk, spices (ginger, sugar) and fat (butter), which is baked slowly on a lower crust in a covered dish on or (normally) in hot coals. The name of this dish, *Tartara juliatica,* may derive in some way from the nature of its crust — this being the only unique feature of this preparation. Our author allows three options for this crust: breadcrumbs, cheese (slices, as in Recipe 126?), or flour (as in the previous recipe).

The concluding phrase of the recipe proper is a little reminiscent of the jaunty end of the recipe for Saracen Sauce (Recipe 113): " . . . Fill dishes with this Saracen Sauce and serve it to tables of Saracens!" Concerning this unidentified name (?), *Catharina Fasanicha,* see the marginal notation at Recipe 191 and our comment to that recipe.

Equally suggestive of jauntiness is the sentence inserted into the bottom margin of the second page, f° 50v. Although not so arranged in the manuscript, the lines of this addition read as if they might be intended as verse or else inspired by some popular song:

A ir' alla Calata
mi sera bono;
he meglio mi sera
de star' cum questa torta
sotto l'omo.

The word for "man" is repeatedly written *homo* in the Menus of this manuscript. If this is indeed the sense that we are to understand here, rather than *lomo* or perhaps a word for elm tree, we may think that the writer is using this footnote to refer to a somewhat ambiguous and *risqué* ditty.

❖ 134. In the Riva del Garda manuscript, the incipit of this recipe reads *Per fare uno milliazo per quatro overo cinque persone*; in the Vatican copy (alone) of the *Arte coquinaria* (f° 35v) the rubric is likewise *Per fare uno migliaccio per quattro ho cinque persone.* However, in the Table of this same Vatican copy the name of this "millet" cheesecake is rendered (in the feminine) as *Migliaza biancha.* The two qualifications that we find used with this *Miliazo* in the Neapolitan manuscript — *fasanitico* and *a lo modo florentino* — are unique to it. They appear to be connected somehow to the Catharina of the previous recipe and perhaps to the marginal notation identifying Recipe 18 as a *menestra fasanica,* as well as to the marginal notation that we read further on at Recipe 191: *He questo he pasto de Catherina fasaniticha Florentina* (see the comment to that recipe).[57] The qualifications may well refer to a person or family known to the author, or famous (or infamous) within the author's circle.

---

[57] Of the four occurrences of the term *fasanica* and *fasanitico* in our manuscript, all but this one appear in appended, marginal notations. The presence of the term in this title, *Miliazo fasanitico,* suggests that our scribe was likely responsible for those other notations as well as the body of the manuscript, and that they were more or less contemporaneous with the making of the manuscript.

This *miliazo* is not what the modern *migliaccio* was to become. Etymologically its name derives from its principal ingredient, the very fine flour called millet.[58] For our author the fine flour still accounts for the essential nature of the preparation. By a century later, however, the determining ingredient in the dish seems to have become animal blood, particularly that of a pig, and this remains so today.[59] For our author, furthermore, a significant element in this torte, and one that relates it to the preceding recipe, seems to be the nature of its "crust." In this case a finger-thick layer of butter or lard is spread on the bottom of the baking dish, melted and then used as a medium in which the millet mixture is to be deep-fried while baking. In both the *Arte coquinaria* and the *Honesta voluptate* the ingredients and procedures are those that we read here. The use of extremely fine wheat flour—*fiore de farina*, "flower of flour," as Riva and the *Arte coquinaria* write in their versions—seems to satisfy the requirement for millet flour in the dish's name.

❖ 135. An Elderflower Torte is a fairly common preparation in late-medieval cookery. Similar recipes are found in English (the *Sambocade* of the *Forme of Cury*, Recipe 179) and in Italian (the *Torta sambugata* of the *Anonimo Veneziano*, Recipe 99). The Martino versions of this dish remain close in their wording. The Riva manuscript explains explicitly why the filling should be relatively thick: the particles of elderflower tend to rise rather than remain evenly suspended in the liquid mixture.

❖ 136. The same abbreviated recipe, with its reference to the Spelt Tort (Recipe 130), is found in Martino (and in Platina, but curiously not in Riva). The later versions require the mixture to be "yellow with saffron"—perhaps because in their particular copy of the earlier recipe they wrote that only a little saffron should be used.

❖ 137. In the *Arte coquinaria* (Recipe 138) the title of this dish is a little more descriptive of its contents: *Torta di cerase et rose rosse*. The recipe there and eventually in Platina remains very similar, except that no mention is made later of the use of butter in the torte's crust. This recipe is not copied in the Riva del Garda manuscript.

❖ 138. This particular Green Torte seems to be a cross between the *Torta bulignesa* (Recipe 126) and the *Herbulata de maio* (Recipe 127). In this regard, the end of this second recipe as it appears in Riva (Recipe 144) and the *Arte coquinaria* (Recipe 126) is significant: *E simille torta sive herbollata quanto piu sera verde tanto piu sera bella*—"Any similar torte or herb dish looks prettier the greener it is." Only one herb is relied upon to provide the green in the *Turta verde* of the *Manoscritto Lucano* (Recipe 47): chard. The sole specific direction in our Neapolitan recipe—that only the green juice of the herbs and chard be used, and not the pureed plants themselves—seems no longer of any importance in the sixteenth-century version of this dish.

---

[58] The *Dizionario etimologico italiano* (4, 24456b) indicates that the word *migliaccio* dates from the fourteenth century and derives from the Latin *miliaceus*, "millet." According to this work also, in Naples in 1016 the Latin derivative *miliaccium* designated a millet bread.

[59] According to the *Vocabulario de las dos lenguas toscana y castellana* of 1570 by Cristóbal de las Casas, the *migliaccio* was a *torta hecha de sangre de puerco*. A modern definition of the dish retains this insistence upon animal blood: in the smit Grande dizionario della lengua italiana, it is a *torta confezionata con sangue di maiale, stemperato con farina, pangrattato, uova, latte e altri ingredienti . . . , cotta in padella con strutto o in teglia nel forno . . . .*"

❖ 139. This Turnip Torte and the following Quince Torte are each given short shrift here. By their placement on the page they seem to be treated separately in our manuscript, though in both Riva and the *Arte coquinaria* they are combined (with yet another variety) and disposed of under a single rubric: *Torta de pere e de rappe e de codogne.* There both the pears and the turnips are to undergo a preliminary cooking under the coals; the quince are first to be boiled in a fat broth and *then* (optionally) to follow the pears and turnips under the coals — *che forsi serano megliori.* According to Riva and Martino, these principal ingredients (each alone or together?) are to be sieved and dealt with in the same way as in the *Torta de zuche* (our Recipe 128).

❖ 140. According to the preceding text in the Neapolitan manuscript, this Quince Torte is apparently likewise to be fashioned on the model of the Common Torte of Recipe 131. The abbreviated directions for this sort of Quince Torte in Riva and the *Arte coquinaria* indicate that the quince are first to be quartered or cut up, cleaned, boiled in fat bouillon, (optionally) baked under the coals, sieved and (optionally) mixed with such seasonings as are found in the recipe for Squash Torte (our Recipe 128). However, this latter preparation calls for the incorporation of porkbelly (or butter or lard) as well as eggs and milk, whereas the Common Torte is a somewhat plainer sort of cheese-and-herb mixture.

The *Manoscritto Lucano* contains an interesting *Turta de cotognie* (Recipe 48) in which the quince are first cooked in honey and then steeped in rosewater. They are then ground with cheese, sugar, cinnamon and egg yolks.

❖ 141. This Cabbage Torte is copied in Riva (alone) where its directions are changed in several respects from those found in the Neapolitan manuscript. The *torsi* or stems are to be sliced into long strips before cooking; then the excess broth is to be squeezed from them and they are to be ground in a mortar before being sieved; rather than a pound of *bono caso veghio he fresco*, Riva specifies half a pound of *caso frescho* and half a pound of *caso permesano*; and Riva adds two or three notes at the end, to the effect that this torte should be quite squat, creamy (*grassa*) with butter, and is good to eat in the winter.

❖ 142. Although there is no rubric to announce it, this paragraph begins a relatively long series of recipes for eggs. The first of these recipes, Eggs Cooked in a Sheet of Paper, is a remarkable *tour de force.* As a culinary procedure it seems to be recognized elsewhere only in the manuscript of Riva del Garda, and there only as an adjunct to a recipe for a *Menestra di fyore de sambucho a tempo di carne* (Recipe 98) — a dish not represented in our collection.[60] The excuse for appending the procedure to that recipe is slim. The Riva author extends his meat-day elderflower recipe by claiming to deal with a contingency: *E notta che, non havendo padella de cocere l'ova, te insegnaro como debi cocere in una carta o vero palpero:* . . . , "And note that, should you not have a pan for

[60] Nor do we find the preceding recipe for twelve servings of its lean, eggless counterpart, a *Menestra di fyore de sambucho in tempo quadragessimalle* (Recipe 97 in Riva). Both elderflower preparations seem to have been added to the compilation by Martino di Rossi who, for some reason — perhaps the small number of eggs to be cooked in the meat-day version — saw the second recipe as offering an opportunity to dispose of these directions that he found, in the Neapolitan Collection or its source, for cooking-in-paper.

cooking the eggs, I shall instruct you on how to cook in a sheet, or rather in paper ... " — and then our present text, somewhat simplified in Riva, follows. The change in the exact wording is significant here: our Neapolitan author clarifies his direction by writing *una carta — dico uno mezo foglio de papiro*; the Riva scribe then writes *una carta o vero palpero*. Our author is clarifying the precise size of paper sheet (a half-sheet) to be used; the Riva scribe understands merely that *carta* and *palpero* are close synonyms. In the case of our author, the half-sheet of paper is a well-known unit: the whole of his manuscript is written on these half-sheets which, folded, form his double-folios.[61] The half-sheet of paper with which to begin this "recipe" would therefore measure roughly 21 cm by 29 cm — that is, perhaps not surprisingly, the size of a standard modern European sheet of paper (the "A4" format, about 8 1/4" by 11 1/2").

The recipe in question, for cooking-in-a-paper-pan, is suitable for three egg yolks, mixed with broth, sugar and elderflowers, ingredients that otherwise might properly be cooked in a pan in lard or butter.

The procedure itself, the use of a paper pan, is remarkable, given that a frying pan of a size adequate for three eggs would surely not be lacking in the kitchen of any noble household where this recipe might be read or known. The procedure is worthy of being classified among the *Mirabilia gule* that begin at Recipe 66. We should, of course, understand that fifteenth-century paper could, if required, be relatively thick and quite tough, of the consistency of cardboard. With the edges of a half-sheet turned up to contain the cooking oil, the horizontal area would be just enough to hold the contents of an average modern frying egg. Yet we must still wonder whether such a manner of cooking is feasible and practical; and, if so, just how frequently it might prove useful.

On the whole it seems highly unlikely, as the Riva manuscript suggests, that any professional cook might have to learn to do without such a fundamental kitchen utensil as a regular bronze or iron pan. A circumstance presenting such a contingency might possibly arise when the cook's master was travelling and his cook was caught, as it were, between kitchens; this paragraph might appropriately be located alongside Recipe 123, *Mostarda per portare cavalcando*. However, the final sentence in our text suggests that the Neapolitan author does not himself care to vouch for the practicality of the procedure — and suggests perhaps, too, that the whole thing may be little more than a joke.[62] Significantly, it is not reproduced in the *Arte coquinaria*.

Just who *was* this Julino de Sozago, *amatore de le gentileze*, of whom our author writes? The only town of this name to which modern gazetteers make any reference is Sozzago (alternatively spelled Sozaggo), in Piamonte in the province of Novara, on the left bank of the Terdoppio (an affluent of the Po River); its population in the twentieth century is about 1500 persons. Julino must surely have enjoyed some significance in Neapolitan society at the time his name was written by our author, but unhappily the personage remains almost as much a mystery as Catherina Fasanitica.[63]

---

[61] See the Introduction, A. (i) Physical description of the manuscript.

[62] In the Riva del Garda text the author likewise feels that a concluding comment is called for. Unfortunately an even more obscure one than is in the Neapolitan text, this bears upon the whole operation: ... *Et questo se fa per excelentia et per piacere*.

[63] In his *Cucina italiana del quattrocento* (Florence: Olschki, 1996), 39, note 6, Claudio Benporat points out the similarity of this *Julino* and the qualification of Tartara Juliatica of Recipe 133.

❖ 143. This particular recipe for scrambled eggs and cheese is unknown elsewhere. The qualification "in the German fashion" is interesting—but not helpful.

❖ 144. With this simple Egg Omelet begins a series of fifteen egg dishes whose sequence and text are faithfully followed at the beginning of the versions in Riva and the *Libro de arte coquinaria.* Both works add directions for coloring the omelet green, and general advice that the egg mixture not be stirred or overcooked.

❖ 145. The flavor and color in this Herb Omelet are contributed by the juice of the herbs listed in the recipe. The compilers of Riva the *Arte coquinaria* (and Platina in his *Honesta voluptate*, Recipe IX,24) have, deliberately or accidentally, overlooked the phrase *et fane suco*: for them the chopped, fried herbs themselves become part of this omelet. The same variant is found in the *Fritelle amare* (Recipe 172).

❖ 146. A *fritella* is a (deep-fried) fritter. Our compiler will write out many varieties of lean-day fritters in the section on dishes for Lent (Recipes 172–179). When it is applied to eggs, the qualification *fritellata* would seem to designate an egg-rich batter that is deep-fried. It is clear, however, and a little disappointing, that this present recipe is for nothing more or less than fried eggs. These eggs are not scrambled, as would be the case for an omelet.

The clarification that is inserted with a personal subjunctive, *a cio che me intenda*, is an interesting justification from the author.

❖ 147, 148. These dishes are produced by variants of a common general procedure.

❖ 149. The series of egg dishes has passed beyond the simple varieties of elementary omelets, scrambled eggs, fried eggs and poached eggs. We now have fancier preparations. The first involves deep-fried deviled eggs.

Because of its relative complexity (at least compared with the simple procedures that have been outlined in previous recipes), this is one of the longer recipes here. A question arises concerning the instruction that only *una parte* of the egg yolks are to be used in the "stuffing." Later, in a similar preparation described in Recipe 157, our author explicitly directs that four yolks be so used—without, however, indicating either there or here the total number of eggs with which the cook is to begin to work. The remainder of the yolks seem to be forgotten or discarded. However, the Riva manuscript and the *Arte coquinaria* enrich this dish a little in an efficient way with directions for an "appropriate" serving garnish: this Riva sauce is a smooth blend of *left-over yolks*, raisins, spices, verjuice and wine syrup. Platina (Recipe IX,28) adds to the role of this sauce by setting his stuffed, fried eggs to boil briefly in it.

❖ 150. The crepe-thin omelet is to be folded twice into a quarter of its original size, so that it is four layers thick. This dish combines two types of egg-cooking procedures. The phrase *che serea a modo de una torta* does not appear in Riva or the *Arte coquinaria*; those two works do, however, direct that the omelet be taken from the grill and served in its folded shape, just as it was cooked and garnished.

❖ 151. Despite reproducing this recipe with care from the *Arte coquinaria*, at the end of it Platina (Recipe IX,30) adds one of his acerbic comments: *Stolidum inventum et coquorum ineptiæ ac ludi!* — "This is a stupid concoction, one of the absurdities and games of cooks!"

❖ 152. ... *he copre con un' altra scutella*: an alternative but larger vessel, specifically designed for this sort of dry cooking, was properly called a *trapa* (see the commentary to Recipe 57, for instance). Significantly, the Italo-Latin *Tractatus* glosses the term *trapa* in a recipe for pullets: *Dequoquitur etiam pullos in trapa, id est inter duas scutellas terreas interius bene plumbatas.*[64] The two *scutelle* called for in the Neapolitan Collection — the upper one presumably dished upwards in order to contain live coals — may have been of a glazed earthenware as in the *Tractatus*. An egg coddler would be used nowdays for this sort of cooking.

❖ 153. The eggs remain in their shells for this dish. The term *sudate* has its literal sense: the albumen transpires through the shell until it hardens on the inside, and then, as our author says, the eggs are done. The text is reproduced in Riva; in the *Arte coquinaria* we read: *Et quando sudano ben forte, cavale, che son cotte.*

❖ 154. The name of the preparation is modified in Riva (*Ove stuffate con la sua scorza*) and the later Martino (*Ova tuffate con la sua cortece*). The length of the eggs' cooking time, *un bullore* according to the Neapolitan cook, becomes *uno pater noster o pocho piu* in the later collections.

❖ 155. The implication in the name of this procedure is that "once (and more) over lightly" was a favorite way to do eggs in Florence. This dish will form the basis for a development in Recipe 157. It is only in this recipe in the Neapolitan Collection, and in Recipe 157, and in the corresponding recipes in Riva and in the *Arte coquinaria* (and the *Honesta voluptate*, Recipes IX,33 and 35), that any dishes at all are qualified as being "Florentine." This seems to indicate a surprising indifference to Florentine cookery at the time.

❖ 156. The *Ova sopra la brasa* is basically a variant of the *Ova in cenere* of Recipe 153. The *brasa viva*, on which the eggs are placed before their tops are broken open, are hotter than the earlier *cenere calda*, in which the whole eggs are rolled around at length. In Riva and the *Arte coquinaria* the dish is called *Ova sperdute nella braxa accesa*.

❖ 157. This recipe amounts to a further variant or development of the *Ova fritellate* of Recipe 155 and offers a counterpart to Recipe 149 for the "plain" *Ova piena*. Though the dish is not expressly associated with Florence by its name in our collection, the other versions of it in Riva, Martino and Platina copy into the rubric the qualification "in the Florentine fashion" that is found here only in the text. Both the procedure and the stuffing itself resemble what we have already seen for the deviled eggs of Recipe 149. The *marangoli* that are to be used in the garnish according to our text and in Riva become specifically *suco di naranci* and *succus malarantii*, "orange juice," in the *Arte coquinaria* and the *Honesta voluptate* (Recipe IX,35).

---

64 The Franco-Latin recipe collection known as the *Modus viaticorum* (see Carole Lambert, op. cit., Recipe 30) directs that a fish pie be baked *in trapa vel furno*, depending upon whether the cook wishes to bake it over and under live coals or (if he has one) in the oven.

The version of the Martino collection that is read in the MS Urbinate latino 1203 bears evidence of a remarkable scribal *lapsus*. At his Recipe 195, in copying the *Arte coquinaria*'s Recipe 194 for *Ova frictellate piene*, the scribe's eye passes from the word *sopra* (which is also in the first line of our text) to the *sopra* written toward the beginning of the following recipe (*buttandogli sopra del zuccharo* in Martino; *butando de sopra zucaro* in our text); thereafter the scribe continues on and finishes copying the text of Martino's recipe for *Ova in forma de raffioli* (our Recipe 158). There can be no question of the Urbinate latino copy being an immediate source for either of the known texts of the *Arte coquinaria*.

❖ 158. The eggs are likely to be broken separately on the sheet of lasagna dough, then the dough is to be cut to a size and perhaps shape suitable for wrapping, like ravioli, around each egg. Lasagna dough is described in Recipe 179 as being not very tough but (according to Riva and Martino in their version of our Recipe 179) *sottile* or "thin." For the present dish of Eggs in the Shape of Ravioli both Riva and the *Arte coquinaria* describe a further procedure — *Simellmente poi fare/conciarai le dicte ove a forma di pastelli* — in which the flat dough, with the seasoned egg on it, is cooked *como una torta* (presumably in the coals in a baking dish with a lid) or else fried. Both caution against overcooking the egg and so making it too hard.

❖ 159. This recipe and the following two are not properly egg dishes, yet they are copied here just before the rubric for "Lenten Dishes" that we shall read at Recipe 162. The logic of the sequence may be that Recipes 159 and 160 are of the same *genre* as the so-called Egg Ravioli of Recipe 158. In Riva they appear together in the midst of *torte*.

❖ 160. This recipe is for an early version of the turnovers that are still known as *calzone* in modern Naples. The word derives from a medieval Latin *calisone* attested in Padua about 1170 and which Battisti and Alessio gloss as a *dolce di farina e mandorle* (*Dizionario etimologico italiano*, 1, 695b). Those authors relate the Italian word to the French *chausson*. Though amplified, the Riva recipe for *Calisoni* and Martino's for *Caliscioni*, are still close to the text we have here.

It would be a mistake to read "as *I have* said" for the passage *como he dito*, and to see this tense as indicating that the Neapolitan writer inherited a text in which the order of the recipes has been altered. Several possible interpretations exist; they should take into account the scribe's deliberate change of his text (see our next paragraph). If the scribe intended "as *is* said," he may merely be anticipating what he knows will appear in a later recipe, the *Torta de Marzapane* of Recipe 180. (The same spelling for the modern Italian word è is quite normal and found, for instance, on f° 2v: . . . *he quando he cotta*.)

Having first written *Torta bianca*, the scribe's correction, or amelioration, to *Torta de marzapane* is itself very interesting. The two fillings bear some resemblance to one another. However, the second lacks the eggs and cheese of the first, and depends on almond milk rather than animal milk. The second preparation seems, in fact, to be a lean (Lenten according to the writer) counterpart of the first. Because the directions for White Torte have indeed already been copied in Recipe 125, the scribe's *original* intent may well have been to write a past tense: " . . . as I have said."

Both Riva and the *Arte coquinaria* add several lines directing the cook on the method of making some sort of attractive impression on the pastry by means of a cleverly carved block of wood.

❖ 161. Appended to the end of this section just before a series of lean dishes that are suitable for preparation during Lent is this remarkable recipe for snails. According to its title at least, this preparation is intended for meat-eating days. Within the recipe's text a variant in the secondary ingredients alone allows the dish to be served on lean days; the snails in themselves must have been conceived as appropriate lean-day fare.

A considerably shortened version of this recipe is copied into the Riva compilation, following the incipit *Per cocere lumaghe* (without the qualification *in tempo grasso*). In particular Riva does not copy the medical information that we read here concerning snails: *queste sono restaurative et lubriche al corpo*; the Riva compiler copies only as far as the Neapolitan's list of herbs. Though Platina does mention snails in his recipe collection (*De cochleis*: Recipe IX,39), he is in no way indebted to what we read here or in Riva.

The author (or his source) clearly is confident about certain medico-physical lore that he has acquired concerning the natural virtues of snails. Even his language echoes that of the medical treatises of the day: ... *Queste sono restaurative et lubriche al corpo.* We find similar analyses and a similar style in Magninus Mediolanensis, *Regimen sanitatis*, Ch. 17, *De carnibus*, with regard to snails: *Preparata enim sic restringit ventrem et alimentum sufficiens corporibus exhibet in tamen etiam que multum competit volentibus impinguari.*[65]

Snails seem not to be an unusual foodstuff in late-medieval Europe. The bourgeois *Menagier de Paris* writes of *lymassons* (which are also called *escargolz*, he says) in §257—although he does add that they are food for the wealthy. And the northern-French *Vivendier* provides directions (in Recipe 57) to prepare a general-purpose sauce from chopped snails. The Neapolitan author (or his source) shows little hesitancy about the proper culinary measures to be taken with snails. The procedures are somewhat complex, the directions are detailed, and the gastronomic "goal," the nature of the finished dish, is clearly understood. Even the added marginal notation (to say nothing of the sketches of snails essayed in two margins, ff° 58r and v) indicates considerable culinary experience with this food.

❖ 162. With this Almond Dish or Almond Paste begins a chapter of dishes that would satisfy the alimentary restrictions laid down by the Church for either Lent or lean days in general.

An enormously large number and range of preparations made use of almonds in the late Middle Ages, and in Italy a particular variety of these dishes was called *Amandolata*. Recipes similar to what we read here can be seen in the *Amandolatas* of the *Anonimo Toscano* (Recipe 169), the *Anonimo Veneziano* (Recipe 41), the Wellcome manuscript (Recipe 212), *Buone vivande* (Recipes 37 and 38) and the Nice Collection (Recipes 16 and 17). The *Armandollata/Mandolata* of the Riva del Garda manuscript and the *Arte coquinaria* closely echo our version of the recipe.

❖ 163. Other than for the chick-peas themselves (where the so-called Martino text increases a pound to a pound and a half), the quantities that we read here for the various foodstuffs are reproduced exactly in the *Brodo de ciceri rossi* of Riva and Martino, as well as in Platina's *Ius in*

---

[65] Rome, Vatican, Palatino latino, MS 1331. The *Regimen sanitatis Magnini Mediolanensis medici famosissimi Attrebatensi Episcopo directum* was published in Louvain by Johannes de Westfalia in 1482.

cicere rubeo (Recipe VII,57). Interestingly, all three of the latter versions add a concluding line to the effect that this *brodo* or *ius* could appropriately be served to a sick person, and that if it is prepared for this purpose it should contain no oil or salt/spice.

❖ 164. This Lenten recipe for peas refers to the preceding treatment of chick-peas as a possible alternative model, though with two changes. In Riva and the *Arte coquinaria*, where this recipe does not appear after the chick-pea recipe, the model to be followed is the Lenten White Dish (Recipes 41 and 91 respectively: our Recipe 6); unfortunately the present recipe for *Piselli in tempo quadragessimalle* has been copied at some distance from the recipe for the Lenten White Dish — some twenty recipes afterwards, in the case of the Riva compilation. The phrases, ... *como e dicto de sopra nel capitolo del biancho mangiare* and ... *como s'e dito di sopra*, make for a rather awkward consultation in the later versions.

❖ 165. The option of purchasing a quantity of the *fava menata* that is called for in this dish indicates that retail merchants or local delicatessens must have stocked cooked bean paste or bean mash as a staple — that is, as a standard food-stuff preparation that was in fairly constant demand among the local population. The cook could then take up a quantity of this paste and dress it as he liked — here with fried onion and raisins.

In both Riva's *Fava menata d'ogni resone* and the *Arte coquinaria*'s *Fava menata* our text is almost lost among a variety of alternative procedures.

❖ 166. This recipe is for an eggless bean "omelet," cooked in a way similar to that used for a normal omelet. It contains herbs and fruit. In the Riva del Garda manuscript the name of this dish is *Fava nela padella*; in the later Martino collection this has become *Friger la fava*.

❖ 167. The series of three "mock" or "pseudo" foods, or pretend-dishes, that begins here is found in both Riva and Martino in detail and in the same order (Recipes 174–76 and 152–54 respectively). Platina likewise reproduces this series in his eighth book (Recipes 54–56).[66] The descriptive name of the first dish in the series, the present recipe for *Jonchada de amandole*, appears in the other two Italian compilations as *Zonchata di quadragessima* and *Gioncata d'amandole in quadragesima*, and then rendered by Platina into Latin not too helpfully: *Concretum amygdalinum in ieiunio*: "Almond Gelatine for Lent." The feature of this recipe that seems significant to Platina is apparently that the almond milk sets or gels; for the Neapolitan author what was important is that the almond curd will imitate dairy cheese. The Latin collection at Châlons contains a similar recipe (Recipe 61) for *Ioncata amigdalata*.

It may be that Platina did not understand the sense of the word *Joncada* or *Gioncata*, though on the surface this is unlikely. The original form of junket was a flavored animal milk — a *jonchata de vero latte*, as our author writes in this recipe. After having set, the substance was conventionally kept and served in a basket made of reeds or rushes. The Latin term for such a reed is *juncus*, *jonco*, hence the name *joncata*.

---

[66] The placement is curious: this Book Eight is entitled *De condimentis quæ vulgo sapores vocant*, "On Condiments Which are Commonly Called 'Flavorings'."

Almond cheese and almond butter, both made from almond milk, were common products in the late-medieval kitchen.[67] Since they made no use of animal milk, this and the following four dishes are valuable preparations for deceiving the appetite on lean days.

Between the versions that we read here in the Neapolitan manuscript and the Riva del Garda and the *Arte coquinaria* texts, at least one passage has been changed. In our version we read, " Mix everything together and strain it forcefully so that its substance comes through"; in the other collections this may have become a little corrupted: "Make sure [the fish broth] is good and substantial and that the fish is very fresh, distempering everything together and straining it forcefully until the almond mixture does not stay in the strainer." The later Italian versions also allow the addition of herbs, "as is done in other [ordinary] *joncate*"; they omit the final phrase in our text, *he falla comer al coco* . . . .

❖ 168. In the Riva del Garda manuscript and the *Arte coquinaria* the title of this recipe bears the qualification *di quaresima / in quadragesima.*

This recipe for *Ricotta contrafatta* benefits from the Neapolitan author's colorful imagination as he describes the normal ricotta and the manner of peddling it through urban streets. This lively evocation is missing in Riva, Martino and Platina.[68]

❖ 169. Almond butter is a fairly common product in the medieval kitchen. It was believed to be an appropriate dish for a sick person, and is so prepared by Chiquart in his *Borre d'amendres* (Recipe 67).

It may seem that a patent error occurs in the first line of the text here: the quantity of almonds specified in the previous recipe is not a pound and a half. What the writer is insisting upon, though, is not the quantity of almonds but the treatment they are to receive, specifically the word *biancate*, and the explanation of that procedure that is given in the preceding recipe: *cio'e, falle stare a moglio una note, he cusi serano piu belle pellate.* Riva and the *Arte coquinaria* write "one pound of almonds" (rather than the pound and a half) as they have just written in their version of the recipe for *Ricotta contrafatta* (our Recipe 168) — perhaps because they or their source misunderstood the sense of that same phrase, "as is said above."

The use of *farina de amido* is not frequent in our collection of recipes. This standard culinary starch is called for in only one other preparation, Recipe 178, where it is qualified as *farina fina de amido.* However, the substance must have been on hand as a staple in the kitchens of noble households throughout the end of the Middle Ages, because a good number and variety of recipes

[67] For a recipe for cheese made from almond milk, see the German *Buch von guter spise*, Recipe 72: *Einen kese von mandel* (Hans Hajek, *Das buch von guter spize aus der Würzburg-Münchener Handschrift.* Text des späten Mittelalters, 8 (Berlin: Erich Schmidt, 1958), 35); or the Dutch *Keukenboek*, Recipe 26: *Botere ende Kaes van Amandelen* (Constant Antoine Serrure, *Keukenboek uitgegeven naar een Hs. der 15e eeuw*, Maatschappij der Vlaamsche Bibliophilen, Werken 10 (Gand: Annoot-Braeckman, 1872), 7).

[68] In Recipe 18 of his Book II the latter does, however, describe the process for making true ricotta: "When the cheese is taken from the bronze kettle, we heat the whey for some time on a slow fire until the fat which is the residue of the cheese rises to the top. Farmers call this ricotta because it is gathered from the milk in a second heating."

do mention it. The technique for making wheat starch was "popularly" known since the time of Pliny the Elder;[69] directions for the procedure continued to be copied, particularly in English recipe collections[70] from which a cook could make up a batch of starch for future use.

❖ 170. The particular root that is identified here as *pastonaca* is debatable. The *Tacuina sanitatis* distinguish two varieties: a white *pastinaca*, which we would call a parsnip, and a "red," sweeter variety, which we would call a carrot. Later, Michele Savonarola further distinguishes between a wild *pastinaca*, which is reddish, and a domestic or domesticated variety, which is somewhat less red in color.

If this recipe is copied directly from a Catalan source, then, given the sense of the Catalan word *pastenaga*, "carrot," our author may very well be writing out a treatment for carrots. One might hesitate to suggest that he didn't know which sort of root his source was referring to. In any case, because this recipe turns up in the Riva collection, it is not apt to have the same sort of immediate Catalan source as we find in so many other of the Neapolitan recipes which do not appear in Riva.

In Riva and the *Arte coquinaria* (and the *Honesta voluptate*, Recipe IX,22) these *Pastonache* turn up at the end of a series of fritters (of which in the Neapolitan Collection we shall see the beginning after another recipe) and before a series of egg dishes (which we have already seen). Because the parsnips/carrots are fried in a batter, these later collections may perhaps have considered them to be significant as a sort of fritter. In any case they constitute an entirely appropriate Lenten dish and belong in the present series of lean preparations. While this recipe is more or less faithfully copied by the compiler of the Riva manuscript, the dish apparently holds little interest for the Martino reviser (or, for that matter, for Platina), who has abbreviated this recipe to the point of leaving out the direction for making the batter in which the parsnips/carrots are to be fried; then the *Arte coquinaria* also omits any mention of an appropriate serving garnish.

❖ 171. Yet another recipe for White Dish is copied here, from some unidentified source. Though this version of what is probably the most widely known of all late-medieval culinary preparations contains such ingredients that it is suitable for lean days and during Lent, and consequently belongs in this particular chapter of the collection, our compiler had already provided a recipe for such a lean White Dish near the very beginning of his work: *Bianchomanghiare per .x. menestre* (Recipe 6). At that point a marginal notation even labels the earlier recipes as "for Lent." Like the present version of the dish, that previous one used fish paste and had a ginger flavor. Previously that fish paste had been mixed with almond milk; here it is mixed with rice flour, pine nuts and goat's milk. This last ingredient is noteworthy, given that this dish is expressly identified as for use during Lent.

---

[69] *Natural History*, book 18, chapter 16.

[70] For instance, in the British Library, MS Harley 5401:

> To make amydon. Recipe whete & stepe it .ix. days, & change the water every day twyes; then bray it in a morter right small & clene it throgh a haryn syve & lat it stonde tyll it he sett; then put onto the morter & bray it in a clothe to it be dry.

Constance Hieatt, "The Middle English Culinary Recipes in MS Harley 5401," *Medium Ævum* 65 (1996): 59; Recipe 23.

❖ 172. The *fritelle* in our collection correspond to the French *beignet* or doughnut. Normally in them some sort of batter (consisting basically of flour or rice flour or almond paste) is deep-fried. However, the term "fritter" can also be applied when the principal foodstuff (figs, for instance, in Recipe 175) is deep-fried apparently without an exterior coating of some sort of batter. It is remarkable that in our recipe collection there are no "standard" meat-day fritters but only fritters whose ingredients make them suitable for serving on lean days. We find the term *fritella* used outside of this series of Lenten dishes only in the name of the *Ova fritelata* (Recipe 146) and in its two variants, *Ova fritellate a lo modo fiorentino* (Recipe 155) and *Ova fritellate piene al modo fiorentino* (Recipe 157).

All of the fritters in this series of eight in the Neapolitan Collection remain copied in close proximity in both Riva and the *Arte coquinaria* (as well as in Book IX of the *Honesta voluptate*). In these latter, the version of the first recipe, for so-called Bitter Fritters, explicitly names the dish "Fritters of Bitter Herbs." The quantities specified in our text are later missing. Then those other texts blunder, or at least risk changing the nature of the fritters substantially, by not clarifying that it is juice extracted from the herbs that is combined with the flour and leavening; the other copies read as if the chopped herbs are themselves to be mixed into the batter mixture. These other copies also add figs to the raisins, but omit any spices or saffron. A serving garnish of sugar and honey, not mentioned by the Neapolitan cook, is appended in each.

❖ 173. To late-medieval prepared dishes elderflowers lend a flavor that is widely appreciated in the gastronomy of the time. We have already seen them used in our manuscript in the Elderflower Torte (Recipe 135). An Elderflower Dish was equally popular, versions of it being found under the names of *Swade, Sambucata, Sambugado* and *Savocata* in the Anglo-Norman "B" collection (Recipe 23), the *Frammento* (Recipe 54), the Anonimo Veneziano (Recipe 72) and the Wellcome manuscript (Recipe 141). The Riva manuscript and Martino's *Libro de arte coquinaria* also contain a version of this recipe, calling it a *Menestra di fyore de sambucho ... in tempo quadragessimalle* (Recipes 97 and 98 respectively).

In the form of a fritter as well, the elderflower flavor was much appreciated by late-medieval gourmets. For meat-eating days a recipe for an elderflower fritter can be seen in the Anonimo Veneziano (Recipe 27), the *Liber de coquina* (Recipe III, 7: *De fristellis*) and the *Anonimo Meridionale* "B" (Recipe 37), as well as in Riva and Martino (Recipes 184 and 161: *Frittelle di fyore de sambugho*) and Platina (IX, 2). For lean days we find the present recipe and its echo in Riva, the *Arte coquinaria* and the *Honesta voluptate* (Recipe IX,10). The major difference between these latter recipes and our Neapolitan recipe is that a little leavening is added into the fritter batter by the latter compilers.

❖ 174. The serving garnish is omitted from the copies of this recipe found in Riva, the *Arte coquinaria* and the *Honesta voluptate* (Recipe IX,12).

❖ 175. Properly speaking, and according to what seems to be the normal sense of the word, this dish may not be a fritter: the term seems to be applied to this preparation solely because the figs are deep-fried in oil. Riva's, Martino's and Platina's fried stuffed figs are to be powdered with a little flour; we may wonder whether our scribe has erred in not noting this step.

The insistence that *ogni cosa sia biancha* is perhaps made a little more comprehensible with the amplification, concerning the treatment of the almonds and the pine nuts, that is found in the

Arte coquinaria alone: *fa che siano bianche et nette*. The skins are to be removed wholly from the nuts.

❖ 176. The choice in the way in which the apples are to be cooked here (and in Recipe 185), whether by boiling or "under the coals," was essentially a choice between a moist or a dry preparation. Cooking *sotto la braxa* would be done in an earthenware or metal dish (normally called a *trapa*) whose convex lid allowed it to hold sufficent coals to provide the heat that was desired.

As in their version of the Elderflower Fritters, Riva, Martino and Platina (Recipe IX,13) direct that a little leavening be put into the apple mixture, but they leave out the spices and rosewater that we see prescribed here.

❖ 177. The name of this dish bears a comparison with ravioli because the fish-and-fruit paste is to be coated with a batter or wrapped in a loose dough like ravioli before being deep-fried. This dish is similar to the preparation described in the second half of Recipe 31 in the *Buone vivande* and which makes *tortelli piccoli con croste sottili*.

Platina occasionally seems surprisingly indifferent as to his recipes' names: this and the following dish (and, in his collection, the previous one as well) are called simply *Aliter*, referring back to the generic name *Frictellæ*. The version of this ravioli-type fritter that we find there and in the *Arte coquinaria* has several of the Neapolitan cook's (and Riva's) ingredients presented as alternatives: "almonds *or* other nuts *or* pine nuts," "fish milt *or* livers." None of the later versions includes mint along with the other herbs.

The term *latte de pesso* refers to the milt or soft roe of male fish. It stands distinct from the *ova de pesso* as is seen in Recipe 183.

❖ 178. This recipe is a variant on the previous one, though with little of its gastronomic interest. A paste of rice and almond milk, sweetened and flavored with rosewater, is coated with pastry and deep-fried. No mention is made of a serving garnish.

In Riva this dish is descriptively renamed *Frittelle in forma di pastelli picolli*; its opening line, however, retains the definite article—*fa cocere lo rixo ben*—which likely refers to the rice of the original title. Riva's new title seems to be derived from the same phrase found later in our text: *le fritelle (ho) in forma de pastelli*. The explanation of that phrase that we read in the Neapolitan manuscript (alone)—*cio'e, pone questa compositione in una pasta fatta como he quella cassa del pastello picolo*—refers to the small casings previously described for the Ravioli Fritters of Recipe 177.

❖ 179. Called *Frictellæ ventosæ* by Platina (Recipe IX,20), this recipe is much abbreviated by this compiler and by the persons responsible for Riva and the *Libro de arte coquinaria*. Missing is much of the detailed explanation, not only of the shapes of various objects that can be made with the dough, but of the actual making and frying of the fritters. To the mind of those later authors, the sculpted, hollow turnovers described here may well be just another instance of foolish fantasy on the part of an idle cook.

❖ 180. Three tortes are inserted into this chapter on Lenten dishes. The first relies upon that dependable staple of late-medieval cookery, almond paste. Marzipan has already been used in other prepared dishes of this collection, the *Menestra de marzapane* (Recipe 35) and the *Calisoni* (Recipe

160). In the text of this latter recipe, the *Torta de marzapane* is expressly identified as being among dishes suitable for Lent.

The shell that will hold the marzipan mixture — a lower crust only, because this is a torte — is to be made with wafers. These wafers will be used by the Neapolitan cook later (in Recipes 185 and 186) as a top garnish for a pie; their use as a lower pie shell is unusual.

As a torte this dish should generically be cooked in a baking dish on and under the hot coals. Our author does not specify this, however. The Riva manuscript and the *Arte coquinaria* (as well as the *Honesta voluptate*, Recipe VIII,48) are more explicit: the preparation is to be cooked in the oven or in the fire like other tortes. The other collections warn the reader to be certain that the torte cook slowly and not burn. In particular they advise that this torte be low and thin rather than tall and thick.

❖ 181. This Rice Torte bears some resemblance to the Rice Fritters *in forma de ravioli* (Recipe 178) we have just seen. Both its lower and upper crusts are made with strips of lasagne.

A similar preparation, but for meat-days, is described in the sixteenth-century *Manoscritto Lucano* (Recipe 59). There the pike eggs are replaced by chicken eggs (yolks alone), three sorts of cheese are prescribed, and pine nuts are not mentioned.

❖ 182. The name that identifies this fish-paste torte is intriguing, and all the moreso that the recipe appears not to have been copied in the *Arte coquinaria*. This recipe is, however, not only picked up by the compiler of the Riva del Garda manuscript but expanded into two recipes. In this latter collection it has been given the names *Una torta papalle in tempo di quaresma* (Recipe 170) and *Una bona torta papalle per fare collatione* (Recipe 171). Only the first of these corresponds roughly to our recipe; the second describes a variant of the dish.

The qualification in the name may recall the *Salsa papale* of Recipe 117, although a similarity between the two preparations does not seem to go beyond their names.

❖ 183. Because it is a lean or Lenten dish, this omelet depends upon fish eggs — a whole "beakerful" of them — rather than chicken eggs. As an optional alternative to the herbs, Riva allows garlic as well as onion.

❖ 184. Recipes 183 and 184 make use of the same secondary ingredients, so that the distinction between them must lie in their primary ingredient. However, modern caviar is understood to be the roe, or eggs, of any large fish though particularly of sturgeon. Because of the way this recipe refers back to the ingredients "for the pike," we may perhaps assume that sturgeon eggs (or those of some other large fish) are involved here, and only half the quantity of them is required relative to the pike eggs (of Recipe 183) and to the other ingredients.

❖ 185. Two dishes, called generically *tartare* and *tartari*, conclude this section of Lenten dishes in the Neapolitan manuscript. Reference has been made earlier to this sort of preparation, in the dishes called *Una tartara alla sienese* (Recipe 133) and *Tartara julatica* (Recipe 134): according to these recipes, a *tartara* is a variety of crustless custard baked in a big, covered pan in the coals. For a lower crust on the buttered baking dish, the *Tartara julatica* gives the cook a choice between breadcrumbs or grated cheese or merely a sprinkling of flour.

In the first of these Lenten *tartare* a beaker of pike eggs is mixed with ground pine nuts and cooked apples and is set to the depth of a finger(-width) on a pastry crust in a low pan. Concerning the consistency of this filling, Riva directs that the mixture be strained "under pressure so that it is somewhat thick but not too much so." Otherwise a couple of passages in our text turn up a little garbled in the Riva copy. In neither copy is there any indication as to why this dish should be qualified as being "in the French fashion."

❖ 186. As is the case for the previous dish, these *Tartari bianchi* seem to be known (by this same name) only in the collection of the Riva del Garda manuscript. They might be thought to be a lean (or Lenten) counterpart to the *Torta biancha* (Recipe 125) which is made of chicken eggs (or just egg whites), cheese, milk and butter.

The marginal insertion of the word *torte* here is a fairly dependable indication that the *tartare* must have been considered a variety of that other dish: mixtures, usually custards, on a lower crust of some sort, enclosed in a baking dish and baked, usually slowly, in moderately hot coals or embers.

The appended note, concerning the judicious use of *sale* and the need for a professional sensitivity on the part of the cook in such matters, are unique to the Neapolitan Collection. Because there is no explicit mention of "salt" as an ingredient in the body of the recipe proper, but rather of sugar, ginger and rosewater, we incline to a broader, generic interpretation of "seasoning" for the word *sale*—fully recognizing that the word here may still be intended in its literal sense.

❖ 187. With this folio we find ourselves in a series of recipes for the preparation of fish. This "chapter" will be the last in the Neapolitan Recipe Collection, as such a chapter frequently is in other recipe collections of the time. Most of these recipes appear in Riva and in the *Libro de arte coquinaria*, and occasionally a sequence of recipes will be the same; Platina shows considerable indifference to considerations of piscatory cuisine.

In the versions of the first recipe here, both Riva and the *Arte coquinaria* allow sardines to be roasted as well; for the garnish, both allow verjuice as an alternative to orange juice.

❖ 188. This carefully detailed recipe for preparing octopus is reproduced in the Riva del Garda manuscript, but in the *Arte coquinaria* it is reduced to merely, "This is a vile fish of no value; therefore cook it however you want."

❖ 189. In both Riva and the *Arte coquinaria* these crabs are assimilated to crayfish (*gambari*), which are dealt with (boiled in water and vinegar) in an earlier recipe in those collections; crayfish do not appear in the Neapolitan Collection.

❖ 190. The warning that the cook should check that the salt fish has not gone bad is enlarged a little in the *Arte coquinaria*: When cut into strips, the flesh should have a good, russet (*roscio*) color. This recipe is passed over by the compiler of the Riva collection. Platina, in the second half of his Recipe X,23 for sturgeon (our Recipe 199), reproduces Martino's text but inserts a useful note toward the beginning of his copy: *Ex stirione sit salitura quam vulgo "schinale" vocant, quasi "spinale", quod ex dorso spina fiat* . . . : "There is a fish pickle also made from sturgeon which is commonly called *schinale*, as if *spinale* because it is made from the back and spine."

❖ 191. Across Europe—from England (Austin, "B," Recipe 163) to France (*Doctrine*, 41; *Viandier*, Recipes 136 and 156; *Menagier de Paris*, Recipes 210 and 273) to Italy (*Tractatus*, III, Recipe 5)—and from the beginning of the fourteenth century throughout the fifteenth, there was general agreement that rayfish should be boiled and that it should be served with a garlic sauce. This seems to have been universal culinary practice. The use of such a "hot" sauce, in a humoral sense,[71] suggests a widespread recognition that the nature of rayfish required forceful correction. Its dietary and gastronomic values were questionable. In fact, rather than copy a recipe for *raie* the compiler of the Riva manuscript rather disdainfully dismisses the fish with the observation, *Per cocere raie, cocello como ti pyace, che non ghe grassa, e poi ha de farne pocha stima* (Recipe 264).

The sense of the notation that continues after this recipe into the bottom margin is obscure. There have been two earlier references to Catharina (in Recipe 25) and to Catharina Fasanicha (in Recipe 133), though neither is qualified by the word "Florentine" as here. The person (if indeed this is a proper noun) seems to have been an acquaintance of the author or patron (or, perhaps, even scribe)—and someone whom his pen could treat with almost playful familiarity; or else she may have been a person whose gastronomic taste enjoyed some sort of general recognition in the circle of the readership of this manuscript.

For the words *fasanica* and *fasanitico*, one possibility occurs: these words may be adjectives derived from *fasano*, "pheasant," a dialectal form attested to in our manuscript. If so, their sense may be erotic. The feminine of the wildfowl, *fagiana* continues in Italian, especially in Tuscan, to be used as a metaphor for the vulva. It is interesting that the foods to which the term is applied in our Collection all have vaguely similar natures: in Recipe 18, the so-called "lasagne" made from boiled pieces of capon skin and called *Menestra fasanica*; in the present Recipe 191, the boiled rayfish, generally despised as a food in other recipe collections, is exalted with the designation of *pasto de Catherina fasaniticha florentina*; and in Recipe 134, the deep-fried cheesecake would take on a rather pliable, undulating skin. The designations of *fasanica* might in every case be a facetious evocation of female genitalia. *Catharina* may be no specific woman; the phrase *Catharina fasanicha* may be a conventional means to evoke a woman of easy virtue.[72]

As for the qualification "Florentine," if the above conjecture about the image of the "pheasant" is correct we may also dare suggest that the modern reputation that north-Italian women enjoy, in southern Italy, for a carnality unfettered by excessive pudicity may indeed date from earlier centuries.

---

[71] The qualities of garlic are hot and dry, both in the fourth degree. See, for instance, the *Régime du corps de maître Aldebrandin de Sienne*, ed. Louis Landouzy and Roger Pépin (Paris: Champion, 1911), 162. An assessment in the fourth, the most extreme, degree indicated that a foodstuff could constitute a mortal danger to any person consuming it; cooks (or physicians) should resort to it only with great caution and primarily as a corrective to other foods whose humoral tendencies are in the opposite directions.

[72] One may hesitate to suggest that the phrase the scribe wrote earlier, about "smelling of Catharina," would also jibe with this interpretation of the name. In Recipe 25, the cook is advised to wash tripe well, *che non sapiano da Catharina*.

❖ 192. This recipe receives a good amount of detailed attention from our author. In Riva the recipe for shad is very much shorter and in several respects quite different;[73] in the *Arte coquinaria* both cooking methods are mentioned but the respective sauces appropriate to each method of preparation are abbreviated to simply two names: Green Sauce (see the comments to Recipe 106) for the one, and White Sauce (our Recipe 104) for the other. The *forzina* or gill rakers in shad are bony processes that are to be removed through the fish's gill.

❖ 193. The identification of the fish that our scribe writes as *bessano* poses a slight problem. In the corresponding recipe in Martino's *Arte coquinaria*, where the text is quite similar, the fish's name is written as *bestino*: "catfish." That later version extends the recipe that we read in our Collection by appending a surprisingly Platinesque comment: "You may be assured that any catfish is most foul (*velissimo* — that is, *vilissimo*) and more suitable for cobblers (to eat) than gentlemen." (Platina reproduces only six of the fish recipes that have survived in the Neapolitan Collection as it now is, and the recipe for *bessano/bestino* is not one of them.) The Riva compiler does not copy this recipe nor the two that follow it here.

❖ 194, 195. Neither of these recipes, for sea bream and turtle, has a counterpart in either the Riva del Garda manuscript or the *Arte coquinaria*. It should be noted, though, that the first of the recipes, for *fravolino*, has been added into the bottom margin of the page. The term *acarpionado* with which this recipe ends is explained by Riva in that collection's Recipe 279 whose incipit reads, *Per fare carpionare tructe a modo di carpioni.*[74] The *carpione* is the carp that is peculiar to Lake Garda. The verb *carpionare* is still today a culinary term derived from this particular fish and referred originally to a peculiar treatment given that carp; nowdays the Italian term is glossed "to souse" in English. According to the Riva author there would seem to be four steps in order to *carpionare* a trout — and, apparently, the sea bream of our Recipe 194: clean, eviscerate and puncture the fish; pickle it in salted vinegar and water; compress it; fry it in oil.

❖ 196. The recipe whose conclusion alone we can read at this point in the Neapolitan manuscript seems to be for eel. Though eel is very common in late-medieval cookery, our collection (in the imperfect state in which we possess it) refers to this fish only here and in Recipe 50 where it is merely an option in an alternative procedure.

Not enough of this recipe is extant for us to be able with any great assurance to identify any cognate reading in another manuscript. However, the *De apereylar be de menyar* does contain directions for *Anguiles en ast fets aytal salse* (Recipe 120: see Appendix C), a recipe that is copied

---

[73] The text of Recipe 267 in the Riva del Garda manuscript is as follows: *Per cocere lasche: volleno essere fritte adaxio, che non si bruxano; e per suo sapore li daray salza verde o vero agresto verde.*

[74] The whole of that Riva recipe is as follows: *Per fare carpionare tructe a modo di carpioni, nettalle et cavalle fora l'interiora, ponzondolle a molti lochi con la puncta del cortello da ogni parte; et faray salmoyra de aqua e de accetto equalmente, mettendoli del salle asay, el qualle faray stringere ben, et dentro li metteray le tructe per mezo giorno et piu; facto questo, li cavaray fora, mettendolli sopra una tavolla et in sopressa tre o quatro hore, et frigendo molto ben in bono ollio; et fa che siano ben cocte et non arse. Et queste tructe potray conservare uno mese, frigendolle dele altre volte, sel te pyacera, reffazendolla a modo di carpione.*

more or less literally into the *Libre de sent soví* (Recipe 198); the end of this text is similar to what we have in the Neapolitan Collection. Both copies of the Catalan version show that the eels are cooked by boiling, then chopped into chunks and the sauce served in bowls. This sauce is hot and has been composed of ground almonds, spices, saffron and boiling water; alternatively, and preferably according to the Catalan text, a Garlic White Sauce could be used for eating these eels.

The Riva and *Arte coquinaria* recipe collections have five recipes involving eel, three of which direct the cook on ways to cook and dress eel as a dish in itself, and two of which are for an eel torte. Only Recipe 273 in Riva, titled *Per cocere le anguille in altro modo,*[75] offers an ending that is suggestive of the brief remnant in our manuscript. The whole of this recipe in Riva reads as follows:

> *Per cocere le anguille in altro modo: dell'anguilla e dicto nel altro capitolo abastanza, ma habi per ricordo che quando mette li pezi de essa nel spedo ad uno ad uno, sempre si volle mettere foglie de lauro e de salvia tra l'uno e l'altro, voltando dicto spedo tanto adaxio quanto sia possibille et spexa bagnarli con salmoyra como di sopra facto; e li altri pezi quando parerano preso cocti, habi uno pocho di farina, pocho pane grattato con pocho di canella e salle miscollato insema, buttandoli destramente sopra l'anguilla per farle con questo a modo de una crosta intorno, che li dara bon gusto; e quando e picolla, la potray allessare in aqua o in vino con herbe e spezie, como e dicto nel altro capitullo.*

In the first line of this Riva and Martino recipe, the reference to what has already been written *nel altro capitolo* seems to be to Riva's previous Recipe 248 (Recipe 219 in the *Arte coquinaria*) where the rubric is merely *Per cocere anguilla.*

❖ 197. The name of this dish points distinctly to an Iberian source, and one is obvious in the Catalan collection, *De apereylar be de menyar*. There a dish called *Calamas farcits* is at Recipe 123 whose text, despite its length, is close throughout to that of this recipe in our manuscript. When the texts are set together (see Appendix C) the only significant variant is that the Catalan recipe includes herbs (parsley and marjoram) in the squid's stuffing whereas our version does not. In the *Libre de sent soví* (Recipe 217) this same recipe appears under the rubric *Con sa deu coura calamas al fforn.*

❖ 198. Clearly, and very regrettably, the recipe for *Tencha reversa* which is referred to here as providing direction of squid stuffing, has been lost from our collection. The "inside-out" procedure is a relatively common treatment for preparing larger fish and small animals; most notable in our collection it is used for the Holy Piglet of Recipe 63.

The very detailed text that we read for *Tencha reversa* in the Riva manuscript is contained within Recipe 254 of that collection: *Per cocere tenche.*[76] The passage reads as follows:

---

[75] This is Recipe 251 in the *Arte coquinaria,* although it lacks a rubric in the Washington manuscript. In the Vatican copy the rubric faithfully reads: *Per quocere l'anguilla in altro modo.*

[76] A similar text is copied for *Tenca reversciata* in the *Arte coquinaria,* within Recipe 229 for *Tenche.*

Per cocere tenche, elli sono tre modi bone . . . .

Lo primo, allesso quando 'l'e grassa . . . .

El secondo modo, la potray fare reversa essendo grossa: rescharalla e nettaralla bene, fendendolla dal collo a la coda per il fillo de la schina, e caveray fora tutta l'interiora e rompera ben suttille sue coste; poy prenderay le sue ova e lo grasso del figato; e non havendo la tencha, serano boni delli altri pessi; e habi bono petreseno e altre bone herbe odoriffere pistandolle insema con li figatelli e ova e grasso de pesso, zonzendolli uno pocho de aglio tagliato minuto, uno pocho de pipero, de zafrano e del salle e uno pocho de ollio; item, dele brugne dalmasine seche e dele visolle o cirexe o dela uga passa o [gigibo][77] *con alquanti pignelli mondi; item uno rosso o due de ova fresche secondo lo tempo; et incorpora molto ben tutte queste cosse insema, le metteray sopra sopra questa tencha e reversata — zioe, sopra la pelle vengha dal lato dentro — e falla cusire, o vero ligarla atorno con uno spagho in modo che rettengha questo pyeno, et mettello sopra la gratticula dandolli lo focho adaxio per che volle essere ben cocta; e, rostendolla, faray una salmora con acceto, ollio, sale, saffrano, pipero et uno pocho de sabba, et spexo la voltaray bagnandolla con questa salmora.*

Tercio et ultimo modo e quando la tengha e picolla . . . .

For his squid stuffing, therefore, the Neapolitan cook was likely intending a composition that included fish eggs, fish fat, fish liver, parsley, savory herbs, finely chopped garlic, pepper, saffron, salt and oil, all beaten together. Optional ingredients in this stuffing are prunes, sweet or sour cherries, raisins or muscat grapes and pine nuts, as are one or two raw egg yolks.

❖ 199. The basic recipe of this paragraph (along with the alternative sauces written at the top of the next page, f° 72v) remains unchanged in the somewhat amplified treatment the dish is given in the versions read in Riva and the *Arte coquinaria.* In both of these later compilations, though, directions are split into two recipes: cooking and garnishing, preparing the *sturiono* (Recipes 229 and 196, respectively) and the *sapore* (Recipes 230 and 197, respectively). Those later versions allow vinegar to be substituted (!) for the white wine of the cooking sauce, add *manzo* ("young steer") to our *vitello*, insert several qualifications to guide the cook when he cuts up the sturgeon, point out that a large pot is needed for cooking it whole, add "as my lord does," and finally lay down the general culinary rule that we read in the Neapolitan manuscript to the effect that any fish is gastronomically "much better whole than in pieces or sliced open."[78]

The second part of the Neapolitan recipe names three suitable serving sauces: White Sauce (with added ginger), White Garlic Sauce, or Mustard Sauce. The other two collections point out that a choice among those sauces depends upon the day (whether a meat or lean day) and upon one's taste; they then indicate that a recipe for each sort of sauce has already be given in a previous chapter. In Platina's *Honesta voluptate* (Recipe X,23) this whole text for both the cooking and the saucing of the sturgeon is condensed to a mere three lines.

---

77 The Riva del Garda manuscript is smudged here and not clearly legible. At this point the text in the *Libro de arte coquinaria* reads *uva passa o gigibo*: "raisins or muscat grapes."

78 The *Libro de arte coquinaria* says, a little more universally, . . . *che in pezi o altramente!*

❖ 200. The recipe for umbrine or corb is (with the previous recipe for sturgeon) one of the rare recipes for fish that Platina cares for enough to bother copying (*Lumbrina*, Recipe X,25). The fish *ombrina* is glossed by the Accademici della Crusca as *un pesce assai simile allo storione*; it is interesting to note that our author also assimilates it to the sturgeon. Though classified today as of a different family, the fish of the next recipe, the *dentale*, has an appearance similar to the corb, and the fish dealt with in Recipe 202, the *corvo grosso*, is likely also related to these in the author's mind.

❖ 201. This recipe for the dentex offers the peculiarity of cooking the fish in vinegar. Our text provides two explanations for this specific procedure, one culinary (so cooked, the fish lasts longer) and one gastronomical (it tastes better that way). The version of this recipe found in Riva and the *Arte coquinaria* tries to elaborate a little on the first explanation, though not too helpfully because it has lost the essential direction that the fish be cooked in vinegar: *Volle essere allesato e tenuto ben frescho; non li bixogna mettere tanto vino o acceto: stringha et fa sodo et fa piu conservare lo pesso* . . . .

❖ 202. According to Riva and the *Arte coquinaria* this large corb may also be fried, and the Green Sauce with which it is to be eaten should "taste slightly of garlic and a lot of ginger."

❖ 203. The reworking of this recipe in Riva and the *Arte coquinaria* has the cook boil the large daurade, then inserts, *et molto ben sasonare*; there is no explanation either why such careful seasoning is required for this particular fish or of what it should consist.

❖ 204. This recipe for turbot is another instance in which the Neapolitan version is simple and straightforward but the persons responsible for the texts found in Riva and in the *Arte coquinaria* seize any chance to expatiate and to transmit a little of the extensive practical culinary experience they believe they possess. Discontent with the mere word *frollo*, Riva has *fragille* whereas Martino writes *molto fragile et si rompe facilemente*; for the *sopra una graticula de canuze*, Riva and Martino write "in a wicker basket or bind it on a cutting board"—then these later compilers feel they should explain, " . . . so as to be able to take it out whole (*integro* / *sano*) when it is cooked, so that it will not break up." In a passage almost twice as long as the recipe has been, the later compilers express a general, and very wordy, rule about how slowly fish should be boiled.[79] In all of this verbosity the reviser of the *Arte coquinaria* overlooks mentioning the appropriate serving sauce for turbot.

❖ 205. The handling of red mullet is developed at greater length in Riva and the *Arte coquinaria* with directions for preserving the fish "for eight or ten days"; no serving sauce is mentioned in either of the later works.

❖ 208. In Riva and the *Arte coquinaria* the *hochiali* or *ochiali* (or saddled bream) are "better fried or roasted than boiled."

---

[79] In the *Riva del Garda* copy we read: . . . *Volle buglire molto a daxio. Et nota che ogni pesso generalmente vole buglire adaxio; et bixogna intendere ben la qualitta del pesso, si sono di piu caldi o dura l'uno ch'al'altro, et delli piu teneri e piu molli: cossi volleno cocere chi piu e chi mancho secundo lo bixogno; ma volleno buglire piano, suavemente, tanto che siano ben cocte.* The wording in the *Arte coquinaria* is similar, if even more inflated: for instance, the last *piano, suavemente* is now *piano, suavemente, ad ascio*.

❖ 209. The sea-bream (spelled *sargho* in Riva and *sorche* in the *Arte coquinaria*) can be "fried or roasted" in the other collections.

❖ 210. As in their version of the recipe for *Corvo grosso* (Recipe 202), Riva and the *Arte coquinaria* specify a garlic-flavored green sauce in this recipe for moray eel. Generally speaking, the person responsible for the Neapolitan Collection does not make as much use of garlic as seems to be normal elsewhere in Italian cookery of the time.

❖ 211. Two rather distinct fish are dealt with together in this recipe, the grey mullet and the mackerel. These are of roughly the same size and shape, though of quite different coloring. The Riva del Garda compilation deals with only the second by name, the *macharella* (Recipe 246); the *Arte coquinaria* treats them in separate paragraphs (*cefalo*, Recipe 215; *maccarella*, Recipe 214), roasting or boiling the first (according to size), frying or boiling the second and then dressing it with "pepper and parsley," a distant echo of the sauce we read of in the Neapolitan recipe.

❖ 212. For the sauce that is appropriate for boiled flounder, if large, the reference is to Recipe 204 for turbot. There the sauce is parsley, pepper and saffron in verjuice. Both Riva and the *Arte coquinaria* add a little parsley to the water in which the fish is to be boiled; and, as an alternative, they allow turbot to be fried and then sauced in orange juice.

❖ 213. The identification of the Venetian way of eating oysters is unique to our manuscript. It seems to apply to the type of dressing set out here, a spiced verjuice. If the sauce is meant to accompany oysters when prepared according to either of the methods mentioned, grilled or fried, then the so-called "Venetian way" might identify fried oysters eaten with this sauce.

❖ 214. In our Collection the name of the subject of this paragraph is written *lampuge*, "black fish." Likewise in the Riva manuscript the name of the fish was first written, *lampuge*, but then someone, the original scribe or someone later, changed the word to *lamprede*. For the *Arte coquinaria*, the untitled text of the same recipe in the Washington manuscript has *la lampuga*; however, in the Vatican manuscript of the same work (at f° 57v), the corresponding recipe bears as a rubric *Per quocere lampugne*, and in the text that follows the scribe has clearly (if erroneously) written *la lampugna*.

❖ 215. The concluding generalization about this being the appropriate treatment for "all shellfish" is found only in our manuscript.

❖ 216. It is perhaps a little surprising that, given the high regard that the pike enjoyed in the repertoire of the Neapolitan cook (particularly because of its eggs and its broth), and in the cookery of the period in general, only one way of preparing the fish itself and only one presentation sauce are provided in this collection. And perhaps surprising, too, that the text of this recipe is as laconic as any.

The Riva del Garda collection abbreviates our short text even more by writing merely "boil the fish" and by not bothering to specify the nature of the broth in which this boiling is to take place. The sauce is to be some sort of *mostarda biancha*. But to this brief recipe the same compiler appends a much longer study of the *luzio d'aqua dolze*, "freshwater pike." The *Libro de arte coquinaria* separates the two varieties of fish into two recipes: the first, our text, is identified as for *Merluzo*; the second (Recipe 227) is for *Luccio d'aqua dolce*. The freshwater variety of pike may not have held much interest for our Neapolitan cook.

❖ 217. This trout recipe seems concerned primarily with ensuring that salt penetrate into the flesh of the fish as it is cooked. Riva and the *Arte coquinaria* try to clarify the way in which the sliced trout is to be laid in the *vaso* (or *caldaro*, as they write): our text has ... *li diti pezi per longo—dico che lo tagliato guarda in su*; the others change this to *che li pezi venghano* (*che quello tagliato venga*) *di sopra e asettando in questa forma a sollo a sollo*. This overlapped layering of the trout slices will expose them as much as possible to the salt as they cook. The later versions of the recipe also add a treatment for small trout.

❖ 218. Roasting, frying and occasional boiling are not unusual methods of cooking fish in fifteenth-century culinary practice. Baking a fish is not common, though. In the Neapolitan Collection the recipe headed by the rubric *Tencha in tegamo* is not only one of the longest and most detailed of the entire compilation, it is also exceptional in that it combines four distinct treatments for this foodstuff.

The name *Tench in a Baking Dish* applies only to the first of the four parts of this recipe. In Riva and the *Arte coquinaria* the name of the recipe is simply *Tenche*. Textually there are few close parallels in the exposition of the various methods of preparing tench.

The *tegamo* in question is a large pot, likely flat-bottomed and of earthenware[80] and perhaps covered; in other recipes in our collection it bears foodstuffs into the oven or into hot coals. The present instance of its use has it as a container for the stuffed tench and a complex cooking broth; there is no mention whether it is to be covered as for a baking process.

While Riva and the *Arte coquinaria* present three methods of preparing tench, and enumerate them quite explicitly, none is a copy of the long initial procedure here, the one that alone is properly named *Tencha in tegamo*. Only the filling described in the first part of the *Tencha in tegamo* turns up in the other versions for *Tengha reversa*. We have already shown (see above in the comment to Recipe 198) that Riva and the *Arte coquinaria* contain, as their second method here in their chapters on *Tenche*, what the Neapolitan Collection referred to as the inside-out procedure, or Reversed Tench. The final method in this recipe in Riva and the *Arte coquinaria*, in which the tench is opened, salted and fried, is the third procedure (for tench of one-half or one pound) of the four possibilities in our collection.

❖ 219. The practice of killing a lamprey in a pot of wine goes back at least several centuries before the time of this particular collection.[81] Undoubtedly related to the doctrine that a lamprey

---

[80] In its version of our next receipe for *Lampreda*, the *Libro de arte coquinaria* calls expressly for a *tegame di terra*.

[81] ... *Salva reverentia utentium, iste piscis* [the *lampreda*] *est valde periculosus, quamvis sit ori saporosus. Horum enim piscium in aqua similis est generatio generationi serpentum in terra. Unde multum dubitandum est que non sint venenosi. Unde eorum capita et caude in quibus venenum consuevit esse, et similiter interior spina, nullo modo sunt edenda. Bonum est etiam propter eorum viscositatem que submergantur in vino optimo vive, et*

possesses a humoral nature that is dangerously cool and moist, entirely analogous to that of a snake and further reinforced by the lamprey's habitat, the practice of killing it in wine sought — by affording an intimate contact with both the relative warmth and "dryness" of red wine — to begin at the earliest moment a warming and drying process that would render the lamprey safe, or at least safer, for human consumption. Red wine possesses those qualities, warmth and dryness, in the second degree.

The notion that the lamprey's blood represents its essence is also of long standing, being reproduced in English and French recipe collections of the fourteenth century. See, for instance, the *Forme of Cury* (Recipe 130), the *Viandier* (Recipe 69: *Gardez bien le sang car c'est la gresse*), and the *Menagier* (Recipe 185).

The Riva del Garda manuscript and the *Libro de arte coquinaria* copy this recipe into their compilations, amplifying a few passages and inserting qualifications in others. In particular the second work omits directing that the lamprey be killed in (sweet) wine; of interest in this regard might be its misreading of the word *morire* as *mollare*. The *Arte coquinaria* specifies that the *tegame* be earthenware. Both later works present an image that this vessel be set on the coals "like a torte"; and both offer the option that the lamprey's blood be drained before the lamprey is set cooking. Our second method appears likewise to have been enlarged upon slightly by Riva the *Arte coquinaria*. At the point at which the text of the Neapolitan manuscript breaks off (at the foot of f° 76v), the text in Riva (and the *Arte coquinaria*) continues, ... *et con questo* [*sangue*] *potray fare uno sapore como si mostra di sopra, loqualle daray con essa lampreda.* The sauce for this roast lamprey is to be the same, then, as for the lamprey cooked in the baking dish.

Following the text we have just quoted from Riva, both of the later versions offer a third recipe, for small lamprey — or as the *Arte coquinaria* writes, *le piccole, cio e le lampredoze*, "lamprill"; whether this recipe was on a page now missing from the Neapolitan manuscript is unknown. In Riva the text runs as follows: *Ma le picolle volleno essere rostite adaxio sopra gratizella, facendoli uno sapore con sugo de ranzi e sabba; et non havendo pome ranzi, metteray uno d'agresto con uno pocho di salle e delle spezie dolze; et mentre se arostisseno, li bagnaray con dicto sapore; et cocte li metteray suxo lo remanente sopra;*[82] *et manda a tavolla (Recipe 256).*

❖ 220. This must be one of the earliest written recipes for zabaglone.[83] Its ingredients are those still required in its more modern treatment: egg yolks, sugar and a sweet wine (today, Marsala).

At Recipe 104 in the Riva del Garda manuscript (but, most curiously, not in the *Arte coquinaria*) a recipe has been written whose text, despite differences in quantities, resembles what someone has written on f° 89v in the Neapolitan manuscript.

---

dimittantur ibidem quo usquem mortue sint, et deinde preparantur cum galentina optimarum specierum, secundum que coci magnorum dominorum consueverunt facere. ... Magninus Mediolanensis, *Regimen sanitatis*, chapter 18, *De piscibus*.

82 In the *Arte coquinaria* this last passage reads, ... *le mettirai sopra il rimanente del sapore sopradditto* (Recipe 231).

83 See the monograph by Simona Leone, "Lo zabaione," in *Appunti di Gastronomia* (Milan: Condeco) 13 (1994): 28.

Per fare bono zabaglione per farne una taza, piglia quatro ova—zoe, lo rossumo—e del zucharo e canella a sufficienzia e de bono vino amabille—e sel fusse troppo fumoso, mettelli uno pocho d'aqua o de brodo magro; poy fa lo cocere como se coce lo brodeto et sempre menalo con lo cugiaro; et quando se imbratta, leva lo zabaglione dal focho, poy mettello in una taza. E questo se da a la sera quando l'homo va a dormir. Et notta ch'el conforta lo cervello.

IV. Translation of the Recipes

In this Translation several regular procedures have been followed. As in the text, the symbols ⌈ and ⌋ enclose text that is marginal and seems to have been added to what was originally copied. Editorial material not explicitly in the manuscript text (though perhaps indicated by a marginal notation), but introduced into this translation, is enclosed in square brackets: [ ]. In most instances we have translated the word *menestre* as "serving" although it should be borne in mind that this measure of quantity of a prepared dish may be sufficient for two or more persons — in fact enough for the number of individuals who would be expected to share food from the same dish, platter or bowl.

1. To make a good Pepper Sauce.

To make a good Pepper Sauce for goat kid, hare, wild boar or any other game animal, get equal amounts of water and red wine and wash the meat in this; strain this washing-liquid, then cook the meat in it, adding a little salt; when the meat is cooked, lift it out. If you wish to make two plates of Pepper Sauce, get a pound and a half of raisins and grind them up well, and as much again of bread, thinly sliced and toasted on the grill and soaked in good vinegar, and grind it with the raisins; if you can get the pluck of those game animals, it would be best to grind this in as well; when everything is ground up well, it ought to be distempered with the broth of the meat along with a little must or vinegar; then strain all this into a pot, adding all sorts of spices and a fair amount of pepper; then boil it for half an hour away from a hot fire, and keep it out of the smoke, stirring it often with a spoon; then fry the meat in good *lardo*,[1] dish it out and cover it with this Pepper Sauce — the darker the prettier. To make it dark take a ram's spleen and grind that up with the above.

⌈Note that, if you wish, there should be a beaker of strong vinegar and strong ginger with this meat.⌋

2. A Consommé Broth.

Get well cleaned capons or partridge, pheasants or pigeons or wood doves; and, if you wish to make a consommé from one capon with two servings of broth, get a large mortar with four jugs of water, and put into it a capon whose bones are ground up, along with an ounce of salt pork, thirty grains of ground pepper, cinnamon, 5 or 6 cloves, 5 or 6 shredded sage leaves and one of bay laurel; let this boil for seven hours, putting in no salt. Also, it will be better to add in the above spices when almost the better part of the broth has boiled away.

[1] For reasons noted in the Glossary, the original term *lardo* is kept throughout this Translation.

3. White Dish of Chickens or Doves.

When they are well cooked, take the breast and grind it up; then get ground rice, and almond milk distempered adequately with the chicken broth and rice, and cook it on the coals; when well cooked and thick, add in fine sugar to cook with it; and when it is cooked and as thick as a thick broth, take it off the fire and serve it up garnished with sugar.

4. Twelve Servings of White Dish to go on Capons.

Get two pounds of blanched almonds and steep them for a day in cool water; then get one or more breasts of capon and grind them up with the almonds and a crustless loaf of white bread soaked in lean broth; then get a little verjuice, half an ounce of peeled ginger and more than half a pound of sugar; distemper all this in lean capon broth and strain it into a pot which you will set against the fire, away from the smoke, constantly stirring with a spoon, and let it cook for half an hour; when cooked, add in three ounces of rosewater; then dish it up or, if you wish, cover capons or any other fowl with this White Dish, and serve; to make it all prettier, garnish with a few pomegranate seeds.

5. Twelve Servings of Catalan-Style White Dish.

Get two jugs of goat's milk, and eight ounces of rice flour and set it to boil in the milk; then get a half-cooked capon breast and shred all this finely like hair, then put it in a mortar and pound it a couple of times with the pestle; when the milk has boiled for half an hour, add the capon breast into it along with a pound of sugar and let it all boil for four hours, stirring continuously with a spoon all the while; you will know it is cooked when it sticks to the spoon; then add in two ounces of rosewater; dish it up garnished on top with sugar unmixed with anything else.

6. Ten Servings of White Dish [for Lent].

Get one and a half pounds of skinned almonds and grind them up; get a crustless loaf of bread soaked in pea broth; get half a pound of boiled fish flesh, and grind everything together; get eight ounces of sugar, half an ounce of ginger and three ounces of rosewater, distemper these together, strain them, and cook the mixture for about an eighth of an hour on the coals, so that it does not pick up smoke.

7. Rice with Almond Milk.

To make ten servings get a pound and a half of almonds and half a pound of rice; wash the rice three times, cook it well and drain it thoroughly; grind the almonds — so they do not make oil as they are ground, add in a little clear water or rosewater — and strain them; set the almond milk to boil in a pot with half a pound of fine sugar; as it begins to boil, add in the rice and put the pot on coals away from the fire, stirring continuously with a spoon, and let it boil for half an hour.

Similarly, you can cook the rice with goat's milk or some other milk.

Nota: To keep any similar dish from picking up smoke, take a cloth folded in three or four layers — but first, remove the preparation from the pot, without scraping the bottom, and put it into another pot; then soak the cloth in clear water, wring it out, place it thus folded over the pot and leave it there for half an hour, or for at least a quarter of an hour; then soak it again, and put it back again on the pot: this is how the smokey taste is drawn out. Proceed likewise for Spelt Porridge [*Recipe* 9]: there is no better way.

8. Rice in the Italian Style.

Put fat and lean broth into a pot and boil it; then get cleaned rice that has been washed several times in warm water, put it in and boil it, giving it a couple of turns with a spoon so that it does not stick to the pot; then, when it is cooked, get eggs and grated cheese, and beat everything together, along with a little pepper; set it out in bowls.

9. Spelt Porridge.

Cook the spelt in a pot with fat and lean broth and, when it is well cooked, add in one or two egg yolks beaten with grated cheese, along with pepper, saffron and cinnamon; and when it is set to cook, add in a piece of cured ham; when it is cooked, put cheese on top and serve it.

10. Ravioli.

Get a pound and a half of old cheese and a little new creamy cheese, and a pound of porkbelly or loin of veal that should be boiled until well cooked, then grind it up well; get well ground fragrant herbs, pepper, cloves, ginger and saffron, adding in a well ground breast of a capon, and mix in all of this together; make a thin dough and wrap nut-sized amounts of the mixture in it; set these ravioli to cook in the fat broth of a capon or of some other good meat, with a little saffron, and let them boil for half an hour; then dish them out, garnishing them with a mixture of grated cheese and good spices.

11. White Ravioli.

Get a good fresh buffalo cheese and grind it up thoroughly and, while grinding, add in a little butter, ginger and cinnamon; and for one cheese add in three well beaten egg whites and a decent amount of sugar; mix everything together; then shape it into ravioli the length and thickness of a finger and coat them with good flour; note that these ravioli are made without dough; boil them gently so that they do not fall apart; when they begin to boil, remove them and set them out in dishes with sugar and cinnamon. You can make them yellow with saffron.

12. Thick White Broth.

Grind almonds and strain them with verjuice; get roast cockerels; temper the almonds with verjuice, cinnamon, cloves and ginger, and pour this mixture over the cockerels and serve.

13. A Fine Thick Broth.

For ten servings, get three egg yolks per serving, good verjuice, good meat broth, a little saffron and fine spices; mix everything together, strain it and put it into a pot on the coals, stirring constantly until it coats the spoon; and so take it off the fire, stirring constantly for the length of two *Our Father*'s; then dish it out, putting mild spices on top. Make it sweet or bitter, depending on your master's taste, with verjuice or lemons [lemon juice].

14. Thick Broth of Bread, Cheese and Eggs.

Boil a grated half loaf of bread in a good meat broth for a quarter of an hour; then beat a little grated cheese with three eggs; let the bread cool a little and add the cheese and eggs into it and mix it thoroughly, making it yellow with saffron; and serve it.

15. Sicilian Macaroni.

Make a dough of the whitest flour, one egg white and rosewater—and should you be preparing two plates of it, put in only two or three egg yolks; make this dough quite tough, and make small round sticks of it a hand's width in length and the thickness of a straw; and get a fine iron rod a hand's width in length and the thickness of a cord, set it on a pastry stick and give them a roll with both hands on a table; then draw out the rod and you have the macaroni hollowed through the middle; these macaroni should dry in the sun and can be kept for two or three years; cook them in water or a good meat broth, and garnish them with grated cheese when you set them out on plates with fresh butter and mild spices. Boil them gently for an hour.

16. Roman Macaroni.

Out of fine flour make a dough that is a little larger than for lasagne, and wrap it around a stick, and cut the dough the width of a finger so that it stays like a ribbon; set it to cook in good broth or in some other liquid depending on the season; let the liquid boil first with a little salt before putting the macaroni in it; and if they are cooking in water, add a little fresh butter to it.

17. Vermicelli.

Cook them in good fat broth for an hour, then set them out garnished with grated Parmesan cheese and mild spices; first make them yellow with saffron. You can make lasagne in the same way.

18. Lasagne of Capon Skins [called a *Fasanica* Dish].

Cook capon skins by boiling—or else get the skins of boiled capons—cut them up and cook them in fat capon broth for half an hour with a little saffron; then set them out in dishes with grated Parmesan cheese and mild spices on top.

19. A Dish of "A Thousand Pageboys."

Take the crust off three loaves of bread, grate them, set this on a table and lay out a pound and a half of good flour around it; and put four or five eggs in with the ground bread and beat that well with a knife, always being careful [to coat] the bread with the flour; and when you have lumps that look to you to be as small as candied aniseed, put everything into a sieve and discard the [excess] flour; then dry them in the sun or by the fire. When you want to cook them, use meat broth made yellow with saffron; boil them gently for half an hour; serve them up garnished with cheese and spices.

20. A Dish of "Cardinals."

Take lean boiled veal and pound it as thin as you can, then boil it in fat broth, adding grated bread crumbs and a little pepper and saffron; let it boil a third of an hour and let it cool a little; then get three beaten eggs, grated cheese, parsley, a little marjoram and mint, and beat everything thoroughly together; put it into the pot, stirring with a spoon and adding a very little good verjuice.

⌈You can do the same with the pluck of goat kid or of any other animal.⌋

21. Peas with Salt Pork.

Get peas in the shell and bring them to a boil; get marbled salt pork and cut it into slices half a finger long, and fry them a little; then set the peas to fry with the pork, and add in a little verjuice, a little must, sugar and cinnamon. The same can be done with beans.

22. *Giusello* or *Zanzarelli*.

To make ten servings of this *Giusello*, get eight fresh eggs and half a pound of grated cheese and one loaf of bread, grated, and mix all this together; then get a pot of meat broth, set it on the fire and, when it begins to boil, put this mixture into it and stir it with a spoon, adding a little saffron; and when you see it thickening, take it off the fire and dish it up, with spices on top [and mixed in].

23. Cabbage in the Roman Style.

Get cabbage and break it up with your hands and put it into boiling water; when it is roughly half cooked, throw all the water away; get a good amount of good *lardo*, beat it and put it into the pot with the drained cabbage, stirring with a spoon; then get good fat broth and boil the mixture in it on the fire for two [three] hours, for it is not an unappetizing dish when one is hungry.

24. Lettuce that Looks Like Squash.

Take the stalk of lettuce and cook it like squash with eggs and verjuice; or else cook it like borrage by itself in a broth.

25. Tripe.

Get whatever tripe you want and clean it thoroughly so that it does not smell of Catharina;[2] then cook it with salt pork, and do not add any salt, so it is whiter; when cooked, cut it into small pieces and add a little sage and boil it again with sufficient salt; then dish it out, garnishing it with pepper, cinnamon and saffron.

26. Turnips.

Clean them carefully and cut them up into large pieces, and cook them till done in a fat meat broth; then sieve them through a perforated spoon, or else grind them, and boil them again briefly with a little salt pork; you dish them up with pepper and saffron on top.

27. Garnished Turnips.

Cook the turnips under the coals, or else boil them whole, then cut them into slices the thickness of a knife blade; get Parmesan cheese or some other good fat cheese cut into slices as broad as the turnip slices but thinner; and get sugar, pepper and mild spices mixed together; lay out these slices in a torte pan in layers—on the bottom the slices of cheese with good fresh butter on top, and then the slices of turnip, and so on from layer to layer always adding the spice mixture everywhere; you cook it like that in the pan, with a good amount of butter, for a quarter of an hour or more as you would a torte. This banquet dish is served after the others.

28. Sicilian Semolina Dish.

Cook the semolina in a fat broth, adding it little by little to the pot, stirring constantly with a spoon; boil it for half an hour on the coals away from the fire; then dish it up and put cheese and spices on top.

During Lent you can make this with almond milk, sugar and rosewater.

---

[2] Both the sense and the translation of the phrase *che non sapiano da Catharina* are uncertain. Our guess is that *Catharina* may have a carnal, even lewd, connotation. See the Comment to Recipe 191 concerning the word *fasanica*.

29. Squash.

Peel them thoroughly and cook them in a fat broth; when cooked, put them through a sieve or grind them [in a mortar], and put them back into a good broth, adding a little verjuice and saffron; then take them off the fire and let them cool; then get a number of egg yolks depending on the amount of the squash, beat them with a little grated old cheese and put that into the pot, constantly stirring with a spoon; then make up the dishes, putting mild spices on top.

30. Catalan-Style Gourds.

Get the gourds — that is, squash — and clean them thoroughly and put them into a mortar with salt pork and good beaten *lardo*, and put the mortar onto the coals and bring it to a boil, constantly stirring with a spoon; they should boil like that for two hours; then get good cheese, good fat broth, saffron, mild spices and a very little verjuice and put them into the pot — except for the cheese which should go in last along with the egg.

31. Broth for a Delicate Person.

Get cockerels and put them in a clean pot, fill it with plenty of water so that the scum can be removed; when skimmed, [add in] a little salt pork and cover the pot quickly, and the broth will become white; if it does not, break open a cockerel's head in the broth — that is, boil it broken open; when the cockerels and salt pork are cooked, boil the broth until it reduces to one or two bowlfuls.

32. Porridge for a Sick Person.

Get barley flour, almond milk and chicken broth, and put the flour, sieved, into the milk and set it to cook till done; dish it out; as it finishes cooking, add fine sugar.

33. Eggplants.

Get eggplants and wash and peel them well, then set a little water on the fire and bring them to a boil; cut them into quarters and add a little salt to the water; do not let them boil more than two *Our Father*'s; then take them out onto a cutting board and let them drain; coat them in flour and fry them; when they have fried, drain off almost all of the oil; get a clove of garlic, grind it up with a quarter-piece of the eggplants; then get a little oregano, of the sort that is put on anchovies, grind it up with the garlic and a little bread, pepper, saffron and salt; then distemper all of this together with verjuice and a little vinegar and throw everything together into the pan to fry a little; then dish it out and serve it with mild spices.

34. Hemp Seed Mustard.

For twelve servings, get one pound of hemp seeds and carefully clear any stones from them, then boil them until they begin to open; then get one pound of well blanched almonds and grind them up, add in a crustless loaf of bread and distemper this with meat broth; then grind up the hemp seeds and strain them with good broth, and put the strained material with the almond milk and set it to boil on the coals away from smoke, stirring constantly with a spoon; then add half a pound of good sugar and half an ounce of white ginger, a little saffron and rosewater; dish it up with mild spices on top.

35. Marzipan Dish.

For ten servings of Marzipan Dish get one pound of marzipan and grind it up thoroughly and put with it a capon wing that has been ground up as much as possible; get crustless bread in the amount of an egg and soak it in lean broth; then get a little verjuice, a little rosewater, a little capon broth, and distemper everything together, and cook it gently on the coals with a little ginger; let it come to a boil or a little more, then dish it up with sugar and cinnamon on top.

36. Melon Dish.

Get good melons and take out the good part and grind it in a mortar and set it to boil in a little fat broth; then take it a little away from the fire and, for every bowl, add in one egg beaten with a little good cheese, a little verjuice, a little ginger or pepper, and saffron; and when dishing up, put sugar and cinnamon on top; this dish should be somewhat thick.

37. Catalan-Style Mirausto.

Begin by getting pigeons or cockerels or capons, prepare them as for a roast and set them to roast on a spit; when they are half cooked, take them down and quarter them, and split each quarter in two, and put them into a pot; then get almonds and grind them up thoroughly, and get two slices of toast and four hard-boiled egg yolks and grind up all this with the almonds and distemper it with a little vinegar or broth and strain it; then put it into the pot on top of the meat, adding in good spices — that is, a good lot of cinnamon and a good lot of sugar; then set the pot on the coals and let it boil for half an hour, stirring constantly with a spoon; when it is cooked, serve this Mirausto in dishes or in bowls, and give it a cameline colour.

38. Stewed Herbs.

Get a little marjoram, mint, chard and a lot of parsley, bring them to a boil, then take them off the fire and squeeze the water out of them; then beat them with a knife and put them in good fat broth with a little salt pork.

39. White Genestrata.

Get almonds, peel them and grind them up thoroughly and, when ground, strain them; put them in a pot with sufficient sugar; then make rice flour and mix it into the almond milk and set it to cook, stirring constantly; when it begins to thicken, add in dates and pinenuts and cook them; when you see it thickening, take it off the fire and set it on some warm cinders; then dish it up, putting sugar, rosewater and cinnamon on top.

40. A Pottage of New Broad Beans.

Get new broad beans or *scafa* beans and set them to cook with a pair of pigeons along with a little salt pork off the bone; with this put marjoram, mint, sweet fennel, pepper, cinnamon and ginger — that is, when the beans and pigeons are almost cooked; and when they are cooked, put the beans and pigeons in the middle of a plate with the herb mixture on top.

41. Kidney Beans.

Cook the kidney beans in pure water or in good broth; when they are cooked, get finely sliced onions and fry them in a pan with good oil and put these fried onions on top [of the beans] along with pepper, cinnamon and saffron; then let this sit a while on the hot coals; dish it up with good spices on top.

42. Stuffed Broad Beans.

Steep the broad beans, then split open the skin [of each bean] where the black [line] is and dig out the bean that is inside gently so as not to break the skin; then get blanched almonds and grind them up well with plenty of sugar and stuff the beans — that is, the skin — with this, and then close them back up together again; then set them to heat, dry, in a pot or pan or some other vessel, watching that they do not burn; when they are hot, dish them up into bowls with a little hot meat broth, a little finely chopped parsley and a little onion fried in good grease, with spices on top. For anyone who does not like onions, leave them out.

[Meats]

43. Boiled Meats.

Cut up the meat and soak it in cool water for half an hour, then wash it well in hot water and then in cool water, and set it on the fire in a vessel that is not too small, adding sufficient salt; in particular, whatever scum is produced should be skimmed off. If the salt is dirty, wash it with hot water. If the meat is old, especially if it is tough as of a fowl, take it quickly out of the boiling water and plunge it into cold water and it will cook better.

44. Chicken with Salt Pork.

Take a chicken and cook it in a pot, and when it is half cooked add in spices, saffron, egg yolks and [chicken] livers, everything all ground up together, and cook it so that the chicken is well cooked; then grind a little garlic, if your master likes it, and put it into the pot.

45. Cockerels Boiled with Verjuice.

They should be boiled with salt pork; when they are half cooked, get whole verjuice grapes and cut them in half, remove the seeds and put the grapes to cook with the cockerels; when cooked, add in finely chopped parsley, and pepper and saffron; after this is cooked, serve it up with fine spices on top.

46. Goat Kid or Mutton, with Thick Broth.

Get kid or mutton and cut it into small pieces, and put it into a pot with salt pork; then get sage, mint and onion, and cook everything together; then get good spices and saffron, distemper them with the meat's broth and let everything boil together until the meat falls apart; then lift the meat out into a dish with the thick broth.

47. Florentine-Style Goat Kid in a Baking Dish.

Get the hind or fore quarters of a goat kid and cut them up and put the pieces into a baking dish with a little water, a little verjuice and fat from the kid or a calf, then put in slices of salt pork and *lardo* and send it off to the oven; when you have roasted one side, turn it over; get parsley, mint, onions, chicken liver, egg yolks and grated bread, and mix everything together — everything must be ground up well; when those pieces of meat are cooked, take them out and put the baking dish with the other things in it back on the coals to boil a very little and, as it is boiling, put the meat back in; then take it off the fire and make up bowls [of the meat] with that broth and with good spices on top.

48. Sheep's Head.

Get a sheep's head and wash it thoroughly, cook it well and, if you are able to remove all of the bones, do so; then cut up all the meat, beat it up finely and put it in a pot; then, when it is almost all cooked, get parsley, mint, marjoram and finely chopped onion and put them together in the pot; get spices, eggs, broth, bread moistened in broth, and liver, grind and mix these things together and put them into the pot away from the fire, and boil it until everything is well cooked; then take it off the fire and make up the dishes with spices on top.

49. Calf's Head.

Get a well blanched and clean calf's head and cook it by boiling; its sauce is Garlic Sauce. If you want to roast it in the oven, stuff it with garlic, herbs, *lardo*, spices, with the brain dug out and mixed with those things and saffron; then bind it around so that the stuffing does not fall out, and put it into a baking dish with half a jug of water, and send it off to the oven, adding verjuice and good spices toward the end [of its baking] and turning it over several times in the baking dish.

50. Florentine-Style Meat in a Baking Dish.

Get veal or another meat with the bone, cut it into pieces as small as a fist, and put them into a baking dish with a little water, a beaker of wine and another of good verjuice; if your master likes, add in a few slices of onion — or, should he not like onions, use parsley, the root, that is — along with raisins, dried prunes and salt; cover the meat by no more than a finger of water, and set it in the oven; when it looks half done, add a few cloves, a good lot of cinnamon, pepper and a good lot of saffron — and let it taste of pepper; when it is half cooked, turn it over; then take it out onto a plate with spices and sugar on top, or else leave it in the baking dish.

You can do the same with fish — that is, grey mullet or eel — cut into pieces four fingers in width, washed well and put into a baking dish with a little oil. Note that you can make these things sweet or tart according to your master's taste.

51. Sugared Capon.

Get big fat capons, two days dead; when they are cleaned well, boil them, but not to the point they are overcooked; take them out of the pot to drain; then get enough fine sugar for the size of the capons you wish to sugar, and break up the sugar and dissolve it in rosewater and boil it a little; then pour the dissolved sugar over the capons so they are completely covered, along with good cinnamon; they are eaten almost immediately.

52. To make a Fine Roast of capons, cockerels, goat kid, and any other meat.

First, if it is a large joint of meat, put it to boil unless it is young veal; if it is capon or any other meat that is worth setting to roast, make it clean, then plunge it into boiling water and take it out immediately and put it into cold water — that is done to make it better; then lard it with good *lardo* and mount it on the spit, cooking it slowly; then, when it is almost done, get a grated piece of bread and mix it with salt and coat the meat. In this way you will have it cooked fine.

53. Roast Cockerels.

For roast cockerels, cook them as directed above and, when done, get orange juice or verjuice with rosewater, sugar and cinnamon; then set out the cockerel on a plate, cover it with this mixture and serve it.

54. Goat Kid in Other Ways.

Clean a kid well and set it to roast, and have the spit come out its snout, and be careful not to burn it; for its sauce, get parsley and toast steeped in vinegar, with a clove of garlic and pepper, and grind everything together and temper it with verjuice or with wine syrup, making it tart or sweet as you wish.

55. Chickens or Capons on a Spit with their Sauce.

When you have roasted them well, take five peeled almonds and grind them up with fine sugar — if you do not have sugar, use honey — and temper that with lemon juice to make it slightly thick; put this over the chickens, or else put the sauce in small bowls and the chickens on plates; serve warm.

56. Lemon Sauce for Chickens or Capons.

Get one or more chickens, capons or cockerels that have been cooked a little in water; take them out of the water and mount them on a spit; then get peeled, well ground almonds and temper them with the bouillon of the chickens; then get lemon juice and mix it all together with good spices; and put it into a saucepan to cook a little; then pour it over the roast with a little fat; serve it very hot.

57. *Pariola* for Chickens, Cockerels or Capons on a Spit.

Get pepper, ginger and saffron and grind them up well; then get the livers of those fowl and hard-boiled egg yolks, and a little onion if you like it, and grind all this together and distemper it with verjuice or some other sweet liquid; then take the chickens or capons or cockerels, cut them up and put them in a pot together with the above-mentioned things, and stew them for a short while; then make up a plate and serve with spices on top.

58. A Dish of Small Birds.

Parboil the small birds, then fry them in good *lardo*; get [chicken] livers, egg yolks and toast steeped in verjuice, and parboiled parsley, and grind everything together, distempering it with the bouillon of the small birds; and when the small birds are well fried, put this sauce over them; then put everything in a mortar so that[3] everything is well cooked.

59. Garden Warblers.

Get fat garden warblers and clean them thoroughly, not eviscerating them if you wish; get vine leaves and wrap the warblers in them with salt, *lardo* and fennel; wrapped like that, put them under hot coals for half an hour. Otherwise you can roast them tying them onto a spit in fours by their head and feet; or else put them in a split cane and bind it all around with cord; they should be eaten very hot.

60. Thrush with their Sauce.

Get thrush, clean them and roast them; for their sauce get almonds and blanch them, grind them up as much as you can and combine with them a good amount of [ground] sandalwood

[3] Properly the sense of the conjunction here, *tanto che*, is temporal: "until."

and distemper this with verjuice and a little broth, adding in sugar and cinnamon, then strain everything; bring this sauce to a boil and pour it over the thrush. If you do not like this sauce, when the thrush are done get lemon juice and strong sweet orange juice, or pomegranate juice, with mild spices; mix these together and pour the mixture on the thrush while they are very hot.

61. Catalan-Style Partridge.

Get the partridge and roast it; when it is cooked, take it down from the spit and slice the wings off at the breast, and into those cuts put the following sauce: get pomegranate juice or verjuice, salt, ground cloves and mild spices, and put this into the cuts while the partridge is hot; and note that the partridge should not be overcooked.

62. French-Style *Tremolette* on Partridge.

Get half a pound of almonds and blanch them, or else toast them under hot coals without burning them; then clean them with a piece of rough cloth and grind them up; get fifty wafers made with sugar and steep them in red wine, grind them and distemper that with the almonds, adding in plenty of cinnamon and enough sugar, with grains of paradise and cloves, everything well ground up, and strain everything with a little verjuice; then put everything in a pot with a little lard, stirring constantly; then put this mixture over the roasted partridge with sugar and cinnamon on top.

63. The Holy Piglet, Roasted Inside-Out.

Get a suckling pig and remove its hair so it can be blanched well and cleaned well with hot water; split it open right along its spine and eviscerate it and wash out everywhere inside, and turn it inside-out as is done with tench; then, for its stuffing, get a clove of garlic, ground, and the piglet's liver, well beaten, and parsley, a *quatrino*'s worth of marjoram, a *baiocho*'s worth of pepper, and other good spices, grated cheese, four eggs, saffron, plums and raisins, and mix everything together with *lardo*; put this everywhere inside the piglet; then sew it up well, turned inside-out that way, mount it on a spit fastened carefully with skewers, or else set it on a grill; cook it well; then, whether it is grilled or roasted on a spit, make the following basting sauce: get good vinegar, ground pepper, a good lot of saffron, and salt, and with this you baste it using a sprig of rosemary. Done this way it is good.

64. Little Livers.

Get the liver of any animal you wish, cut it up into pieces the size of a walnut, and coat the pieces with good spices and salt; then tie them up one by one in a clean piece of mesentery, and mount them on a spit; they should not be overcooked.

65. *Tomaselle.*

Get pork liver or veal liver and boil it, but not too much, then grate it; get a pound of pork belly, cook it well and pound it thoroughly; then get a little old cheese and creamy cheese and grate them, and well ground parsley and marjoram, along with raisins, eggs, saffron and good spices, and mix everything together; then get a piece of mesentery and in it wrap that stuffing in wads the size of a walnut — and they should be no larger than a walnut; then cook them gently in good *lardo* in a pan on hot coals.

Here Begin Gastronomical Marvels

66. To Cook a Pigeon and make it be without bones.

Get a pigeon and clean it well, then set it to steep — I mean, immerse it — in strong vinegar for twenty-five hours; then wash it well and make a stuffing for it of cheese, eggs, spices and raisins, and mount it on a spit or roast it; in this way you will find it has no bones.

67. To Make Two Pigeons of One.

Skin a pigeon without water — and be careful not to rip its skin — and then remove the entrails; and reverse the whole skin so carefully that it remains whole; where the skin is torn, sew it; then make a stuffing for it as I said above [*Recipe* 66], and with a needle sew up again wherever you have inserted the stuffing, and boil it; set the other one, that is, the skinless carcass, to roast or to boil; if roasted, get a little grated bread and salt and, when [the carcass is] half cooked, spread this salt and bread together over it; get an egg yolk and beat it well, and baste the pigeon with a feather so as to give it colour, and this way it will look as if it has not been skinned; and so one pigeon will seem to be two.

68. To Cook a Chicken in a Carafe.

In the morning take a chicken that was killed the night before and skin it without hot water so the skin does not tear, then eviscerate it and from that spot begin the skinning, pulling it back up to the neck; then cook the meat without the skin; when it is cooked, take the breast and grind it up thoroughly with a little cheese, parsley, marjoram and other fragrant herbs, and mix this into the chicken breast and grind it all again with a little cloves, pepper, cinnamon, saffron and a little veal fat; and mix everything together, adding in two eggs; make this mixture a little on the soft side. Then get a carafe big enough to hold a chicken or capon, and see that the mouth of the carafe is rather wide; then stuff the chicken skin and sew it where you cut it; stick its feet into the carafe and have its neck stick out of the neck of the carafe — for, before inserting the skin, you should make sure that the carafe will be big enough to hold [the whole of the stuffed skin]; if it is big enough, stuff the chicken through its neck which will be sticking out of the neck of the carafe, but do not overstuff it; then tie up the neck and let the chicken swell to take up the space in the carafe; then settle the chicken properly in the carafe by means of a stick; fill the carafe with slightly salted water, and set the carafe to boil inside a cauldron or else gently by the fire — but it would really be better to fill a cauldron with water and boil it, and then, or before it boils, to set the carafe in it; it will be cooked in an hour's time; send it off to be served, leaving to those whose job it is the weighty problem of carving it up.

69. Redressed Peacocks which Seem Living; and How to Make them Breathe Fire through their Mouth.

You should first kill the peacock with a feather, driving it in upon its head, or else drain its blood from under its throat as with a pig; but it is better to take out its tongue and then to slice it under its body — that is, from the top of its breast to its tail — slicing only the skin and removing it gently so that it is not damaged; when you have skinned it, pull the skin back right up to the head, then cut away the head, which will remain attached to the skin; do the same with the legs, and likewise the tail, taking out the leg bones so that the iron which will make the peacock stand up will not be seen; then take the skinned carcass and set it to roast stuck with lardoons, or else baste it with grease often enough that it will not burn, and stick it with whole cloves, and fill it with the Piglet stuffing [*Recipe* 63] but without garlic; cook it gently so its neck does not burn; if the neck should get too much heat, cover it with a damp cloth; when it is cooked, take it down and redress it in its skin, whose inside you have coated with spices, salt and cinnamon. Then, when you have put its skin back on, get an apparatus of iron driven into a large cutting board and shove this iron through its feet and legs so it cannot be seen; in this way the peacock will be standing so that it will seem to be alive.

And to make it breathe fire through its mouth, get a little camphor with a little fine cotton-wool around it and put this into the peacock's beak and soak it with a little aquavita or else with a little fumey old wine that is volatile; when you want to serve it, set fire to the cotton-wool: in this way it will breathe fire for a long time. To make it more magnificent you can cover the peacock with gold leaf and then cover it with its skin.

The same can be done with pheasants, cranes, geese and other birds.

70. To Make a Cow, a Calf or a Stag Look Alive.

First kill the cow or calf normally, then skin it beginning at the hooves — but keep the hooves and the horns attached to the hide; when skinned, stretch the hide; then get cumin, fennel, cloves, pepper and salt, all ground up to a powder, and sprinkle it over the inside of the hide; then cut away the shin-bone downward from the knee, and remove the tripe through the flank; if you wish, you can roast capons, pheasants or other creatures and put them into the cow's body. If you want to bake it in the oven, lay it on a grill; if you want to roast it over the fire, get a piece of wood — that is, a pole like a spit — insert it, lard it well and roast it slowly so as not to burn it. Then make iron bars large enough to hold it standing up; when it is cooked, set up the bar on a large plank and bind it [*i.e.*, the animal] so that it stands on its feet; then dress it in its hide as if it were alive; if the meat has shrunk anywhere because of the cooking, replace it with bay- laurel, sage, rosemary and myrtle; draw the hide back [in place] and sew it so the iron cannot be seen, and give it a posture as if it were alive.

The same can be done with a deer, a sow and a chicken, and with any other animal you wish. Note that preparing this sort of animal requires a cook who is neither foolish nor simple-minded, but rather he must be quite clever. And note, my lord, that if your cook is not skillful he will never prepare anything good that *is* good, no matter how hard he tries.

71. Veal Pies in a Baking Dish.

Get meat from the haunch of a calf, chop it up with a little veal fat and a little cured ham; when thus chopped up, put it in a pot or baking dish away from the fire, and have it well skimmed; you can put in pigeons, thrush, and other small birds and cockerels; when these meats are half-cooked, get a small onion and chop it well, a little *lardo*, a small amount of good spices and raisins, put this into the pot and cook it a little more; then get verjuice, beaten eggs and more good spices and put everything together in the baking dish and let it finish cooking; and you can put in four or five whole egg yolks.

Note that the cook must be judicious in using those ingredients in quantities appropriate to the amount of the meat and according to his master's taste.

72. Pies of Good Capons, Cockerels, Pigeons and with Veal.

Get lean veal or the meat of the above-mentioned fowl, chop it up with a knife along with a little veal fat; when it is ground and chopped — I mean, in the shape of small playing dice — mix in all sorts of good spices; then make a pastry crust as is used in pies, put the fowl with the meat into it and bake it in the oven; when it looks like they are cooked, get eggs and beat them, verjuice, good spices, fat broth and saffron, mix everything together and put this into the pie through a little hole in the top.

73. Pie of Cock's Combs with the Testicles.

Get combs and cut them into three, and livers into four, and leave the testicles whole; get a little *lardo* and cut it very small and do not pound it; get three ounces of veal fat and pound it well — veal or beef marrow would be better; then get thirty dry sour cherries, cinnamon, ginger and plenty of sugar, and mix all that together; make a good pie and bake it in the oven — and make its crust as is used in pies; alternatively, put it into a pan; when it is cooked, get an egg yolk, verjuice and saffron and, mixed together, put all that into the pie and heat it again, then take it out.

74. Kid Pie.

Get goat-kid meat and cut it into small pieces; then make up the dough with egg yolks and fine oil, form the pastry shell and into it put the kid meat: make a layer of pieces of meat, then another of spices — that is, cinnamon, ginger, pepper and saffron — along with a piece of good cured ham; then cook it in the oven; when it is cooked, make its sauce: get beaten egg yolks, rosewater, verjuice, sugar, spices and saffron, temper them together and put it over this preparation so carefully that the pastry cover does not burst. I repeat: the cook must be judicious.

75. A Pigeon Pasty or Pie.

Get pigeons and cut them up, with or without the crupper; make up the pastry shell with eggs, sugar and rosewater, and put the pigeon pieces into it: a layer of the pieces of pigeon, another of slices of cured ham and another of good spices, sugar and saffron; then make the sauce by grinding chicken liver, and the pigeons' liver and their meat, and along with those things grind marjoram, sugar and egg yolks, with verjuice for distempering, and rosewater; add in this sauce when everything is cooked.

76. Fish Tart.

Take the fish and cut it into large pieces and cook it with salt, wine and something tart — do this with any fish you wish to do in pastry; bonito, bleak, mackerel, bass and mullet, to be put on a spit [or] set on grills, to be served when cooked; then get pepper, saffron, vinegar, finely chopped onion, mixed together, and put that on top.

I do not propose to deal at length with this coarse material.

77. Quince Pie.

Prepare the dough as I have said for the other tarts; then get peeled quince and remove the hard part in their centre, and do not let the hole you make to remove it go all the way through; into this hole put good beef marrow with plenty of sugar and cinnamon; and lay the quince in the pies, adding the marrow to them inside and out; mind that it is not too salty; put another crust on top, cooking it as with the other tarts.

Stuffings or Fillings

78. A Stuffing for a Shoulder of Ram.

Get a shoulder and bring it to a boil; cleave it and remove the bone up to the joint; then get good spices, salt pork and mutton and grind that, get eggs and mix everything together and put it into the shoulder; if you like, when it is stuffed get a slice of some more mutton and with it cover the whole of the shoulder; then put the shoulder on the grill or over hot coals; when it is cooked, serve Parsley Sauce for its garnish.

79. Stuffing for a Fish.

Get ginger, saffron, figs and peeled apples and grind up everything together; then get good pinenuts and crush them finely; then slice the fish through its [ ] stuff the fish through its mouth — first carefully cleaning the mouth and pouring a drop of oil down it; then set it on the grill with rosemary, and make a basting sauce for it of vinegar, spices and saffron.

80. Stuffing for Kid.

Take the boiled pluck of a kid and chop it so that it is all minced up — but first cooked; then get raisins, dates, pinenuts, cured ham, cinnamon, pepper, ginger and sugar, and grind everything together; then stuff the kid, and baste it with fine oil or with good grease, water and salt so that its glazing is pretty.

81. Stuffing for a Capon.

Get marjoram and parsley and grind them up; get one or two breasts of capons and grind them with the other; get a little Parmesan cheese, two egg yolks, cinnamon, pepper, saffron and ginger, with a little *lardo* or cured ham, and grind everything together; stuff the capon and set it to boil or to roast; make its glazing with egg yolks and rosewater.

82. Stuffing for a Calf's Intestine.

Get an intestine, clean it thoroughly and scrape it — it should be fat; then get clean walnuts, half a clove of garlic, a little old Parmesan cheese, fine spices, saffron and raisins, with a little veal fat that is cut as finely as possible but not ground up, and two eggs, and mix all this together; stuff the intestine so that it is a little more than half full.

With these same ingredients you can stuff goat kids — I mean, quarters of a boiled kid — and capons as well.

83. *Cirvelato* of Pork or Veal.

Get meat from the haunch of these animals along with their fat and cut it up small, so it can be well beaten with the knife; then get good Parmesan cheese and new fat cheese, good spices and three or two fresh eggs depending on the amount of the meat, and mix all this together with a little saffron; then get large intestines as are normally used, clean them thoroughly so that no fat is left, stuff them with this mixture and pack it tightly into the intestines, making [the sausages] as long or as short as you like; cook them by boiling; they will not be finished [*i.e.*, ready for eating] for two days.

84. Good Sausages.

Get lean pork or lean and fat veal and beat it well—and mind that there is no gristle in it; if there is ten pounds of meat, use half a pound of salt, two ounces of well cleaned fennel and two ounces of roughly ground pepper; mix everything together and let it stand for a day; then get very well cleaned intestines and stuff them with this mixture, and set the sausages to dry in smoke.

85. Good Cured Ham for Keeping, Cooked.

Test the cured ham, shoving a knife into the middle of it: if the knife smells clean, the cured ham is good, and vice versa; then get equal quantities of wine and water or vinegar—but it would be better without water—and cook it, but not too much; then take it off the fire and add sage and rosemary into the mortar in which it cooked, and let it stand until it is cool. Like that it will keep for ten days.

86. Salt Loin of Pork.

Salt loin of pork should not be too fat, it should be red and cooked as just described for ham.

The same can be done with salt tongues, but they should be cooked more than ham. Any salt meat should be done that way.

87. To Make Good Bolognese Sausage.

Get twenty-five pounds of pork or veal from the haunch, without gristle or fat, and beat it as much as you can; for these twenty-five pounds of meat add in fifteen ounces of salt and one and a half ounces of ground and whole pepper; then get large intestines, clean and wash them well and fill them as tightly as you can with the meat and make them a hand's length long after the Bolognese custom; then set them to dry in smoke.

This is how a prince has them made. In truth they would be even better with two ounces more salt and half an ounce more pepper, too. And see that in these seventeen ounces of salt there is at least two ounces of the white sort, unground. Furthermore, you can make fat ones by taking half lean [meat] and half fat, adding in a good lot of fennel, but those ones are not for keeping.

88. Meat or Fish Jelly in Various Colors.

Get equal amounts of white vinegar and water; get well cleaned sheep or calf hooves and split them in half, throwing away the long fibrous parts; set the feet to boil in the mixture of vinegar and water, and boil them gently, adding in grains of paradise and ginger; when the feet seem cooked to you, take them out and bring the broth back up to a boil; then get four well beaten egg whites and strain them with the broth—otherwise it is better to filter it through a linen cloth since the tighter [the weave] the nicer and clearer it will turn out; make it smell of grains of paradise; then get capons or some other cooked meat, by itself or with the broth, and cast it onto the concoction and set it in a cool place.

To make it in several colors: when the first, which will jell white, is set in a dish, remove a quarter of the jelly from the dish and dissolve it by the fire and put a little saffron into it; then, yellow and almost cool, put it back in its place; when that has jelled, remove another quarter and make it red with cornels, and set it back like the yellow; and so on, you can make as many colors as you wish: to make a green quarter, get new shoots of wheat and some parsley, grind them up, extract the juice and repeat as before; for a peacock-blue color, take cooked carrots and grind some of their skin and do the same as above and following that procedure. Should you run out of jelly, have clear gelatine ready and add it as it is needed. And so it is of various colors.

89. Jelly in a Reed Basket.

Have the decoction made as I directed above; get a new reed basket and in it lay either chicken or some other meat; then get another vessel large enough to hold the basket and pour the decoction into it, and let it jell in a cool place; when it is set, get a hot knife and run it around the basket so that it separates from the vessel; then clean the basket all around with a cloth; and so you can carry the basket wherever you wish. You can do the same with a cage; and likewise in Lent, putting a whole fish in the cage for a pretty effect.

Let the cook be judicious and never stop trying to learn.

90. Jelly Like a Checkerboard.

Get a lot of hooves because the jelly will be all the more substantial, and make a white broth with a little ginger; when the broth is made, get four or five capon or chicken wings and put them in the dish; then get broth—I mean, the decoction from the hooves, strained—and cover the wings with it by a finger width; when the broth has jelled, take one of the intended checkboard squares and cut it out; when you have lifted out a clear square, replace it with one made green, following the directions for coloring I gave in the recipe for Meat Jelly [*Recipe* 88]; in this way you can make as many colors as you wish.

91. Golden Sops.

Get slices of white bread, remove their crust, toast them and soak them in a mixture of fresh eggs beaten with a little rosewater; then take them out and fry them in good butter, turning them often; when they are cooked, which will not take long, remove them from the pan and put sugar, rosewater and saffron on top.

92. Aragonese Sops.

Get chicken livers and cook them in water; when they are done, grind them with a slice of bread soaked in lean broth, and strain; then add in pepper, saffron and ginger, and set this mixture to cook in a small pot away from the fire; when cooked, remove it from the fire; get slices of bread and toast them on the fire and, when toasted, pour the mixture on them hot and serve.

93. Sauteed Cockerel or Pigeon.

Get whichever meat you like, cockerels or pigeons, clean and quarter it and fry it in good *lardo*; when it seems well fried, remove most of the grease from the pan; then get verjuice, two egg yolks, fine spices and a little broth, mix everything together with a little saffron and bring the mixture to a boil with the meat, whether chicken or some other meat; then get a little parsley and marjoram, beat everything well and add it to the sauteed meat in the pan. You can make this dish bitter or sweet: [for the latter], get either must syrup or honey or sugar and cinnamon.

94. Baked Cheese, Bread, etc.

Get bread, remove the crust, slice it thin and toast it on the fire to color it, then coat the slices with fresh butter and put sugar and cinnamon on top; then get slices of creamy cheese and put them on the toast with sugar and cinnamon on top; then put the slices into a torte pan and put this on the coals with its lid on and coals on top; when the cheese has melted, serve it quickly.

95. Applesauce.

Get almonds, grind them thoroughly and make milk; then get ten or twelve cooked apples, grind them up and sieve them, mix them with the almond milk and a little rosewater and sugar, and cook the mixture until it is thick; then take it off the fire and make up dishes of it.

96. *Sfresurato.*

Get well cooked kid pluck, chop it up finely with parsley and marjoram, then put it all into a pot with good fat broth and pepper, saffron, eggs beaten with a slice of cured ham and a very little rosewater and verjuice, and a little sugar, and cook it well; when cooked, serve it up.

97. Distillate of a Leg.

Get a pot large enough for a haunch, into it put the leg studded with good cloves and cinnamon, along with a little rosewater, and cover it with a lid.

98. Distillate of a Leg or of Chicken in a Carafe.

Get a chicken and cut it up very small and put it in a carafe with a little rosewater and a little whole cinnamon; put this carafe in a cauldron full of water and boil it; when the cauldron boils, make sure the carafe is fastened and sealed: put something on it that holds it down steady in the water; in order to know how the meat in the carafe is, put a chicken foot to cook in the cauldron: when this is cooked, so will the rest be; then take out the carafe and pour out the juice in it, and serve it to be drunk or else eaten together with the cooked meat, with sugar on top. This is no food for your mouth, my dear cook!

99. A Hunger Killer.

Get salt pork, parsley, marjoram and minced onions; when the salt meat [is done], take it out and beat a few eggs, spices and saffron with what remains; after it has cooked, serve it.

Various Serving Sauces

100. Sauce for Cockerel Pieces.

Get marjoram and the cockerels' livers, egg yolks, pepper and cinnamon, grind everything together and strain it with verjuice and a little rosewater; when enough of it has strained for the number of bowls you want of it, put the proper amount of sugar on top; alternatively, pour this sauce over the cockerels that you have first cut up and fried in good lard; when they have fried, remove the lard, put in the sauce and bring it to a boil with the pieces of cockerel; serve it in plates.

101. Sauce for Hare.

Take the hare, cut it up and parboil it, then fry it in good lard with a chopped onion; for its sauce, get the hare's liver, roast and grind it; then get a slice of toast and strain everything with must syrup; when it is strained, add in pepper, cinnamon, ginger, cloves and saffron; make it tart with verjuice and sweet with must; pour this sauce over the hare and serve it hot.

⌈102. A Good Sauce.

Get strong, sweet pomegranates and take out a beaker of [their] wine and boil it with half a pound of sugar and half an ounce of cinnamon; note that it should boil a lot and slowly.⌋

103. Sauce for Sauteed Pigeon Pieces.

Get a pigeon, cut it up and fry it in lard; for its sauce, get beaten eggs, cinnamon, pepper, saffron and sugar, mix all this together with verjuice and pour it over the fried pieces and serve it in dishes or in bowls.

104. White Sauce.

Get almonds for the amount [of sauce] you wish to make, blanch them and grind them as much as you can; get a crustless loaf of white bread soaked in verjuice and pound it with sugar and white ginger, and distemper it with verjuice or lemon juice or orange juice; make it quite white.

[Note that any sauce should be rather thick.]

105. Cameline Sauce.

Get raisins and grind them up as much as you can; get three or four ounces of almonds and grind them with the raisins, and two or three slices of toast soaked in red wine, and grind them together; then get a little good red wine, must and verjuice, making it sweet or tart as you wish; strain all this, then adding in a lot of cinnamon, and cloves and nutmegs.

106. A Sauce called Peach Blossom.

Get peeled almonds and grind them with a crustless loaf of white bread, a little ginger and cinnamon, and distemper with verjuice, pomegranate juice and sandalwood, and strain everything; it will be good.

[Note that when you grind almonds, you should add a dose of fresh water or of rosewater so that they do not make oil.]

107. A Sauce called Broom Blossom.

Get almonds, saffron and egg yolks, grind them all together and distemper, straining the mixture, and adding in ground ginger and verjuice.

108. Black Grape Sauce.

Get good black grapes, crush them carefully into a vessel with a crustless loaf of bread, and add in a little verjuice so the grapes will not be so sweet; boil this, but first strain it; when you have boiled it, add cinnamon, ginger and other sorts of spices. Note that this strained sauce should boil half an hour so that it is somewhat thick.

109. Sauce of Sour Cherries or of Ordinary Cherries.

Follow the directions for the Black Grape Sauce but, since the sour cherries are tart, add in all the sugar and cinnamon your master may wish.

110. Lemon Sauce.

Get almonds, blanch them, grind them up, make milk of them and boil this with cinnamon, ginger and saffron; the milk — I mean, the almonds — is strained with lemon juice or pomegranate juice and a very little verjuice and lean broth; and if you want it quite strong, put in more lemons or other citrus juice.

111. Marzipan Sauce.

Get four fingers of marzipan, grind it up with a little good ginger and distemper it with lemon juice and strong, sweet pomegranate juice. This is a good sauce.

Various Cooking Sauces

112. Sauce for Any Game Animal (stag, bear, deer or other).

Clean the meat and roast or boil it; then make this sauce: get a toasted, crustless loaf of bread with a handful of the animal's meat and pepper, ginger and saffron, and grind it up together; distemper this with lean broth, verjuice and honey, and boil it until it is thick; put it into bowls.

113. Saracen Sauce.

When you cook in the Saracen fashion, cut the meat into pieces, wash it well with hot water, put it in a pot without its bouillon and add *lardo*, bitter wine, finely chopped onion, parsley, sage and marjoram, and sautee all this with the meat; when it has sauteed a while until it is cooked, make up platesful of this sauce and serve it to Saracens.

114. Daily Sauce.

Get an ounce and a half of ginger, an ounce of pepper and eight *tornesi*-worth of saffron, and boil it with vinegar or bitter wine until these unground spices have given their flavor to the bitter wine.

115. Lombard Sauce.

Get parsley, mint, sage, garlic, pepper, thyme, a chard leaf, and toasted bread soaked in vinegar, and grind everything together and distemper with vinegar; if it is too strong, add in must or a little broth.

116. French-Style Sauce for Partridge, Chicken or Other.

Get pinenuts and almonds, grind them up with good cinnamon, pepper, cloves, ginger and saffron, and distemper with bitter wine or vinegar or sweet or bitter pomegranate [juice]; dish up into bowls.

117. Papal Sauce.

When carrots are half cooked under the coals, take a finger-length of the reddish bit that looks dark; then get a crushed ginger root, plenty of cinnamon and fine sugar, and mix all this together and let it sit for a night; then sieve it as jelly is sieved, and make up small bowls of it.

118. Royal Sauce.

Get strong white vinegar and a crushed ginger root; for twelve small bowlsful, get an ounce of good, whole cinnamon, only crushed, and half a pound of sugar, put everything together in a small clean pot and let it boil gently on the coals for an hour; then strain it and make up little bowls of it topped with sugar and cinnamon.

119. Verjuice with Garlic.

Get a little garlic, fresh fennel and basil, grind this with a little pepper and distemper it with good verjuice.

120. Vine-Shoot Sauce.

Get vine tendrils, grind them up well along with a shoot of fresh garlic, a crustless loaf of bread and salt; distemper this with verjuice or vinegar and strain it.

121. French Mustard.

It is distempered with only tart wine or must. This is the French Mustard, with neither head nor feet.

122. Italian Mustard.

Get the seed which is called *sinapo* and steep it for a day or two, changing the water often; get blanched almonds and grind them up and put them with the mustard seed grinding it all together; then get good must syrup to make it sweet, and for a tart taste use verjuice, and strain everything and make it thick. Add spices if you want it with spices.

123. Balled Mustard for Trips.

Get mustard seed and, when it has steeped a day, grind it up with a handful of raisins, cloves, cinnamon and a little pepper, and with this paste form balls, small or as large as a walnut; then set them to dry on a board; when dry, you can take them when you go riding; to distemper them, use verjuice or must or wine or vinegar.

124. Slavic Cooking Sauce or Serving Sauce: Garlic Sauce.

Get good walnuts and grind them; when ground, add in as much garlic as you wish; then get a crustless loaf of white bread and soak it in broth, grind it again and distemper it with broth; make up small bowls with pepper on top. If you want it yellow, add saffron; if you want it peacock-blue, add black grapes or cherries — I mean, their juice.

Note that in grinding walnuts, or even almonds, you should always add a drop of fresh water or rosewater into the mortar as you grind.

125. To Make a White Torte.

Get ten or twelve eggs, as you prefer, beat them thoroughly; cut up small a pound and a half of new cheese, then grind it with half a pound of fine sugar, a further half ounce of peeled ginger, half a pound of lard or butter, and a small *fogleta* of milk; then mix the milk, eggs, cheese, sugar, ginger and butter thoroughly together — and note that, to make it whiter, there should be fifteen egg whites; then make thin pastry on the bottom of the pan, put this mixture on it, and cook it slowly over a moderate fire; when it is almost done, give it a little color on top with a hotter fire; when it looks done, take it out and put rosewater and sugar on top, and serve it.

⌈Note that, when it is done, the top of this pie should be sprinkled with an egg yolk beaten with saffron, and then put on plenty of well ground sugar.⌋

126. Bolognese Torte.

Get a pound of new cheese and of old cheese, and grate it; get well cleaned chard, parsley and marjoram, and beat them as much as you can with a knife and fry them in a little good butter, then take them out; get four eggs, saffron and a good lot of pepper, and lard or good butter, and mix everything together; make a thin pastry crust on the bottom of the pan and put this mixture in it; have another crust on top, or else get buffalo cheese, cut it into strips and cover the mixture with it instead of a crust. Note that it should have a good smell of pepper, and cook it slowly; when the upper crust puffs up — I mean, rises — then it is done.

127. May Herb Dish.

Get a pound of creamy new cheese and grind it up; then get twelve or fifteen eggs and about half a pint of milk; then get a lot of chard, a little marjoram, mint and a lot of parsley, grind all these herbs, drain off their juice and put them in with the above ingredients; also add in half a pound of lard or butter, half an ounce of ginger and eight ounces of sugar, and mix everything together; then get a pan with a pastry crust on the bottom, put the mixture in it and cook it slowly with a little heat on top and beneath; when it is cooked — that is, set — put sugar and rosewater on top.

128. Squash Torte.

Get a good squash, scrape and grate it, and bring it to a boil in fat broth or milk; get a pound of new and old cheese; get a pound of pork — I mean, porkbelly — or veal, boil it until it is well done, then beat it with a knife; if you like, instead of the belly you can use good butter or lard, along with half a pound of sugar, ginger and cinnamon, with a beaker of milk and eight eggs; when the squash is cooked in the broth, take it out and strain it; make the mixture yellow with saffron and put it in a pan with a moderate fire above and below; when it looks half done, put small lasagne on top; when it is well done, put sugar and rosewater on top.

129. Rich Rice Torte.

Get rice, clean it thoroughly, cook it in fat broth until it is well done, then set it on a cutting board to cool; get good new cheese, a little Parmesan cheese, ten egg whites, ginger, rosewater and half a beaker of milk — the cheese should be well ground up; mix everything together, as directed in the recipe for White Torte [*Recipe 125*]; serve it like that. This torte takes little cheese.

130. Spelt Torte.

Clean the spelt very well and cook it in fat broth, then drain it; get a pound of new cheese and half a pound of old, grinding or grating both; get a veal belly that is well cooked by boiling and almost disintegrating, beat it with a knife, add fine spices, sugar and saffron with fifteen eggs, and mix everything together; make a pastry crust on the bottom of a pan, put the mixture in it with enough butter; when half cooked, put lasagne closely together on top, then let it cook a little more; take it out and garnish it with sugar, cinnamon and rosewater.

131. Common Torte.

Get good cheese, eggs, butter or other grease, saffron, pepper, ginger, cinnamon, grated bread and fat broth, and blend everything together, along with chard, marjoram and parsley, and bring it to a boil; then take it out and beat it with a knife and put the herbs in with the other ingredients; make a pastry crust on the bottom of a pan, put the mixture in it and cook it on the coals, and cover the pan so that moderate heat can be put under and over it; when it is cooked, nothing else is needed on top, but serve it.

132. A Sienese-Style *Tartara*.

Get twenty almonds, blanch them and grind them up as well as you can; get half a pound of sugar, twelve eggs, a *fogletta* of milk, two *quatrini* of cinnamon, sufficient salt, an eighth of a fresh buffalo cheese ground up so much that it does not need any more grinding; then grease an earthenware dish with butter and flour it and put the mixture into it; set the baking dish or pan away from the fire and covered with a moderate heat. Note that into that mixture you can put a ladleful of lasagne cooked in good broth. When the mixture is done, put sugar and rosewater on top.

133. *Tartara Julatica.*

Get an ounce of good Parmesan cheese and have it thoroughly ground up; get twenty eggs and beat them very well, half a jug of milk, half an ounce of well ground white ginger, half a pound of good butter and half a pound of fine sugar, and mix everything together; then get a big pan and make the following crust on its bottom: get grated bread and first grease the pan with butter; if you do not like to put such a mixture as this on bread stuck to the bottom of the pan, instead of bread get grated cheese or flour, and see that the pan is layered and greased with good butter; then put in the mixture and cook it slowly; put a lot of sugar on top as if it were a marzipan, and rosewater; serve it very hot to Catherina Fasanica.

⌈ [*at the foot of f. 50r, just after the beginning of Recipe 133*] This is much the best of all *Tartare* to take on a promenade. ⌋

⌈ [*at the foot of f. 50v, following Recipe 133*] I like to go strolling, but I prefer to stay with this torte beneath the man (?). ⌋

134. Florentine-Style *Fasanitico* Millet Pudding.

For a good Millet Pudding for ten, get a pound of the newest cheese and grind it up very well—that is, until it is like milk; then get four ounces of the finest flour, twelve egg whites and half a pound of fine sugar, and mix everything together; if you do not have fine flour, use a crustless loaf of bread, grated, instead; get a pan without a pastry crust on its bottom, and put the mixture in it; but before doing this, put in a layer of good lard a finger-width's deep, put the pan on the coals and, when the butter or lard has melted, immediately put the mixture in, applying a moderate fire above and below; when it is cooked, remove it and put sugar and rosewater on top.

135. Elderflower Torte.

Get elderflowers when they have fully bloomed, shake the branch-ends so that all the blossom petals fall off and mix these into the White Torte mixture described above [*Recipe 125*], though this flower mixture should be stiffer and thicker; cook it as I directed for the other tortes, not forgetting the sugar and rosewater.

136. Chestnut Torte.

Get chestnuts, cook them by boiling, grind and strain them with a little milk, adding everything contained in the Spelt Torte [*Recipe 130*].

137. Cherry Torte.

Get red cherries or the darkest available, remove their pit and grind them in a mortar; then get red roses and crush them well—I mean, the petals alone—with a knife; get a little new and old cheese with a reasonable amount of spices, cinnamon and good ginger with a little pepper and sugar, and mix everything together, adding in six eggs; make a pastry crust for the pan with half a pound of butter and set it to cook giving it a moderate fire; when it is cooked, put on sugar and rosewater.

138. Green Torte is made as I said for the Bolognese Torte [*Recipe 126*], except that the juice is extracted from the herbs.

139. Turnip Torte is made like the Common Torte [*Recipe 131*].

140. Quince Torte is similar.

141. Cabbage Torte.

Get those stalks that look like turnips and cook them in good fat broth; when well done, remove them from the broth and push them through the strainer — or, better yet, grind them up as much as possible; then get a pound of good old and new cheese, with pepper, saffron, eight eggs and sufficient butter, and cook them as for the Bolognese Torte [*Recipe 126*].

142. Eggs Cooked in a Sheet of Paper.

Get a sheet — I mean, a half folio — of paper and form it, round or square, [with edges turned up] like a pan in such a way that oil cannot escape from it; put oil up to two fingers deep in this sheet, then set the sheet on the coals, far enough away that it warms up, or else over a candle — that is, two fingers away from its flame so the paper does not burn; when the oil is hot, break two eggs very gently into it and fry them until they are as if cooked in an iron pan. Make sure the eggs are fresh. This dish has been proved by Julino de Sozago, a lover of fine things.

143. German-Style Scrambled Eggs.

Get eggs and beat them well, and add in a little cheese; for ten eggs, add in two ounces of sugar, a little cinnamon, ginger, saffron and an ounce of rosewater or a little verjuice or orange juice; cook it in good butter and, when the butter is hot, put the eggs in the pan stirring constantly with a spoon so they do not overcook; then dish it out into small plates with sugar and cinnamon on top.

144. Egg Omelet.

Get as many eggs as you wish, beat them thoroughly and add in a little milk to make it softer; similarly, add in a little grated cheese with a decent amount of salt, and cook it in good butter.

145. Herb Omelet.

Get chard, parsley, a little marjoram and mint and extract their juice; get grated cheese, cinnamon and sugar, and distemper everything together; then get a pan and fry it in good butter; garnish it with fine spices.

146. Deep-Fried Eggs.

Put a little good oil in a pan and heat it; put whole eggs in it — without the shell, as I see it; when they set and become white on top, they are cooked.

147. Eggs Poached in Water.

Boil water and break fresh eggs into it; when they become white — I mean, when they look quite whitened — remove them from the water, and garnish them with sugar, rosewater, a little orange juice and mild spices with verjuice. Likewise, you can put on grated cheese with spices alone.

148. Eggs Poached in Milk or Wine.

You can do the same as I said above, except that they do not take grated cheese on them.

149. Stuffed Eggs.

Boil fresh eggs whole in water until they are quite hard; shell them carefully, cut them in half and then lift out the yolk without breaking the white; of the yolks grind a part with a few raisins, a little old and new cheese, parsley, marjoram and finely chopped mint, adding in two egg whites with mild spices depending on the amount you are making; mix all of this together with saffron and fill up the hollows left by the yolks, and fry the "eggs" gently in good oil; see that a lot of cloves and cinnamon are in the filling; when they are fried, serve them.

150. Eggs on the Grill.

Beat two fresh eggs, then heat a pan hot and pour them into it letting them run all over it as for a paper-thin omelet; when it looks cooked, make [*i.e.* fold] it into square quarters and set these quarters on the grill; break over them as many eggs as they will hold, in the manner of a torte, garnishing them with sugar and cinnamon; when they look done, take them off the fire.

151. Eggs on a Spit.

Heat the spit hot, mount the eggs through the ends or crosswise, and turn them on the spit as for a roast; when they look done, take them off and serve them.

152. Eggs in Cups.

Get fresh eggs, get a cup or bowl and grease it with butter, break the eggs into it, sprinkle them with sugar, cinnamon and salt, cover with another bowl and put it on hot coals and they will cook quickly; then you can put orange juice or verjuice on top.

153. Eggs on the Coals.

Get fresh eggs and set them on hot coals, turning them often; when they have perspired freely, they are done.

154. Eggs in Cold Water.

Put eggs in cold water and bring it to a boil; then take them out quickly for they are done.

155. Florentine-Style Deep-Fried Eggs.

Get fresh eggs and break them one by one into very hot oil and quickly push them inward with a spatula, making [each of] them as circular as you can; turn them often so they take on a little color and are not too hard or too cooked on the inside but still soft; then eat.

156. Eggs on the Coals.

Get whole fresh eggs, put them on live coals and strike them on top with a stick so they break, and let them cook; when this trifle is cooked, take it out and put a little vinegar and parsley on top. They are good.

157. [Florentine-Style] Stuffed Deep-Fried Eggs.

Make Florentine-Style Deep-Fried Eggs, as directed above [*Recipe 155*], but not too cooked; then from one side remove all of the yolks one by one; get grated old cheese, mint, parsley, marjoram, raisins, pepper and four of the egg yolks — and more depending on the quantity you want to make; mix everything together and refill the eggs through the hole, and set them to fry again until it is likely that the filling is cooked; then take them out and garnish with verjuice or oranges with a little ginger, and serve.

158. Eggs in the Shape of Ravioli.

Make a dough as for lasagne, neither too thick nor too thin; break fresh eggs into it and sprinkle sugar and salt over it; one by one bind them up — I mean, wrap the eggs — in the dough in the way you make ravioli, and fry them.

159. *Offelle.*

Get good soft cheese with little salt, and have it grated; get eggs, whole raisins, cinnamon, ginger and saffron, mix all this together and make this filling rather thick; get a thin pastry dough as for lasagne and bind [*i.e.*, wrap] the filling in the dough like lasagne, making them large or small as you wish, yellowing the top; bake in an oven that is not too hot; they should not be overcooked.

160. Good *Calisoni.*

Make a filling as is described for the Marzipan Torte [*Recipe 180*],[4] copied among Lenten Dishes; make up a dough with sugar and rosewater and spread it out as if you intended to make ravioli, and so wrap the mixture in this dough, making the *Calisoni* as large or small as you wish.

161. Snails for Meat-Days.

Get only those snails found on rosemary, vines, fennel, vines or grapes, because these are restaurative and moistening for the body; to clean them out, get bran flour and put the snails in an earthenware pot [with the bran], and in this way they are cleaned out; leave them a day and a night in the bran flour; when you want to prepare them for eating, wash them well so that no bran is left, bring them to a boil, discard the water and wash them again thoroughly; get the amount of water you want for the broth, boil them, and with them put in rosemary, pepper, a lot of fennel, and mint; when they are well cooked, and if it is a meat-day, put a good ham-bone in to boil; if it is a lean-day, put in good oil; dish them out into small plates with good, fine mild spices. Note that they should have a good smell of pepper, and pick them out with a small pin. If you have large snails, boil them in a kettle, pick them out and wash them thoroughly; remove the fore part, throw away the bowels, flour the rest and fry them in good oil.

⌈Note that all of them are cooked in their shell, except for the large ones which are picked out for frying, yet they are first boiled in their shell.⌋

[4] The scribe first wrote " . . . as is described for the White Torte" but then replaced "White" with "Marzipan." The White Torte is found in Recipe 125.

Lenten Dishes

162. Almond Paste.

For eight or ten servings, get a pound and a half of almonds, blanch them and grind them up, always adding a little fresh water so they do not make oil; get a crustless loaf of good white bread steeped in water, temper everything with fresh water, strain it and set it to boil in a mortar away from the fire; let it boil half an hour or even an eighth of an hour, adding half a pound of fine sugar; let it boil slowly so that it is slightly liquid and not too thick; when grinding and distempering make it liquid like milk, adding in a little rosewater.

163. Chick-Pea Broth.

To make eight servings of red Chick-Pea Broth get a pound of chick-peas, wash them in hot water and put them in a pot where you want to cook them dry; get half an ounce of good flour, a little oil, salt, twenty peppercorns, crushed, and a little ground cinnamon, and stir everything together with a spoon; then add into the pot three jugs of water — that is, the water in which the chick-peas have soaked for the night — and boil them; when they are thoroughly stewed and decomposed, add in rosemary, sage and parsley with a little more good oil; if you like, you can add a clove of garlic; dish up.

164. Pea Dish.

Cook peas in Lent with almond milk, or else as I said for the chick-peas [*Recipe 163*]; but they should not soak, and they do not take flour.

165. Broad Beans.

Get or purchase broad-bean paste and put it in a pot with good oil; fry an onion and put it in the pot with an ounce of raisins; dish it up garnished with spices and sugar.

166. Broad Beans in a Pan.

Get enough broad-bean paste for the size of fritter you want to make, and get chervil, a little sage, chopped figs, apples, mint and parsley, mix everything together and fry it in good oil; remove it onto a round platter with fine spices on top.

167. Almond Junket-Cheese.

Get almonds, blanch and grind them, adding rosewater while grinding; get two ounces of sugar, two ounces of rosewater and a *fogleta* of very fresh pike broth; mix everything together and strain it finely so that all of the substance comes through; let this strained material sit a night in a small dish and in the morning you will find it curdled like fresh cheese from real milk; sprinkle the dish with sugar and candied aniseed; have the cook taste it, for it should taste sweet to him.

168. Fake Ricotta.

Get a pound of almonds, blanch them — that is, let them steep a night so their skins will come off more neatly — and grind them up; then get four ounces of sugar, one ounce of rosewater, half a beaker of fish broth — that is, of pike or good tench — distemper everything together and strain it finely; place this mixture into a mold like those carried by peddlers who cry out, 'Ricotta! Ricotta!'; when you have put the mixture into the mold, put it in a cool place in the evening for the following morning, then dump it out on a trencher board, not forgetting the garnish of sugar, rosewater and candied aniseed.

169. Fake Butter.

Get, as above, a pound and a half of blanched, well ground almonds; get half a beaker of good rosewater and strain the almonds — if that rosewater is not enough, use however much you need so that that amount of almonds can be strained; then, so the almond milk will bind well, get a little starch, a little saffron if you want, and fine sugar, and lay this mixture into a mold as if it were butter; like that it is good to eat.

170. Parsnips.[5]

Clean big ones well and remove the woody part in the middle, and boil them; when they are cooked, flour them and fry them in good oil — but before that, dry them well on a small board; then, to make them better, get a bowl of flour tempered with water, add sugar, cinnamon, saffron and rosewater, coat the parsnips with this mixture and put them in the pan with hot oil; then put spices on top of them and serve them properly seasoned like that.

171. [Lenten] White Dish.

To make six servings of Lenten White Dish: one pound of rice — I mean, rice flour — a jug of goat's milk, four ounces of sugar and a little ginger; boil this, stirring constantly with a spoon; then grind an ounce or two of fish flesh and two ounces of pinenuts, and boil it together; when thick, it is cooked.

172. Bitter Fritters.

Get fine flour and a little leaven; get three *quatrini* of bitter herbs and extract the juice from them — if this is difficult, add a little water; get a *quatrino* of raisins, and good spices and saffron, and mix everything together in the evening for the following morning; then fry it in good oil.

173. Elderflower Fritters.

Get elderflowers; first grind a pound of blanched almonds or pinenuts and strain them with rosewater and pea broth; then get a little good flour, enough for the milk to have the proper liquid consistency, and mix everything together with the flowers — that is, make the mixture in the evening for the following morning; add in sugar, and cook slowly in good oil.

174. Rice Fritters.

Cook the rice and drain it; get peeled almonds in the amount you want to make, grind them and strain them with rosewater and the rice broth, and make the almond milk thick; get fine flour and sugar and mix everything together with the amount of rice you want; make fritters long or broad as you wish, and fry them in good oil; when they are cooked, do not forget to put sugar and cinnamon on top and sprinkle them with rosewater.

175. Stuffed Fig Fritters.

Get almonds and pinenuts and grind them up thoroughly — I say everything must be white — and grind in two good figs and a few raisins; cut up a little well chopped parsley and mix in good spices; if this mixture is too thick, add in a little rosewater; then get fine big figs, make a hole in them where their flower is, fill them with the mixture and fry them in good oil — slowly, I say.

---

[5] For the meaning of *pastonache*, see the commentary to this recipe.

176. Apple Fritters.

Peel and clean the apples carefully and boil them or else cook them under the coals; then remove the good part, grind it up, put with it flour and sugar, distemper it with either rosewater or plain water, with good spices, and fry it in good oil.

177. Fritters Shaped Like Ravioli.

Get almonds, clean pinenuts, walnuts, raisins, figs, milt of good fish and their liver, marjoram, mint, parsley and good spices, and grind everything together with saffron; make the Fritters as you saw for Ravioli [*Recipe 10*] — that is, with the mixture wrapped in a dough made with sugar and rosewater — and fry them in good oil.

178. Rice Fritters Shaped Like Ravioli.

Cook rice, grind almonds, first blanching them, and strain them hard — I mean, as thick as you can — with rosewater; mix the almond milk well with the rice, and add in sugar with a little fine starch; then make the Fritters, or else make them in the shape of pasties — that is, put the mixture into a dough made like the shell of a small pasty, frying in good oil.

179. Puff Fritters.

Get fine flour, water, salt and sugar, and distemper this so that it is not too stiff; then roll out the dough on a table by hand with a bit of round wood and cut it to the size you want it to be when shaped like fritters; fry it in good oil. With this dough you can make pears, apples, walnuts and sprigs of cloves, of rosemary and of sage, shaping the dough however you wish, and quickly dipping it briefly into good hot oil; when they are cooked, color them yellow with saffron tempered with rosewater. Note that, should you want to make the above-mentioned things — that is, pears and so forth — make the dough as broad as a wafer, and dip them in hot oil; or else coat a pan with oil and put the wafer-sized dough in it, then quickly remove it and shape it by hand like a pear or apple or whatever you like; then cook these fritters, shaped like pears or apples or however, in fine oil another short while.

180. Marzipan Torte.

Get almonds, soak them a night, skin them so they are quite white, grind them thoroughly and add to them the same amount of sugar; to make this Torte better, use a pound of the one — that is, of almonds — and a pound of fine sugar, either more or less depending on the amount you want to make, and add to them an ounce of rosewater; mix it all together; get good wafers, made with sugar and rosewater, first soaked in rosewater, lay them on the bottom of a baking dish and put the mixture over them, spreading it carefully with a spoon, and make it low, adding sugar and rosewater on top; then cook it slowly. That is what Marzipan Torte is like.

181. Rice Torte.

Get a pound of rice and a pound of peeled, well ground almonds, and temper them with the broth of the rice; then take the rice, crush it thoroughly when it is cooked and incorporate it into the almonds; get a little pike eggs, grind and strain them, and mix them with a pound of sugar; get two ounces of whole pinenuts and mix everything together; then get a pan and make a lower and an upper crust for it with broad, thin lasagne; when it has finished cooking, put sugar and rosewater on top; this Torte should not be overcooked.

182. Papal Torte.

Get a pound and a half of soft-textured sturgeon or a good pike, well cooked by boiling, and be careful not to leave any bones, then grind it up thoroughly; when ground, take it out of the mortar, get half a pound of almonds and a few pinenuts and grind them together; then get half a pound of rice well cooked in almond milk and grind it with the above; add in a pound of sugar, half an ounce of ginger, a little cinnamon, salt, saffron and a beaker of pike eggs, and strain everything; make a crust in the pan as is directed above, putting the mixture onto it.

183. Fish-Egg Omelet.

Use pike eggs, for they are good. Get pike eggs, about a beakerful, and a beaker of water; get marjoram, mint, very finely beaten parsley, a little pepper and saffron, mix everything together and fry it in a pan with good oil, turning it once. If you do not have herbs, make it with onion that has first been boiled.

184. Caviar Omelet.

Soak caviar in luke-warm water for half an hour, throw away the water and grind up the caviar well in a mortar; if there is half a pound of caviar, put in a beaker of water, pepper, saffron and the ingredients listed for the Pike [*Recipe 183?*], in that same way.

185. French-Style Apple Tart.

Cook whatever apples you want, whether in water or in must syrup, whether in a baking dish in the oven or under the coals; then get pinenuts that have soaked a night in water, and are not rancid, grind them up with the apples; get a lot of sugar, a little cinnamon, a little ginger, a little saffron and a beaker of ground and strained pike eggs, and mix and strain everything with rosewater or some other water; then make a dough of sugar, flour, oil, water and salt, mix them together to make the dough, spread it over the bottom of a low pan, and put the mixture in so that it is no more than a finger deep; cook it in the oven or on the fire as is directed for the other tortes; when almost cooked, get wafers, crumble them over the Tart — those wafers should be made with good sugar; when cooked, garnish with sugar and rosewater.

186. White Tart.

Get the belly of a good fish, boiled and well ground up; get almond milk, pike eggs, sugar and ginger, distemper everything with rosewater or some other water, and strain it; then cook it as with the other tortes, again adding on those crumbled wafers when it is almost done; when it is all done, stick candied pinenuts into the top of the torte — but first wash rosewater over the top; take it out of the pan, with sugar and a little rosewater on top.

Note that a proper amount of seasoning should be put in everything; if the cook is not discriminating, you can be sure that everything he makes will be either overly seasoned or too bland. Let the cook be a gourmand, not for his own sake but for that of his master.

[*missing folio(s)?*]

[Fish]

187. Sardines.

In their natural state they should be fried; when done, garnish them with orange juice and a little of the frying oil and salt; they are eaten hot.

188. Octopus.

If it is alive, beat it forcefully on a stone with a club; then get a little hot water, blanch the octopus well, cut it into bite-sized pieces a finger's length long, and put them into a pot with some oil on top of the coals away from the fire; do not put in water, rather cook them very slowly in oil; then get a little fried onion and fragrant herbs with spices, verjuice and a little water, mix everything together and boil it a short while; then serve it.

189. Crabs.

Cook them in wine, with or without water, and a lot of salt; for its sauce, get vinegar.

190. Kippers.

Cut up the salted fillet crosswise in slices the width of a finger, clean the pieces, cook them on the grill basting each with a mixture of vinegar, salt, spices and oil, and turning them often; serve. Similarly you can fry it, and also put it to boil, and cut it up into pieces of whatever size seems reasonable to you. Mind that it has not gone bad.

191. Rayfish.

It is good only if boiled, and then with Garlic Sauce on top.

⌈This is food for Florentine *fasaniticha* Catherina.⌋

192. Shad.

Remove its gill rakers or gut through its gill, and roast it on the grill basting it with salt, vinegar, pepper, saffron and oil; for its sauce, orange [juice]; otherwise get a leaf of chard, a little parsley, mint, marjoram and pepper, and grind them up with a little bread soaked in vinegar, and distemper with vinegar: that is for its sauce. Similarly you can cook it by boiling; then for its sauce get fifteen walnuts, grind them with a little sugar and good ginger, and distemper with verjuice or lemon juice.

193. Catfish (?)

Boil it in wine, water and vinegar; for its sauce, it takes Garlic Sauce.

⌈194. Sea Bream is good roasted and boiled and on the grill and soused in vinegar.⌋

195. Tortoises.

Get the largest tortoises, for they are the best, boil them alive in a cauldron and let them boil until they are well cooked; remove them from their shell, cut away their head, tail and feet, clean them well so nothing dirty remains, and remove the gallbladder from the liver; then get *lardo* and put it in a pan; get parsley, mint, marjoram, half a clove of garlic, and, when everything is ground, temper it with good spices and verjuice; fry this with the tortoises; then serve. Make the mixture yellow with saffron.

[*missing folio(s)*]

196. [*The name of the dish and the beginning of the recipe are missing.*]
. . . [when] the pieces of the eel are cooked, pour this sauce over them; serve the eel pieces in small plates and the sauce in small bowls.

197. Spanish Squid Sauce.

Get squid and clean them well so that nothing bad is left; take and parboil the legs and head of the squid, and grind or chop them; get walnuts, grind them up with good spices and stuff the squid with the walnuts, spices, the heads and legs of the squid; bind them up and send them off to the oven in a baking dish; when they are almost cooked, to make another sauce for them get a lot of toast soaked in bitter wine or water and grind it with pinenuts and a lot of spices; when you have ground it well, distemper it with water; when the squid are done, take them out of the pot or earthenware dish, put the sauce in the dish and boil it, then put the squid in with that too; when everything has boiled a while, set out the squid in small plates and the sauce in bowls.

198. Squid.

When they are smaller they are better for frying, [serving them] with spices and orange juice on top. The big ones should be well cleaned and stuffed with the stuffing for Reversed Tench; otherwise, if they are quite big, cook them in a mortar with oil, first cut up into small pieces like tripe; place them away from the fire, stirring often; when they are almost cooked, add into the mortar all sorts of spices along with a little sugar and verjuice, and let it come to a boil again; then take it out.

199. Sturgeon with Sauce.

Kill the sturgeon and leave it for two days to become more tender; cook it in good white wine mixed with an equal amount of water, and enough salt; boil the sturgeon as long as for veal, and break it into pieces—although it is prettier to serve it whole because any fish is better whole than in pieces; when it is cooked, take it out and color it yellow with saffron and orange juice if you like; the sauce for it should be White Sauce as I said above, but with more ginger. As well, you can serve White Garlic Sauce or else Mustard Sauce with it.

⌈Note that any fish should be well seasoned.⌋

200. Corb.

It should be prepared like the sturgeon [*Recipe 199*], except that it should boil less; for its sauce, the same sauce.

201. Dentex.

It should be boiled with vinegar because it lasts longer that way, and it tastes better than if cooked in water.

202. Large Corb.

It should be boiled; if small, it should be roasted; for its sauce, Green Sauce or Mustard Sauce.

203. Gilthead.

If large, boil it; otherwise, fry it.

[Note that any fish should be boiled slowly.]

204. Turbot.

Boil it, and because it is so soft, tie it to a reed tray and boil it gently in a large vessel; for its sauce, it takes verjuice, ground parsley, pepper and saffron on top.

205. Red Mullet.

They should be roasted; for their sauce, orange [juice], spices and salt on top.

206. Salpa.

Eviscerate them and roast the fish; with orange [juice] on top.

207. Goby.

They are better boiled than roasted.

208. Saddled Bream.

The are better fried than boiled.

209. Sea-Bream.

It is good boiled and roasted.

[Note that any fish should be eviscerated.]

210. Moray Eel.

Skin the eel, or else skin it with hot water, throwing away its head and tail — I mean, a piece of it — then fry it; for its sauce, Green Sauce.

211. Grey Mullet or Mackerel.

They are good fried if they are small; if large, boiled; when half-cooked, cover them with good pepper, verjuice, parsley and butter or oil.

212. Flounder.

If large, boil it; it should be prepared like a turbot [*Recipe 204*].

213. Oysters.

They are cooked on the coals, and when they open they are cooked; or else you can dig them out and fry them in oil; when cooked, garnish them with strong spices — this is the Venetian way of doing them.

214. Black Fish.

They should be fried; then garnish them with orange [juice] and pepper.

215. Clams, Mussels.

Get a dry pan and into it set the clams on the fire; when they begin to open, they are done; you can quickly add verjuice, pepper and finely chopped parsley, and heat them up again, and take them out for serving. Similarly you can cook them on the coals. To remove any sand from them, let them sit a night in water.

Other shellfish are done the same way.

216. Pike.

It should be boiled in vinegar, wine and water; for its sauce, Mustard Sauce.

[Note than any fish should be thoroughly cleaned of its scales.]

217. Trout.

Clean large trout well and cut them up into pieces the width of a hand; to cook them, get a vessel large enough to hold the pieces and put them into it lengthwise—I mean, with the cut part facing upwards; having bled like this, sprinkle salt on top, then pour in water in such a way that it does not wash away the salt you put there, and bring the water to only two fingers above the fish, and cook slowly; when froth begins to form, remove enough of the fire from underneath for it to boil very gently; when they are cooked, take them out, set them to dry on a large trencher board with mild spices on top; for its sauce serve White Sauce.

218. Tench in a Baking Dish.

Get a good three-pound tench, scrape it until it becomes white, and remove its teeth; get ten walnuts, half a *quatrino* of parsley, marjoram, a little mint, a chick-pea-sized amount of garlic and a lot of pepper, and grind everything together with saffron, a little oil, unground raisins and the tench's liver; when you have ground it all up, push the mixture through the tench's throat—but first remove its insides through its mouth with some sort of hook that will not break the gallbladder; alternatively, open it slightly near its head and put in the filling through the opening; then set it in a baking dish large enough for the tench and boil it with half a beaker of vinegar, half a beaker of verjuice and two beakers of water with an ounce of must syrup, more or less depending on whether you want it sweet; add in whole raisins, plums, sour cherries and an onion fried in good oil; at the end get chopped parsley, mint and marjoram, and add them in for a boiling; remove the tench from the baking dish, put it in a small plate with good spices and lemon juice, and serve it with everything that was in the baking dish.

If the tench is small, fry it.

Those that are between one-half and one pound, split them along the spine and fry them; [serve them] garnished with orange [juice] or verjuice.

Moreover, you can cook a large tench on the grill, making for it the filling described above in the Three-Pound Tench [*first paragraph, above*]; make a basting sauce for it of vinegar, pepper, salt and saffron, cooking it slowly and using a sprig of rosemary to baste it often with that sauce.

219. Large Lamprey.

Lamprey should be killed in a semi-sweet wine, then it should be put into hot water to rub away its skin-oil—but be careful not to remove or harm its skin; remove its tongue and teeth, and see that the bowels are removed with some sort of hook that will not harm its body, because the lamprey has nothing else to be discarded than its bowels; do not waste its blood because its sauce is made with it; put a nutmeg into its mouth and cloves into the holes of its neck; put the lamprey into a baking dish with an ounce of oil, verjuice and good white wine, making enough of this liquid to cover the lamprey, then put a little salt on top of it; cook it slowly on the coals. As it has cooked, make this sauce for it: get almonds or walnuts, grind them up with a few raisins and a slice of toast, distemper with verjuice or must or whatever other liquid you like, and strain it all; then add in cloves, ginger and cinnamon, and serve it.

Prepare it in another way—that is, roasted on a spit, holding under it, as you turn it, something to catch its blood, for that is its goodness; with it you can make its [sauce] . . . .

---

220. Zabaglone.[6]

For four cups of Zabaglone get twelve fresh egg yolks, three ounces of sugar, half an ounce of good cinnamon and a beaker of good sweet wine; cook this until it is as thick as a broth; then take it out and set it on a plate in front of the boys. And if you like you can add a bit of fresh butter.

The end.

[6] This recipe is not part of the corpus of recipes compiled by the Neapolitan cook but is found by itself on f° 89v, following the series of banquet menus.

V. Ingredients, Utensils and Glossary

A. Ingredients in the Recipes

Variant spellings are indicated in parentheses.

animal (unspecified): animale (animali), bestia salvatica, salvasina (salvasine);
(domestic): bove, capra, capreto, carnero, castrado, montone (monthone), porcheta, porco (porcho), scroffa, vacha, vitello (vitella);
(game): capriolo, cervo, cervia, lepore, limache (lumache), urso;
(viscera and products): budella (budelle, budello), coglioni, coradella (coratella, coradelle), creste, ficatelli (figatelli), figato (figatto), milza, reticella, sangue, testa, testiculi, trippa (trippe), ventresca;
(preserved meats): carne salata, persuto (persutto, presutto), somata.

fowl (unspecified): ucelli (ucelletti), volatili;
(domestic): capono (caponi, capone), galina (galine), galli, oche, pavone, polastro (polastri, pollastri, pullastro, pulastri, pullastri), pulli;
(game) bechafichi, columbi salvatici, fasani, grue, palumbi, pernice, pipione (pipioni, pizone, pizone), starna (starne), tordi (turdi).

seafood (unspecified): pesso;
(fish): alice, alose, anguilla, bessano, calamari, ciffalo (zefali), corvo, dentale, fravolino, goze, hoghiali, lampreda, lampuge, laze, luzo, macarella, morena, muiols, ombrina, orata, passara, raye, rombo, salpani, sarde, sardelle, sargo, scinale, spinole, sturiono, tenca (tencha, tenghe), triglie, trotte, varats;
(molluscs, crustaceans, etc.): calamari, cappe, concule, granci, hostriche, polpi, testudine (testidine);
(fish products): caviaro, latte.

dairy products: butiro, caso (fresco, veghio), caso parmesano (permesano, parmisano, permisano), latte, probatura.

eggs: ova (ovo), bianchi, ghiari, rossi.

grains and their products: amido, cemolella, farina, farro, grano, molica (molicha), nevola (nevole), orzo, pane (pani), pasta, riso, semula.

vegetables and herbs (unspecificied): herbe, herbe odorifere, herbuze (herbuce, arbuze);
(above ground): basilico, biete, boragine, caule, cicero (ciceri), fasoli, fava (fave), finochio (finoghio), fiore (fiori) de sambuco, juivert, lactucha, lauro, maiorana (maiorano), marignani, menta, mortella, pampani, petrosillo, piselli, rigano, rose, rosmarino, salvia, sambuco, sarfoglio, scaffe, serpillo, vite, zuca (zucha, zuche);
(below ground): agleto, aglio (alio), carotte, ceba (cepa), cipolla (cipolle), cipolletta, pastonache, rape.

spices, etc. (unspecified): specie, specierie;
canela (canella), garofali (garofoli), grana paradisi, mostarda, pepe (pipero, pipere, pepero, pebro, pebre), sale, senipa (sinapo), zenzaro (zenzero, zenzevero, zinzibero, zinzivero, gingibero, gingibro);
(colorants): sandalo (sandali), zafrano (zaffrano, saffrano);
(sweeteners): mel (mele), zucharo.

fruit, nuts, seeds: agrume, amandole (amandoli), anesi (anasi), aranze, canepa (canipa), carabace, castagne, cerase (cesrase), cimino, codogne (pome codogne), cornali, datili, fiche, granate (pome granate, melagranata), limoni, marangoli, mela, meloni, noce, noce moscata (moscate), noghie, pere, persico, pignolli, pome, prune, uva, uva negra, uva passa, visole (vissole).

liquids and fats:
(grape products): aceto (acito), agresto, mosto, mosto cotto, saba (sabba), vinagro, vino (vino dolce), vino cotto;
(other liquids): aqua, aqua rosata (rosada, rosa), aqua vita, brodeto (brodetto), brodo, licore, latte (late, de amandole, de capra), suco (sugo);
(fats): lardo, medula, oleo, saimo, struto (strutto).

B. Utensils and Heat Sources

As in the preceding listing, variant spellings are indicated here in parentheses.

Utensils: aco, bastone (bastoni), bichero (bicheri), bucale (bucali, buchali), caldaro (caldare), candela, canevazo, canistro, canna, caraffa, cazola, cultello (cortello), cughiaro (cughiara forata), filo (filo de ferro), papiro (carta papiro), forma (for ricotta, butter), gabia, gradelle, graticula (graticula de canuze), legno (legno tondo, legno ... como un spito), mortaro, olla, padella (padela, padella de torta, patella), paletta, panno (panno lino), penna, piatello (piatelli), piatto (piato, piatti), pignata (pignatta, pignatella), pila (pilla), pistono, ramo de rosmarino, rampino, saxo, scala, scutella (scutelle, scudella, scudelle, scutellini, scudelini, scudellini), sedazo, seta, spito (spido), spileto, stamegna (stamigna), stanga, taglero (tagliero), tavola (tavoleta), taza, tegamo, tiella (tiela), tondo, vaso (vasso).

Heat sources: brasa (braxa, braxe), cenere (cenere calda, cinere, cinere calda), foco (focho, fogo), forno, sole.

◈

C. Glossary of the Recipes

This Glossary is intended as well to function as an index. To this end, all dishnames are listed here with their recipe number, with both name and number printed in bold type. Verbs appearing in finite forms are normally glossed by an infinitive.

Resources and *sigla*:

The following dictionaries and glossaries are cited partly for their authority and partly in order to indicate possible lexical relations between the Anonimo Napolitano and Italian and Catalan usage of the time or of more modern times.

The symbol > indicates the eventual Italian form of a word. An asterisk identifies a hypothetical word.

Altamura: Antonio Altamura, *Dizionario dialettale napolitano*, 2nd ed. (Napoli: Fausto Fiorentino Editore, 1968).

Casas: Cristóbal de las Casas, *Vocabulario de las dos lenguas toscana y castellana* (Sevilla, 1570; reprint: Madrid: Ediciones Istmo, 1988).

CID: *The Cambridge Italian Dictionary*, general ed. Barbara Reynols (Cambridge: Cambridge University Press, 1962); vol. I: Italian–English.

Cobarruvias: Sebastián de Cobarruvias, *Tesoro de la Lengua Castellana o Española* (Madrid, 1611; reprint: Madrid, n.d.).

Cotgrave: Randle Cotgrave, *A Dictionarie of the French and English Tongues* (London, 1611).

Crusca: *Vocabolario degli Accademici della Crusca*, 2d ed. (Venezia: Iacopo Sarzina, 1623).

DEI: Carlo Battisti & Giovanni Alessio, *Dizionario etimologico italiano*, 5 vols. (Firenze: Barbèra, 1950–57).

DuCange: Carolo Du Fresne, Domino DuCange, *Glossarium Mediæ et Infimæ Latinitatis*, editio nova a L. Favre, 10 vols. (Niort, 1883–87).

DCVB: A. Alcover, F. Moll, *Diccionari Català–Valencià–Balear*, 10 vols. (Palma de Mallorca, 1930–62).

GDLI: Salvatore Battaglia, *Grande dizionario della lingua italiana*, to Vol. 18 (sik-) (Torino: Unione Tipografica – Editrice Torinese, 1961–).

Gual Camarena: Miguel Gual Camarena, *Vocabulario del comercio medieval* (Barcelona: El Albir, 1976).

REW: W. Meyer-Lübke, *Romanisches Etymologisches Wörterbuch* (Heidelberg, 1972).

abrusar 54, abrusi 69, abruxi 69, abrusano 42, 62 > abbruciare: "consumar col fuoco" (*GDLI*); " . . . di cibo che è stato cotto oltre misura" (Altamura); to burn, scorch; see also *brusi*, below

acarpionado 189 > accarpionare, carpionare: to cook a fish in the same way as a carp; *cf.* the modern gloss, "to souse (fish) in vinegar to be eaten cold"

aceto 1, passim, acceto 37, acito 193, accito 1 > aceto: vinegar

acio 25, passim, azo 106 > acciò, azzò: (conj.) "affinché, acciocché" (Altamura); so, so that

aco 67 > ago: needle

aconzare 70, aconciar 161, aconza 69, passim, aconcerai 157, aconzarai 27, aconzata 69, 200, 212, aconci 15 > acconciare: "accomodare, contrario di guastare" (*Crusca*); to arrange, prepare; see also *conza*, below

ad 9, 61, 74: (Latin) to, in; the letter *d* is retained before a vowel, as *ad uno* 16, passim

adasio 11, passim > adasio (obsolete), adaso (Altamura), adagio: slowly

adiunge 178, agionge 108, 219, azonze 11, passim, adiongera 180, agiongera 173, adiongendoli 167, agiongendo 22, 25 passim, agiongiendo 173, azongendo 20, azonzendo 136 > aggiungere: to add in; (in reflexive) to be added in; sopragiongendo 77, 150, 180: adding on top

adoso 69, 70 > addosso: on, upon; on its, one's back

aggiungere: see *adiunge*, above

agleto 120 > aglietto: "dim. d'aglio, ne si dice aglietto, se non quando egli è fresco, et non ancor capituto" (*Crusca*); fresh garlic; see also *foglia*, below

agliata 49, 124, 191, 193, 199: Garlic Sauce (Altamura)

aglio 33, 49, 54, 63, 69, 82, 119, 124, 163, 195, 218, alio 44, 115 > aglio: (bot.) *Allium sativum*, garlic; **Agresto cum aglio 119**

agresto 4, passim > agresto: verjuice; **Agresto cum aglio 119**

agro 13, 93, 101 bitter, tart; *cf. brusco*; see also *vino*

agrore 76: bitterness, tartness, tang

agrume 110 > agrume: citrus fruit (juice)

alessare 51, passim, allessare 27, passim, alessato 191, 201, 216, allessati 208 > lessare: to boil, boil slowly, cook by boiling, stew; (adj.) alesso 6, passim, alleso 182, allesso 20, a alesso 49 (adv. phr.): boiled; *cf. bollita*, below; **Alesso 43**

alice 33 > alice: (ichth.) *Engraulis encrasicholus*, anchovy

almancho 7: at least

alose 76 > alosa: (ichth.) *Alosa alosa*, shad

amabile 219 > amabile: "è quel sapore, che forse i latini dicean *suavis*, che l'attribuiamo al vino, contrario al brusco, e piccante, e pende più tosto al dolce" (*Crusca*); semisweet (said of wine)

Amandolata 162: almond paste

amandole 3, passim, amandoli 4: almond; *cf.* It. *mandorla*

amazare 69, amaza 70, 199 > ammazzare: to kill, slaughter

amido 169, 178 > amido: starch

anesi 19, 167, anasi 168 > anice: aniseed (always qualified as *confetti*, "candied")

anguilla 50, 196 > anguilla: (ichth.) *Anguilla anguilla*, eel; **[Anguilla 196]**

appareghio 58: arrangement, preparation, specif. a prepared dish; *cf. apparecchiare*: "mettere in ordine, in punto, preparare, apprestare" (*Crusca*); **Appareghio de ucelletti 58**

apichi 8, apiza 69 > appiccare: "unire, e congiungnere, l'una cosa all'altra, o con l'altra" (*Crusca*); to attach, join; (in reflexive) to cling, stick; *cf. spichi*, below

aqua rosata 4, passim, aqua rosada 169, passim, aqua rosa 5, passim: distilled rosewater; see *aqua rosata* in Gual Camarena, *s.v. aqua rosacea*

aqua vita 69: distilled wine, (wine) spirits

aranze 199 > arancia: orange

arbuze: see *herbuze*, below

armate 27 (**Rape Armate**): prepared, done up (lit. "fortified")

arusti 101 > arrostire: roasted, grilled

asutto 23 > asciutto: (past part.) drained, dried; *cf. sutta*, below

ascalda 142 > scaldare: (refl.) to become overheated (*cf. scaldare*, below)

atorno 19, atorno a 89 > attorno: (prep.) around, about

attacara 5, atacato 69, 133, attacata 98, attacate 70 > attacare: to attach, stick

aureghia 192 > orecchia: gill (of fish)

azo: see *acio*, above

azonze: see *adiunge*, above

baiocho 63 > baiocco: (numis.) "moneda baxa" (Casas); "moneta di rame, che si coniava nella Roma pontifica e circolava negli Stati della Chiesa; equivaleva a circa sei centesimi di franco e si divideva in cinque quattrini" (*GDLI*); fifteenth-century coin; see also *quatrino*, below

balotte 123 > ballotta: chestnut-sized balls

bambace 69 > bambagia, bambace (Altamura): cotton, cotton wool, wadding

basilico 119 > basilico: (bot.) *Ocimum basilicum*, basil

bastonceli 15: "piccolo bastone, bastoncino; ramo, fusto appena appena dirozzato" (*GDLI*); small sticks, (wooden) rods

batere (*carne*) 87, battere (*lardo*) 73, (*carne*) 84, bate (*vitella*) 10, (*herbe*) 38, (*vitello*) 73, (*herbe*) 93, (*ova*) 150, (*polpo*, to kill) 188, bati (*ova*) 19, (*panzeta*) 65, (*ova*) 125, (*herbe*) 126, (*ventresca*) 128, (*ventresca*) 130, (*rose*) 137, (*ova*) 144, batti (*vitella*) 20, batuto (*lardo*) 30, (*ovo*) 36, batuta (*ova*) 11, (*ova*) 74, (*carne*) 83, (*ova*) 88, (*ova*) 96, batute (*herbe*) 10, batudo (*petrosillo*) 183 > battere: to beat

bechafichi 59 > beccafico: (orn.) figpecker, garden warbler; **Bechafichi 59**

Bessano 193: (ichth.) perhaps a scribal error for *bestino*, catfish

bestia salvatica 112: game animal; **Salsa ad ogni bestia salvatica 112**

biancho manghiare 4, 171, bianchomanghiare 3, 4, 5, 6: white dish (a sort of prepared dish); **Biancho manghiare 171, ~ de galine ho palumbi 3, ~ per coprire caponi 4, ~ alla cathalana 5, ~ [de quaresima] 6**

bianco 87, passim, biancho 4, bianca 88, 106, 125, 160 (note), biancha 63, 63, 88, 129, 135, 175, 218, bianche 34, 60, 62, 104: (adj.) white, blanched; biancho 149, biancho 15, bianchi 88, 125, 129, 134, 149: (subst.) white (of an egg); bianchata 49, biancate 4, 122, 169, 173, bianchate 42, inbiancate 147: whitened, blanched (by parboiling); Agliata biancha 199, **Brodeto biancho 12, Genestrata biancha 39, Ravioli bianchi 11, Sapore biancho 104, Tartari bianchi 186, Torta biancha 125**

bichero 1, passim, bicheri 218 > bichiere: drinking-glass, tumbler, cup, beaker

biete 38, passim > bieta (obsolete): "acelga" (Casas); (bot.) *Beta vulgaris*, subspecies *cicla*, (Swiss) chard

bisogna 68, passim > bisognare: to be necessary

bisogno 169 > bisogno: need

boca 79, 98 > bocca: mouth

bollita 80 > bollire: boiled; *cf. alessare*, above

boragine 24 > borragine: (bot.) *Borago officinalis*, borage

botti 5 > botto: "colpo, percossa" (*GDLI*, Altamura); stroke, blow

bove 73, 77: ox

brasa 156, brase 6, braxa 27, passim, braxe 3, passim > brace: embers, coals

brodeto 3, passim, brodetto 46 > brodetto: "minestra d'uova dibattute con broda, o acqua" (*Crusca*); a prepared dish made from thickened bouillon, perhaps containing cooked foodstuffs; a thick broth; a thin stew, of thicker consistency than a *brodo*; **Brodeto**

bello 13, ~ biancho 12, ~ de pane he caso he cum ova

brodo 1, passim > brodo: brewet, broth; **Brodo consumado 1, ~ de amandole a homo delicato 31, ~ de ciceri 163**

brusca 62, 91, bruscato 54 > bruscare: "chamuscar [to singe], perdigar [to broil slightly, brown]" (Casas); to toast; *cf. torrato*, below

brusco 54, 105, brusca 122, brusce 109, 116, brusche 50 > brusco: sharp (in taste), bitter, tart; see also *agro*

bruscula 92, bruscule 94, brusculato 37, 58, 112, brusculado 1, passim, brusculate 92 > brusculare: probably the same as *bruscare*, to toast

brusi 142 > bruciare: *brusciare*, "abrasar" (Casas); to burn, set on fire

bruto 43, 197: dirty, unclean (salt, squid)

bucale 49, 102, 133, 171, 220, bucali 2, 163, buchali 5 > boccale: pot; measure for wine or other liquids (*DEI*)

buconi 188 > boccone: mouthful, morsel (*DEI*)

budella 68, 83, 84, 87, budelle 83, budello 82, 161, 192, 219: bowel, intestine

buglore 11, bullore 21, passim > bollore: a boil, (a state of) boiling; dare uno bullore 21, 25, 33, 60, levare uno bullore 35 (*hano levato uno buglore*, "they have come to a boil"), trare uno bullore 78, 154, 198

bulignesa 87, 126, 138, 141, bulignesi 87: Bolognese

buso 72, 77, busso 77, busi 219, bussi 157, buco 175 > buso: (small) hole ("tosc." *DEI*)

bussato 15: (past part.) holed

butando 158 > buttare: to throw, cast

butiro 11, passim: butter; **Butiro contrafato 169**

cacia 3, passim, caza 45, passim, caciara 7, cazarai 7, cazato 77, caciando 59, cazando 69, 85 > cacciare (Altamura): "arrojar, echar" (Casas); to throw, cast; *cf. cavare*, below

calamari 197, 198 > calamaro: (ichth.) *Loligo vulgaris*, squid, calamary; **Calamari 198, Salsa hispana a calamari 197**

calata 133, calate 133 > calata: "ant. aria musicale e ballo caratterizzati da un ritmo veloce; '*Ballare di calata*' danzare la calata" (*GDLI*); "cfr. fr. *calade -ate* (sec. XVI), discesa; tuffo nell'acqua; colpo scherzoso sul cappello altrui" (Altamura); "*callata*: (vox Italica) ambulacrum, gall. *promenade*. Locus commodum ad ambulandum animi gratia" (Du Cange); dance (perhaps walk, stroll)

calda 73, 179, 215: subst., in the phrase *dare una calda a*, to heat briefly

caldaro 68, 98, 161, 195, caldare 98: vat, kettle

calisoni 160 > caliscione: "morselletto fatto di marzapane" (*Crusca*); a marzipan turnover; *cf.* "dial., spezie di raviuolo o agnellotto" (*DEI*); "*cazone*, calzone, ... focaccia ripiena di salumi e latticini" (Altamura); **Calisoni boni 160**

camfora 69, canfora 69: (bot.) *Cinnamomum camphora*, camphor

canela 149, 150, canella 2, passim > cannella: (bot.) *Cinnamomum*, cinnamon

canepa 34, canipa 34 > canapa: (bot.) *Cannabis sativa*, hemp, hemp seed

canestro 89, canistro 89 > canestro: "spezie di paniere" (*Crusca*); (tightly woven) basket, hamper; *cf.* Cat. *canastra*, "recipient fet de canyes o de viments entreteixits, de forma tronco cònica invertida i de boca redona ... que serveix per traginar roba, fruita o altres coses; cast. canasta" (*DCVB*); the *Arte coquinaria* has *canestro o cistello* (Recipe 256)

canevazo 62 > canevaccio, canovaccio: canvas rag, coarsely woven cloth

canna 59: cane

canti 59 > canto: side

canuze 204 > cannuccia: "dim. di canna, sottilissima canna" (*Crusca*); (slender) reeds, perhaps woven as a mat; *cf.* can(n)iccio: reed matting, tray made of reeds

capono 56, caponi 2, passim, capone 2, passim: capon, castrated (young) rooster; **Bello rosto de caponi, polastri, capreto 52, Caponi inzucarati 51, Galine ho caponi in spito cum suo sapore 55, Limonata a galine ho ha caponi 56, Pariola con galine ho ha pollastri ho ha caponi in spito 57, Pastizi de boni caponi, polastri, pizoni 72, Sfarcimento a capone 81**

Cappe 215 > cappa: (zool.) bivalve molluscs of various species; *Ensis ensis*; *Meretrix chione*; *Chamelaea gallina*; *Venus verrucosa*; clams, mussels

capra 7, 171 > capra: goat

capreto 20, passim, capretto 46, capreti 82 > capretto: goat kid; **Bello rosto de caponi, polastri, capreto 52, Carne de capreto in tegamo alla fiorentina 47, Carne de capretto ho de carnero cum brodetto 46, Capreto in piu modi 54, Pastello de capreto 74, Sfarcimento a capreto 80**

capriolo 1, 112: deer; **Salsa ad ogni bestia salvatica ho de cervo ho urso ho capriolo ho de altra carne 112**

capsa 74, 75: probably a borrowing from Cat. *capsa*; box; *cf.* mod. It. dim. *capsula*; see also *cassa*, below

carabace 30: probably a borrowing from Cat. *carabassa, carbassa*; gourd, pumpkin; see Gual Camarena, *s.v. carabassa*; **Carabace alla catalana 30**

caraffa 68, 98: carafe

Cardinale 20: (orn.?) cardinal

carne 1, passim: meat; **Carne de capreto in tegamo alla fiorentina 47, Carne de capretto ho de carnero cum brodetto 46; Carne in tegamo alla fiorentina 50, Gelatina de carne ho de pesso 88**

carne salata 2, passim > carne-salata: "*cansalada*: antigament escrit també *carnsalada*, part grassa del porc, situada entre la pell i la carn, que és de color blanc i es guarda salada per a tirar a l'olla i altres guisats. Cast. *tocino*; *cansalada entreviradá*: la que es treu dels cuixots, que té vies de carn magra" (*DCVB*); salt pork, preserved pork; see Gual Camarena, *s.v. carnsalada*

carnero 1, 46, 78: perhaps a borrowing from Sp. *carnero*, ram; see also *castrado, montone*, below; **Carne de capretto ho de carnero cum brodetto 46, Pieno ad una spalla de carnero 78**

carotte 88, 177: (bot.) *Daucus carota*, carrot; *cf. pastonache*, below

carta 142: "foglio di carta, foglio scritto" (*DEI*, 13th–14th c.); a sheet (of paper)

caso 8, passim: cheese; see also *parmesano, probatura*

cassa 178 > cassa: box, container; *cf.* Cat. *caixa*; see Gual Camarena, *s.v. caxa*; see also *capsa*, above

castagne 136 > castagna: (bot.) *Castanea sativa*, chestnut; **Torta de castagne 136**

castrado 46, 78, 88 > castrato: sheep, mutton; see also *carnero, montone*

cathalano 61, catalana 30, 37, cathalana 5: Catalan

Catharina 25, 133, Catherina 191: seems to be a proper noun

caule 23, 141 > caule, caulo: "cavolo" (Altamura): (bot.) cabbage; **Caule alla romanesca 23, Torta de caule 141**

cavare 209, passim, cavato 49, cavati 149, cava 1, passim, cavano 161, cavara 206, caverai 137, 157, cave 137 > cavare: to extract, remove (esp. out of), dig out; *cf. cacia*, above; cava (la pignata) dal focho 48: remove (pot) from fire, take (up) off fire

caviaro 184: caviar, roe, fish eggs (partic. of sturgeon?); *cf. latte*; **Fritata de caviaro 184**

caza, etc.: see *cacia*, above

cazola 9, 39: probably a borrowing from Cat. *cassola*; pot

ceba 76, cepa 46: onion; the first form is probably a borrowing from Cat. *ceba* "onion"; see Gual Camarena, *s.v. cebes*; *cf. cipolla*, below

cemolella 28 > sĕmmŭlella: "semolino" (Altamura); semolina; **Cemolella ciciliana 28**

cenere 39, 59, 62, 65, 152, 153, cinere 41, 94 > cenere, "ashes"; embers, coals

cerase 109, 124, 137, cesrase 137 > cĕràsa, "ciliegia, *majàteca* 'marchiana'" (Altamura): (bot.) *Prunus cerasus*, (sour) cherry; **Sapore de visole ho de cerase 109, Torta de cerase 137**

cerco 69 > cerco (obsolete), cerchio: circle, ring

cervia 70: hind

cervo 70, 112: stag; **A fare che una vacina, una vitella, uno cervo parano vivi 70, Salsa ad ogni bestia salvatica ho de cervo ho urso ho capriolo ho de altra carne 112**

cicero 218, ciceri 163, 164 > cìcĕrĕ, "cece" (Altamura): (bot.) *Cicer arietenum*, chick-pea; **Brodo de ciceri 163**

ciciliana 28, ciciliani 15: Sicilian

ciffalo 50, zefali 211 > cefalo: (ichth.) *Mugil cephalus*, common grey mullet; **Zefali ho macarella 211**

cimino 70 > cimino, comino: (bot.) *Cuminum cyminum*, cummin

cinere: see *cenere*, above

cinna 10: perhaps same as *scina*, spine, back, (hence) loin; otherwise udder, dug, (hence) belly; *cf. cinna*, "Ant. zinna, mammella" (*GDLI*)

cipolla 48, passim, cipolle 41, passim > cipolla: onion; *cf. cepa, ceba*, above

cipolletta 71: small onion (?)

cirvelato 83 > cervellato: a variety of sausage; *cf.* a modern gloss: "salsiccia (tipico un temp di Milano), composto da carne, sangue e cervello di maiale, con formaggio e aromi" (*GDLI*); **Cirvelato de carne de porco ho de vitella 83**

coco 70, 71, 74, 89, 98, 167, cocho 186 > cuoco: cook

codogne, pome (pomi) codogne 77, 140 > cotogna: (bot.) *Cydonia oblonga*, quince; **Pastizi de pome codogne 77, Torta de codogne 140**

coglioni 73 > coglione: testicles

columbi salvatici 2: (orn.) of the family *Columbidæ*, wood doves; see also *pipione*, below

compagnone 220 > compagnone: "e huono gioviale, piacevole, e di buon tempo. Lat. *homo voluptarius*" (*Crusca*); comrade, chum, buddy, (merry) fellow

concule 215 > còncola: "conchiglia" (Altamura); shell, conch (of a mollusc, gastropod); such shellfish

confetti 19, 167, 168, 186: candied (by means of a sweet substance; said of aniseed, pinenuts)

consumare 2, consumado 2, consumati 163 > consumare: "lograre, finire, ridurre al niente, torre l'essere" (*Crusca*); to consume, boil down (a liquid), concentrate; (pp. as adj.) concentrated, condensed

contrafato 169, contrafatta 168: counterfeit, fake, mock

contrario, e[x] contrario 85: (Latin) on the contrary

conza 37, 70: to arrange, mount (as on a spit or sloping grill); see also *aconzare*, above

coppo 75: a variety of pasty; "*coppo*: crosta di pasta a foggia di tegola, nome di pietanza" (Sŭthold, *Manoscritto Lucano*, p. 236)

coradella 80, coratella 96, coradelle 1, 20 > coradella: "entrañas" (Casas); from recipe 96 it is clear that the term corresponds to Cat. *freixura*, Fr. *fressure*, *i.e.* the lungs, and, more often, the lungs, heart, and liver of an animal; lights and organs, pluck

cornali 88 > corognàlĕ, "corniolo" (Altamura), cornalina: (bot.) *Cornus mas*, cornelian cherry

corpo 75 > groppone: (ornith.) crupper, rump (of fowl); see *DEI*, *s.v. groppa*

corso 74, 75 > corso: layer, bed

cortelo 27, cortello 38, cultello 19, passim > cortello (dial. Ven., Tusc.), coltello: knife corvo 202 > corvo: (ichth.) *Johnius umbra*, brown meagre, corb; or *Sciaena cirrhosa*, corb; *cf. ombrina*, below; **Corvo grosso 202**

cossa 71, 97, 98: upper leg, thigh, haunch; **Cossa stillata 97, Stillato de cossa ho de galina in caraffa 98**

costa 27: blade (of a knife)

cotto: see *mosto* and *vino*, below

creste 73: coxcombs

crosta 19, passim: (pastry) crust; 80, 81: glazing

crostata 94 > crostata: variety of prepared dish baked on toast; *cf.* the modern sense: "torta salata di pasta fatta cuocere al forno" (*GDLI*); **Crostata de caso, pane 94**

cuce 63, 68, 197; recuce 67 > cucire: "coser" (Casas), *cuscire*; to sew (up)

cughiaro 1, passim: spoon; cughiara forata 26: holed (stirring) spoon (used as a strainer)

cultello: see *cortelo*, above

cum 1, passim: (Latin) with

dadi 72: dice; *dadi da iocare*: gaming dice

datili 39, 80: (bot.) dates; see Gual Camarena, *s.v. datil*

denanze 47, 161 > dĕnantĕ, "avanti, davanti, innanzi" (Altamura): (adj.) fore (quarters of an animal); *cf. dreto*

Dentale 201: *cf.* Cat. *dèntol*, "sea bream"; (ichth.) *Dentex dentex*, dentex

diffacia 46, diffata 130, disfallo 5 > disfare: to disintegrate (of boiled meat)

discordare (te) 174, discordandote 168, discordanti 135 > scordarsi: to forget

discreto 74, 89, 186, discretto 70, descretto 71: "che ha discrezione" (*Crusca*); judicious, discriminating, astute

disfallo: see *diffacia*, above

distempera 4, passim, distempara 111, distempra 104, distemperare 58, 62, 75, 162, distemprare 1, distemperato 3, distemperando 58: to moderate the (unhealthy) humoral temper (of a foodstuff by the admixture of a tempering agent); see also *stempera*, below

dito 11, 90, 117, 188, 190: finger, finger's width (as a unit of measurement)

dolce 167: sweet; 186: dainty, fine; as opposed to agro: 13, 93, 101; as opposed to brusco: 50, 54, 105, 116; see also *finoghio, granate, licore, marangoli, specie, vino*

dopia 7: (adj.) folded (of fabric)

dreto 47: hind (quarters of an animal); *cf. denanze*

dritto (*per lo dritto de*) 63 > diritto: right along

etiam 42, 190: (Latin) likewise, furthermore

exire 142: (Latin) escape, overflow

fanti: see *milli fanti*, below

farcimento: see *sfarcimento*, below

farina 5, passim: (wheat) flour; *fiore de farina* 134, 170, 172, 174, 179: fine (wheat) flour

farinata 32: "vivanda fatta d'aqua, e farina, cotta nella pentola al fuoco, usata da' poveri huomini, e contadini. Paniccia. Lat. *pulsiis*" (*Crusca*); porridge (of cereal grain), gruel; **Farinata ad homo infermo 32**

farro 7, 9, 130, 136 > farro: spelt; **Potagio de farro 9, Torta de farro 130**

fasani 2, 69, 70 > fasàno: (orn.) "fagiano" (Altamura); pheasant

fasanica 18 (marginal), fasanicha 133, fasanitico 134, fasaniticha 191: perhaps with reference to a *fasano*, "pheasant," with erotic connotations

fasoli 21, 41: (bot.) *Phaseolus vulgaris*, kidney bean; **Fasoli 41**

fatue 186: bland, insipid; opposed to *salato*, *q.v.*, below

fava 42, 165, 166, fave 40, 42: (bot.) *Vicia faba*, broad bean; **Fava 165, ~ in padella 166, Fave piene 42**

fele 195, 218 > fiele: gall

fende 42, 63, 79, 218, fender 69 > fendere: to split, break, cut in two, cleave; see also *sfendo*, below

fetine 1: thin slices; *cf. fetta*, below

fetta 78, passim, fette 21, passim: slice; *cf.* *fetine*, above

fiche 79, 166, 175, 177: figs; *fiore* [of a fig] 175, fig blossom; **Fritelle de fiche piene 175**

figato 48, passim, figatto 65, 101, ficatelli 73, passim, figatelli 44, passim: liver; **Figatelli 64**

filo 59: cord; filo de ferro 15: wire, fine rod

finochio 161, finoghio 59, 84, 87, 119, 161, fenoghio 70, finoghio dolce 40: (bot.) *Fœniculum vulgare*, fennel

fiore, fiori: see *farina, genestra, persico, sambuco*

fixure 61: fissures, slits, openings

florentino 134, florentina 191, fiorentino 155, 157, fiorentina 47, 50: Florentine

foco 22, passim, focho 3, passim, fogo 92 (reading uncertain): fire

fogleta 125, 127, 167, fogletta 132 > foglietta: "antica misura di capacità per liquidi, equivalante a circa mezzo litro in uso nelle regioni centro-settentrionali . . . e giunta a Roma intorno al 1500" (*GDLI*); about half a pint

foglia (de agleto) 120: leaf, shoot (of garlic plant); foglie (de vite) 59, (de oro) 69, (de rose) 137: leaves, petals

foglio (de papiro) 142: sheet (of paper); *cf.* *carta*, above

forata 26: holed, perforated (spoon)

forma (for ricotta) 168, (for butter) 169: mold, form (for cheese, butter)

forma, in forma de (prep. phr.) 5, 72, 158, 177, 178, 179: in the shape of; 24, 30: in the manner of

fornire 71, fornita 181 > fornire: "finire. Lat. *conficere, perficere*" (*Crusca*); fornì, "provvedere compiutamente a qualche cosa, portare a termine un lavoro o altra impresa" (Altamura): to conclude, finish (off)

forno 47, 49, 50, 70, 72, 73, 74, 159, 185, 197: oven

forzina 192 > forcina: gill-rakers, numerous long thin cartilaginous or bony processes on the inner side of the (shad's) gill-arch

franceso 62, francesa 121, franzesa 116, 121, 185: French

frascaria 156 > frascherìa: "chiacchiere, fantoccerie, vanità, baie, bagattelle. Lat. nugae, gerrae" (*Crusca*); "cosa di poco o nessun conto; inezia; fantasticheria" (*GDLI*); trifle, simple thing, triviality

Fravolino 194 > fravolino, fragolino: (ichth.) *Pagellus erythrinus*, sea bream, pandora

fritata 144, 145, 150, 166, 183, 184 > frittata: "modo di cucinare l'uovo in padella con olio" (Altamura): fried dish of eggs, omelet; **Fritata de herbe 145, ~ de ova 144**

fritelata 146, fritellate 155, 157: (past part.) deep-fried

fritelle 172, passim > frittella: pancake, (deep-fried) fritter; **Fritelle amare 172, ~ piene de vento 179**; for other *fritelle*, see Recipes 172–79 or, in this Glossary, the significant qualification in their name

fritura 195: (the action of) frying

frollo 182, 204, frolle 199 > frollo: (adj.) "tiglioso aggiunto de carne da mangiare, che abbia ammollito il tiglio, e sia diventata tenera" (*Crusca*); tender

fume 7: (masc. sing. subst.) smoky taste, fumes

fusti 88: fibrous processes (in hoof), shank

gabia 89 > gabbia: cage, bird-cage

galina 44, passim, galine 3, passim: hen, chicken; **Galine ho caponi in spito cum suo sapore 55, Galine cum carne salata 44, Per cocere una galina in una caraffa 68, Limonata a galine ho ha caponi 56, Pariola con galine ho ha pollastri ho ha caponi in spito 57, Salsa ala franzesa a pernice, a galine 116, Stillato de cossa ho de galina in caraffa 98**

galli 73: rooster; **Pastello de creste de galli cum li testiculi73**

gamellino 37, gamelino 105: brownish, camel-colored, the color of cameline sauce; **Sapore gamelino 105**

garofali 101, 123, garofoli 2, passim: (bot.) *Eugenia caryophyllus*, cloves

gelare 89, gelato 88, 90, gelata 88, 89: to jell, set (with a gellant, gelatin) gelatina 88, 89, 90, 117: a dish including jelled gelatin, jelly: **Gelatina de carne ho de pesso 88, ~ in uno canistro 89, ~ a modo de uno scachero 90**

genestra 107 > ginestra: (bot.) *Spartium junceum*, (color of) broom, Spanish broom, with brilliant yellow blossoms; *cf* Cat. *ginesta, ginestra*; **Sapore ditto fiore de genestra 107**

genestrata 39: a dish with (normally) a color of *genestra*; Cat. *ginestrada* (*cf. Libre de sent soví*, Recipe 56); **Genestrata biancha 39**

gentileze 142: "astratto di gentile, nobilità. Lat. *generositas, nobilitas*" (*Crusca*); courtly refinements

ghialdo 19, 88, 198, ghialda 14, 124, 128, 195, ghialdi 11, 17, ghialde 159, 179: yellow

ghiari 11 > chiara: whites, albumen (of eggs)

ghiotto 186 > ghiotto: "vizioso di vizio di gola, goloso, avido di cibi dilicati" (*Crusca*); gluttonous person, gourmand

gingibero: see *zenzaro*, below

gio 70, 79, 217 > probably *giù*: "abaxo" (Casas); down, below

Giusello 22: a cheese custard; see also *zanzarelli*, below

gola 69, 218 > gola: throat, gullet

Goze 207 > probably ghiozzo: (ichth.) species *Gobius*, goby

gozolo 106: small amount, dose; *cf. gozzo*, crop (of a bird), (pop.) throat

gradelle 76 > gradella: "parrillas" (Casas); *cf.* Cat. *graella*; see Gual Camarena, *s.v. grailles*; grill, gridiron; see also *graticula*, below

grado 27 (*de grado in grado*): layer (of a prepared dish); *cf. solo*

grana paradisi 62, 88: (bot.) *Amomum melegueta*, grains of paradise, melegueta pepper

granate 60, 61, 106, 110, granate dolce 102, 111, 116; granate brusce 116; (grani di) melagranata 4: (bot.) pomegranate; *granate* is qualified with the word *pome* in 106 alone; see Gual Camarena, *s.v. malgranas*

Granci 189 > granchìo: (zool.) crab

grano 88: wheat

graticula 1, 63, 78, 79, 150, 190, 194, 204, 218: grill, gridiron (Altamura); see also *gradella*, above

gratusato 47, 67 > grattugiare: to grate

grue 69 > gru: (orn.) of the family *Gruidæ*, crane

guasti 69, 219, guastare 219 > guastare: to spoil, ruin, mar

gule (before 66): (Latin, genitive), of taste, of gluttony; epicurean

gussa 146, gusso 161, 195 > guscio: husk, pod, shell (of an egg)

hage 170: subjunctive, 3rd pers. sing. of *havere*

hene: see *-ne* (enclitic), below

herba 88, herbe 10, 127, 131, 138, 145, 172, 183: herbs; **Fritata de herbe 145**

Herbicine 38: an herb dish

Herbulata de maio 127: an herb dish

herbuze 40, 49, herbuce 68, arbuze 188 > erbucce: "erbe da mangiare odorifere, e saporite. Qui è preso largamente in significato d'erbette. Lat. *herbula*" (*Crusca*); herbs (collectively)

hispana 197: Spanish

Hoghiali 208 > probably occhiata: (ichth.) *Oblada melanura*, a variety of sea bream, saddled bream

Hostriche 213 > ostrica: *Ostrea edulis*, oyster

imbandisone 27 > imbandigione: "(dial. ant.) preparazione e disposizione di cibi e bevande per un pranzo sontuoso, per un banchetto, per un invito" (*GDLI*); dish appropriate for a banquet

imbotita 97 > imbottire: interlarded, stuck (with cloves); *cf.* "riempire di lana, cotone o sim., riferendosi a coltre, vestiti; spagn. *embutir* (dal lat. *buttis*, 'botte')" (*DEI*): *i.e.* to stuff, pad, wad

imbrata 13, 170, inbrata 94, 132, 133, imbrate 11 > imbrattare: "quasi imbruttare, intridere, che è mettere in su che che sia sporcizia, e lordura" (*Crusca*); to dirty, stain, smear (with a substance)

imo 70, 155: (Latin) rather, on the other hand

impasta 15, inpastata 160: to put into pastry

impazo 68 > impaccio: "noia, impedimento, fastidio, briga, intrigo. Lat. *molestia, impedimentum*" (*Crusca*); impazzo, 'mpazzuto: "ammattito, impazzito; in alcune zone della Campania, specialmente nel Salernitano, si preferisce la forma *'mpacci* da *paccio* anziché *pazzo*" (Altamura); "impedimento" (Casas); problem, irritation, bother; see also *pazo*, below

impiede 69: = *in piede*, standing

impitura 63, passim, impiture 77: filling; *cf. sfarcimento*, below

inbiancate: see *bianco*, above

infilza 69, infilzato 69 > infilzare: to pierce, stick, prick (with a lardoon or clove)

infonde 43, 66, infuso 54, passim: to dip, immerse, infuse

ingegni: see *inzengno*, below

inghioda 70, inghiodato 69 > inchiodare: *enclavar* (Casas); to nail

iteriora 59, 63, 67, 209, 218 > interiora: entrails, viscera (of fowl, piglet, fish)

involupati 59: (past part.) to envelop, wrap; *cf. involtare* 59

inzengno 69, ingegni 70 > ingegno: contrivance, mechanism; *cf.* Sp. *ingenio*: "apparatus"

italiana 8, 122: Italian

item 2, passim (Latin): likewise, also

joncata 167, jonchada 167 > giuncata: "(XV sec.) latte rapreso; da 'giunco' . . . perché si pone e si conserva su stoini di g." (*DEI*); pressed unsalted curds (which used to be served on a mat of little rushes: *giunco*, "rush"); *cf.* Eng. junket; **Jonchada de amandole 167**

joveneta 52 > giovanetta: young, with diminutive

juivert 54, 58, 78, 96, 113, 115: probably from Cat. *juyvert* (obsolete), *julivert*: parsley; *cf. petrosillo*, below

julatica 133: with reference to a region in Italy, Giulatica?; **Tartara julatica 133**

laborata 74 > lavorare: to knead

lactucha 24: (bot.) *Lactuca sativa*, lettuce; **Lactucha che para zucha 24**

lampreda 219 > lampreda: (ichth.) *Petromyzon*, lamprey; **Lampreda grossa 219**

Lampuge 214 > lampuga: (ichth.) "(XIX sec.) pesce marino simile alla salpa, col dorso ceruleo e attraversato da linee dorate, *Stomateus fiatola*" (*DEI*); *Stromateus fiatola* or *Centrolophus niger*, black fish

lardo 1, passim: likely the same as Fr. *lard*, *i.e.* the highly fatty tissue under the skin of swine, available in solid slabs, untreated; if salted or pickled it became *carne salata* (*q.v.*). The term cannot be translated as "lard," which is a rendered fat, Fr. *saindoux*, It. *strutto*, Sp. *manteca*: *cf. saimo, struto*, below; nor can the English word "bacon" be used, which is usually a smoked or cured *lard maigre, i.e.* meat veined or marbled with fat; as there seems to be no satisfactory English equivalent to this term, we leave it untranslated throughout this edition.

lasagne 16, 17, 18, 128, 130, 132, 158, 181, lassagne 159: lasagna; **Lassagne de pelle de caponi 18**

latte 3, passim, late 125, 162, 173, 178: milk; latte (de pesso) 177: (fish) milt, soft roe; *cf. caviaro*

lauro 2, 70: (bot.) *Laurus nobilis*, (leaf of) bay laurel, sweet laurel

lavadura 1 > lavatura: "lo liquore, nel quale s'e alcuna cosa lavata" (*Crusca*); wash water

Laze 192 > laccia: (ichth.) *Alosa alosa*, shad

legno 70: wooden shaft (as for a spit); legno tondo 179: smooth bar of wood (as for a rolling pin)

lepore 1, 101 > lepre: hare; **Sapore a lepore 101**

levato 172 > lievito: leaven

licore 219, licore dolce 57 (comparable with verjuice) > liquore: liquid, juice

limache 161, lumache 161 > lumaca: (zool.) snail; **Limache in tempo grasso 161**

limonata 56, 110: dish flavored with lemon juice; **Limonata 110, ~ a galine ho ha caponi 56**

limoni 13, 55, 56, 60, 104, 110, 111, 192, 218: lemon; see Gual Camarena, *s.v. limós*

lino 88: linen

lombarda 115: Lombard

lomo 133: back, loin (?); perhaps *omo, q.v.*

lubriche 161: (medical term) possessing laxative qualities

luzo 167, 168, 181, 182, 183, 184, 185, 186, 216 > luccio: (ichth.) *Esox lucius*, pike; **Luzo 216**

macarella 211 > maccarello: (ichth.) *Scomber scomber*, mackerel; **Zefali ho macarella 211**

macharoni 15, 16, machoroni 15, macharone 15: macaroni; **Macharoni ciciliani 15, ~ romaneschi 16**

macina 181, macinato 3 > macinare: to grind, mill, crush, pound

maiorana 20, passim, maiorano 157: (bot.) *Origanum vulgare*, marjoram

manducare 51, 59, 133: (Latin) to eat

manghiare: see *biancho*, above

marangoli 53, 104, 143, 147, 152, 157, 187, 192, 198, 205, 206, 214, 218: (bitter) oranges, orange juice; marangoli dolce 60: sweet oranges

marignani 33 > marignani: (bot.) "(region.) melanzana" (*GDLI*); *Solanum melongena*, eggplant, aubergine; **Marignani 33**

marzapane 35, 111, 133, 160, 180: marzipan; **Menestra de marzapane 35, Sapore de marzapane 111, Torta de marzapane 180**

Matta fama 99: a prepared dish

medula 73, 77 > medùllo: "midollo" (Altamura); marrow

mel 55, mele 93, 112: honey

mela 79: apple

melagranata: see *granate*

meloni 36: melons; **Menestra de meloni 36**

menata (*ova menata* 143, *fava menata* 165, 166) > menà: "battere, percuotere" (Altamura); scrambled, beaten

menestra 13, passim, minestra 7, 36, menestre 2, passim, minestre 4 > menestre: "guisado" (Casas); (a) serving (of a prepared dish); see also *minestra* (verb), below

menta 20, passim: (bot.) *Mentha*, mint

messeda 73, miseda 131 > mescidare: "mescolare rimestando in continuazione; stemperare, impastare, mischiare" (*GDLI*); *REW*, #5605: **miscitare*, "mischen," aital. *mescitare*; to mix, blend

miliazo 134 > migliaccio: millet pudding; < Lat. *miliaceus*, millet (*DEI*); **Miliazo fasanitico alo modo fiorentino 134**

Milli fanti 19 > millinfànte: "pastina fine fatta a mano, gragnuola" (Altamura); variety of pasta made from granular dough

milza 1: spleen

minestra (subst.): see *menestra*, above

minestra 3 (verb) > menestrà: "minestrare, scodellare, far le porzioni a tavola" (Altamura); to dish out, serve; see also *menestra* (subst.), above

minutato (lardo) 73, (petrosillo) 215, minuzato (aglio) 63, minuzata (cipolla) 48, minuzate (cipolle) 99 > minuzzare: "tritare minutissimamente, sbricciolare" (*DEI*, derived from Lat. **minutiare* and late Lat. *minutare*); chopped finely, minced

minuto 19, 42, 44, 48, 82, 125, minudo 183, minuta 20, 83, 149: small, fine; *minuto minudo* 183: very small

mirabilia (in rubric before Recipe 66): Latin (subst. pl.), miracles, marvels

mirausto 37: *cf.* Cat. *mig-raust* (*Libre de sent soví*, Recipes 54 and 55); lit. "half-roast(ed)," dish in which fowl is half-cooked by roasting, then finished by being boiled in a sauce; **Mirausto alla catalana 37**

miscola 13, passim, miscolare 159, 172, miscolarai 127, 137, miscolato 49, 76, misculato

10, misculado 199, miscolada 188, 190, miscolate 22, 27, miscolando 4, misculando 5 > mescolare: to mix, blend *cf.* It. *mischiare*, Cat. *mesclar*

miscolanza 53, passim: mixture

moglio: stare a ~ 122, 123, 124, 163, 164, 168, 180, 165; stare in ~ 4; ponere a ~ 66, 104, 105, 184; mettere a ~ 43, 62; mettere in ~ 42, mogliare 91, mogliato 48: to soak, steep (in a liquid)

molica 4, passim, molicha 34, 35: the crumb or soft part of bread (as opposed to the crust)

monda 29, 39, 91, 176, mondare 33, mondato 4, 125, mondate 55, 56, 77, 106, (adj.) monda 79 > mondare: to peel, hull, husk (usually nuts); 91 to remove crust (from bread)

montone 48, monthone 48 > montone: ram, mutton; sheep; *cf. carnero*, *castrado*, above; **Testa de montone 48**

morbida 144, morbide 155: soft

Morena 210 > murena: (ichth.) *Muraena helena*, moray, murry-eel

mortaro 5, 36, 124, 137, 182, 184 > mortaio: mortar; *cf. pila*, below

mortella 70 > mortella: (bot.) *Myrtus communis*, myrtle (Altamura)

moscata: see *noce*

mostarda 121, 122, 123, 199, 202, 216: mustard (sauce); **Mostarda franzesa 121, ~ ytaliana 122, ~ per portare cavalcando in balotte 123**

mosto cotto 93, 101, 122, 185, 218: must syrup (made by reducing must by boiling); see also *saba*

muiols 76: *cf.* Cat. *mùjol*, "peix de l'espècie *Mugil cephalus*, semblant a la llissa, amb el cap pla i la boca petita; cast. *mùjol*" (*DCVB*); grey mullet

-ne (enclitic) passim: generally with the modern partitive sense, *e.g. coprine* 78, *farane* 219, *voleme* 22; note particularly *hene* 42, 199, 204 and *serane* 1, 202

nervi 84, 87: gristle

nevola 179, nevole 62, 180, 185, 186 > nevola: "cialda sottilissima e leggera, appunto come una nuvola" (*GDLI*); (very thin, light) wafer

noce 10, 219, passim > noce: (bot.) walnut; see also *noghie*, below; noce moscata 219, noce moscate 105: (bot.) *Myristica fragrans*, nutmeg

nodo 78 : joint (of bone)

noghie 192, 219: (bot.) walnuts; *cf.* Cat. *noga*, (dialectal), "nou" (*DCVB*); see also *noce*, above

oche 69: geese

Offelle 159: "(region.) piccola pasta dolce, confezionata con diversi ingredienti in varie regioni italiane" (*GDLI*); derived perhaps from L. *offa* and *ofella*, "bit, morsel"; a ravioli-like preparation, "dainty bites"

oleo 146, 155, olio 7, passim: (olive) oil; see Gual Camarena, *s.v. oli*

olla 31, 113, 197: pot, small cauldron; probably a borrowing from Cat. *olla*, "pot"; see *olles* in Gual Camarena; *cf. pastizo*, *pignata*, below

Ombrina 200 > ombrina: (ichth.) "dim d'ombra, oggi con questa voce, comunemente si chiama solo un pesce assai simile allo storione" (*Crusca*); *Umbrina cirrosa* or *Sciaena cirrosa* (*GDLI*), umbrine, corb; *cf. corvo*, above

omo 133 > olmo, uomo (?): elm tree (?); "*homo*, hombre" (Casas); "*ommo*, uomo, maschio" (Altamura); man (?); perhaps also *lomo*, *q.v.*

Orata 203 > orata: (ichth.) *Chrysophrys aurata*, kind of Mediterranean sea bream, gilthead

ordine, tale ordine 88: (Latin) in a similar way

oro, foglie de oro 69: goldleaf; see also *suppa*

orzo 32: barley

ossa, tuta l'ossa 48: "*ossa*, huesos" (Casas); (collective singular) bones ovo 35, 36, 67, 125, ova 8, passim > uovo: egg; ova de pesso 183: fish egg; **Ova in aqua freda 154, ~ in cenere 153, ~ cotta in carta papirea 142, ~ fritelata 146, ~ fritellate a lo modo fiorentino 155, ~ fritellate piene al modo fiorentino 157, ~ in forma de ravioli 158, ~ menata alla todesca 143, ~ piena 149, ~ sopra la brasa 156, ~ sopra la graticula 150, ~ sperduta in latte ho in vino 148, ~ sperduta in aqua 147, ~ in spito 151, ~ in taze 152, Fritata de ~ de pesso 183**

padela 143, 182, padella 33, 91, 93, 125, 126, 127, 128, 130, 131, 133, 134, 143, 145, 146, 150, 165, 166, 170, 181, 183, 195, 215; patella 41, 42, 65, 73, 186 > padella: (frying-)pan; padella bassa 185, ~ da (de) torta 27, 94, ~ de ferro 142, ~ grande 133

pagla 15 > paglia: straw

paletta 155 > paletta: "piccola pala, e tutta di ferro, e dicesi propriamente di quella, che s'adopra nel focolare" (*Crusca*); "piccola pala (in gen., metallica) per raccogliere spazzatura" (Altamura); spatula

palumbi 3: dove

pampani 120: vine-shoots, vine-sprouts; **Salsa de pampani 120**

pane 1, passim, pani 19: (loaf of) bread; *pane biancho* 4, 91, 104, 124, 162

panno 89, panno lino 88: (linen) cloth

panza 186 > panza, "pancia, ventre" (Altamura), pancia: belly (of a fish)

panzeta 65: belly (of a pig)

papale 117, 182: papal; **Salsa papale 117, Torta ~ 182**

papiro 142, papirea 142 > papiro ("papyrus"): (subst. and adj.) paper; see Gual Camarena, *s.v. paper*; see also *carta* and *foglio*, above

paradisi: see *grana*

pariola 57: a sauce of liver and spices; *cf.* Cat. *porriola, puriola* (*Libre de sent soví*, Recipes 72 and 87, and Nola, *Libro de guisados*, f° 22); **Pariola con galine ho ha pollastri ho ha caponi in spito 57**

parmesano 129, parmisano 133, permesano 17, 18, 27, 83, permisano 81, 82: Parmesan (var. of cheese)

passa 1, passim, passara 167, 169, passarai 168, passato 100, passata 32, passati 92, passate 185 (per la stamegna, per la cughiara forata, per sedazo, per la seta) > passà': "setacciare" (Altamura); to strain, filter, sift (flour in 32); see also the substantives *passada, passato*, below

passada 167: (substantified past part.) a strained substance; see also *passato*

Passara 212 > passera: (ichth.) *Pleuronectes flessus*, flounder

passato 34: (substantified past part.) a strained substance; see also *passada*

pasta 10, passim: dough; see also *impasta*

pasta 123, 159: paste, ground mixture

pastello 73, 74, 76, 178, pastillo 74, pastelli 73, 77, 178: (a covered, standing) tart; *cf.* Cat. *pastell*, Sp. *pastel*; *pastelli, pastelillos* (Casas)

pastizo 72, 75, pastizi 71, 72, 77 > pasticcio: a variety of cooking dish; by extension a (covered, standing) pie made in such a dish; *cf. olla, pignata*

pasto 191: pie

pastonache 170 > pastinaca: (bot.) "spezie di radice d'acuto sapore, e si mangia cotta. Lat. *pastinaca*"; "çanahoria" (Casas), *i.e. Daucus carota*, carrot or *Pastinaca sativa*, parsnip; *cf.* Cat. *pastenaga*, carrot; **Pastonache 170**

patella: see *padela*

patrone 13, 44, 50, 70, 71, 109 > patrono: "amo, señor, dueño" (Casas); "padrone" (Altamura); lord, master, employer

pavonaza 124, pavonazi 88 > paonazzo: "viola scuro, violaceo, di una tonalità più o meno tendente al porpora o al bluastro" (*GDLI*); peacock-blue, violet, purple

pavone 69, pavoni 69: peacock; **Pavoni revestiti 69**

pazo 70 > pazzo, "oppresso da pazzia. Lat. *insanus, mentecapius*" (*Crusca*), pàccio, "pazzo, folle, matto" (Altamura): foolish, mad, insane; see also *impazo*, above

pebro 84, passim, pebre 76: pepper; probably a borrowing from Cat. *pebre*: see Gual Camarena, *s.v. pebre*; *cf. pepe, pipero* and *pepero*, below

pellare 210, pellate 168, pellara 67 > pelare: to skin (fowl, eel, almonds); *cf. scorticare*

penna 67, 69: feather

pensero 68 > pensiero: "inquietudine di mente, afflizion d'animo. Lat. *cura, anxietas*" (*Crusca*); thought, concern, worry

pepe 25, passim, pipero 2, passim, pipere 8, pepero 1 > pepe: (bot.) *Piper nigrum*, pepper; *cf. pebro, pebre*, above

perbulle 58, perbulire 101, perbullire 197, perbulito 58: to parboil

pere 179: pear

pernice 116 > pernice: (orn.) *Perdix*, (common grey) partridge; see also *starna*, below; **Salsa ala franzesa a pernice, a galine 116**

persico, fiore de 106: (bot.) *Malum persicum*, peach blossom (color); **Sapore dito fiore de persico 106**

perso 114: part. of *perdere*, to give over, yield up

persuto 7, passim, persutto 74, passim, presutto 161 > presùtto: "< lat. *prae exsuctus*, prosciutto" (Altamura); *persuto*: "torrezno" (Casas: Old Sp. *torrezno* is glossed by Cobarruvias as "el pedaço de la lunada [midhaunch] que assamos"); the ham (probably cured); **Persutto bono da servare cotto 85**

pesso 6, passim: fish; *cf.* Cat. *peix*, It. *pesce*; **Pastello de pesso 76, Sfarcimento a pesso 79**

petrosillo 20, passim: (bot.) *Petroselinum crispum*, parsley; *cf. juivert*, above

peza 7, 69 > pezza: piece of (linen) cloth, napkin (*DEI*)

pezo 220: bit, piece

pezoli 166 > pezzùllo: "dim. di *piézzo*, pezzetto, minuzzulo, frustolo" (Altamura); small pieces

piato 88, piatto 53, 57, 88, piatti 1, 33, 103: plate, platter; piatello 40, passim, piatelli 15, passim: small plate

pige 7 > piega: folds

piglare 161, pigliando 87, 185, piglia 1, passim, pigla 182, pigli (pr.subj.3) 6, pigliano (pr.subj.6) 7, pigliarai 23, 127, piglarai 130, 145, 180, piglerai 128, pigliera 124 > pigliare: to take, get

pignata 1, passim, pignatta 62, > pignata: "olla" (Casas); pot (earthenware or metal); pignata de terra 161: earthenware pot; pignatella 56, 92, 118: small pot; *cf. olla, pastizo*

pignolli 39, 79, 80, 116, 171, 173, 175, 177, 181, 182, 185, 186, 197: (bot.) *Pinus pinea*, pinenuts

pila 2, 6 (marginal), 30, 58, 162, 198, pilla 30, 85, 198 > pila: "pila" (Casas); "XIV sec.; vaso di pietra, recipiente di pietra" (*DEI*, 4,2919a and 2921a); a sort of basin or bowl (perhaps of stone); in the Neapolitan Collection always used for cooking, in 30 serves as an alternative to a *pignata*; *cf. mortaro*, above

Piperata 1: pepper sauce

pipero: see *pepe*, above

pipione 67, 103, pipioni 2, 75, 93, pizone 66, 67, pizoni 37, 40, 71, 72 > piccione: (orn.) *Columba livia*, pigeon; see also *columbi*, above; **Coppo sive pastizo de pipioni 75, Per cocere uno pizone et farlo senza ossa 66, Per fare de uno pizone dos 67, Pastizi de boni caponi, polastri, pizoni 72, Sapore a pipione spezato he soffrito 103, Sofritto de carne de pulastri ho de pipioni 93**

piselli 6, 21, 164, 173 > pisello: pea; **Piselli cum carne salada 21, Menestra de piselli 164**

pistare 62, passim, pista 1, passim, repista 68, 124, piste (pr.subj.3) 106, pistarai 149, pistando 7, passim, pistado 84, passim, pisto 10, passim, pistata 44, passim, pistada 195, pisti 61, 62, 70, piste 39, 56, 124 > pistà': "ammaccare, frantumare, stritolare col pestello" (Altamura); to grind (in a mortar)

pistono 5 > pistóne: "pestone: ceppo de forma conica con manico diritto" (Altamura); piston, pestle pizone, pizoni: see *pipione*, above

pocoto 110: a small quantity

polastro 53, pullastro 31, 100, polastri 37, passim, pollastri 57, pulastri 12, 93, pullastri 12, passim > pollastro: cockerel, young rooster; **Bello rosto de caponi, polastri, capreto 52, Polastri alesso cum agresto 45, ~ arosto 53, Pariola con galine ho ha ~ ho ha caponi in spito 57, Pastizi de boni caponi, ~, pizoni 72, Sapore a ~ spezati 100, Sofritto de carne de pulastri ho de pipioni 93**

Polpi 188: (ichth.) *Octopus vulgaris*, octopus

pome 95, 166, 176, 179, 185: apple; see also *codogne*, *granate*, above; **Fritelle de pome 176, Tartare alla franzesa de pome 185**

porcheta 63, 69 > porchetta: "(gastron.) vivanda, tipica della cucina rustica sarda, toscana, romana, ... costituita da un maiale da latte ... intero ... spesso in occasione di feste populari" (*GDLI*; roast suckling-pig; **La sancta porcheta arosto reversata 63**

porco 83, 87, 128, porcho 1, 65, 69, 84: pig; **Cirvelato de carne de porco ho de vitella 83**

potagio 9, 40: pottage; **Potagio de fave fresche 40, ~ de farro 9**

preme 7, 98 > premere: to press

presertim 43: (Latin) for instance

preso 220: thick

presutto: see *persuto*, above

probatura 11, 126, 132 > provatura: "queso de bufalo" (Casas); a kind of fresh cheese made from buffalo milk

prune 63, 218: plums; prune seche 50: prunes; see Gual Camarena, *s.v. prunis* (*siccis*)

pullastro: see *polastro*, above

pulli 47, 89, 93 > pollo: chickens

Pumata 95: applesauce; *cf.* old Cat. *pomada*, "menja composta de pomes cuitas" (*DCVB*)

pur 68, pure 161 > pure: yet, nevertheless, also

qua 131: (Latin) there

Quaresima 28, 89, 164, 171: Lent; quadragesimali 160: Lenten

quagliata 167 > quaglià': "qualgliare, coagulare, rapprendere" (Altamura); to curdle, coagulate (as milk)

quarto 132: quarter (of a round of cheese) (?)

quatrino 63, 172, 218, quatrini 132, 172 > quatrino: (numis.) "denomizione di una piccola moneta ... " (*GDLI*); a coin of small value; the sixtieth part of a Tuscan lira, equal to four *denari*, a quarter of a Neapolitan *grano*; see also *baiocho*, above

ragonisi 92: Aragonese; **Suppa de ragonisi 92**

ramaiolo 132 > ramaio(u)lo: "strumento da cucina, che, per lo più, si fa di ferro stagnato, fatto a guisa di meza pala vota, con manico stretto, e sottile. Lat. *tudicula*" (*Crusca*); ladle, ladleful

ramo 218, rami 179 > ramo: branch; ramicioli 135 > ramoscello: twig, sprig

rampino 218, 219 > rampino: "*Raffio*, strumento di ferro adunco, graffi ... ; dicesi anche *rampino*" (*Crusca*); hook, hooked implement

ranzo 190, ranzi 185 > rancio: "rancio" (Casas); rancid

rape 27, 139, 141, rappe 26, 27 > rapa: (bot.) *Brassica rapa*, turnip; **Rappe 26, ~ armate 27, Torta de rape 139**

rasca 128, 218 > raschiare: to rub, scrape

ravioli 10, 11, 158, 160, 177, 178: ravioli; **Ravioli 10, ~ bianchi 11, Fritelle in forma de ~ 177, Fritelle in forma de ~ cum riso 178, Ova in forma de ~ 158**

Raye 191 > raia, razza: (ichth.) *Raja*, ray, skate

recuce: see *cuce*, above

restaurative 161: (medical term) restorative, therapeutic

reticella 64, 65 > reticella: (lit.) little net; (anat.) *reticulum*, peritoneal membrane, mesentery, omentum

ricotta 168: var. of cheese; **Ricotta contrafatta 168**

rigano 33 > regamo: (bot.) *Origanum vulgare*, oregano, wild marjoram

risguardando 19 > riguardare: to take care

riso 3, passim: rice; **Riso cum latte de amandole 7, ~ alla italiana 8, Fritelle de ~ 174, Torta grassa cum ~ 129, Torta de ~ 181**

roba 100 > roba, ròbba: "roba, stoffa, proprietà" (Altamura): things, goods, material, substance

romanesca 23, romaneschi 16: Roman; **Caule alla romanesca 23, Macharoni romaneschi 16**

Rombo 204, 212 > rombo: (ichth.) *Rhombus maximus*, turbot; *Rhombus levis, Platophrys podas*, brill

rosa, rosata, rosada: see *aqua*, above

rose 137: roses

rosmarino 70, 85, 161, 163, rossmarino 79, rosomarino 63: (bot.) *Rosmarinus officinalis*, rosemary; ramo de rosmarino 218: sprig of rosemary (used to baste a roast)

rossi 9, 13, 15, passim, egg yolk; see also *vino*

saba 115, sabba 1, 21, 101, 105, 121, 123, 219 > saba: "arrope" (Casas); must, must syrup; see also *mosto cotto*

sabrero 56, 58, 113: probably related to old Cat. *sabrer*, "brou o salsa" (*DCVB*); bouillon of juices from boiled meat

saffrano: see *zafrano*, below

saimo 100, 101, 103 > saime: fat, grease; *cf.* Cat. *saïm*: see Gual Camarena, *s.v. sagí*; grease, especially lard

salato 77, salado 86, 199, salata 2, passim, salada 21, 31, salate 86, salade 170, 186: seasoned; opposed to *fatue, q.v.*, above

sale 1, passim: salt; 186 and perhaps elsewhere: seasoning, condiment

salmora 63, 79, 218 > salimòja: "acqua salata per conservarvi pesci, funghi, olive, ecc." (Altamura); probably a borrowing from Cat. *salmorra*; *cf.* Sp. *salmuera*, "pickle, brine"; *salmoia*, "salmuera" (Casas); a vinegar pickle, acid preservative sauce, (specifically) a basting sauce

Salpani 206 > probably salpa: (ichth.) *Boops salpa, Sarpa salpa*, salpa

salsa 78, passim: sauce, seasoning (commonly used during the preparation of a foodstuff); **Salsa cotidiana 114, ~ lombarda 115, ~ papale 117, ~ regale 118, ~ o sapore sclavonesco, ho vero agliata 124**; for other *salse*, see Recipes 112–24 or, in this Glossary, the significant qualification in their name

salsize 84, salzize 84, salsizoni 87 > salsiccia: (pork) sausage; **Salsize bone 84; Boni salsizoni bulignesi 87**

saltem 87: (Latin) at least

salvasina 1, salvasine 1: "*salvaggina*, carne d'animal salvatico, buona a mangiare" (*Crusca*); wild animal (meat), game (meat); see Gual Camarena, *s.v. salvagina*

salvatico 1, salvatica 112, salvatici 2: (adj.) wild, game (of animal); see *bestia*, above

salvia 2, passim: (bot.) *Salvia officinalis*, sage

sambuco 135, 173 > sambuco: (bot.) *Sambucus nigra*, elder; *fiori, fiore de sambuco*, elderflower; **Fritelle de fiore de sambuco 173, Torta de fiori de ~ 135**

sandalo 60, sandali 106 > sandalo: (bot.) *Santalum*, sandal, sandalwood; see Gual Camarena, *s.v. sàndjl*

sangue 69, 219: blood

sanguinato 217 > sanguinare: to bleed

sano 87, sana 67, 98, 118, 146, 159, 218, sani 69, 71, 181, sane 149 > sano: "intero, senza magagna. Lat. *integer*" (*Crusca*); whole, unground or uncut; see also *sodo*

sapere 89, 98, sapi 186: to know, understand, learn; sapera 85, 167, sapi 50, sapiano 25 > sapere: "aver sapore" (*Crusca*); sapé', "aver sapore" (Altamura); to taste, have a flavor

sapore 49, passim, sapor 199, 217: sauce (commonly used as a serving garnish: *pone de sopra questo sapore*, 58); **Sapore biancha 104**, 199, 217, **~ bono 102, ~ gamelino 105, Salsa o sapore sclavonesco, ho vero agliata 124**; for particular *sapore*, see Recipes 100–111 or, in this Glossary, the significant qualification in their name

sarazini 113: Saracens; sarazinesca 113: Saracen; **Salsa sarazinesca 113**

sarde 76 > sarda: (ichth.) *Clupea pilchardus*, pilchard (adult sardine); also perhaps *Clupea sprattus, Sarda mediterranea*, sprat; *Sarda sarda*, bonito

Sardelle 187: (ichth.) *Sardina pilchardus sardina*, sardine

sarfoglio 166 > cerfoglio: (bot.) *Anthriscus cerefolium*, chervil

Sargo 209 > sargo: (ichth.) various species of edible marine fish; *sargo* or *sargus*, a fish of the genus *Sargus*, the type of the family *Sparidæ*, the sea-breams

saxo 188, saxi 34 > sasso: stone, rock, pebble

sbrufa 174 > sbruffare: to squirt, besprinkle, spray

scachero 90 > scacchiera: chess board, checkerboard

scaco 90, scachi 90 > scacco: square, check

scaffe 40 > scafa: (bot.) a variety of bean; *DEI* derives the word from med. Latin *scafus*, "baccello della fava," pod, hull (of a bean); yet *DEI* (with DuCange) cites *fabas sive scafos* and the twentieth serving of Menu [2] includes *piselli he scaffe*: perhaps therefore a variety of bean of which the pod is edible

scala 70: grill (for roasting)

scaldare 42, 150, scalda 151, scaldato 89: "indurre il caldo in che che sia. Lat. *calefacere*" (*Crusca*); to (over)heat

scina 63, 218 > schiena: spine, backbone, back; *cf.* Cat. *esquena*, "back"; *REW*, #7994 *skina*, "smalles Stück Knochen, Schiene"; see also *cinna*, above

Scinale 190 > schinale: "(ant. XIV sec.) schiena" (*DEI*); salted fillet (from back of fish); kipper

sclavonesco 124: Slav, Slavic; **Salsa o sapore sclavonesco 124**

scola 33 > scolare: (trans.) "dicesi de' liquore, quando sgorgata, o versatane la maggior parte, n'esce a poco poco il residuo. Lat. *guttatim effluere*" (*Crusca*); to drip, drain, pass through a strainer

scorticare 68, 70, scortica 210, scorticato 67, 69, scorticata 68, 70, scorticando 69: to skin (fowl, calf, eel); *cf. pellare*

scorza 21 (*piselli*), 42 (*fave*), 88 (*carotte*): "corteza, cascara" (Casas); "corteccia, crosta, guscio, buccia, baccello" (Altamura); pod, shell, skin

scroffa 70 > scrofa: sow

scrola 135 > scrollare: to shake, toss

scutella 36, 152, 170, scudella 152, scutelle 8, 11, 37, 42, 47, 103, 112, scudelle 31, 116, 197 > scodella: bowl; scutellini 55, 100, scudelini 117, 118, 124, scudellini 196 > scodellino: small bowl

sedazo 19, 32: probably a borrowing from Cat. *sedàs*: see *cedaz* in Gual Camarena, *s.v. sedaços*; sieve; *cf. seta* and *stamegna*, below

semula 161 > semola: bran, chaff; see Gual Camarena, *s.v. sèmola*

senese 132: Sienese; **Tartara alla senese 132**

senipa 34, sinapo 122 > sĕnàpo ("senapa": Altamura), senape: (bot.) *Sinapis*, mustard; mustardseed; **Senipa di canepa 34**

sequitarai 109 > seguitare: to follow, continue; the form suggests a Latin influence

serago 156, 196, 208: probably *serano*

serane: see *-ne* (enclitic), above

serpillo 115 > serpillo: (bot.) *Thymus serpyllum*, wild thyme

servare 85: to keep (in a preserved state)

seta 95 > seta: silk, probably in the sense of *setaccio, staccio*, "sieve," made of silk; *cf. sedazo*, above, and Cat. *sedàs*

sfarcimento 65, 79, sfarsimento 81, 82, farcimento 80: filling, stuffing; probably a borrowing from Cat. *farciment*; *cf. impitura*, above; **Sfarcimento ad uno budello de vitella 82, ~ a capone 81, ~ a capreto 80, ~ a pesso 79**

sfendo 88: "*sfendere*: hender" (Casas); to split, cleave; see also *fende*, above

Sfresurato 96: a prepared dish of animal pluck, *fresura*

similiter 17, 69, 86: (Latin) similarly

simul 58, 60, 67, 83, 101: (Latin) together

sinapo: see *senipa*, above

sive 40, 65, 75, rubric before 78, 132, 192, 197: (Latin) or

sodo 45 > sodo: solid, whole, unground; see also *sano*

sofritto 93 > soffriggere: "(XVI sec. vivanda soffritta" (*DEI*); a sauteed dish; **Sofritto de carne de pulastri ho de pipioni 93**

sole 15, 19: sun

solo 135 > solo, suolo: layer, stratum; *cf. grado*

sopragiongendo: see *adiunge*, above

Somata 86 > summata, somata: salt loin of pork

spaca 78, spacata 59 > spaccare: to split, break open, cleave

spago 15 > spago: "funicella sottile. Lat. *funiculus, filum*" (*Crusca*); "cordel, cuerda, hilo de cañamo" (Casas); string, cord

sparte 61 > spartire: cleave, sever, cut away

specie 1, passim: spices (variously); specie dolce 13, 15, 17, 18, 27, 29, 30, 34, 60, 61, 147, 149, 161, 217: mild spices

specierie 114: spices (*specie* collectively)

spela 63, 68, spella 180 > spelare: to clean, strip (hair from), pluck (feathers from); in this last context (Recipe 68) the Riva del Garda MS shows *pilla*

sperduta 147, 148: poached (of eggs)

spexe 7 > spesso: "continuo" (Casas); continuously

speza 103, spezato 103, spezati 100 > spezzare: to break apart (a fowl), cut up

spiana 180 > spianare: "ridurre in piano, pareggiare" (*Crusca*); to smooth (out), spread (level)

spica 33, 82, 195, spicha 63, spico 54 > spicchio: clove (of garlic)

spichi 89 > spiccare: to detach, cut off

spileto 161 > spilletto: (dim.) "un sottil fil di rame, corto, e acuto da una extremità, a guisa d'ago, e dall'altra con un poco di capo rotondo, del quale le donne si servono, per fermarsi i veli in testa, o per altra simil cosa, il che chiamano appuntare. Lat. *acicula*" (*Crusca*); (small) pin

spinole 76 > spinola: (ichth.) a common dialect name for the bass, *Morone labrax* (*CID*)

spito 52, 54, 55, 56, 57, 59, 61, 63, 64, 66, 76, 151, spido 37, 219: spit

squagliare 51, 88, squagliato 51, 94, 134 > squagliare: to melt, melt down, dissolve, liquefy

squame 216 > squama: (fish) scales

stamegna 1, passim, stamigna 107 > stamigna: "tela rada fatta di pelo di capra" (*Crusca*); sieve, filter (of matted goat fleece fibers); see Gual Camarena, *s.v. stamenya*; see also *sedazo, seta*, above

stanga 70 > stanga: bar, shaft, pole (as a spit)

starna 61, starne 2, 61 > starna: (orn.) *Perdix perdix*, (grey) (common grey) partridge; see also *pernice*, above; **Starne al modo cathalano 61, Tremolette sopra starne al modo franceso 62**

steccho 170 > stecco: stick, dry twig, wooden pin

stempera 12, 54, 55, 74, 162, 195, stempra 56, 170, 181, stemperato 179: to moderate the (unhealthy) humoral temper (of a foodstuff by the admixture of a tempering agent); see also *distempera*, above

stillato (ablative) 98, stillata 97 > stillare: "cavar l'umor di qualunque cosa, per forza di caldo, e col mezzo d'alcuni strumenti fatti per ciò. Lat. *stillare, guttos emittere*" (*Crusca*); to distill; the distillate

stinchi 70 > stinco: tibia, shin-bone

stringa 16 > stringa: *cinta* (*i.e.* ribbon) (Casas); lace, thong

stringe 83, strenge 155, stingere 169 > stringere: to draw tight, bind together

struto 125, 128, 134, strutto 62, 100, 126, 127 > strutto: lard

stuffate 57 > stuffare: to stew (in a *bain Marie*); *cf.* "*stuffa*: stanza calda, riscaldata da fuoco, chele si fa sotto, o da lato. Lat. *balnea, -arum*" (*Crusca*); the medieval sense of *balnea* was an alchemical *bain Marie*

sturiono 182, 199, sturione 199, 200: (ichth.) *Acipenser sturio*, sturgeon; **Sturiono cum sapore 199**

suco 98, passim, sugo 53, passim > succo, sugo: juice

sudate 153 > sudare: (of cooking eggs) to sweat, perspire

sufficienter 62: (Latin) sufficiently

sufficientia, a sufficientia 3, 43, 130, 132, 186, 199: (Latin) sufficiently

sugare 7, passim > asciugare: to dry, drain, dry up, wipe

sugo: see *suco*, above

suppa 92, zupa 91: sop(s) (var. of prepared dish); **Suppa de ragonisi 92, Zupa d'oro 91**

supra, ut supra 88: (Latin) as above

suso 5, 27: on, upon; *cf.* It. *suso* (obsolete): up, upwards

sutta 215, sutti 163: (adj.) dry, *i.e.* without (cooking) liquid; *cf. asutto*, above

svozato 76 > sbozzato: (subst.) crude, shabby, unworthy piece of work; *cf.* "*sbozzare*: produrre un manufatto semilavorato; per estens. fabbricare in modo rudimentale un oggetto" (*GDLI*; *DEI* dates this verb from only the 17th c.)

taglero 69, 129, tagliero 33, 168, 217 > tagliero (obsolete): cutting board, trencher board

tapola 80, 197, tapolata 71, seem to be misreadings of Cat. *capola, capolada*, left untranslated from the original Catalan recipes; "*capolar*, tallar a trossets petits, cast. *triturar, picar*" (*DCVB*); to chop finely

tartara 132, 133, 185, tartare 133, 185, tartari 186: a kind of large, low, custard torte; *cf. torta*; **Una tartara alla senese 132, Tartari bianchi 186, Tartara julatica 133**

tavola 15, 19, 70, 123, 179: table; tavoleta 170: small table

taza 152, taze 220: cup

tegamo 47, 49, 50, 71, 185, 197, 218, 219 > tegame: pan, frying pan; baking dish

temperato 128, 131, 137: moderate (said of fire)

tenca 218, tencha 168, 198, 218, tenghe 63 > tinca: (ichth.) *Tinca tinca*, tench; **Tencha in tegamo 218**

Testa de montone 48, ~ de vitello 49

testiculi 73: testicles

Testudine 195, testidine 195 > testudine: *tortuga* (Casas); tortoise

tiela 132, tiella 132, 180, 197 > tièlla: "horno, hornaza" (Casas); "afer. del lat. *patella*, padella metallica" (Altamura); large pan, earthenware baking dish

tinge 179 > tingere: to dye, paint, stain

todesca 142: German; **Ova menata alla todesca 143**

tolle 2, passim, tole 41, 123 > togliere: to take

Tomaselle 65 > tomacello, tomasella: variety of sausage

tondo 142, 179, tonde 155 > tondo: (adj.) round, circular; tondo 166 > *tóndo*: (subst.) "tavolino dal ripiano rotondo" (Altamura); small round board

tordi 60, turdi 71 > tordo: (orn.) *Turdus*, thrush; **Tordi cum suo sapore 60**

tornesi 114 > tornese: (numis.) a coin first used in Tours and subsequently used in Italy and given different values; in the Kingdom of Naples its value was two centesimi or half a *grano*; see also *baiocho, quatrino*

torrato (pane torrato) 197: probably a borrowing from Cat. *torrat*, "toasted"; *cf. brusca, bruscato*, above

torsi 141 > torso: (bot.) "il gambo del cavolo sfogliato" (*Crusca*); stalks (of cabbage), sprouts

torta 27, passim, torte 135, 185, 186 > torta: *torta* (Casas); (open-faced) pie, tart; **Torta biancha 125, ~ bulignesa 126, ~ comuna**

131, ~ grassa cum riso 129, ~ papale 182, ~ verde 138

trare (uno bullore) 78, 154, 198 > trarre: to draw, come (to a boil)

tremolette 62: var. of prepared dish consisting of a sauce on partridge; **Tremolette sopra starne al modo franceso 62**

Triglie 205 > triglia: (ichth.) *Mullus surmuletus*, red mullet

trippa 25, 198, trippe 25, 70, 206 > trippa: tripe; **Trippa 25**

tristo 219 > tristo: "malvagio, cattivo" (Altamura); bad, impure, harmful; the *Libro de arte coquinaria* (Recipe 231) shows the word *gattivo* instead of *tristo*: ... *perche la lampreda non ha in corpo niente di gattivo, excepto questo budello*

trita 65, passim, (past part.) trito 175, 204, 218, trita 47, 80, 101, tritata 72 > tritare: to mince, chop

Trotte 217 > trota: (ichth.) *Salmo trutta*, trout

turdi: see *tordi*, above

ucelli 58, 69, 71: birds; ucelletti 58: small birds; **Appareghio de ucelletti 58**

urso 112: bear; **Salsa ad ogni bestia salvatica ho de cervo ho urso ho capriolo ho de altra carne 112**

usanza 70, 83, 87, uxanza 72 > usanza: usage, custom

ut: see *supra*, above

uva 108, 161: grapes; uva negra 108, 109, 124: black grapes; uva passa 1, 50, 63, 65, 66, 71, 80, 82, 105, 123, 149, 157, 159, 165, 172, 175, 177, 218, 219: raisins; **Sapore de uva negra 108**

uxire 172 > uscire: go out, leave

vacha 70, vacina 70: cow; **A fare che una vacina, una vitella, uno cervo parano vivi 70**

varats 76: Cat. *verat*, "peix de l'espècie *Scomber scomber* ... cast. *estornino, caballa*" (*DCVB*); see Gual Camarena, *s.v. verat*; mackerel

vaso 42, 43, 89, 108, 208, vasso 217: vessel, container

veneciana 213: Venetian

ventresca 10, 128, 130 > ventresca: "lardo" (Casas); "cansalada prima que té el porc sota el ventre" (*DCVB*); belly, porkbelly, a kind of *lard maigre* from the belly; *cf.* Middle Fr. *ventresque*, "generally, th'offalls, intralls, inwards, guts, or pauch of an (edible) creature; as a calves pluck, a hogs haslet, a sheeps gather, etc; but particularly, the bellie (which is the daintiest) part of a Tunnie" (Cotgrave); *cf.* also "Ventresca: pancia, e ventresca, ventre di porco ripieno di carne, uova, cacio, ed erbe battute insieme, e messo in sorpressa" (*Crusca*)

Vermicelli 17: vermicelli

verzellata 21 > vergellato, verzellato: marbled (lean meat with fat)

via 23, passim; getta via 23, 94, 161, geta ~ 184, gitando ~ 88, gittando ~ 210, taglia ~ 69, 195, cava ~ 88, rascare ~ 219 > via: (adv.) away

vinagro 54, 76: probably a borrowing from Cat. *vinagre*, vinegar; *cf. aceto*, above

vino 1, 50, 76, 85, 102, 123, 189, 193, 216: wine; vino agro 113, 114, 116, 121, 197; vino amabile 219: semi-sweet wine; vino bianco 219, vino biancho 199; vino cotto 54: wine syrup (made by reducing wine by boiling); vino dolce 220: sweet wine; vino rosso 1, 62, 105; vino veghio fumoso 69: old, fumy (gaseous) wine

visole 109, vissole 73, 218 > visciola: sour cherry; **Sapore de visole ho de cerase 109**

vita: see *aqua*, above

vite 59, 120, 161: (grape) vine

vitella 10, passim, vitello 49, 72, 73, 199, calf; **Cirvelato de carne de porco ho de vitella 83, Pastizi de vitella in tegamo 71, Sfarcimento ad uno budello de vitella 82, Testa de vitello 49, A fare che una vacina, una vitella, uno cervo parano vivi 70**

volatili 4, 43: fowl

vole 4 (understand *si vole*): if you wish, optionally

Zabaglone 220 > zabaglione: a sort of sweet pudding

zafrano 63, 172, zaffrano 9, passim, saffrano 33 > zafferano: (bot.) *Crocus sativus*, saffron; see Gual Camarena, *s.v. safrà*

zanzarelli 22 > zanzarelli: a cheese custard, synonym for *giusello* (*q.v.*, above)

zefali: see *ciffalo*, above

zenzaro 1, passim, zenzero, 10, zenzevero 11, passim, zinzibero, 80, zinzivero 92, gingibero 57, 112, 118, gingibro 74 > zenzero: (bot.) *Zingiber officinale*, ginger

zo 218 > ciò: that

zuca 128, zucha 24, zuche 24, 29, 30, 128 > zucca: (bot.) *Cucurbita*, squash, pumpkin; **Zuche 29, Torta de ~ 128**

zucaro 3, passim: sugar; see Gual Camarena, *s.v. sucre*

zupa: see *suppa*, above

◈

D. Particular Words and Expressions in the Recipes

Numbers in bold face in the first of the following lists identify recipes in the Neapolitan Collection for which Catalan counterparts are not known to exist. The presence of Catalan (and Castillian) words in those recipes may indicate that those recipes are Iberian in origin.[1]

In the third list words in parentheses are variant forms found in the Neapolitan manuscript.

(i) Catalan words in the manuscript

capsa: 74, **75**
carabace (It. *zucca*): 30
carnero (Cast.): 1, 46, 78
cazola (Cat. *cassola*): 9, 39
ceba, cepa (Cat. *ceba*, It. *cipolla*): 46, 76
gingibero, gingibro (Cat. *gingebre*, It. *zenzaro, zenzevero*): 57, 74, 112, **118**
gradelle (Cat. *graella*, It. *graticula*): 76
juivert (It. *petrosillo*): 54, 58, 78, **96**, 113, **115**
mujol (Cat. *mujol*, It. *cefalo*, a fish): 76
olla (It. *pignata*): 31, 113, 197
pebro (Cat. *pebre*, It. *pipero, pepe*): **84**, **100**, 101, 112, 114, **126**, **183**, **184**, **192**
sabrero (Cat. *sabrer*): 56, 58, 113
sedazo (Cat. *sedas*, It. *stamegna*): 19, 32
[s]farcimento (med. Cat. *ffarciment*, spelled with two *ff*): **65**, **79**, 80, 81, 82
tapola, tapolata (Cat. *capola*): **71**, 80, 197
torrato (Cat. *torrat*, It. *bruscato, brusculato*): 197
varats (Cat. *verat*, It. *maccarello*, a fish): 76
vinagro (Cat. *vinagre*, It. *aceto*): 54, 76
vino agro: 113, 114, 116, 121, 197

---

[1] Carmelo Spadaro di Passanitello (in "Il codice Bühler 19 della Pierpont Morgan Library di New York," *Appunti di Gastronomia* 9 (1992): 13) identifies *comer, castrados, carnero, zabaglion* [*sic*] and *discordandote* as terms of Spanish origin in our manuscript; he further identifies *patruni, capolato, torrati, sfusiata, pignata* and *minuzzato* as characteristically Sicilian words, though without indicating where he read them in the manuscript.

(ii) Latin words and expressions

ad (*before a consonant*), cum, e[x] contrario, et, etiam, exire, imo, incipiunt mirabilia gule, item, manducare, presertim, qua, saltem, sequitarai, similiter, simul, sive, sufficienter, a sufficientia, ut supra, tale ordine

(iii) Geographic and proper names

[a]ragonisi, bulignesa (bulignesi), cathalano (catalana, cathalana), Catharina (Catherina), ciciliana (ciciliani), florentino (florentina, fiorentino, fiorentina), franceso (francesa, franzesa), hispana, italiana, julatica, lombarda, papale, permesano (permisano), romanesca (romaneschi), sarazini (sarazinesca), sclavonesco, senese, todesca, veneciana

VI. Appendices

A. Composition of the Neapolitan Recipe Collection
with correspondences to recipes in other collections

Our intention in presenting this table is both to allow the reader to visualize a little more clearly the arrangement of the contents of the Neapolitan manuscript and, modestly, to encourage study of fifteenth-century Catalan and Italian cookery by facilitating comparisons among the recipes of this Collection and corresponding recipes reproduced in other recipe collections of the time. Some of these texts are close to being literal copies; others, indicated by parentheses here, are similar enough to suggest the trace of an influence in one direction or another.

Gathering	Folio	Recipe #	Recipe name[1]	Riva[2]	*Arte*, etc.[3]
A	1r	1	Per fare bona piperata	4	5
	1v	2	Brodo consumado	42	43
	2r	3	Biancho manghiare de galine ho palumbi		AM 40
		4	.xii. Minestre de biancho manghiare per coprire caponi	39	41
	2v	5	.xii. Menestre de bianchomanghiare alla cathalana	40	42
	3r	6	Bianchomanghiare [de quaresima] per .x. menestre	41	91
	3v	7	Riso cum latte de amandole	53	81
	4r	8	Riso alla italiana		

---

[1] The symbol 6 that precedes some of the recipe names reproduces a similar one written in the manuscript's margin close to the rubric of the recipes so indicated here.

[2] The numbers assigned to the recipes in the Riva del Garda manuscript are those in the transcription by Benporat, *Cucina italiana del quattrocento* up to 228; he does not number the paragraph that outlines general directions for preparing fish (*Et notta che in questo tractato che generalmente che ogni rasone di pesso* . . .), which should be numbered Recipe 228. From that point in the collection up to the end (Recipe 281) my numbering of Riva del Garda recipes is one more than in Benporat.

[3] The edition of Martino's *Libro de arte coquinaria* is that of Emilio Faccioli in his *Arte della cucina*, 1:117–204. Other references in this column are to *De apereylar bé de menyar* (AM), to the Primitive *Sent soví* (PSS) and to the *Libre del coch* of Mestre Robert (Robert). The specific texts in these last three collections can be read in Appendix C (p. 249).

Gathering	Folio	Recipe #	Recipe name	Riva	*Arte*, etc.
	4v	9	Potagio de farro	51	51
		10	Ravioli	85	77
	5r	11	Ravioli bianchi	88	
	5v	12	Brodeto biancho		AM 19
		13	Brodeto bello	43	
	6r	14	Brodeto de pane he caso he cum ova	45	54
	6v	15	Macharoni ciciliani	74	78
	7r	16	Macharoni romaneschi	72	68
		17	Vermicelli	76	79
	7v	18	Lasagne de pelle de caponi	90	83
		19	Milli fanti in menestra	93	85
	8r	20	Cardinale in menestra	63	59
	8v	21	Piselli cum carne salada	61	57
		22	Giusello ho Zanzarelli	47	47
b	9r	23	Caule alla romanesca	95	96
		24	Lactucha che para zucha	67	64
		25	Trippa	64	60
	9v	26	Rappe	70	66
		27	Rappe armate	181	159
	10r	28	Cemolella ciciliana	69	65
	10v	29	Zuche	78	86
		30	Carabace alla catalana	80	88
	11r	31	Brodo [de amandolo] a homo delicato		PSS 205
	11v	32	Farinata ad homo infermo		PSS 187
		33	Marignani		
	12r	34	Senipa di canepa	177	76
	12v	35	Menestra de marzapane	106	
	13r	36	Menestra de meloni	107	
	13v	37	Mirausto alla catalana	16	13
	14r	38	Herbicine	(89)	(80)
		39	Genestrata biancha		
	14v	40	Potagio de fave fresche		
		41	Fasoli		
	15r	42	Fave piene	59	75
[*meats*]					
	15v	43	Alesso	2	3
		44	Galine cum carne salata		AM 20
	16r	45	Polastri alesso cum agresto	30	16

Gathering	Folio	Recipe #	Recipe name	Riva	*Arte*, etc.
		46	Carne de capretto ho de carnero cum brodetto		AM 16
	16v	47	Carne de capreto in tegamo alla fiorentina		AM 57
c	17r	48	Testa de montone		AM 85
	17v	49	Testa de vitello	25	30
	18r	50	Carne in tegamo alla fiorentina		
	18v	51	Caponi inzucarati		
	19r	52	Per fare bello rosto de caponi, polastri, capreto he de qualunche altra carne	3	4
		53	Polastri arosto	17	17
	19v	54	Capreto in piu modi		AM 58
		55	Galine ho caponi in spito cum suo sapore		AM 35
	20r	56	Limonata a galine ho ha caponi		AM 31
	20v	57	Pariola con galine ho ha pollastri ho ha caponi in spito		AM 23
		58	Appareghio de ucelletti		AM 110
	21r	59	Bechafichi	27	32
		60	Tordi cum suo sapore	24	29
	21v	61	Starne al modo cathalano	28	33
	22r	62	Tremolette sopra starne al modo franceso		
	22v	63	La Sancta Porcheta arosto reversata	29	15
	23r	64	Figatelli	22	27
		65	Tomaselle	32	21
	[23v–24r] Incipiunt mirabilia gule				
	23v	66	Per cocere uno pizone et farlo senza ossa		39
	24r	67	Per fare de uno pizone dos		40
	24v	68	Per cocere una galina in una caraffa	211	
d	25r				
	25v	69	Pavoni revestiti che parano vivi, et per farli gittare focho per bocha		14
	26v	70	A fare che una vacina, una vitella, uno cervo parano vivi		
	[*pasties*]				
	28r	71	Pastizi de vitella in tegamo	9	12
	28v	72	Pastizi de boni caponi, polastri, pizoni et cum carne de vitella	8	9
	29r	73	Pastello de creste de galli cum li testiculi	10	38

Gathering	Folio	Recipe #		Recipe name	Riva	*Arte*, etc.
	29v	74		Pastello de capreto		Robert 66
	30r	75		Coppo sive pastizo de pipioni		
		76		Pastello de pesso		PSS 217
	30v	77	6	Pastizi de pome codogne	12	151

[31r] Farcimenti sive impiture

Gathering	Folio	Recipe #		Recipe name	Riva	*Arte*, etc.
	31r	78	6	Pieno ad una spalla de carnero		AM 88
	31v	79		Sfarcimento a pesso		
		80		Sfarcimento a capreto		PSS 189
	32r	81		Sfarsimento a capone		
	32v	82		Sfarsimento ad uno budello de vitella		
		83		Cirvelato de carne de porco ho de vitella	33	22
	33r	84		Salsize bone	34	23
	33v	85		Persutto bono da servare cotto	37	36
	34r	86	6	Somata	38	37
		87	6	Per fare fare boni salsizoni bulignesi		

[*miscellaneous preparations*]

Gathering	Folio	Recipe #		Recipe name	Riva	*Arte*, etc.
e	35r	88	6	Gelatina de carne ho de pesso, et de piu colori	208	255,beg. Cap.VI
	36r	89	6	Gelatina in uno canistro	209	256
	36v	90	6	Gelatina a modo de uno scachero		
	37r	91	6	Zupa d'oro	182	160
		92	6	Suppa de ragonisi		
	37v	93	6	Sofritto de carne de pulastri ho de pipioni	15	11
	38r	94	6	Crostata de caso, pane, etc.		
	38v	95		Pumata		Robert 35
	39r	96	6	Sfresurato		Robert 42
		97	6	Cossa stillata		
	39v	98	6	Stillato de cossa ho de galina in caraffa		Robert 101
	40r	99	6	Matta fame		

[40r] Sapori de piu sorte [*cooking sauces*]

Gathering	Folio	Recipe #		Recipe name	Riva	*Arte*, etc.
		100	6	Sapore a Polastri spezati		
	40v	101	6	Sapore a lepore		AM 63
		102		Sapore bono		
	41r	103	6	Sapore a pipione spezato he soffrito		
		104	6	Sapore biancho	120	101

Gathering	Folio	Recipe #		Recipe name	Riva	*Arte*, etc.
	41v	105		Sapore gamelino	121	102
		106		Sapore dito fiore de persico	125	106
	42r	107		Sapore ditto fiore de genestra	126	107
		108		Sapore de uva negra	127	108
	42v	109		Sapore de visole ho de cerase	129	110
		110		Limonata		AM 96
		111		Sapore de marzapane		
[43r] Salsa de piu sorte [*serving sauces*]						
	43r	112		Salsa ad ogni bestia salvatica, ho de cervo ho urso ho capriolo ho de altra carne		AM 97, 95
		113		Salsa sarazinesca		AM 111
	43v	114	6	Salsa cotidiana		AM 148
		115	6	Salsa lombarda		
	44r	116		Salsa ala franzesa a pernice, a galine o altri		Robert 85
		117		Salsa papale		
	44v	118		Salsa regale		
		119		Agresto cum aglio	139	121
f	45r	120		Salsa de pampani	138	120
		121	6	Mostarda franzesa		PSS 209
		122		Mostarda ytaliana	132	112
	45v	123	6	Mostarda per portare cavalcando in balotte	134	114
	46r	124	6	Salsa o sapore sclavonesco, ho vero Agliata	135	
[*pies*]						
	46v	125		A fare torta biancha	142	124
	47r	126		Torta bulignesa	143	125
	47v	127		Herbulata de maio	144	126
	48r	128		Torta de zuche	145	127
	48v	129		Torta grassa cum riso	150	132
		130		Torta de farro	151	133
	49r	131		Torta comuna		136
	49v	132	6	Una tartara alla senese		
	50r	133		Tartara julatica		
	51r	134	6	Miliazo Fasanitico alo modo florentino	147	129
	51v	135		Torta de fiori de sambuco	148	130
		136		Torta de castagne		135
	52r	137		Torta de cerase		138

Gathering	Folio	Recipe #		Recipe name	Riva	*Arte*, etc.
	52v	138		Torta verde		
		139		Torta de rape	146	128
		140		Torta de codogne	146	128
		141		Torta de caule	167	
[*egg dishes*]						
G	53r	142	6	Ova cotta in carta papirea	99	
	53v	143	6	Ova menata alla todesca		
		144		Fritata de ova	212	182
	54r	145		Fritata de herbe	213	182
		146		Ova fritelata	214	183
		147		Ova sperduta in aqua	215	184
	54v	148		Ova sperduta in latte ho in vino	216	185
		149		Ova piena	217	186
	55r	150		Ova sopra la graticula	218	187
	55v	151		Ova in spito	219	188
		152		Ova in taze		
	56r	153		Ova in cenere	221	190
		154		Ova in aqua freda	222	191
		155		Ova fritellate a lo modo fiorentino	223	192
	56v	156		Ova sopra la brasa	224	193
		157		Ova fritellate piene [al modo fiorentino]	225	194
	57r	158		Ova in forma de ravioli	226	195
	57v	159		Offelle	165	148
		160		Calisoni boni	164	147
	58r	161		Limache in tempo grasso	117	
[59r] Menestre de Quadragesima						
k	59r	162		Amandolata	91	82
[*legumes*]						
	59v	163		Brodo de ciceri	92	84
	60r	164		Menestra de piselli		92
		165		Fava	57	
		166		Fava in padella	58	58

Gathering	Folio	Recipe #		Recipe name	Riva	*Arte*, etc.
[*counterfeit dishes*]						
	60v	167		Jonchada de amandole	174	152
		168		Ricotta contrafatta	175	153
	61r	169		Butiro contrafato	176	154
	61v	170		Pastonache	204	181
	62r	171		Biancho manghiare		
[*lean fritters and pies*]						
	62v	172		Fritelle amare	193	170
		173		Fritelle de fiore de sambuco	192	169
	63r	174		Fritelle de riso	194	171
	63v	175		Fritelle de fiche piene	196	173
		176		Fritelle de pome	195	172
	64r	177		Fritelle in forma de ravioli	200	177
		178		Fritelle in forma de ravioli cum riso	201	178
	64v	179		Fritelle piene de vento	202	179
	65v	180		Torta de marzapane	163	146
	66r	181		Torta de riso	156	142
	66v	182		Torta papale	170	
[i ?]	69r	183		Fritata de ova de pesso	173	
		184		Fritata de caviaro	172	
	69v	185		Tartare alla franzesa de pome	160	
	70r	186		Tartari bianchi	161	
[*fish*]						
i[4]	67r	187	6	Sardelle	271	248
		188		Polpi	274	249; Robert 213
	67v	189		Granci	272	(250)
		190		Scinale		257
		191		Raye	264	
	68r	192		Laze	267	224
		193		Bessano		217
		194		Fravolino		
	68v	195		Testudine		

---

4 The signature of the gathering was originally written as "*k*"; at some time this was stroked out. Both the original letter and the apparent correction seem to be of an early hand resembling that of the scribe.

Gathering	Folio	Recipe #	Recipe name	Riva	*Arte*, etc.
k[5]	71r	196	[Anguilla ?: *beginning missing*]	273?	251?; AM 120
		197	Salsa hispana a calamari		AM 123
	71v	198	Calamari		(253)
	72r	199	Sturiono cum sapore	229–30	196–7
	72v	200	Ombrina	231	198
		201	Dentale	232	199
		202	Corvo grosso	234	201
		203	Orata	235	202
	73r	204	Rombo	236	203
		205	Triglie	239	207
		206	Salpani	240	208
		207	Goze	241	209
		208	Hoghiali	243	211
		209	Sargo	244	212
	73v	210	Morena	245	213
		211	Zefali ho Macarella	246	215,214
		212	Passara	247	216
		213	Hostriche	249	222
	74r	214	Lampuge	250	223
		215	Cappe	251	225
		216	Luzo	252	226
	74v	217	Trotte	253	228
	75r	218	Tencha in tegamo	254	(229)
	76r	219	Lampreda Grossa [*unfinished at foot of f. 76v*]	256	231

[*menus*]

Gathering	Folio	Title
l	77r	Convito de lo archiepo de Benevento Primo
	77v	Convito del conte Jeronimo
	80r	Un'altro convito
	83r	Altra rasone de convito
m	85r	Ordine del pranzo fatto da monsignore Ascanio allo principe de Capua

[*isolated recipe*]

Folio	Recipe #	Recipe name	Riva
89v	220	Zabaglone	(Riva 102)

---

[5] In small, fine lettering in black ink, this signature seems to have identified the beginning of a gathering at some point in time *after* the original scribe's "*k*" had identified the eighth gathering of the present manuscript. This f° 71 is currently within the ninth gathering, whose signature "*k*" seems to have been corrected to "*i*". See the previous note.

B. The Neapolitan Collection and Martino de Rossi

A substantial number and variety of significant clues exist that argue the primacy of the Neapolitan Collection of recipes over either of the collections attributed to Martino, the *Libro de cosina* or the *Libro de arte coquinaria*. The following enumeration presents an illustrative assortment of these clues. For the most part the evidence is textual in nature. In most cases it is enough to compare the text of the Neapolitan manuscript (on the left, below) with the text of the Riva del Garda manuscript (on the right, below) alone, without referring to the text of the recipes in *Arte coquinaria*, because this latter is normally relatively close to what the Riva scribe has written.[6]

Recipe 14. Several misreadings in Riva?

Fa bullire mezo uno pane gratato per uno quarto de hora	*Fa buglire lo pane gratusato per lo quinto de hora*

Recipe 24. The word *pede* is glossed in Riva by a phrase and a synonym:

piglia lo pede de la lactuche	*piglia quello de sotto piu blanco dela lactuca, zioe lo fustono*

Recipe 26. The dishname is qualified in Riva:

Rappe	*Rape ala lombardescha*

Recipe 37. Further specifications in Riva concerning the preparation of an ingredient:

piglia amandole he pistale	*tolle amendole bruschollate sotto la cenere calda et nettali in uno pano senza nettare altramente et pistale*

Recipe 43. Amplifications and a clarification in Riva:

se la carne fusse veghia, presertim dura como volatile	*se la carne fusse vegia e dura, presertim caponi, galline, pollastri*
et sera piu cocibile	*et cossi sera piu bella et piu ben cocta e presto*

Recipe 45. An explanation in Riva of an obscure phrase:

agresto sodo	*agresto in uga*

---

6 The full text of the Riva del Garda manuscript can now be read in Benporat, *Cucina italiana del quattrocento*, 157–231, although it is still advisable to check the facsimile in Bertoluzza, *Libro di Cucina del maestro Martino de Rossi*.

Recipe 52. Much amplification in Riva, perhaps by way of explanation:

poi lardala	*et mello si possia conzare poy lardella*
cum bono lardo	*zoe, con lardo batuto et altre cosse conveniente odorifere oncha bene secondo el gusto del tuo patrone, et drento, sel te piace, de bone herbe con brugne seche o visole o in tempo del agresto o altre cosse simelle*
metela in spito	*mettilla ornatamente nel spedo al focho*
miscola cum sale he sallalo	*miscolla salle como ti pare necessario et gettalo sopra lo rosto da ogni canto*
[ ]	*dandoli una bona volta calda di focho et fazendolo voltare presto*
he cusi lo haverai cotto bello	*et in questo modo haray il tuo rosto bello et collorito et quanto piu presto, sara melio per che sapera meliore caldo caldo*

Recipe 53. Change of sequence in Riva makes nonsense of the text. In the Neapolitan sequence *Polastri arosto* follows general instructions on roasting meats; in Riva the dish is reclassified as a poultry dish and follows *Miraustro ala catellana.*

Per fare polastri arosto, coceli cum l'ordine sopra ditto he, quando serano cotti	*Per fare polastri a rosto e se vole cocere a rosto e, quando e cocto*

Recipe 60. Riva explains the purpose of an ingredient:

pone simul assai sandolo	*mette con esse asay sandoli azio chel sapore sia rosso*

Recipe 63. Riva explains a procedure:

riversala como se fa cum le tenghe	*reversandolla a modo se fano le tenche—zioe, ponendo fora quello ch'e de drento*

Recipe 64. Riva specifies what in the Neapolitan manuscript is only generalized:

figato de qualunche animale te pare	*figatelli de vittello, polastri, porcho o de altro animale*
ligali in una reticella	*passali in rette di porcho o de vittella—et meglio e de capreto*

Recipe 88. Riva glosses an unusual term:

gitando via quilli fusti longi	*cavandolli fora l'osso dele gambe*

Recipe 109. Riva (and the *Arte coquinaria*) transmit nonsense:

ma per esser le visole brusce, azonze zucaro he canella assai	*ma lo potray fare differente de collore piu o mancho secundo lo subyecto li metteray*

Recipe 123. A scribal lapsus appears in Riva. No quantity has been written in the recipe before this point.

cum uno pugno de uva passa	*con uno de uga passa*[7]

Recipe 127. A translation in Riva of a measure of quantity has to be approximate:

una fogleta de latte	*uno quarto o cercha di lacte*

Recipe 134. Riva misreads:

habi una padella senza crosta sopra lo fondo, he meteralli dentro . . .	*haveray la padella senza pasta o crosta sopra lo focho, et dentro li metteray . . .*

Recipe 163. Riva explains the value of an ingredient (the water in which chickpeas have steeped):

mette . . . aqua — cioe de quella dove son stati a moglio ala notte	*mettelli . . . aqua — de quella dove li hay fati state a moglio la nocte, pero che quella aqua ha tutta la substantia in se*

Recipe 164. Rearrangement of the sequence of recipes and the omission of an alternative makes a reference in Riva both awkward and useless. In the Neapolitan Collection a preparation for peas follows one for chickpeas and is based upon it. However, in Riva the recipe for chickpeas is copied some thirty recipes later; the significant reference is changed to a procedure read some twenty recipes before but absolutely commonplace.

cum latte de amandole, ho vero como he diti de li ciceri	*con lacte de armandolle como e dicto de sopra nel capitolo del biancho mangiare*

Recipe 172. A precise quantity is supressed in Riva:

piglia tre quatrini de herbe amare	*con le herbete* [mentioned in the title]

Recipes 173, 174 and 176. Riva duplicates this series of lean fritters with meat-day counterparts. In each case (Riva Recipes 184, 187 and 189, respectively) the principal difference is that the meat-day versions of the fritters are fried in animal fat (*structo, grasso*); the additional Elderflower Fritters (Riva Recipe 184) also contain cheese, egg whites and milk, much as the *Torta de fiori de sambuco* of the Neapolitan's Recipe 135.

Recipe 178. A slight change in the title in Riva, but a definite article, referring to the title, is kept:

Fritelle in forma de ravioli cum riso: Fa cocere del riso	*Per fare le frittelle in forma di pastelli picolli, fa cocere lo rixo*

Recipe 181. Riva's changing of wording becomes awkward and nonsensical:

una crosta de sotto he de sopra cum lasagne larghe he sotile	*la crosta di sotto e di sopra li metteray dele lassagne seche e suttille*

[7] The error is partially corrected, or at least avoided, in the *Arte coquinaria*. There the compiler has written simply, *habi de l'uva passa*.

Recipe 184. A change of sequence in Riva makes reference awkward. In the Neapolitan Collection, a reference is made to ingredients already listed in the preceding recipe as well as to the procedure set forth there; in Riva the same reference is made to ingredients yet to be read in the next recipe — yet nevertheless these ingredients are still written out as well as the reference.

zaffrano he quelle cose dite del luzo in quello modo	*zaffrano, herbete e cipolle secundo che e ditto di sotto de la frittata de ove del luzo*

Recipe 185. A nonsensical misreading in Riva:

una crosta de sotto he de sopra cum lasagne larghe *he sotile*	*la crosta di sotto e di sopra li metteray dele lassagne* seche *e suttille*

C. Catalan Recipes in the Neapolitan Collection

A number of the recipes in the Neapolitan Collection have a counterpart in one of three Catalan recipe collections, *De apereylar bé de menyar*, the Primitive *Sent soví*, and the *Libre del coch* of Mestre Robert. Those Neapolitan recipes are the following: 3, 12, 31, 32, 39, 44, 46, 47, 48, 54, 55, 56, 57, 58, 74, 76, 78, 80, 95, 96, 98, 101, 110, 112, 113, 114, 116, 121, 188, 196 and 197. The text of the Catalan recipe to which one of the above Neapolitan recipes bears a relatively close resemblance is reproduced here.

(i) *De apereylar bé de menyar*

16. Cabrit e molto ab broet. (Neapolitan 46)

Cabrit ab broet, o molto o vacha ho crestat. Pren hom la carn, e fa'n hom pecetes poques, e van en la ola ab carn salade. E pren hom juivert e salvia e mente e cebes, e cou tot ensemps en la dita olla. E puys destempre-ho ab de bones especies picades ab safra, e van en la ola, e cou tot ensemps tant tro que le carn se desfassa. E puys trau-ne hom la carn en teyladors, e fa'n hom sopes ab la salsa.

Libre de sent soví, p. 187, Recipe 180: *Qui parla con sa deu ffer carn ab brou, moltó o vaca o crestat o cabrit*

19. Broet blanc. (Neapolitan 12)

Si vols fer broet blanc prin amenles picades e colades, e mit-hi agras; e sien be rostits los polastres; puys fes tot bulir ab lart de porch; e quant deuras manyar, mit-hi los polastres e ayes bonas especias gingebre, girofle d'ultra mar; e cant deuras anar a taula torna-ls-hi.

20. Gualines ab carn selade. (Neapolitan 44)

Gualines, si les dats ab carn salade, metets ne .i. pertida en ast, si tantes ni ha, e les altres en ola ab carn selade. E sien meses en aygua que en la primera couguen. E si son gualines qui no vuylen coure tost, trets les de le olla e muylats les ab aygua freda per so que pus tost coguen.

E picats de les especies ab del safra e ab los fetges e ab muyols [ms: mugols] d'ous cuyts, e ab lo sabrer de les gualines destrempats-ho. E puys cougua per sao. E picats a .i. depart del ayl qui ni volra. E dats les gualines ensemps del ast e de la olla, e si es temps d'agras [ms reading not clear], metets-ny.

Libre de sent soví, p. 102, Recipe 58: *Qui parla con se coen qualines en olla*

23. Puriola a galinas o capons en ast. (Neapolitan 57)

Prin pebre e gingebre e safra, e pica-ho be, e pren hom los fetges e muyols d'ous cuyts en brases e pique'ls hom be. E com son be picats, destempre'ls hom be ab brou. E pren hom ceba escaldade be, e puys va en la salsa. E qui le vol bulir, pot-ho hom fer, e pot-se bullir ab teulles bullens.

E pren hom los capons o les gualines ho pols, e esquartere'ls hom, qui's vol, e puys van en la purriola. E con es ben mesclat, van los quartés per tayladors e la salse per escudeles.

Libre de sent soví, p. 121, Recipe 87: *Qui parla con se deu ffer puriola a gualines ho a capons ho a pols en ast*

31. Si vols fer limonia. (Neapolitan 56)

Prin los pols o galines ho capons, qui sien primerament cuyts .i. poc en aygue. Puys trets-los de l'aygua, e mit-les en [ms: e] ast.

E ayes amenles perades, e destempre-les ab lo sebrer dels capons. E d'altre part prin del suc dels limons, e met-ne ab la [ms: le] polvora de les species, e puys passa-o [ms partly unreadable] tot sobre les brases, e estia tro que sia be espés, empero primerament hi deu hom metre del lart del porc en la caçola. E sie donat per tayladors.

A .xx. persones .iiii. llibres d'amenles.

35. Gualines o capons en ast. (Neapolitan 55)

Altre salse qui vol dar gualines en ast o capons.

Prenets .v. grans de menles perades e sien be picades ab lo sucre, e sia axetat ab suc de limons o de teronges, e no's vol bulir, e sia be espessa. E si no avets sucre, metets-hi mel. E fets-ne escudeles, e gualines per tayladors.

Libre de sent soví, p. 104, Recipe 60: *Qui parla con se ffa salsa a gualines en ast cens bolir*

40. Manyar blanch. (Neapolitan 3)

Pren gualinas e cou-les. E quant seran be cuytes, prin lo blanc dels pits e de les ales e tayle-u ben manut, e puys pique-o com mils pusques.

E puys prin arros, e mol-lo axi com a farina. E ayes let d'amenles destemprades ab lo brou de les gualines, e mescle-hi l'arros, e puys vaye tot en .i. ola. E met-y hom del arros per guise que torn espés. E cougue be, e vol-se coure en bon brasquet de brases o de carbo per paor de fum. E non deu hom pertir la ma per ço com tem mo[lt lo] foch.

E puys pren hom sucre blanch, e met-n-y hom mentre cou. E com es espés axi com a morterol, leve-l hom del foch. E va sempre per escude[le]s. [Prin hom del sucre, e met-ne hom] axi com a polvora.

Libre de sent soví, p. 93, Recipe 49: *Qui parla con sa deu ffer manjar blanch*

57. Cabrits en caçola. (Neapolitan 47)

Si vols fer caçoles [ms: caorles] de cabrits, fets ne primerament quartes, e fets ne de cascun quarter .iiii. o .v. parts. E ayats les caçoles, e metets-hi queacom d'oli e de grex fus, e posats en la caçola dejus canyes per tal que la carn no's pusque tenir a la caçola. E posats hi los cabrits ab taylades de carn selade amples, e vaye al forn [ms: el foch]. E quant sera colrat de quela part, girats lo de l'altre en la caçola.

E ayats picades especias ab safra e ab juivert e ab cebe, ab fetges e ab muyols d'ous debatuts ab de bon vinagre, e sia temprat ab aygua lo vinagre, e debatets-ho be tot encemps. E cant la cassola venra del forn, que'l cabrit vos parra colrat, trets-lo de la casçola, e metets [la salsa en] la casçola ab lo grex que la carn hi aura lexat, e posats la cassola sobre'l foch, e sie be menat [ms: menut) per ço que'ls ous no's pusquen desliguar tote vegade a .i. ma. E ayats del vinagre en guisa que no y sapie gayre. E cant començara de bolir, tornats hi lo cabrit en la caçola e la carn selade, e bule tro que sie be espesse. E tastats ho de sal e de vinagre, e ayats queacom de cebe prim taylade. E puys fets ne escudeles.

Libre de sent soví, p. 156, Recipe 136: *Qui parla con sa deu ffer casola de cabrits ab salsa*

58. Si vols saber [fer] cabrit en totes maneres. (Neapolitan 54)

Si vols dar cabrit en ast, fe'l bel, e mit-lo en l'ast, e fe-li exir l'ast sobre'l nas, e guarde'l d'escarmar.

E fe-li aquesta salsa: prin juyvert e pa torrat remuylat en vinagra e .i. gran d'ayl e pebre e avalanes torrades, e pica-u be a enug. E axeta-ho tot ab [ms: e] mel o arrop segons que't sera viares. E destempre-u tot ab vin, e romangue espés.

63. Cunils ab sosengua. (Neapolitan 101)

Si vols cunils ab sosengua, sien perbulits .i. poc, e fets-ne quartés. E ayats del lart fos, e metets-hi de la ceba taylada, frita ab lo lart. E vayen los cunils leyns, e frigen ensemps. Vaya-y de la aygua a poc a poch.

E ayats de les especias ab del safra, e els fetges dels cunils cuyts en caliu, e del pa torrat muylat ab vinagre, e picats-ho tot ensemps, e vaya en la olla ab los cunils. E cogue be tot ensemps. E tastats-ho de sal e de vinagre, e levats-ho del foch, e laxats-ho posar .i. poc, que prou espés ne sera. E fets-ne escudeles.

E si hi picats dels ous, mes ne valra.

Libre de sent soví, p. 119, Recipe 82: *Qui parla en altra manera con se ffa sosengua a conils o a lebres*

85. Cabayat. (Neapolitan 48)

Cabayat se fa exi del cap del molto: pren hom .i. cap de molto, e soquerre'l hom be e lava'l be, e puys pren hom aygua calent e sia be blanch. E puys cou lo. Con se pot desossar [ms: desnosssar], trau-ne hom los ossos [ms: osses] e leva'n hom la carn tota, e puys tayla hom menut—e dels peus fa'n hom peçes menudes—e met-ho hom en .i. ola ab lo brou del cap del molto tot encemps.

En apres pren hom juyvert e cebes menut taylades, e van en la ola. E puys pren hom especies e ous cuyts, e pica-u be, e van en la olla. E cou tot encemps. E con es tot cuyt, leva-u hom del foc, e fa-y hom escudeles.

Libre de sent soví, p. 188, Recipe 182: *Qui parla con sa deu ffer de aperellar tota cabadura e peus, e con sa deu menyar*

88. Spatle farcide. (Neapolitan 78)

Qui vol fercir espatle, pren hom le espatle [e met-la en la olla]. E con es perbulide, fen-le hom, e trau-ne hom la post tro al nou.

E puys aya hom species e carn de molto e carn selade, e capole-u hom e mescle-y ous com a ferciment. E puys fercex-ne hom l'espatle. E con es farcide, pren hom .i. tela de molto, e cobre-y hom tota l'espatle. E puys vaya sobre lo bresquet o sobre graeles. E con es cuyta, tayla hom, e dona-la hom ab salsa e ab juyvert.

Libre de sent soví, p. 67, Recipe 8: *Qui parla con se ffercex espatla de moltó en altra manera*

96. Limonia. (Neapolitan 110)

Si vols fer limonia, ayes bone leyt d'emenles, e mit-le a coure, e aye-y gingebre, canela, safra. E si no pots aver limons, mit-hi vin de megranes o vinagre, que aytant hi valra.

97. Salsa a tota salvatgina, cervo e porch senglar, ors o cabirol, e tota altre bestia salvatya. (Neapolitan 112)

Primerament sia ben cuyta, e qui le volra metre en sols, pot-le y metre, ho, si.s vol, pot-le metre en ast, segons que l'hom se n'alte.

E fets-hi aquestes salses: prenets moleda de pa, e parats-le e muylats en vinagre, e de le carn de le bestie matexa, qui sia magre e capola-le hom, e pebre e gingibre. E sia be picat, e axetat ab lo sabrer .i. poch, e ab molt vinagre e ab mel, per ço que sia agradolç. E sia be bolide e espessa.

E si ny volets, metets-hi safra, mas no si tayn.

Libre de sent soví, p. 123, Recipe 90: *Qui parla con se ffa salsa a servo ho porc senglar ho hors ho cabirol ho tota bestia salvatge*

110. Qui vol apereylar aucels menuts. (Neapolitan 58)

Aucels menuts perbul hom, e puys pren hom lart de carn selade e sofrig- los.

Puys pren hom los fetges e vermeys d'ous e pa torrat remuylat en vinagre e juyvert perbulit, e pica-u hom tot ensems, e puys destempre-u hom ab del sobrer dels aucels.

E con los aucels son be sofrits, vaya la salse en la caçole e bule tot ensems tro que'ls aucels sien cuyts. E puys vayen per tayladors e la salsa per escudeles.

Libre de sent soví, p. 155, Recipe 133: *Qui parla con sa deu ffer en alcels menuts alidem*

111. Carn a la sarraynesque. (Neapolitan 113)

Con cuynaras carn a la sarraynesque, fe peces de le carn, e lave-les be ab ayga calenta. Puys mit la carn en la olla meyns de sebrer; e met-hi hom lart de carn salade be grasse e .i. poch de vinagre, e cebe taylade menut, o salsa e juyvert e salvia e moradux taylat, e sofriges tota la carn. E quant aura bona pessa sofrit, met-hi hom aygua calenta que tengues ya pres lo foc. E cogue tro que le carn sie be cuyte.

Libre de sent soví, p. 188, Recipe 181: *Qui parla con cuynarets carn a la sarreynesca*

120. Anguiles en ast fets aytal salse. (Neapolitan 196)

Anguiles escorxa hom. E qui les vol en ast fa-y aytal salsa: pica-y hom amenles perades e moltes species e molt safra. E con es picat, tempre-u hom ab aygue bolide. E con les enguiles son cuytes, van per tayladors e la salsa per escudeles.

E qui s'en [?] alte mes valen ab alade.

Libre de sent soví, p. 203, Recipe 198: *Qui parla con a anguila en ast quina salsa s'i deu ffer ab amelles*

123. Calamas farcits. (Neapolitan 197)

Si vols coure calamas farcits al forn; primerament los nedeya, que no y lexs res qui avol sie. Aprés prin les cames dels calamars e'ls caps, e perbul-los, e capolats tots ensemps. E puys ayats juyvert e moradux, e capole-ls ab les cames e ab los caps; e ayats nous qui sien be picades, e tot encemps capolats-ho ab de bones species. E puys fercits-ne los calamars, e met-hi hom de bon oli dintre. E puys cosits-ho, que lo ferciment no.n pusque exir. E met hom los calamas [en una casola] ab del oli, e va al forn.

E puys fa hom salsa. Primerament ayats pa remuylat molt en aygua, e picats-lo be, e metets-hi pinyons, e pich-se tot encemps, e metets-hi de bones species. E con sie be picat, exetats-ho ab aygue. E con los calamas seran cuyts, trau-los hom de la caçola, e met-hi hom la salsa, e bule. E con deura bulir, met-hi hom los calamas. E con aura bulit .i. peça, vayen los calamas per tayladors, e la salsa per escudeles.

Libre de sent soví, p. 214, Recipe 217: *Qui parla con sa deu coura calamas al fforn*

148. Salse cotidiane. (Neapolitan 114)

Salse de tot die comunament: onça e mitga de gingebre, e .i. once de pebre, [e] .viii. diners de safra.

(ii) Primitive *Sent soví*

187. [in part] Farine a hom levat de malaltia, e tempre lo ventre. (Neapolitan 32)

E ayes farina d'ordi, e fe let d'emenles ab brou de galines. E la let feta, mit-hi farine berutelade, e mit-ho a coure, e cougue molt.

E fe'n escudela, e a le derreria al coure pots hi metre .i. poch de sucre blanch.

Libre de sent soví, p. 224, Recipe 35: *Farines*

189. Cabrit farcit en ast. (Neapolitan 80)

Pren la resole levade, e mit-le a coure ab lo cor e ab lo leu e carn selade. E con sera cuyt, mit-hi juivert, qui hi bule i. poch, e moradux, e .i. poch de cebe. E capole-ho be ab la çebe e ab les erbes.

E con sera be capolat, mit-hi species. E si't vols, ayes ayls escaldats, e panses netes, e mit-les hi entegres. E a farciment de .i. cabrit [e] mit-hi .iiii. ous, e mescle-ho be, e mit-ho leyns.

Libre de sent soví, p. 65, Recipe 4: *Qui parla con se ffercex cabrit*

205. Brou ab amenles a hom delicat. (Neapolitan 31)

Pren brou de pols o de pole escaldades, e mit-les en la ola ben nete, e umpli-le be d'aygua per tal que pusque be escumar. E escumade, ayats .i. poc de carn salade axi com demunt es dit. E con la ola aura bolit .i. pega, de guise que pusque estar cuberta sens sobrexir, mit le carn selade, e cubri-le tantost, e ago fera tornar lo brou tan blanch com leyt. E puys, si no era blanc a ta guisa, esclafares-hi lo cap del pol en la ole, [e sera blanch]. E es cert que del brou no deu hom fer sino .i. escudele.

Libre de sent soví, p. 191, Recipe 187: *Qui parla com se ffa brou amellat a hom deliquat*

209. Mostayla francesa. (Neapolitan 121)

Solament se destempre ab vinagre, o ab arrop la pots fer.

Libre de sent soví, p. 177, Recipe 162: *Qui parla con se fa mostaya nostrada*

217. Penades de pex. (Neapolitan 76)

Ffe les peçes grosses, e mit lo pex [a coure] ab sal e ab salse. E si les fas d'anguiles [ms reading uncertain), pots hi metre juyvert cruu a la derreria, un poch de vinagre e agror. E axi de tot pex que vuyles metre en pa, e serdine, e senogues, e verats.

Lops [o] muyols en ast o en greles.

Donat con sera cuyt. Pots aver pebre e safra e vinagre e çebe gros taylade, e mescle-u tot, e gita-li-u desus.

(iii) Robert, *Libre del coch*

35. De pomada. (Neapolitan 95)

Pren pomes que sien agres e dolçes e fes-ne quatre parts de cascuna, e part-les e leva'ls lo cor, e apres met-les en aygua freda e si son massa agres dona'ls un bull. E apres pren ametlles netes e blanques e pica-les be. E, com sien picades, met les pomes ensemps dins lo morter ab les ametles e torna-ho a picar fort. E, com sia picat, destempprar-ho has ab bon brou de gallines e passar-ho has tot pe estamenya. E met-ho tot en la olla ahon ha de bullir. E apres pren gingebre que sia fi e fes-lo net de la escorça fins que sia blanch. E apres fes-ne troços axi com un mig dau, e met-lo a remullar de part de vespre en aygua-ros que sia fina, fins al mati. E apres pren canyella que sia cencera e ligada ab un fil ensemps ab clavells de giroffle e escalda-u ab bon brou callent. E quant sia escaldat los clavells e la canyella, met la olla al foch ab les pomes e met-hi bona quantitat de sucre dintre. Quant sia mes de mig cuit, pendras lo gingebre remullat e la canyella escaldada e los clavells e metras-ho tot en la olla. E, si no sap prou al gingebre, met-n'hi un poch de picat fins que la salsa sapia al gingebre. E apres que sia cuyt, metras aygua-ros en la olla, e apres fes escudelles, e damunt les escudelles metras sucre tres m per cada escudella.

42. Potatge que-s diu frexurat. (Neapolitan 96)

Hajes frexuras e met-les a coure en una olla per si a part, e apres, com sien cuytes, trau-les de la olla e fes-ne tallades tant grans com un dau e redones. E apres çoffregir-les has ab un poch de carn salada e ab ceba e met-ho tot plegat. Apres pren ametlles que sien ben torrades, e pica-les en un morter ab fetge de molto que sie cuyt en brases e una molla de pa torrat e remullat en vinagre blanch, e pica-u tot ensemps. E, com tot sie ben picat, destempra-u ab bon brou de molto, e apres passar-ho has tot per estamenya. E, com sia passat, mescla-u tot, ço es la frexura e la salsa e vaja al foc a bullir. E met en la olla de totes salses fines empero met-hi un parell de ous per cada escudella. Fes que sapia un poch lo potatge a vinagre.

58. Potatge que·s diu genestada. (Neapolitan 39)

Hajes arros e fes-ne farina e passa-la per un cedaç. E apres pren let de ovelles o de cabres. E, si no·n tens, ajes let de ametles. E destempra la farina del arros en dites ametles o let de cabres de manera que sie ben clar, e apres met-ho en la olla perque bulla. E met aquestes coses que·t diré en la olla: sucre e datils mundats e pinyons e avellanes entegres que sien belles e blanques e los datils tallats axi com un dau. E met-hi de totes salses fines en la olla e mena tostemps ab una menadora de fust. E, si vols fer la genestada blanca, e axi ho poras fer. E axi mateix poras metre en loch de sucre [canyella]. Desobre les scudelles poras metre grans de magranes agres. Empero es menester que repos un poch la olla ans de fer escudelles.

66. Bon farciment de cabrit. (Neapolitan 74)

Pren mulles de molto e frexures de cabrit e metles a coure en la olla ab un troç de carnsalada que sia entreverada. Com sia cuyt, capolau-la be. E apres met-hi un poch de pa rallat ensemps ab un poch de formatge rallat, e axi mateix mescla-u tot plegat. E capola-u be ab un poch de polivert tallat menut. E com sia ben mesclat, pren ous ab los blanchs, e ab tot ensemps vaja ab les altres coses; e met-y axi mateix de totes salses fines e molt çaffra, perque molt vol esser groch. E apres mescla-u tot molt e que sia fort capolat. E apres çoffrogiras ton cabrit o porcell, empero, quant es porcell, no si met jolivert.

E si per ventura eren massa grassos los cabrits per metre en ast, pots-ne fer troços e fer-ne panades. E pots pendre la salsa fina e jolivert tallat. E met-los en panades ab un poch de oli dolç e vaja la dita vianda al forn. E com la volras traure del forn un poch abans, debat los ous ab agresta o such de toronges. E com sien ben debatuts, metras ho dins la panada per lo spirall que damunt te. E apres torna-la en lo forn per spay de tres Pater Nostres, e apres trau-la gentilment e porta-la davant ton senyor. E quant seras davant ell rompras-la, e, bona y rompuda en un bell plat, donar-la has a ell.

85. Bona salsa francesa. (Neapolitan 116)

Aquesta salsa francesa es bona a tota volateria que sia en ast cuyta. Pren ametles que sien netes e blanques e pinyons, e pica-u be ab gingebre e pebre e met-y molta canyella. E destempra-u ab vi de magranes agres e assaborir-ho has que sia agra dolç. E axi mateix pots fer salsa ab such de magranes agres e ab canyella sola mesclara e lançada damunt e es fet.

101. De estillat. (Neapolitan 98)

Una gallina pendras e fer-l'as neta e talla-la a troços, de manera que los troços puguen passar per un coll de ampolla. He trosseja [ms. *troreja*] los ossos, de manera que·n hisqua be la sustancia. E quant sera dins la ampolla, metras a una gallina un got de aygua-ros e quinze o vint grans de girofle, e met-ho tot dins la ampolla. E apres tapa-la molt fort de manera que la vapor no puga exir. E apres pren una caldera e fes que sia plena de aygua neta e vaja al foch a bullir. E met dins la caldera un manat de palla de ordi. E sobre la palla metras la ampolla, axi com la caldera bullira, perque bulla tambe la ampolla. E coga de aquesta manera grosses tres ores e mija. E sapies que y haura una bona quantitat de brou; e aquest brou e una cosa la mes maravellosa para malalts del mon. E la palla se met en la caldera, perque la ampolla no toca al sol de la caldera, correria gran arrisch la ampolla de rompre's, e si no se rompia, sabria a la sabor de la caldera lo brou.

213. De polp. (Neapolitan 188)

Capitol que tracta en quina manera se deu aparellar lo polp.

Primerament bat-lo fort, perque aquest peix es molt dur, e per ço vol esser molt batut. E apres pren lo polp e renta'l. E apres vaja dins la olla a coure ab una ceba e ab un poch de oli. E guarda que no·y metes sal, perque aquest peix es de natura ja prou salat, ni aygua tan poch, perque ell mateix ne fara prou, e aquella aygua tomaria com un brou roig. E si hi vols metre unes poques de especies no faras mal. Empero tapa la olla molt be, que no·n hisca lo fum. E axi se aparella lo polp, empero leva-li un budel que te al cap. E com lo metras a coure, met-hi una poca de aygua. E menges aquest negoci ab salsa verda, e es fet.